No. 3204
$31.95

DacEasy™ Accounting and Payroll Made Easy

Version 3.0

Gary West and William Mills

Published by **Windcrest Books**
FIRST EDITION/FIRST PRINTING

Library of Congress Cataloging-in-Publication Data

West, Gary, 1947-
 DacEasy accounting and payroll made easy: version 3.0 / by Gary
West and William Mills.
  p. cm.
 Includes index.
 ISBN 0-8306-3204-2 (pbk.)   ISBN 0-8306-9204-5
 1. DacEasy accounting (Computer program) 2. DacEasy payroll
(Computer program) 3. Accounting—Data processing. 4. Payrolls-
-Data process. I. Mills, William R. II. Title.
 HF5679.W474 1989
657′55369—dc19   89-4259
                                                      CIP

TAB BOOKS Inc. offers software for sale. For information and a catalog, please contact TAB Software Department, Blue Ridge Summit, PA 17294-0850.

Questions regarding the content of this book should be addressed to:
Windcrest Books
Division of TAB BOOKS Inc.
Blue Ridge Summit, PA 17294-0850

Ron Powers: Director of Acquisitions
Lori Flaherty: Technical Editor
Katherine Brown: Production

Contents

Introduction

In 1985, Dac Software, Inc., introduced Version 1.0 of *DacEasy Accounting* and changed the computer/accounting world. Prior to that introduction, the average cost of a complete accounting system was about $6,000—if you wanted to use a computer to do the books.

When *DacEasy Accounting* sold—complete with payroll capabilities—for under $125, other accounting marketers snickered that it couldn't possibly be more than a toy. When it received a product-of-the-year award and a world-class-software award within the first year, other accounting marketers began looking at the price-to-performance value of their products. So did those who were looking for accounting software.

Version 1.0 of *DacEasy Accounting* and *Payroll* became the industry standard. It sold almost 200,000 copies during its first year and a half and climbed to sixth place on the software sales charts.

Version 2.0 was released in May 1987. Every review was positive. Every user was thrilled.

Version 2.0 was not merely an upgrade; it was a major revision. The new version was written in the C language instead of compiled BASIC. The speed showed. The "user interface"—computerese for the menu and structure—was better organized. The ease showed.

Version 2.0 added departments and multiple-company capabilities to its power. It simplified the initial setup routine so that novice computer users had no trouble getting started. The program's capabilities were expanded to support service-based companies as well as product-based companies. Other enhancements were added to the major revisions—and another 100,000 copies were sold within the first six months of its release.

Consequently *DacEasy Accounting* and *Payroll* received another world-class-software award and a product-of-the-year award in 1987.

In July 1988, Dac Software released Version 3.0 for *DacEasy Accounting* and *Payroll*. With the third addition came several major enhancements. The user interface changed again, with the introduction of "pull-down" menus attached to a "top-line" selection bar. The main user menu changed to indicate actions and functions. Previous versions had listed the journals in which those actions and functions were performed.

DacEasy Graph + Mate was added as a utility program. It provides two very important functions: (1) Graph + Mate provides a "front-end access" system for the complete *DacEasy* series of software; and (2) Graph + Mate provides analysis tools in the form of direct graphing of data from within the DacEasy data files.

The "front-end access" displays a list of software that is available from your fixed disk and lets you select the application you want to use. When you have completed your work in the accounting module, you are returned to the applications menu in Graph + Mate and you can select the payroll module from that menu. This makes the entire package much easier to use. In addition, you can add other *DacEasy* programs to the menu.

The graphic analysis of your data will provide information for decision-making purposes. You will be able to analyze, at a glance, patterns in your sales, in your customer records, and in other files in your accounting system.

DacEasy Accounting has increased the number of items available on-screen for customers and vendors. These include identification numbers and codes for tax purposes and additional information on balances, owed and due. The data entry of new customers and vendors, as well as in other files, has also been streamlined. New records can be added "on-the-fly"—without leaving the transaction you are in. The same is true for adding new accounts to the Chart of Accounts. It is no wonder then, that in October, 1988 *DacEasy Accounting* and *Payroll* received its third consecutive world-class software award.

The Purpose of This Book

As with the first two editions of *DacEasy Accounting* and *Payroll Made Easy*, our intent is to describe the *DacEasy* system in terms that the average business owner and operator can understand. Computerizing the accounting, payroll, and inventory functions of even the smallest business can add power and performance to operations. Time and resources generally given to those tasks are reduced significantly, and the return-on-investment, for software, hardware, and training, is immediate and valuable.

We will show you that *DacEasy* is capable of handling the smallest recordkeeping tasks, the largest recordkeeping tasks, and everything in between. Finally, we emphasize the ease with which these tasks can be accomplished.

Version 3.0 of *DacEasy Accounting* and *Payroll* is one of today's rare commodities in the software industry; it has significantly enhanced its power and performance while making the program easier to use and operate. Our task, throughout this book, is to point out the power, describe the performance, and refine the use of the program in terms you can understand.

In addition, we spend a great deal of time on the output processes—creating and printing reports that you can produce from the records you keep. We define standard reports and show you how to create and use reports you can tailor to your specific needs. You will have a greater understanding of the financial status of your business and, consequently, be able to make informed decisions about what to do in the day-to-day operations of your business as well as in yourlong-term planning.

Who Can Benefit from this Book

We continue to believe that small businesses can benefit greatly from using *DacEasy Accounting* and *Payroll*. With this in mind, we have continued to write for those small business owners and operators who might have little, or no computer experience, and who might have little, or no accounting experience.

Many of you understand that computerizing the books is essential to remaining competitive in the market place. This book helps you achieve that goal.

We provide a logical discussion of the principles of accounting and payroll, a step-by-step procedure for using *DacEasy Accounting* and *Payroll*, and a series of tutorials that will take you through the set up and operation of a fictitious company.

The language used in this book is ''conversational English''—it is not filled with technical jargon that makes most accounting texts and computer texts so difficult to read and understand.

Writing Conventions

Throughout the book, we discuss the use of specific keys or key combinations that you must know to complete certain tasks, and to move from one task to another. When we name keys to be pressed, we enclose the key names in ''pointed brackets''—such as: <SPACEBAR> indicates that the <SPACEBAR> key should be pressed. A key combination is written in much the same way, except the keys are separated by a ''plus symbol''—such as: <CTRL+X> indicates that you must hold down the control key—<CTRL>—and press the <X> key.

Information that you are to type is boldfaced. For example, in a sample record you might be asked to type Sam Jones' name. We write such an instruction as:

''At the next field, type **Jones, Sam**.''

Other writing conventions will be logical and intuitive.

Conclusion

If you are upgrading a previous version of the *DacEasy* series, or if Version 3.0 is your first attempt at computerizing your recordkeeping, this book can make the process easier. We will help you understand the accounting part, as well as the computer part of recordkeeping. We explain how the system works so you can track and analyze the information you need to make your business more profitable. Because you will understand your business in ways you never thought possible, your productivity will improve.

The power of the *DacEasy* software is ready to be put to work. Our goal is to assist you in turning that power into a profit.

Introduction to *DacEasy* and the Computer

Chapter Goals

- *This chapter is devoted to two basic topics: (1) the* DacEasy *diskettes, program modules, and utilities; and (2) the keys used by* DacEasy *for accomplishing the tasks you choose.*

- *Our discussion of the* DacEasy *diskettes includes the purpose of the files on the disks and the special utilities that make* DacEasy *so easy to use. The discussion of the keyboard focuses on the keystrokes needed to move from one function or activity to another, to undo something you wish you hadn't done, and to ensure that your work has been saved for later use.*

If you have been using a previous version of the *DacEasy* series and are now upgrading to Version 3.0, you should turn to Appendix A. After following the procedures described in that appendix, you can return to this chapter to begin learning about the things that have happened to your files as you upgraded.

Basic Assumptions

We do not make too many assumptions in our discussions with you. We must, however, make a few in order to discuss how *DacEasy* software works.

One of the assumptions we will make is that you are using an IBM or an IBM-compatible computer. Your computer might be compatible with a PC, a XT, an AT, or one of the PS/2 models. You may be using either a color system or a monochrome (one-color) system.

We will also assume that your system has at least one disk drive, one fixed disk (sometimes called a ''hard disk''), and at least 384K (kilobytes) of memory (RAM). You will note, in the original *DacEasy Accounting* and *Payroll* manuals, that a mere 256K is required for those programs to run. We are recommending 384K so you can use *DacEasy Graph + Mate*, which is one of the fine utilities you might consider using to help with your accounting and payroll tasks. *DacEasy Graph + Mate* is described later in this chapter.

We are assuming that you have a fixed disk drive for two reasons: (1) Version 3.0 of *DacEasy Accounting* and *Payroll* is contained on multiple diskettes, making it necessary to swap disks during many of the tasks you will be asking the program to complete; and (2) the cost of a fixed disk is so low that the investment will pay for itself within the week. In addition, if you have even a moderate number of customers, want to keep inventory, and will be using the payroll module, the data files will not fit on one floppy disk—you will need the additional storage space offered by a fixed disk.

Our discussion can be translated into procedures for systems that include only two disk drives—if you understand the logic of swapping disks and if your data files will fit on one floppy disk. In cases where features for two-drive systems are worth special mention, we will explain the differences between those and the fixed disk systems.

You should have a printer available to print reports, purchase orders, customer invoices, accounts payable and payroll checks, and other information. Many of the *DacEasy* reports require 132 columns; so if your printer is the standard width, you must be sure it can condense print to get 132 columns of text on an 80-column page (8 ½ by 11 inches).

Our last assumption is that you have the *DacEasy Accounting* and the *DacEasy Payroll* modules and that you want to learn to use both.

A Recommendation

If you have not purchased *DacEasy Graph + Mate*, we strongly recommend that you buy and use it.

DacEasy Graph + Mate

DacEasy Graph + Mate is a program that runs with the *DacEasy* series, providing several very handy features such as:

(1) *DacEasy Graph + Mate* provides a ''pop-up'' calculator that can be used to calculate answers used in your accounting entries.

(2) There is a ''pop-up'' note pad—sort of an electronic ''sticky notes''—on which you can make notes to yourself for later use.

(3) A feature that can record keystrokes so they can be assigned to one key is also included. Later, when you need to use the same sequence of keys, you can press that one key and all of the keystrokes will be automatically repeated. This process permits you to build and assign ''macros''—keys that have expanded functions as a result of the definition and assignment of a series of keystrokes to one key.

(4) *DacEasy Graph + Mate* lets you see your reports on-screen before you print them. This feature can save you considerable time and effort in creating and using reports that contain data from within the *DacEasy* programs.

(5) A key feature of *DacEasy Graph + Mate* is a utility for making back-up copies of your data files—a procedure you should follow every day.

(6) The most-used feature of *DacEasy Graph + Mate* will be the viewing of files through "windows", which can be opened with the touch of a key. Each type of file (chart of accounts, customers, vendors, inventory, employee, etc.) can be viewed on-screen as you work. This means that you do not have to keep printed lists of files on hand to find, for example, customer numbers as you are working with your record keeping.

(7) *DacEasy Graph + Mate* provides some very powerful tools for printing reports from your data files. You can customize reports so that you have up-to-the-minute information about all aspects of your business. You can send copies of these reports to your printer, your screen, or to a disk file to be used later with other data.

(8) *DacEasy Graph + Mate* also lets you export your data to other types of software, such as word processors or spreadsheets so you can further analyze your company's growth and needs.

(9) You can also create graphs that display your records in pictorial format so you can make quick, informed decisions about patterns in the operation of your business. These graphs can also be printed so that you can analyze long-term patterns.

We discuss *DacEasy Graph + Mate* as we work our way through the book. You are, however, not required to have *DacEasy Graph + Mate* in order to use *DacEasy Accounting* and *Payroll*. You will be able to do the things we discuss and you will be able to operate your business without it. It does, however, provide powerful tools for getting the most out of your record-keeping system.

Understanding Common Procedures

Types of Disks

We use the terms "disk" and "diskette" to refer to those floppy disks that contain your programs and on which some of your files will be kept. The two terms mean exactly the same thing. These diskettes come in two basic formats for personal computers: (1) 5.25-inch format and (2) 3.5-inch format.

You have seen the terms "fixed disk" and "hard disk" used in this book. We use those terms interchangeably, as well. A fixed disk is usually inside your computer and is fixed there so that you cannot remove it (as you can floppy diskettes). Fixed disks have a much greater data capacity than floppy diskettes and operate at far greater speeds.

With most computers, the term "applications software" is used to describe software used only for a particular task (or application). You will be using floppy diskettes for two distinct purposes. The disks containing the software you've purchased are called the "program disks" or the "master disks." The disks on which the program creates and maintains your information are called "data disks" or "file disks." Typically, when you are using a two-drive system, a program disk will be placed in drive A:, and a data disk will be placed in drive B:.

When using a fixed disk, you will define subdirectories on your fixed disk that will serve the same purpose as using two floppy diskettes. One subdirectory on your fixed disk will contain your program software, which you will copy into that subdirectory. Another subdirectory will be used to create and maintain your data files.

If you are using a fixed disk or "hard disk", you will copy your program disks onto the fixed disk. Then you can have the computer keep your data on the fixed disk or on one of your floppies. As we indicated earlier in the chapter, floppy disks can contain a much more limited amount of data, compared to fixed disks, and, we assume that you are using a fixed disk.

Naming Disk Drives

When discussing disk drives, we refer to the standard configuration that drive A: is on the left and drive B: is on the right, if you are using a PC or a PC/XT. For an AT-type computer, drive A: usually is the drive on top, with drive B:, if present, immediately under it. These configurations can vary depending on the actual brand of the computer you are using. When we discuss a fixed or hard disk drive, it is named drive C:.

Menus and Work Screens

DacEasy software makes extensive use of menus. That is one of its strengths because menus make the work easier for people who have little computer background. Instead of spending too much time learning a set of commands, a new user can simply consult the displayed menu and select a function to start or complete a task. Each of the menus is pictured and explained throughout this book.

Some of those menus will have sub-menus, which can also have sub-menus. Each menu sequence ends in a "work screen," where you can enter or change data.

At a menu screen, you will simply make a choice. This is usually done by pressing a letter or by moving a highlight bar across or down to the desired selection and pressing <ENTER>. At a work screen, you enter the actual data to be used by the *DacEasy* programs.

Work Screens and Windows

In our discussions of the several *DacEasy* screens, we refer to your "current work screen." By that, we mean the work screen at which you are currently completing a task.

At times, when you are using "*DacEasy*" software, you will have one or more "windows" open on the screen. Each of these windows can contain information you need, or it can let you enter new information the program might need. Windows can be opened on menu screens or on work screens as they are needed.

The Disk Operating System DOS

When you first turn on your computer, you must have a copy of the disk operating system—DOS—on drive C: (for fixed disk systems) or in drive A: (for floppy disk only systems). If the computer does not find DOS on the appropriate disk, it will not be able to use the disk drives.

After starting your computer with DOS in the proper drive, you can take a look at the names of the files on each of the program disks that came with your *DacEasy* packages. Starting your computer, in the "computerese" language, is called "booting" your computer.

The following discussion includes the *DacEasy Accounting* and *Payroll* disks that contain the original programs you will use. We also discuss the disks that contain *DacEasy Graph+Mate*, which is optional but highly recommended.

The *DacEasy Accounting* Disks

After turning on, or booting, your computer with DOS with a fixed disk, you will see the standard DOS prompt—the C>—where you can enter commands to the computer. Place the *DacEasy Accounting* disk 1 in drive A:, close the door and type in the DIR command to display the directory (or contents) of the disk:

DIR A: <ENTER>

Figure 1-1 displays the directory for the *DacEasy Accounting* disk 1. The largest file on the disk, DEA3.EXE, is the *DacEasy Accounting* program. The other files are used for various purposes when DEA3.EXE calls on them to complete a task or when you are setting up the program before using it for the first time. For example, before beginning a new set up, the INSTALL.BAT starts the installation process by asking that you insert Disk 2 so it can use a file called DSETUP.EXE. This file asks questions about

```
C:\>dir a:

   Volume in drive A has no label
   Directory of  A:\

   DEA3      EXE    228326    6-24-88    3:00a
   DEAU      EXE     62433    6-24-88    3:00a
   DA3-F00   DA1     21725    6-24-88    3:00a
   DA3-HLP1  DAT     18278    6-24-88    3:00a
   DA3-F17   DA1      6581    6-24-88    3:00a
   DA3-RA2   REP      5248    6-24-88    3:00a
   DA3-INC   REP      4096    6-24-88    3:00a
   DA3-BAL   REP      3614    6-24-88    3:00a
   DA3-F00   KA1      2200    6-24-88    3:00a
   DA3-RA1   REP      1920    6-24-88    3:00a
   DA3-HLP1  KEY       140    6-24-88    3:00a
   INSTALL   BAT        84    6-24-88    3:00a
        12 File(s)      2048 bytes free
```

Fig. 1-1. The Directory of the Install/Program Disk No. 1 for DacEasy Accounting.

```
C:\>dir a:

   Volume in drive A has no label
   Directory of  A:\

DA3-00     EXE     285728     6-24-88     3:00a
DSETUP     EXE      32386     6-24-88     3:00a
DA3-HLP2   DAT      29554     6-24-88     3:00a
INSTALL    TXT       3552     6-24-88     3:00a
DA3-HLP2   KEY        136     6-24-88     3:00a
INSTALL    BAT         84     6-24-88     3:00a
READ       ME        4787     6-24-88     3:00a
          7 File(s)        2048 bytes free
```

Fig. 1-2. The Directory of Disk No. 2 for DacEasy Accounting.

the types of data files you will have and then reserves the space on your disk for the new data. The DEAU.EXE file is used to upgrade your data to Version 3.0. It re-organizes the data so Version 3.0 can read it.

After you have viewed the directory for Disk 1, remove it from drive A: and replace it with Disk 2 for *DacEasy Accounting*. Figure 1-2 shows the directory of the second accounting disk. It contains the names of two files that are used anytime you ask for help (anytime during your work with *DacEasy*, just press <F1> for help).

If you are using a two-drive system without a fixed disk, you must swap Disk 1 and Disk 2 at various times so *DacEasy* can find the appropriate information with which to work.

The *DacEasy Payroll* Disks

Figure 1-3 displays the directory for *DacEasy Payroll* Disk 1.

The first payroll disk contains DEP3.EXE and two files used to display help screens when using the payroll module. As described in a "loose" page in the program manual, the README.TXT file contains information about using the program.

```
C:\>dir a:

   Volume in drive A has no label
   Directory of  A:\

DEP3       EXE     311088     7-28-88     3:02a
DP3-HLP    DAT      27587     7-28-88     3:02a
README     TXT       5504     7-28-88     3:02a
DP3-HLP    KEY        184     7-28-88     3:02a
INSTALL    BAT         74     7-28-88     3:02a
          5 File(s)       15360 bytes free
```

Fig. 1-3. The Directory of the Install/Program Disk No. 1 for DacEasy Payroll.

```
C:\>dir a:

   Volume in drive A has no label
   Directory of  A:\

DEPU      EXE    65641    7-28-88   3:02a
DP3-F04   DAT    35035    7-28-88   3:02a
DSETUP    EXE    34778    7-28-88   3:02a
PUPGRADE  TXT     3361    7-28-88   3:02a
INSTALL   TXT     3040    7-28-88   3:02a
INSTALL   BAT       74    7-28-88   3:02a
PUPGRADE  KEY        6    7-28-88   3:02a
        7 File(s)      216064 bytes free
```

Fig. 1-4. The Directory of the Tax File Disk No. 2 for DacEasy Payroll.

Disk 2 also contains the files needed to upgrade your files from a previous version and to install Version 3.0 for the first time. One file, DP3-F04.DAT, is a data file that will be copied onto your fixed disk. It contains tables of information to be used in the payroll program.

The *DacEasy Payroll* Disk 1 contains the payroll program (DEP3.EXE), the help files, and the screen files. This disk will be used after the installation procedures have been completed.

The *DacEasy Graph+Mate* Disk

DacEasy Graph+Mate incorporates most of the features of its predecessors— *DacEasy Mate* and *DacEasy RePort*, which are no longer part of the *DacEasy* series.

The *DacEasy Graph+Mate* Disk 1 contains an installation file, a configuration file, a help file, and program files, GM.EXE, GMREPORT.EXE, and GMEXPORT.EXE.

```
C:\>dir a:

   Volume in drive A has no label
   Directory of  A:\

GM        EXE    86249    6-28-88   3:00a
INSTALL   EXE    75345    6-28-88   3:00a
GMREPORT  EXE    72349    6-28-88   3:00a
GMEXPORT  EXE    65449    6-28-88   3:00a
GRAFMATE  DD     19850    6-28-88   3:00a
GRAFMATE  HLP    14863    6-28-88   3:00a
READ      ME     11180    6-28-88   3:00a
GMDRIVER  COM     6749    6-28-88   3:00a
        8 File(s)       7168 bytes free
```

Fig. 1-5. The Directory of Disk No. 1 for DacEasy Graph+Mate.

```
C:\>dir a

   Volume in drive A has no label
   Directory of  A:\

GMGRAPHS EXE    121219    6-28-88    3:00a
GRAFMATE DD      19850    6-28-88    3:00a
GRAFMATE HLP     14863    6-28-88    3:00a
READ     ME      11180    6-28-88    3:00a
GMDRIVER COM      6749    6-28-88    3:00a
GRAPHICS PRN       335    6-28-88    3:00a
         6 File(s)     185344 bytes free
```

Fig. 1-6. The Directory of Disk No. 2 for DacEasy Graph+Mate.

Its directory is shown in Fig. 1-5. The configuration file and the program file are used each time you start *DacEasy* with *DacEasy Graph+Mate*. The disk also contains a file, GMDRIVER.COM, that must be used if your computer system has a monochrome graphics adapter (instead of a standard monochrome adapter or a color adapter).

The *DacEasy Graph+Mate* Disk 2 contains the program file GMGRAPHS.EXE, which is used to create, edit, and print graphic representation of your accounting and payroll information. See Fig. 1-6. This disk also contains three files that are also on the first *Graph+Mate* diskette. These files must be on this disk so that the system will work with a two-floppy drive computer. When you copy these two disks to your fixed disk, only one copy of each of the three files is saved on the fixed disk.

Figure 1-7 shows the basic relationships among the *DacEasy* programs.

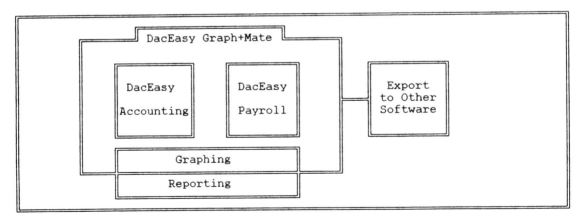

Fig. 1-7. DacEasy Graph+Mate brings together the entire DacEasy series, with links to other types of software, as well.

DacEasy and the Keyboard

The Keyboard
DacEasy software uses all IBM-type keyboards and several Keytronic-styles without difficulty. The basic functions of *DacEasy* have been simplified enough to use only a few keys—and those keys are common to all IBM-type keyboards.

The Alphabetic Keys
As you might expect, the standard alphabetic keys are used for putting information onto the *DacEasy* work screens.

The Numeric Keys and the Calculator Pad
There are two sets of numeric keys on the IBM-type keyboards: one set across the top of the keyboard and another set in a "calculator pad" on the right side. The top row will print numbers normally; the "calculator pad" must be turned on by pressing the <NUM LOCK> key.

If the <NUM LOCK> key is off, the "calculator pad" becomes a "cursor control pad." You can then move the screen cursor (the little line or box that flashes to let you know where you're typing) in the direction of the arrows printed on those keys.

Using Upper-Case Letters
Version 3.0 of *DacEasy* does not require that most information be entered as "all caps"—that is, as all upper-case letters. You can choose to use all upper-case letters by pressing the <CAPS LOCK> key, which locks the keys the same as on a typewriter keyboard.

It is important to note that <CAPS LOCK> affects only the 26 alphabetic keys. Other keys must still be "shifted" to type the characters printed at the top of the key cap. (For example: You might want to print a "percent sign" on the screen. If <CAPS LOCK> is off, you must hold down a <SHIFT> key and press the key with the percent sign on it—the numeric "5" on the top row of the keyboard. If <CAPS LOCK> is on, you must do exactly the same thing since <CAPS LOCK> does not affect the numeric keys.) Also, if <CAPS LOCK> is on, holding down a <SHIFT> key and pressing a letter key will print a lower-case letter on the screen. As soon as you release the <SHIFT> key, <CAPS LOCK is restored.

Entering Your Information
The *DacEasy* screens show you where to type your information by flashing a "cursor"—a line or a box (depending on your computer)—at the location for the next letter or number to be typed. Information can be entered only at the cursor.

The <ENTER> key, which is sometimes called the <RETURN> key, is the key that will "enter" your information into the *DacEasy* programs. After typing any piece of information, you will press <ENTER> to send the information to the actual files. (Note that many IBM-type keyboards do not have the word "ENTER" printed on that key; instead, there is a "broken arrow", which is located to the right of the alphabetic keys.)

Correcting Mistakes before Entering Your Data

If you make a mistake while typing, and if you have not pressed the <ENTER> key, you can erase and correct the mistake by pressing the <BACKSPACE> key. The <BACKSPACE> key is usually labeled with an arrow that points to the left and is located at the top of the keyboard above the <ENTER> key. <BACKSPACE> deletes characters to the left of the cursor as it is pressed.

If you hold down the <CTRL> key—which is labeled but may be in one of several places on your keyboard—and press <BACKSPACE> at the same time, all the information on the cursor line will be deleted. This can save time in erasing long strings of unwanted information.

The <ESC> key—the "escape" key—is used to leave a task and to return to the previous menu, cancelling whatever has been done on the current task. This provides a way to quit in the middle of a task without completing it. The <ESC> key, though clearly labeled, may be located in one of three different places on your keyboard. The traditional location is at the upper left corner of the keyboard, adjacent to the <1> key. The newer AT-type keyboards include the <ESC> key near the upper right of the keyboard, above the "calculator pad." The newest enhanced keyboards locate the <ESC> key in the upper left corner again, but away from all the other keys.

Table 1-1. Keys and Key Combinations Used for Data Entry and Editing.

KEY	FUNCTION
<NUM LOCK>	Turns on or off the "calculator pad" at the right of the keyboard (except PCjr and PS/2 Model 25)
<CAPS LOCK>	Turns on or off the "all caps" typing with alphabetic characters; does not affect non-alphabetic keys
<ENTER>	Instructs computer to accept the information you have just typed
<BACKSPACE>	Deletes the character immediately to the left of the cursor; pulls back all characters from the right to fill in the gap
<CTRL+BACKSPACE>	Deletes all information on the line in which the cursor rests
<ESC>	Aborts the current task and returns to the previous menu; all information on the current screen is lost
<CTRL+X>	Aborts the current task and returns to the top of the same work screen; all information is lost, but can be re-entered immediately

The "function keys"—labeled <F1> through <F10> on most keyboards, although the newer keyboards have <F1> through <F12>—have specific functions, depending on the module in which you happen to be working. The bottom line of each screen will indicate the available function keys and will provide a one- or two-word label to indicate the actual function. The normal functions of those keys are described in Table 1-1.

Correcting Mistakes after Entering Your Data

On each *DacEasy* work screen, you will see labels for the information you are to enter. After typing the information beside or under one of these labels, you will press <ENTER> to put the information into the program. When you press the <ENTER> key, the cursor moves to the space beside the next label. To correct errors in a previous entry, press the <LEFT ARROW> key. The <RIGHT ARROW> key moves the cursor to the next field ("field" is used to denote the kinds of data common to all fields in your file).

Because the <LEFT ARROW> and <RIGHT ARROW> keys are used to move from one "field" to another, you must use another pair of keys to move to the left and right within a field. To do this, hold down the <CTRL> key and press the appropriate arrow key. The cursor will then move to the next character in that field.

Table 1-2. Function Keys Used in DacEasy Accounting Version 3.0.

KEYS	FUNCTION
<F1>	Displays help directly relevant to the work screen on which you are working
<F2>	Has different functions, depending on the module in which you are working
<F3>	Not used in Version 3.0
<F4>	Change date used for recording or posting items to the system
<F5>	Shows balance for given invoice when in Accounts Receivable or Accounts Payable
<F6>	Deletes the current record
<F7>	Enter beginning balances for customer file, vendor file, and inventory file
<F8>	Sorts certain data in Cash Receipts and Enter Payments routines
<F9>	Automatically applies receipts and payments to the appropriate Accounts Receivable and Accounts Payable transactions
<F10>	Reports to system that all data have been entered for the displayed record

Table 1-3. Keys and Key Combinations for Moving the Cursor within DacEasy.

KEYS	FUNCTION
<LEFT ARROW>	IN A MENU: moves selection bar up DATA ENTRY: moves cursor to previous field
<RIGHT ARROW>	IN A MENU: moves selection bar down DATA ENTRY: moves cursor to next field
<UP ARROW>	IN A MENU: moves selection bar up DATA ENTRY: moves cursor to previous field
<DOWN ARROW>	IN A MENU: moves selection bar up DATA ENTRY: moves cursor to next field
<HOME>	IN A MENU: moves selection bar to top DATA ENTRY: moves cursor to beginning of field
<END>	IN A MENU: moves selection bar to bottom DATA ENTRY: moves cursor to end of field
<INS>	DATA ENTRY: begins and ends inserting text in existing text
<DEL>	DATA ENTRY: deletes character at cursor
<BACKSPACE>	DATA ENTRY: backspaces and deletes to left of cursor
<CTRL+HOME>	DATA ENTRY: moves cursor to first field on screen
<CTRL+END>	DATA ENTRY: moves cursor to last field on screen
<CTRL+ LEFT ARROW>	DATA ENTRY: moves cursor one character left in field; does not delete character to left
<CTRL+ RIGHT ARROW>	DATA ENTRY: moves cursor one character right in field; does not over-write character to right
<ALT+D>	TRANSACTIONS: deletes entire line
<ALT+I>	TRANSACTIONS: inserts blank line

If you want to insert a set of characters in the information in a field, first move the cursor to where you want to enter the characters, press <INS> to tell *DacEasy* that you want to begin to insert your characters. When you have completed the task, press <INS> again to turn off the insert operation. You can then move to another location in the field and repeat the process, if necessary.

Errors can also be corrected by pressing the <CTRL+X> key combination. This will erase everything on the current work screen and will let you start over on that screen.

A "Normal End"

There is one final comment to be made about using the keyboard: When you have finished a work session, always return to the main *DacEasy* menu and "escape to DOS" before turning off your computer. Some computer systems keep small amounts of information in memory as they work and later move that information to a disk only when there is no room left in memory to hold it. That information is also moved to disk when the program ends in a normal manner. If you turn off the computer without going through a "normal" end, some of your information may still be in memory when the power is turned off. It will be lost.

Be sure to end each session "normally" by escaping to DOS from the main menu.

Summary

The DacEasy disks contain the programs to be used in accounting for your company's business. The programs use a menu system that permits you to make choices from lists until you reach a work screen. Work screens are used for putting information into the data files.

The DacEasy Graph+Mate utility is recommended because of its ability to dissimulate information to operate your business more efficiently. It allows you to find information as you needed it without printing a long list of your files. And, when you need printouts of your information, you can design and print them immediately.

The DacEasy software packages work equally well with any of the various types of keyboards used with IBM and IBM-compatible computers. The DacEasy programs make use of keys that are common to all the keyboard types. Tables 1-1, 1-2, and 1-3 show the key functions and operations available in DacEasy.

Your Disks and Computer System

Chapter Goals

• *This chapter describes setting up your fixed disk so you can use* DacEasy Accounting *and* DacEasy Payroll *with the least amount of effort. There will be three focal points: (1) Making backup copies of your program disks; (2) installing the* DacEasy *program disk on your fixed disk; and (3) making regular backup copies of your data files. The result will be an efficient and safe way of keeping your business records.*

Before proceeding, you should make backup copies of your program disks—the disks you purchased from Dac Software. This backup procedure should not be confused with the backup procedure for data files, which will be discussed later in the chapter.

Keep in mind that the intent of the copyright law is to permit you to have one copy of the software in operation and the other copy for backup. You cannot, legally, make a backup copy and use it while a friend or colleague uses the original disk. One software publisher sums up the software copyright law by comparing it to the copyright law for books: One book cannot be read by two different people in two different places at the same time. Therefore, computer users should not use copies of the same software in two different computers at the same time.

Making Backup Copies of Your *DacEasy* Program Diskettes

To protect your financial investment in computer software, you should never use the original disks for anything except to make copies that are your working copies. If you use your original disks and something happens, your only option, in most cases, is to buy another set of software disks.

If you have two disk drives that use the same format, you can use the DOS command DISKCOPY to make the appropriate backup copies. This will copy the original disk onto a second disk. The second disk will be an exact duplicate of the first. If you have two disk drives with different formats—such as a 5.25-inch drive and a 3.5-inch drive—you must use the COPY or XCOPY command to copy files from the original to the backup diskette. (XCOPY is available only if you use DOS version 3.2 or greater.)

Before beginning the copying process, place write-protect tabs over the notches in each of the original disks. If you are using 3.5-inch diskettes, slide the write-protect tab so it opens the notch on each of your original diskettes. Finally, label each disk copy.

The following procedure will enable you to make your backup copies, provided your disk drives have similar formats:

(1) Place the DOS disk in drive A: and turn on your computer.

(2) Give the appropriate date and time.

(3) At the DOS prompt, type:

DISKCOPY A: B: <ENTER>

(4) When prompted, place the first original disk in drive A:, and a new, blank disk in drive B:. (For systems with only one drive, you must use the one drive as though it were two. DOS will instruct you when to insert and remove each disk.)

(5) After the copy of the first disk is completed, answer "Y" (for "Yes") to copy another disk. Insert the next original and a new blank disk as instructed. Repeat the process until all the program disks are copied and labeled.

(6) When the last disk has been copied, answer "No" to indicate that you have no more disks to copy.

If your disk drives are different formats, use COPY or XCOPY to make your backups. That process is different, depending on the capacity of the original disk and the capacity of the target disk. Refer to your DOS manual to determine the exact procedure. (When using different disk drive formats is a problem, create a subdirectory on your fixed disk and copy the originals to that subdirectory. Then, using the newly formatted diskettes, copy the files out of that subdirectory to create your backups.)

After your program copies are made, place the originals in a safe place—somewhere away from your work area—and use the backup diskettes for of the installation procedures.

Installing the *DacEasy* Software on your Fixed Disk

When using *DacEasy* (or any other software) on a fixed disk, you will need to set up subdirectories that contain (the program files) and data files. By placing files in subdirectories, you will not have problems with adding other programs that might overwrite some of the files that are already on the disk. In addition, when upgrading your software, these upgraded programs can be placed in the appropriate subdirectories without interfering with other files and programs.

If you are planning to use *DacEasy Accounting* and *Payroll* with more than one company or with several departments within one company, you will need to create one subdirectory for the *DacEasy* programs and one subdirectory for each company and department that will be keeping records. *DacEasy* lets you create subdirectories from within the programs; so you do not have to do it before beginning to use the software.

The net effect of using subdirectories is that your fixed disk acts like a stack of floppy disks, with each subdirectory representing one of those floppy disks.

Installing *DacEasy Accounting* and *Payroll*

Each of the *DacEasy* programs has an installation program on the disk (on Disk 1 in each set with more than one disk). These installation programs will create whatever subdirectories as necessary, copy the appropriate files from the program disks, and place them in subdirectories.

The following procedure installs all of the *DacEasy* software to your fixed disk. (If you are using a two-drive system that does not include a fixed disk, you can turn to Appendix A and follow the installation procedures described there.):

(1) "Boot" your system, provide the appropriate date and time, and wait for the C> DOS prompt to be displayed.

(2) Put the *DacEasy Accounting* Disk 1 (Install/Program) into drive A:.

(3) Type:

A:<ENTER>

(4) At the A> prompt, type:

INSTALL <ENTER>

(5) When asked to identify the type of system you have, select "H" for hard disk.

(6) The installation program will display information about a file that must be on your disk when you "boot" the system. The CONFIG.SYS file provides information to the computer about your system configuration. The *DacEasy* programs will have several files open at once, as you work with your recordkeeping tasks. The CONFIG.SYS file can include the commands to reserve space in memory for those files. If you do not have a CONFIG.SYS file, the installation program will create it for you; if you do have such a file and it does not have the appropriate commands, the installation program will add these commands to the file.

(7) After the CONFIG.SYS file is confirmed, you will be asked to name the subdirectory where you want the accounting files copied. Refer to Fig. 2-1. The installation program will recommend C:\DEA3. If this is acceptable, simply press <ENTER>, otherwise type the subdirectory name you want and press <ENTER>.

(8) If the subdirectory does not already exist, you will be asked to confirm that you want it created.

(9) You will be instructed to insert Disk 2 and press <ENTER>. When the files from Disk 2 are copied into the subdirectory, you will be prompted to re-insert Disk 1. The files from that disk will then be copied to your fixed disk.

(10) When the installation is completed, the program will display an appropriately worded message and the DOS prompt will be redisplayed.

```
╔═══════════════════════════════════════════════════════════════════════╗
║ ┌─────────────────────────────────────────────────────────────────────┐ ║
║ │                      DACEASY INSTALLATION                           │ ║
║ ├─────────────────────────────────────────────────────────────────────┤ ║
║ │The DacEasy Program files will now be copied to your hard disk.  Specify│ ║
║ │the path name for the directory where you would like the program files │ ║
║ │stored.  If the path name does not exist, the system will create it for you.│ ║
║ │                                                                       │ ║
║ │Enter path name: C:\DEA3                                               │ ║
║ │                                                                       │ ║
║ │                                                                       │ ║
║ │                                                                       │ ║
║ │                                                                       │ ║
║ │                                                                       │ ║
║ │                                                                       │ ║
║ └─────────────────────────────────────────────────────────────────────┘ ║
║ Press <─┘ to continue, ESC to exit.                                      ║
╚═══════════════════════════════════════════════════════════════════════╝
```

Fig. 2-1. Naming the subdirectory (path) to which the accounting system will be installed.

```
╔═══════════════════════════════════════════════════════════════════════╗
║ ┌─────────────────────────────────────────────────────────────────────┐ ║
║ │                      DACEASY INSTALLATION                           │ ║
║ ├─────────────────────────────────────────────────────────────────────┤ ║
║ │The DacEasy Program files will now be copied to your hard disk.  Specify│ ║
║ │the path name for the directory where you would like the program files │ ║
║ │stored.  If the path name does not exist, the system will create it for you.│ ║
║ │                                                                       │ ║
║ │Enter path name: C:\DEP3                                               │ ║
║ │                                                                       │ ║
║ │                                                                       │ ║
║ │                                                                       │ ║
║ │                                                                       │ ║
║ │                                                                       │ ║
║ │                                                                       │ ║
║ └─────────────────────────────────────────────────────────────────────┘ ║
║ Press <─┘ to continue, ESC to exit.                                      ║
╚═══════════════════════════════════════════════════════════════════════╝
```

Fig. 2-2. Naming the subdirectory (path) to which the payroll system will be installed.

(11) Repeat the process with the *DacEasy Payroll* diskettes. You should, however, name a different subdirectory were the payroll files will be copied. The installation program will recommend C: \ DEP3. See Fig. 2-2.

Installing *DacEasy Graph + Mate*

Installation procedures for *DacEasy Graph + Mate* are different from the main accounting and payroll programs. To install *Graph + Mate*:

(1) At the C < 1 > prompt, type:

MD C: \ GRAFMATE < ENTER >

This command will create a drive C: subdirectory named GRAFMATE. If you would prefer a different subdirectory name, enter that name instead of GRAFMATE. Remember to use eight, or fewer, legal DOS characters.

(2) Insert the *DacEasy Graph + Mate* disk into drive A:.

(3) To copy the files on the *Graph + Mate* disk into the GRAFMATE subdirectory, type:

COPY A:*.* C: \ GRAFMATE < ENTER >

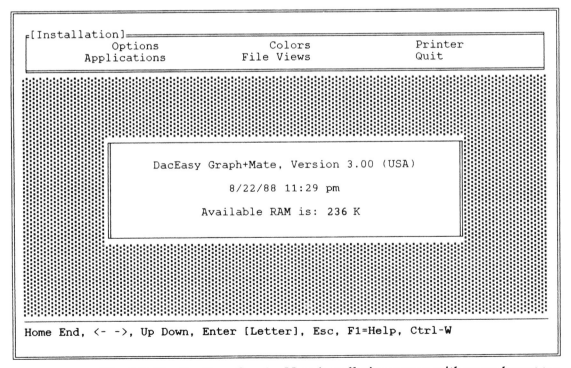

```
┌[Installation]══════════════════════════════════════════════
│         Options              Colors              Printer
│       Applications         File Views            Quit
├─────────────────────────────────────────────────────────────





              DacEasy Graph+Mate, Version 3.00 (USA)

                       8/22/88 11:29 pm

                    Available RAM is: 236 K





─────────────────────────────────────────────────────────────
Home End, <- ->, Up Down, Enter [Letter], Esc, F1=Help, Ctrl-W
```

Fig. 2-3. The DacEasy Graph + Mate installation screen with menu box at top.

(4) Change the current directory by typing:

CD C:\GRAFMATE <ENTER>

The computer will use files in that subdirectory as it completes the installation.

(5) To start the actual installation, type:

INSTALL <ENTER>

Figure 2-3 shows the installation screen for *DacEasy Graph + Mate*. It displays the amount of memory (RAM) that is available during the installation process. The screen that you see when your computer starts the installation might show a different amount of available RAM, depending on your operating systems. There can be other differences, depending on your computer.

There are several basic set up procedures that should be completed at this time.

Defining the *DacEasy Graph + Mate* Options

From the Installation Menu, you can select from among six options. We will discuss each of these in depth. To select an option, move the highlight bar to the desired option and press <ENTER> or press the key for the first letter of the option name. To select Options, press <O>.

A small window will appear under the OPTIONS heading. It displays seven options that must be considered before continuing with the installation process. Four of the options

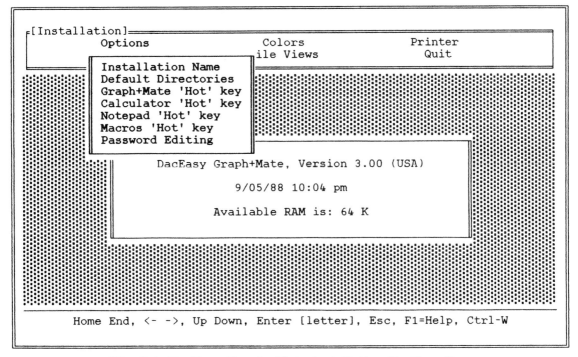

Fig. 2-4. DacEasy Graph + Mate installation "options."

are "hot keys", which are used to access features in *DacEasy Graph + Mate*, and will not be discussed here.

Move the highlight bar to "Installation Name" and press <ENTER>. A second window will open (see Fig. 2-5) permitting you to enter information about the company or department for which *DacEasy* is to do the accounting and payroll. In the tutorials that appear later, we will build recordkeeping systems for a company called Parts and Parcels, Inc., which is a hardware store. The information shown in Fig. 2-5 will be used in those tutorials.

Enter the appropriate information for your company.

When you have completed the last line and pressed <ENTER> —or <F10> —the company information will be filed on a disk and the OPTIONS window will be re-displayed.

Move the highlight bar to the second selection in the window to define the Default Directories where *DacEasy* can expect to find your programs and files. Figure 2-6 shows the resulting window.

You will be asked to name the subdirectory where your *DacEasy Accounting* files are located. For example, a subdirectory named C: \ DEA3 \ PARTS, indicates that the files are on drive C:, in a subdirectory named PARTS (for Parts and Parcels, Inc.) which is a subdirectory of DEA3, or where the accounting program files are located. (See the accounting installation procedures described earlier in the chapter). You will also be asked to give the subdirectory name where *Graph + Mate* files are located. We've given

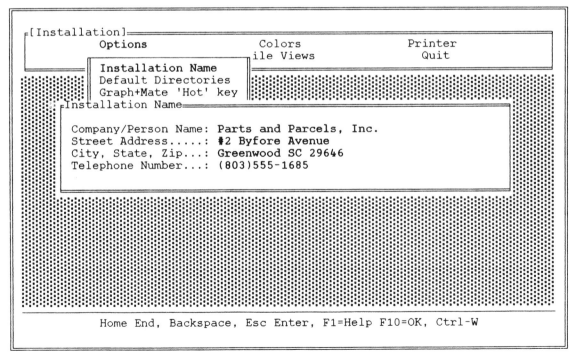

Fig. 2-5. The Installation Name window for identifying your company within DacEasy Graph + Mate.

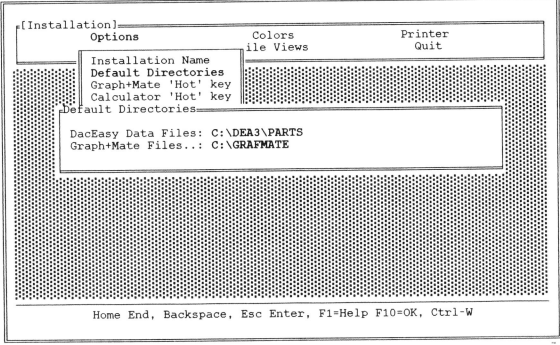

```
┌[Installation]══════════════════════════════════════════════════
│         Options              Colors            Printer
│                              ile Views           Quit
│         ┌────────────────────┐
│         │ Installation Name  │
│         │ Default Directories│
│         │ Graph+Mate 'Hot' key│
│         │ Calculator 'Hot' key│
│       ┌─Default Directories══════════════════════════════════════┐
│       │                                                          │
│       │  DacEasy Data Files: C:\DEA3\PARTS                       │
│       │  Graph+Mate Files..: C:\GRAFMATE                         │
│       │                                                          │
│       └──────────────────────────────────────────────────────────┘
│
│
│
│
│
│
│
│
│         Home End, Backspace, Esc Enter, F1=Help F10=OK, Ctrl-W
```

Fig. 2-6. Naming the subdirectories (paths) where DacEasy can find your accounting files.

C:\GRAFMATE because that's the name of the subdirectory in which we are making this installation. You should use the subdirectory names you have selected for your business.

After giving the information press <ENTER> or <F10>, to save the information to disk and return to the OPTIONS window.

When you select the next four items from the menu in the OPTIONS window, you will see the "hot key" combinations that are built into *DacEasy Graph + Mate*. Each of these combinations can be changed; however, there is no need to change any unless they conflict with another program that you are running at the same time you are running *DacEasy* software. One example would be a "memory resident" program such as Sidekick, which can be loaded into your computer's memory and will stay there—in the background—while other software is running. Sometimes the key needed to access that background program will be the same as one of the *DacEasy* "hot keys." In that case, one of the combination keys will have to be changed to avoid conflicts.

DacEasy Graph + Mate has four utilities that can be "popped up" from any work screens while using the *DacEasy Accounting* and *Payroll* programs. Table 2-1 lists the utilities and the default "hot keys" used to access the utilities. Within the Graph + Mate installation process, you can change those "hot keys" if you need to do so.

DacEasy Graph + Mate utilities are discussed in a Chapter. We recommend that you skip changing the "hot keys" at this point—unless you feel comfortable about going on at this time.

Table 2-1. "Hot keys" for Using DacEasy Graph+Mate.

```
"Hot Key"        Function
==========       =========================================
<ALT+F10>        Start DacEasy Graph+Mate from within
                 DacEasy Accounting or DacEasy Payroll

<ALT+N>          Pop-up DacEasy Notepad from within
                 DacEasy Accounting or DacEasy Payroll

<ALT+C>          Pop-up DacEasy Calculator from within
                 DacEasy Accounting or DacEasy Payroll

<ALT+M>          Pop-up DacEasy Macro Facility from within
                 DacEasy Accounting or DacEasy Payroll
```

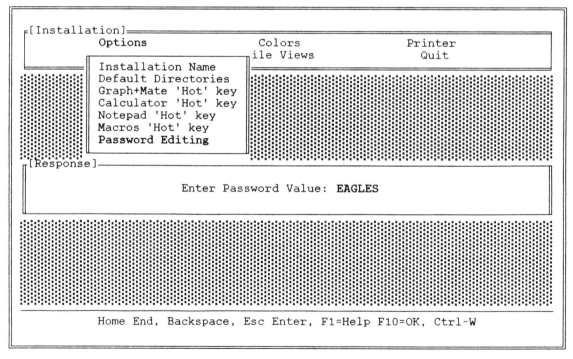

Fig. 2-7. Entering a password that restricts casual access to your data files.

The last item on the OPTIONS menu is Password Editing, as shown in Fig. 2-7. At this screen, you can enter an eight-character (or fewer) password that will restrict access to the *DacEasy Graph + Mate* program. After it is entered, you will be asked to "validate" it by retyping it blindly. The password will be assigned only if your blind validation is exactly the same as the original. Figure 2-8 shows the screen as it validated our password.

When you include a password, the program will request it each time the program starts. The password must be entered exactly before access will be permitted. The password can be changed only by someone who can give the current password first.

Security is an important issue for keeping your company's financial records, whether you do that manually or with a computer. Passwording is a means of protecting your records from unauthorized prying. More important, it is a means of protecting your records from unauthorized tampering. We strongly recommend that you consider passwording.

There are several considerations in the use of passwording. The specific password provided here, is restricted to entering *DacEasy Graph + Mate* only. It does not restrict access to the accounting or payroll modules (these can be accessed without going through *Graph + Mate*). Separate passwords are entered in the accounting and payroll modules, providing several levels of access to those records.

Be careful to use passwords that people will not easily guess. It is unwise to use first or last names, initials or other obvious clues that can lead to unauthorized access.

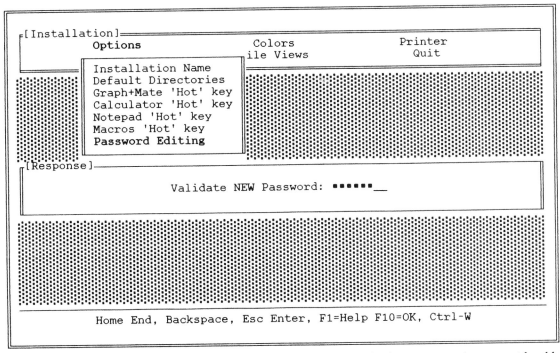

Fig. 2-8. Validating a new password. *After assigning a password, you must be able to blindly re-type it before it is officially assigned to the system.*

Obviously, you will want to use a password you will not easily forget, but use caution. Figure 2-7 uses the password EAGLES, which is a favorite high school team mascot. If, however, a co-worker knows this, it might prove to be too easy to guess and, therefore, by pass the secret system.

Another factor in using passwords concerns problems that can arise when the person keeping your records leaves the company—especially if it is under less-than-pleasant circumstances (not that that could ever happen with your company). You must set up a system that can protect your company from unauthorized password changing before that person leaves. This happened to a major eastern city within the last couple of years: The city manager was fired after a heated discussion by the city council. The manager went back to the municipal office building, entered the city's management software on his password, and with the authority granted his password, changed all the passwords for all other city employees, and left town.

Security is a major issue when setting up your system and you should consider it an important part of the operating procedures.

After the system validation of the password you selected, the OPTIONS menu will be displayed again. Because passwording is the last item we will consider at this time, you can press <ESC> to close the menu window.

When the main installation menu reappears, move the highlight bar to the COLORS

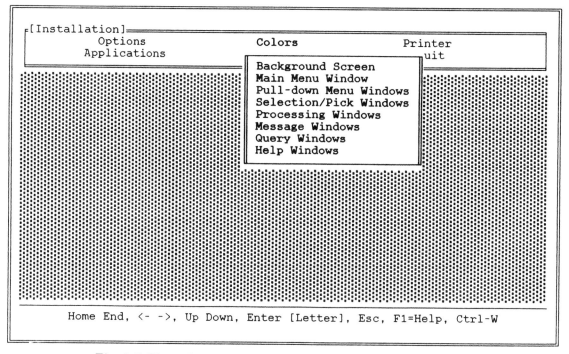

Fig. 2-9. The colors window shows all the possible screens and windows that you can see while using DacEasy Accounting. *You can define different colors for each of them.*

option and press <ENTER>. Figure 2-9 shows the color options; these options are discussed in Chapter 6.

Press <ESC> to return to the main installation menu and select the PRINTER option. Figure 2-10 shows the list of printers for which automatic configuration is available. If you use one of these printers, you can move the highlight bar to the printer's name, press <ENTER>, and save the information to your disk. From that point on, *DacEasy* will know how to operate your printer.

If your printer is not listed among those automatically supported by *DacEasy Graph+Mate*, you must define the printer data manually, including specific codes for specific printer functions. This is discussed in detail in Chapter 7, which describes the setup procedures for the accounting module. (We have placed printer information in that chapter for two major reasons: (1) The setup procedures for the accounting module include printer set up; and (2) some users may not be using *DacEasy Graph+Mate* and need the printer information in the accounting and payroll setup.)

Adding Accounting and Payroll
to the *DacEasy Graph+Mate* Applications Menu

The APPLICATIONS options from the Installation Menu provides a means of listing and accessing the *DacEasy* programs that you will use. Figure 2-11 shows the window with your options and Fig. 2-12 shows a listing of the items we added to our applications

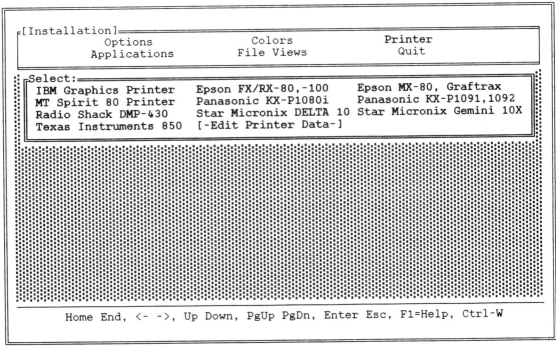

```
┌[Installation]════════════════════════════════════════════════════════
│           Options              Colors              Printer
│           Applications         File Views          Quit
│
│┌Select:═══════════════════════════════════════════════════════════
││ IBM Graphics Printer    Epson FX/RX-80,-100    Epson MX-80, Graftrax
││ MT Spirit 80 Printer    Panasonic KX-P1080i    Panasonic KX-P1091,1092
││ Radio Shack DMP-430     Star Micronix DELTA 10 Star Micronix Gemini 10X
││ Texas Instruments 850   [-Edit Printer Data-]
│
│
│
│
│
│
│
│           Home End, <- ->, Up Down, PgUp PgDn, Enter Esc, F1=Help, Ctrl-W
```

Fig. 2-10. Printer options. You must select the printer that you will be using or you can define your own printer parameters.

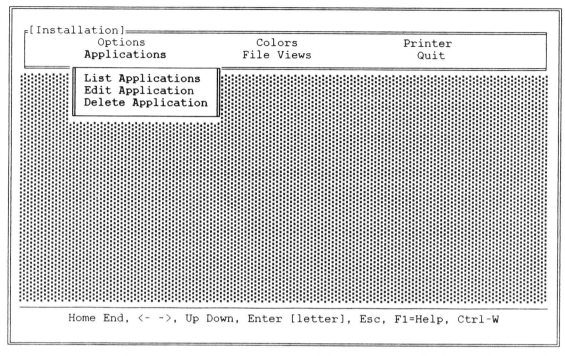

```
┌[Installation]══════════════════════════════════════════════════════════
│        Options                  Colors              Printer
│        Applications             File Views          Quit
└─────────────────────────────────────────────────────────────────────────
      ┌─────────────────────┐
      │ List Applications   │
      │ Edit Application    │
      │ Delete Application  │
      └─────────────────────┘


      Home End, <- ->, Up Down, Enter [letter], Esc, F1=Help, Ctrl-W
```

Fig. 2-11. Applications operations. *You create and edit the DacEasy Graph+ Mate Applications Menu from this window.*

options. (We discuss adding menus to the list in the following paragraphs.)

The Applications listings allows you to build a menu of modules from which to select. From the menu you create, you can move the highlight bar to the program you want to run, press <ENTER>, and work in that module. When you are finished working in the module, you return to the *Graph + Mate* menu and select another application. The information provided in this installation process is used by *Graph + Mate* to display the menu listing. The advantage of the menu system is that you do not have to remember DOS commands.

We will add two modules to the menu listing so that you can immediately see the benefits and can begin using the system with your software. This is discussed in further detail in Chapter 6.

Figure 2-12 provides a summary of the items we are adding to our menu options. This list, however, is not available in this format until after the choices are added. (This reflects our main means of completing Algebra in high school—see the answer in the back of the book, then solve the problem by working toward the answer. Figure 2-12 is the answer; Fig. 2-13 is the problem to be solved.)

When you select Edit Application from the APPLICATIONS menu window, you will see a screen similar to that shown in Fig. 2-13. We have added *DacEasy Accounting* to the list by providing the name we want to see on the menu, the program name that starts the accounting module, the path to that program, and by giving the complete path to the data files kept for the program to use. You can see, in our example, that we have told the program to look for our files in a subdirectory called C:\DEA3\PARTS. After giving those four pieces of information, the menu will know how to start the program for us.

Looking at Fig. 2-12, you can see the options we added to our menu, including the

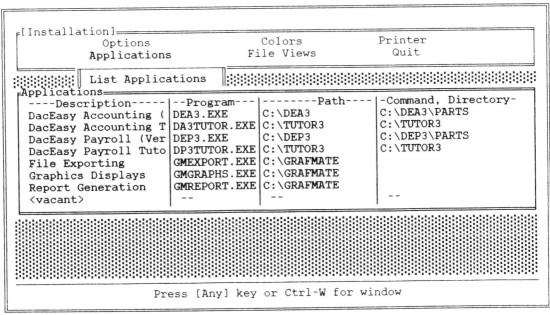

Fig. 2-12. A list of the DacEasy applications that are automatically installed on the Graph+Mate menu.

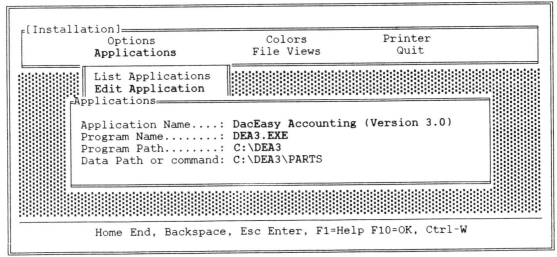

Fig. 2-13. Editing one of the Applications Menu selections. You can provide the name of your choice and define the program and data paths.

27

payroll module and the two tutorials that can be purchased from Dac Software, Inc. You should add the information for the payroll module before you continue with this chapter. (Be sure to use the subdirectory names that apply to your system.)

This menu can be of particular importance to you if you are operating two different companies or setting up different departments. Instead of using *DacEasy Accounting* as a menu choice, you can place both your companies or departments in separate menu options. For example, you can place one company in the menu by giving the company name in the Application Name line when you edit the application list. Then you can give a specific data path for that company. The second company could be added under a different Application Name with a different data path. The same program name and program path could be given for both because they help the computer find the accounting program. After adding two companies, you can elect to work with either of these by moving the highlight bar and pressing <ENTER>.

Viewing Data Files from Within *DacEasy Graph+Mate*

The fifth option on the Installation Menu allows you to list the information you want to see when you look into your data files. Figure 2-14 lists the files you can see as you work with the accounting and payroll modules. Procedures for setting up these files are discussed more fully in Chapter 6.

The last option on the Installation Menu is the Quit option, which allows you to quit

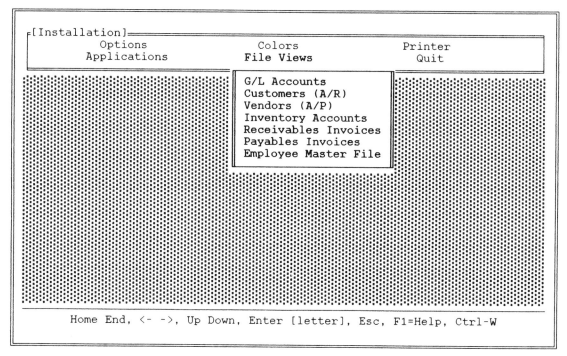

Fig. 2-14. List of files that can be viewed from within DacEasy Graph+Mate.
Once you select one, you can define the information to be included in the displayed data.

the Installation process and return to DOS. After completing the above procedures, you can exit the installation program, and put the menu system to work.

Making Backup Copies of Your Data Files

Although we have not yet created any data files, you should know that data files contain all of the accounting and payroll information for your business. If you were to lose these files, you would lose all of your records for the normal operation of your business, as well as all the tax-related data for the current year. You would lose all the information you will need in order to bill your customers. In effect, your data files are the life blood of your business and you must take precautions not to loose them.

Because data files are so important, you must make backup copies daily. Then, should you lose your files, you can simply restore your backup copy to the fixed disk and continue without loss of time and the tears needed for re-building a business' day-to-day data.

The preceding warning is not an attempt to scare you by making you believe your computer is unreliable. It's just an acknowledgment that all machines break and that all disks fail. That doesn't mean this happens frequently. It means, simply, that these things do happen.

Types of Backup Systems

There are several ways you can backup your data files. The most common way is to copy up files onto a floppy disk. There are, however, other ways to make backups.

One method of backing up the files on your fixed disk is to purchase and install a tape system. Tape systems can store all the data on your fixed disk onto one tape cartridge. This process, can be completed without requiring you to stand around and watch. (That is the biggest advantage, along with getting everything on one tape.)

If you have an AT-tape machine, and if you are planning to use floppy disks to backup your data files, you should buy high-density disks and use drive A: for your backups. If you are using an XT-type or a PC-type computer, you are limited to using standard, double-density disks. The advantage to using high-density disks is they can hold four times as much data, reducing the number of disks needed for each backup.

If you are using a floppy diskette backup system, use the DOS command BACKUP to save your data files. Do not use the COPY command, because it cannot copy large files to one disk. On the other hand, the BACKUP command can copy very large files onto a series of disks, and, using the RESTORE command, put all the files on a fixed disk.

To use BACKUP, you must have a sufficient number of formatted disks to hold all of your data. Be sure to buy several boxes of disks so you can keep two sets of backup disks. Do not do a backup onto the set of disks you backed up to yesterday. Keep yesterday's disk and use a new set for the second day's backup. Then rotate the two sets so that the previous day's backup is always available if you need it.

Refer to your DOS manual for further information on BACKUP or RESTORE.

And remember: Backup your data files every day.

For those of you who get caught up in fine details of using computers, we want to provide this caution. DOS Version 3.3 and later versions use a BACKUP/RESTORE system that is totally different from—and incompatible with—earlier versions of DOS.

Files backed up with DOS 3.3 cannot be restored with DOS 3.2 (or earlier). The same is true, going the other way.

To further complicate matters, DOS will not allow you to start one version of RESTORE if you booted your system with an earlier version. You will receive an "Incorrect DOS version" message when you try.

You can backup your files using the BACKUP procedure provided in *DacEasy Graph + Mate*. This process is discussed in Chapter 6, written specifically for *Graph + Mate*.

Summary

This chapter describes the procedures for making backup copies of your original program disks, for installing the DacEasy *programs onto your fixed disk, and for backing up your data files on a daily basis.*

The procedures for using the DacEasy *series with a two-floppy system with no fixed disk are described in Appendix A.*

The Basics of Accounting

Chapter Goals

- *Chapter 3 presents some basic accounting terms, their definitions, and the way they are used in general accounting. The discussion will center on the terms you "must" know in order to perform basic accounting tasks. There will be no advanced material presented here.*

- *This chapter includes a discussion of the basic structure within an accounting system, as well as the relationships among the various levels of any accounting package—whether or not it is computerized. The definitions presented here will focus on the "must" relationships and will not enter into basic accounting "theory." The focus will be practical and purposeful.*

There is a special "language" used by the people in any area of specialized skill and knowledge. Those of us who use computers develop a special set of terms that we use— and then we reduce those terms to three- or four-letter abbreviations—RAM, ROM, CPU, and IBM are but a few examples.

Accounting has it's own language as well, and it is necessary to understand some of the basic terms in order to comprehend the accounting and payroll processes. With this in mind, we will define the terms you may need to understand some of the functions of *DacEasy Accounting.*

Business Basics

Besides having a language all its own, accounting is considered to be "the language of business." It provides financial information, expressed in terms of money, about everyday business transactions.

A business transaction is usually defined as anything that must be recorded as it relates to the business. This would apply to purchases, sales, returns of sales, payroll, adjustments made because of lost or damaged stock, and all other activities within a business that involve the margins between profit and loss.

There are three major types of small businesses. A sole proprietorship is owned by one person, who makes all the decisions, has all the responsibilities, and keeps all the profits. A partnership is owned by two or more people who have a contractual agreement that defines decision-making, responsibilities, and distribution of profits. A corporation is owned by the people who have purchased shares of stock, and is regulated by state and federal laws that define decision-making processes, responsibilities, and distribution of profits.

DacEasy Accounting and *Payroll* is designed to handle the recordkeeping for all three types of small businesses. The *DacEasy* programs are also designed for use by service-based businesses as well as product-oriented businesses.

Accounting Basics

Accounts

There are five basic types of accounts that business information is placed in during the accounting process.

Assets: Anything the business owns or is owed.

Liabilities: The debts of the business, or anything the business owes.

Owner's Equity: The original investment of the owner, plus any net earnings resulting from operations; this type of account is also referred to as capital.

Expenses: Costs incurred in the process of doing business.

Revenue: The money made in the operation of the business.

Assets, liabilities, and owner's equity are permanent accounts that define the continuing status of the business. The value of these accounts change as the business grows and are carried over from one year to the next.

Expenses and revenues, however, are not permanent accounts. These accounts are emptied at the end of each business year. The values contained in expenses and revenues are subtracted at the end of each year to determine the profit (or, on some occasions, the loss) for that year. This calculated value is placed into an equity account and becomes a permanent part of the business records. At that time the expenses and revenues are "zeroed" and the business starts a new year.

The five types of accounts are classified according to how they express value in the business. Each account has subdivisions that, ultimately, can help a business define trends in its operations and new operations. These subdivisions are eventually defined by individual accounts that contain detailed information on the daily operations of business.

Assets can be divided into three major subdivisions. Current assets are cash and other assets that can be sold or consumed, usually within one year or less, through the normal operations of the business. Fixed assets are assets of a permanent or relatively fixed nature. These might include buildings, machinery, and other property items used in the business. Other assets include any asset that does not fit into the previous two categories.

Liabilities can be divided into two major subdivisions: Current liabilities are those that will be due within one year, or less, and are to be paid out of current assets, long-term liabilities are those that will not be due for more than one year.

Owners' equity can also be divided into two major subdivisions. Capital is the investment in the business by the owner(s)—usually the initial start-up funding for a small business—and is to be payed at some time; retained earnings are the accumulated profits and earnings of the business. These funds are retained for business investment and are not withdrawn by the owners. In corporations, retained earnings initially include dividends, which are later paid back to stockholders.

There are no subdivisions within the revenue and expense categories other than individual accounts.

Double Entry Accounting

Basic accounting uses a "double-entry" accounting system that requires that every transaction be entered into a minimum of two different accounts. The purpose of the double-entry process is to ensure that each entry is balanced by another entry. This process makes it more difficult to make a mistake, because a single error must be made twice—in each part of the double-entry—in order to pass the test of balance.

In accounting terms, one entry must be a "debit" and the other entry a "credit." In effect, the system keeps records for every dollar spent or earned. The dollar spent is recorded in one place, while the sources of the dollar is recorded in another place. When one number is added to the books, another must be subtracted. The net result is zero. And whenever the net result is zero, the books are in "balance."

In a standard paper-and-pencil accounting system, a ledger sheet will contain columns

	Description	Acct. No.	Debit	Credit	Balance
1	Sales	41		2000.00	<2000.00>
2	Cash on Deposit	111	2000.00		-0-
3	Telephone	60	113.13		113.13
4	Cash on Deposit	111		113.13	-0-
5					

Fig. 3-1. A typical ledger sheet used in accounting.

```
                 ACCOUNTS PAYABLE TRANSACTION ENTRY
 Trans. #   :  ████████            Reference/Check #  :
 Vendor Code:                      Transaction Date   :    /  /
 Vendor Name:                      Due Date           :    /  /
 Trans. Code:                      Discount Date      :    /  /
 Invoice #  :                      Discount Available :          0.00

 Acct.#   Account Name         Description          Debit      Credit



 Total Debits :              │  Total Credits :

 F1-Help F6-Delete F9-Auto Entry F10-Process ALT D-Delete line
```

Fig. 3-2. DacEasy Accounting debits and credits are similar to those on a regular ledger sheet.

for the debits and credits. Figure 3-1 shows a typical ledger sheet, including sample entries in the debit and credit columns.

Figure 3-2 shows a work screen from *DacEasy Accounting*. It contains columns for an account number, an account name, amounts to be debited, and amounts to be credited. Note that the *DacEasy* work screen is very similar to the standard ledger sheet in that both request the same information. Entering amounts into *DacEasy Accounting* is very similar to entering information onto a ledger sheet.

Increasing Your Assets

In a double-entry accounting system such as *DacEasy Accounting*, you will almost always enter positive numbers. The accounting system will know when to subtract your number and when to add it—by looking at the account where you placed the number. When negative adjustments are made, the system will treat them appropriately.

A double-entry system works something like this:

(1) Every asset account is a "debit" account. Any positive amount entered into an asset account is added to the value of the business. Assets have some value to the company and should be increased.

(2) Every liability account is a "credit" account. Any positive amount entered into a liability account is subtracted from the value of the business. The amount is

subtracted because it was placed in a "credit" account. Liabilities take value from the company.

(3) All owners' equity accounts are "credit" accounts because the values placed in these accounts represent amounts owed to the owner or owners. The value of the owners' equity is subtracted from the value of the company because it is a debt owed the owners. See Fig. 3-3.

The following is an example of a first transaction for a new company:

(1) A business receives $1,000 in cash and deposits it in the company bank account.

(2) The first entry into the accounting system will be a debit to Cash, which increases that asset account.

(3) The balancing credit will be the second entry, and assuming the $1,000 resulted from a sale, that entry will be to sales—which increases the revenue account.

Both of the entries increased the affected accounts even though one entry was a debit and the other was a credit. The accounting process is balanced at zero because each debit is matched to a credit of equal value. In effect, the use of the funds has been balanced with source for the funds used in this business transaction.

Increasing Revenues

The rule of debit and credit, in its application to revenue and expense accounts, is based on its relationship to the value of the business. The net income, or the net loss for a period, as reported on the income statement, is the net increase or the net decrease in the business' value resulting from operations. For a business year, the net value of operations is measured by subtracting the expenses from the revenues to determine if money was made or lost.

Revenues increase the company's value and are recorded as credits, while expenses

	Account Description	Acct. Type	Debit	Credit	
1	Assets	Debit	Increase	Decrease	
2	Liability	Credit	Decrease	Increase	
3	Owners' Equity	Credit	Decrease	Increase	
4	Expenses	Debit	Increase	Decrease	
5	Revenues	Credit	Decrease	Increase	

Fig. 3-3. Results of debits and credits for different account types.

decrease value and are recorded as debits. Revenue and expense accounts are "operation" accounts.

Accounting In The Real World

There are three ways for a business to approach its accounting tasks: (1) the cash basis accounting system; (2) the accrual basis accounting system; and (3) a blend of the two. (Of course, there may be several other "creative" approaches to accounting. The *DacEasy* series can assist you in adding the flexibility you need while restricting certain forms of creativity that may provide an unrealistic picture of your business operations.)

Cash Basis Accounting

The cash basis of accounting is used when you want to record expenses when they are paid and record revenues when they are collected. Inventories, accounts receivable, and accounts payable are not used in a true cash-basis accounting system. Sales are not recorded until payment is rendered by the buyer and expenses are not recorded until actual payment is made. In a retail business, purchases are not recorded until actual payment is made, even though the physical possession of the merchandise may precede payment by some length of time. The cash basis accounting system requires the least amount of record-keeping among the systems discussed here.

Accrual Basis Accounting

The accrual basis of accounting is used when a company wants to match revenues with expenses. Revenues are recorded when earned and expenses are recorded when they are incurred. The accrual basis of accounting requires the use of accounts receivable, accounts payable, and inventories.

The basic principles of accrual accounting involve the time at which expenses are incurred and the time revenues are earned. Expenses incurred, but not paid and not recorded on the books at the end of an accounting period, are still considered expenses for that period. The amount owed should be shown as a current liability on the balance sheet and included among the expenses on the income statement at the end of the period. Revenues earned, but not yet collected and recorded on the books at the end of an accounting period, are still considered revenues for that period. The amount to be collected should be shown as a current asset on the balance sheet and included among the revenues on the income statement at the end of the period. In addition, in a retail business, purchases are recorded either when the order is placed or when the company takes possession of the merchandise. The purchase can be recorded directly in the inventory account and then charged to expenses, with the expense and inventory accounts adjusted at the end of the accounting period.

Combining Cash *and* Accrual Basis Accounting

The third accounting system combines elements of the cash basis and the accrual basis systems. Many small businesses do not perceive the need for the detailed records required by the accrual system, but want or need to maintain inventory records as well as sell on credit. Usually the inventory records and accounts receivable records are maintained in subsidiary ledgers but not in the main records of the company. For instance, cash-basis accounting sales are not recorded until cash is received. Those sales made on credit are not recorded on the companies main records at the time of the sale, but only at the time cash is received. Inventories are maintained for all the same reasons as under the accrual system, but are not reflected in the financial statements. This hybrid accounting system is more common than would be expected, and many businesses perceive it to be the best of two worlds.

You might prefer one of these three types of accounting approaches. *DacEasy* can provide immediate assistance for either the cash-basis (receipts-and-disbursements) approach or the accrual approach. *DacEasy* cannot, however, provide complete control over combination of both accounting methods. That lack of control is not based on a fault of the software; it's based on the full integration of the accounting modules and that full integration insists on the interfacing of inventory records with the accounting system if the inventory module is used.

As you work your way through the rest of this book, you may discover innovative ways to adapt *DacEasy Accounting* to your accounting needs by integrating both the cash and accrual basis of recordkeeping.

Summary

The basics of accounting has been presented and includes definitions of terms and their application in the accounting setting. You should study the examples provided to determine your course of action. When you have decided which examples and which models apply to your specific needs, then continue with DacEasy.

4

The Basics of Payroll Management

Chapter Goals
- *This chapter presents some basic payroll terms, their definitions, and the way they are used in an accounting system. As in Chapter 3, the discussion concentrates on the terms one "must" know in order to accomplish the basic payroll functions and how they relate to the general accounting system. Practical approaches to payroll accounting also are presented.*

If accounting is the language of business, then payroll is certainly the language of those hired to work for the business. And without the employees who look forward to payday, most companies could not conduct business. And without the sales and services provided by those employees, most companies could not attract customers to the business.

All in all, payroll will take a large portion of accounting time and resources.

Business Basics

Payroll can be the largest expense a company has. In addition to the payroll itself, there are fixed charges and fringe benefits that must be accounted for in the payroll process. In addition, there are the hidden costs in the time required to follow up on that accounting process—the time accounting for leave and vacation, W-2 forms, for 1099's, quarterly Social Security reports, consolidating numbers with the general ledger, and countless other tasks involving the shuffling of figures for financial accounting.

Payroll Basics

As all of us know, there are two kinds of pay—gross pay and net pay. The gross pay is the total earnings of an employee before deductions are made. The amount left after deductions is the net pay—or, more informally, the take-home pay.

There are several other terms and abbreviations that are commonly used when discussing payroll and payroll management. These are listed below and described in the following paragraphs:

(1) Minimum wages: the lowest hourly rate allowed by law.

(2) Overtime pay: the hourly rate required when an employee works more than 40 hours per week.

(3) Payroll deductions: taxes and other amounts deducted from an employee's earned pay.

(4) Payroll exemptions: number of dependents for an employee; this number can determine which tax tables are used to calculate deductible taxes.

(5) FICA: Federal Insurance Contribution Act; the Social Security law.

(6) FUTA: Federal Unemployment Tax Act.

(7) SUTA: State Unemployment Tax Act.

(8) EIC: Earned Income Credit; a tax refund for some employees whose pay is below a specified minimum and who maintain a home for at least one dependent.

(9) Vacation and sick leave: time to which employees are entitled as specified by the company's benefits plan.

Minimum Wages and Overtime

Federal and state laws regulate most business payroll functions. The Federal Fair Labor Standards Act sets minimum wages, requires overtime, and regulates the use of children in the labor force. Individual state laws might provide standards higher than the federal laws; that is, a state might require that employers pay a higher minimum wage than the federal law requires.

The minimum wage provision requires that employees, not specifically exempted, be paid a minimum hourly rate and an overtime wage of one and one-half the regular wage for time worked in excess of 40 hours per week. Overtime is not required for working days in excess of eight hours, provided the total number of hours in one week does not exceed 40.

Payroll Deductions

An employer is also responsible for withholding certain amounts from the total gross pay. These payroll deductions must be strictly accounted for and reported to the appropriate agencies. Periodically, the employer is required to make a payment to those agencies so the employee's benefits and taxes can be updated.

Deductions may be grouped in two basic categories:

(1) Payroll taxes, which include Social Security taxes, federal income taxes, state income taxes, and local income taxes.

(2) Voluntary deductions, which may include pension and retirement plans, group insurance, union dues, charitable contributions, and others.

Social Security Taxes

Under the Federal Insurance Contribution Act (FICA), both the employer and the employee contribute to the employee's social security account. The contribution amount is a percentage of the employee's wages. The law requires that the employer withhold the employee's share and send it to the appropriate agency each quarter. Along with the employee's share, the employer must pay a matching amount into each employee's account.

Federal and State Income Taxes

Based on the gross amount of wages and the number of exemptions to which an employee is entitled, the employer must deduct amounts for federal and state income taxes. As with other deductions, these tax amounts must be strictly accounted for and paid periodically to the appropriate agencies. At the end of each calendar year, these amounts must be reported to the employee, the Internal Revenue Service, and the state's tax commission.

Two forms are important in the collection and reporting of social security and income taxes: (1) the federal W-4 Form is used by the employee to document the number of exemptions to which he or she is entitled; and (2) the federal W-2 Form is used by the employer to report earnings and deductions. Both forms are also used by state governments for documenting earnings and deductions.

Other Income Taxes

Many cities and counties also levy income taxes on the gross earnings of employees. These must also be accounted for and reported on W-2 Forms at the end of each calendar year.

Federal and State Unemployment Taxes

The Federal Unemployment Tax Act (FUTA) establishes a joint federal and state program to make payments to persons who become unemployed. Each state has a State Unemployment Tax Act (SUTA) that requires employers to pay a percentage of their payrolls to an insurance fund from which unemployment benefits are paid to former employees. FUTA and SUTA are employer taxes and are not deducted from employee payrolls.

Earned Income Credit

For some employees whose wages are below the minimum set by federal law, the employer may be responsible for paying an earned income credit in addition to the regular salary. If such an employee—and possibly that employee's spouse—makes less than the specified minimum and maintains a home for a dependent, he or she can qualify for a tax "refund" although he or she pays no taxes.

Whenever an employee asks that the employer verify and pay the earned income credit, the employer is obligated to do so. The record-keeping for such payments is the responsibility of the employer.

Payroll in the Real World

Accurate payroll records are necessary to determine operating expenses for your business and to report earnings information to employees and to federal, state, and other governmental agencies.

Keeping Payroll Records

The payroll register is the business document through which all those payroll records are kept. The payroll register is prepared at the end of each payroll period. It shows the names of employees and their gross earnings, deductions, and net pay for the given period. Annual reports, including the federal W-2 Forms, are calculated from the periodic payroll registers.

Reporting and Paying Payroll Taxes

On or before the last day of the month following the end of each quarter, an employer must file an "Employer's Quarterly Federal Tax Return," reporting the federal income taxes withheld and the amount of FICA taxes collected from all employees. These amounts must be deposited in a federally approved bank according to a prescribed schedule.

At the end of each year, the employer must provide a "Wage and Tax Statement" (the W-2 Form) to each employee. The form must show the amounts of taxable wages paid, federal income taxes withheld, FICA taxes withheld, and state income taxes withheld. Local income taxes (city or county) must also be shown, if those are withheld.

Copies of the W-2 Form are sent, by the employer, to the Social Security Administration and to the appropriate federal, state, and local tax commissions. An appropriate number of copies must be given to each employee.

Deposits must also be made for the FUTA taxes—if the FUTA liability is greater than $100. These deposits are required before the end of each month, following the end of a calendar quarter. If the employer's FUTA liability is less than $100, the actual amount must be sent to the IRS with the annual FUTA return (Form 940). That form is due to the IRS on or before January 31 of each year.

Controlling Payroll Records

As indicated at the beginning of this chapter, payroll can be a significant part of a business' expenses. In addition to the actual payroll, there are matching FICA taxes and FUTA and SUTA taxes that must be considered when planning payroll management. The record-keeping must include records for the business, for the employees, and for various and sundry other agencies of the federal, state, and local governments.

The business has a large responsibility for keeping payroll records. The use of a computerized accounting and payroll system will greatly reduce the time necessary for keeping those records and for reporting to the appropriate agencies. The use of a computerized system, however, does not lessen the responsibility for that record-keeping.

Acct Type	Description	Debit	Credit
	[TO RECORD PAYROLL]		
Exp	Wages	10,000.00	
Exp	FICA Employer	715.00	
Exp	FUTA	76.00	
Exp	SUTA	87.00	
Liab	FICA W/H Employee		715.00
Liab	FICA Employer		715.00
Liab	FUTA		76.00
Liab	SUTA		87.00
Liab	Federal Income W/H		2,000.00
Liab	State Income W/H		1,285.00
Asset	Payroll Account (Cash)		6,000.00
	TOTALS	10,878.00	10,878.00
	[TO RECORD TAX DEPOSITS]		
Liab	FICA W/H Employee	715.00	
Liab	FICA Employer	715.00	
Liab	FUTA	76.00	
Liab	SUTA	87.00	
Liab	Federal Income W/H	2,000.00	
Liab	State Income W/H	1,285.00	
Asset	Checking Account (Cash)		4,878.00
	TOTALS	4,878.00	4,878.00

Fig. 4-1. The typical accounting entries for one payroll period.

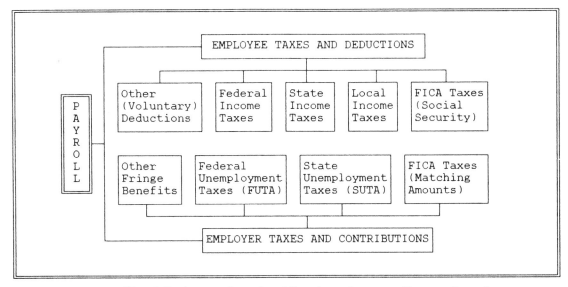

Fig. 4-2. An employer's obligations for payroll recordkeeping.

Effective payroll management and control require all of the following:

(1) The person(s) who must authorize payments for payroll before checks are distributed.

(2) Wages paid are correct and received only by the appropriate employees.

(3) The various reports based on payroll information are reliable and are filed in a timely manner.

(4) Adequate security systems and procedures prevent unauthorized access to computer payroll records.

These management procedures would apply to any aspect of a business operation but are especially important in the payroll area because it involves so many other individuals.

Summary

The basics of payroll management have been presented and include the definitions of common payroll terms and how they are applied in the accounting setting, as well as the types of reports that are necessary in the payroll process.

The *DacEasy* Accounting Process

> **Chapter Goals**
>
> - *In this chapter, you will learn how* DacEasy Accounting *handles the numbers you put into the accounts and journals. You will see the relationships among the separate program modules. As a result, you will be able to make real decisions about how you want to use* DacEasy *in your business, including the levels of simplicity and detail you want to keep.*

When some people begin using a new software package for the first time, they have trouble following the flow of the program. This can be particularly true for accounting and payroll software because of the sophistication—real or perceived—of the software. In many cases, the difficulty comes from a very simple source: There is some difficulty in making the physical move from working on paper (usually a horizontal task) to working on a screen (usually a vertical task). In other cases, the difficulty comes from a lack of understanding that an entry in one module of the software will affect data in other modules.

This chapter addresses the latter issue. Only practice and willingness to learn will help with the former.

The *DacEasy* Program Modules

The *DacEasy Accounting* Main Menu, shown in Fig. 5-1, permits you to access the accounting functions whenever you need to make an entry. The functions themselves represent the various tasks you can complete using the *DacEasy* software. Once you select a function from the menu, you will be able to select a specific accounting operation choose a function from a list of options.

The options list will be displayed in a window attached to your function selection. Figure 5-2 shows the window attached to the Transaction function from the Main Menu. It lists the six program modules where transactions can be directly entered. When you

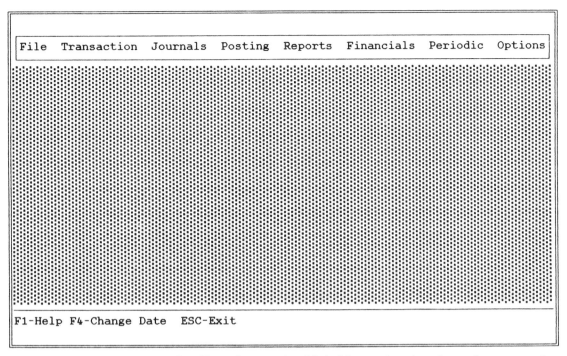

| File | Transaction | Journals | Posting | Reports | Financials | Periodic | Options |

F1-Help F4-Change Date   ESC-Exit

Fig. 5-1. The DacEasy Accounting Main Menu, showing the major accounting functions. DacEasy Payroll runs from a separate program.

make a selection from the Main Menu, the window will display a list of options directly related to those program modules.

The *DacEasy Accounting* program modules include the general ledger, accounts receivable, accounts payable, purchasing, billing, and inventory.

In addition, you can edit your files and run the end-of-period routines, as needed. By selecting the Options function, you can increase the capacity of your files when your company's growth requires it. These are but a few of the things you can do while you're using *DacEasy Accounting* and *Payroll*.

The *DacEasy Payroll* Main Menu also displays the functions that can be accessed in the payroll module. Figure 5-3 shows the *DacEasy Payroll* Main Menu. You can see that it offers only one option not included on the Accounting Main Menu: Payroll Processing.

Although the payroll module is sold separately from the accounting module, it is simply another module of the whole accounting system. When integrated with the *DacEasy Accounting* system, it functions exactly as other modules. Consequently, we will include payroll as a module of the accounting system. The specific functions of the payroll module are discussed in Chapter 4 and as needed in other chapters throughout the book.

What Many Businesses Don't Have and Why

In many cases, business owners or operators will not use receivables or payables

45

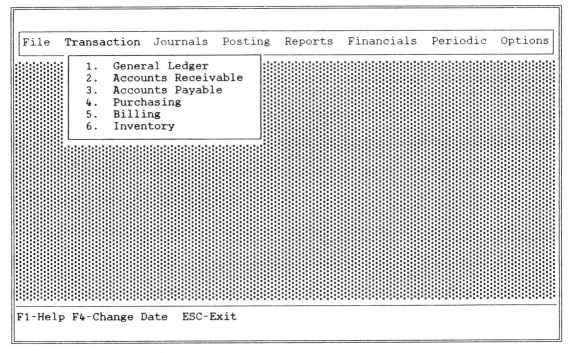

Fig. 5-2. The Transaction window on DacEasy Accounting Main Menu. *The major program modules are listed in the "pull-down" window.*

because the paper work becomes too cumbersome to maintain. Many small businesses will not even consider keeping up-to-date inventory records because of the time and expense involved. Purchasing and billing are necessary evils because you can't sell what you don't have and you can't collect from customers to whom you can't send invoices. Seeing reports of the company's overall activities for the current year and making forecasts for future years are almost unheard of in the small paper-and-pencil business setting.

The primary reason for not collecting the data include the time it takes to gather it and the expense of paying someone else to do it for you.

Needing Your Information and Having It Too

With *DacEasy Accounting* and *Payroll*, you can keep track of information for up to three years and have that information available simply by pressing a few keys. Best of all, you can have it on the screen or on paper.

In addition, all the recordkeeping that goes with having that information is done automatically for you by the "integrated" *DacEasy Accounting* and *Payroll* modules.

Integrating Your Recordkeeping

DacEasy Accounting is designed to do most of the work in accounting for you. Work completed in one module will automatically update all other modules where there would be some change as a result of the work you've done. Because the modules of the

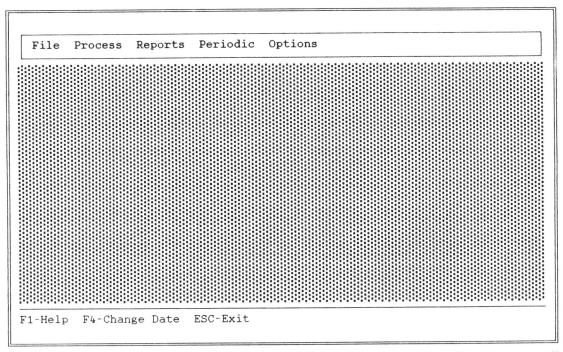

```
  File   Process   Reports   Periodic   Options
```

```
  F1-Help   F4-Change Date   ESC-Exit
```

Fig. 5-3. The DacEasy Payroll Main Menu, *showing the major payroll* **functions.** *DacEasy Accounting runs from a separate program.*

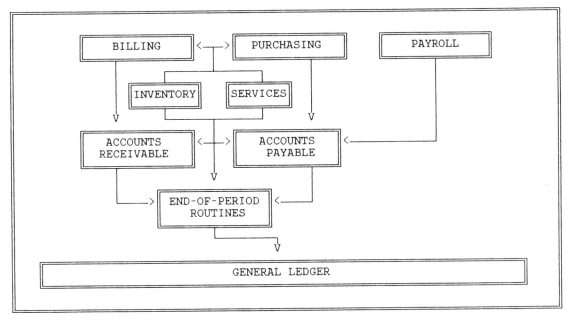

Fig. 5-4. The relationships among the DacEasy Accounting and Payroll modules. *Action in one updates all others.*

accounting package work together in keeping your records, the software is said to be "integrated" (see Fig. 5-4).

As an example of "integrated" recordkeeping, let's look briefly at the inventory process. After you define the items to be included in your inventory and assign each item a unique inventory number, you can have your inventory updated automatically each time you purchase additional stock and each time you sell an item from stock.

The integration of the *DacEasy Accounting* modules is the best reason for learning to use the program.

The General Ledger Module

The general ledger is a summary of all the detailed activity that has gone on in your company. In the ledger, you enter the totals from the other journals in your recordkeeping system. ("Journals" might include a cash disbursements journal, a payroll journal, a general journal, and several other books-of-record where parts of your information are kept.)

If you are keeping your records by hand, you (late into the night when you've finally decided you can't put it off any longer) or someone else, (whom you pay with part of the money you could be using on your next vacation—if you ever get to take one) will calculate the totals from the various journals and will enter those into the general ledger. It is no small task, and it is to be taken seriously because the general ledger is the official financial record for your company.

DacEasy Accounting will automatically calculate and post the summaries from your various journals and records without your turning on a calculator. It is that simple (and if you do need a calculator, *DacEasy Graph + Mate* will pop it up for you).

Accounts receivable, accounts payable, billing, purchasing, and inventory automatically send information to the general ledger whenever the end-of-period routines are run.

The Accounts Receivable Module

Accounts receivable is where the records for individuals and companies who owe you money are kept. In a paper-based accounting system, a ticket is made up at the time of the credit sale and the information from that ticket is posted to accounts receivable by hand. At the end of the recordkeeping period, these amounts are totaled and transferred to the general ledger—again, by hand.

With *DacEasy Accounting*, all you need to do is complete the purchase ticket in the billing module. Accounts receivable and the general ledger will be automatically updated. In addition, your inventory will be decreased, automatically, by the number of each item purchased through the purchase ticket.

The Accounts Payable Module

Accounts payable is where the records are kept for the individuals and companies you owe money for the products and services you purchase to operate your business. Normally, you would create some type of purchase order, send it to your vendor or give it to a representative of that vendor, receive the merchandise and the invoice, and, eventually, write the check to pay for the merchandise or service.

If you maintain a detailed inventory on paper, you must adjust your on-order and on-hand counts for each item received, post the invoice to payables, and make the necessary entries when the check is written to pay for everything. Finally, at the end of the recordkeeping period, the appropriate amounts would be calculated and transferred to the general ledger.

With *DacEasy Accounting*, you simply fill out your purchase order, using the inventory numbers you previously set up. The purchase order automatically updates your on-order counts in inventory. When the merchandise and invoice are received, you update the purchase order to reflect the actual items received and the amounts due. From that point, the on-order counts in inventory are decreased, the on-hand counts are automatically increased, and accounts payable is updated to include the newly received invoice.

When you are ready to pay your vendors, you simply tell *DacEasy Accounting* that you are ready to print the checks, you confirm the amounts to be paid, and you arrange to do something useful while the program prints all your checks.

When it is time to run end-of-the-period procedures, the general ledger is automatically updated and your printed reports will describe, in detail, the activity within each account during that period and for the year-to-date.

Other Activities In Accounts Receivable and Accounts Payable

In addition to the accounting aspects of what has been described for accounts receivable and accounts payable, *DacEasy Accounting* keeps records of spending with each of your vendors and records of payment from each of your customers. At any time, you can check to see how much you have spent with each vendor or you can create a list of customers who have spent over a certain amount with you during the current period (sometimes useful for special sales to preferred customers).

In addition to providing information to vendor and customer files, *DacEasy Accounting* provides information to inventory so that you are always aware of what's moving and what's not. The information can also be used to provide a warning list for items whose numbers have reached levels below your predetermined counts. In addition, the cash value of your inventory (based on the inventory costing system you select) is immediately available whenever you need to see it.

The Purchase Orders Module

The purchase orders module helps you control your purchasing, your inventory, and your billing. Indirectly, it also helps control your accounts payable and the general ledger. Many small businesses, however, tend to overlook the value of a purchasing procedure and do not use it because they believe it takes too much time. Just the opposite is true for the *DacEasy* system.

For *DacEasy Accounting*, the purchasing process requires that your inventory be set up (although the level of detail in that inventory is up to you). On a purchase order, you would list items by your inventory number and the program will mark your inventory with on-order counts. When the items are received from your vendor, you will mark each item received and the program will change its counts to include stock on-hand (instead of on-order).

Your accounts payable is automatically updated so that *DacEasy Accounting* can print the checks to all your vendors whenever your ready.

Note that you don't have to memorize inventory numbers or keep on-hand printed lists if you are using *DacEasy Graph + Mate*. By just pressing a few keys, you can see, on-screen, the complete inventory listing as well as select the appropriate number to be "pasted" on your purchase order.

The Billing Module

If you use the inventory and purchasing modules when you buy products to sell, you will save yourself much time and effort in the billing process. When a customer purchases an item, you can create a sales ticket (for a cash sale) or a customer invoice (for a cash sale) or a customer invoice (for a credit sale) that includes each item's inventory number. The *DacEasy Accounting* program will automatically revise your on-hand inventory counts, using the sales figures from the ticket/invoice.

The billing module updates accounts receivable, inventory, and the general ledger, as well. Updates are done without additional work on your part.

The Inventory Module

One of the real powers of *DacEasy Accounting* is the manner with which it handles your inventory—if you are willing to make the initial investment in time to create a good and logical structure for it to follow.

To keep up-to-the-minute inventory records requires only that you use the purchase order module and the billing module to track purchases and sales. You never have to manually update your inventory if you use the other two modules properly.

The inventory module will also give you lists of products that are not selling, lists of products that are below your desired on-hand minimum counts, and many other reports

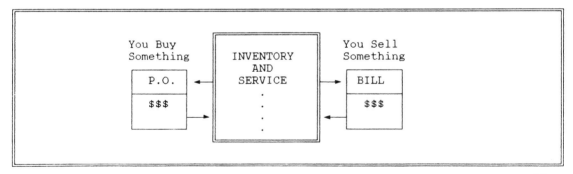

Fig. 5-5. The relationships among purchasing, billing, and inventory. *When you include your inventory numbers for products and services on your purchase orders, your inventory is updated with the number of each item you have "on-order." When you confirm receipt of the items you have ordered, the "on-order" count is changed to "on-hand." When you include your inventory numbers on your customer bills, your inventory is updated by decreasing the "on-hand" counts.*

directly related to inventory control. Consequently, you can make effective decisions about handling your inventory.

Figure 5-5 shows the relationships among the purchasing, billing, and inventory modules.

The Reports Module

One of the special features of *DacEasy Accounting* is that it allows you to print reports from data stored in its files. In addition to several predefined basic reports, it also provides a special function that allows you to design special reports that can call up and use any of the data in your files.

The Payroll Module

The payroll module is sold as a separate program package. It is, however, fully compatible with the other *DacEasy Accounting* modules. The payroll data can be transferred directly to the general ledger.

The payroll module provides a straightforward approach to paying employees. It determines the employer's share of social security taxes as well as the employee's share of social security taxes, state taxes, and federal taxes, based on the number of exemptions and the appropriate tax table. It also provides a means of keeping records for other payroll deductions.

The payroll module will save hours of your time (or the time of someone you pay) just in calculating and printing federal W-2 Forms. Finally, it will print quarterly reports for the state and federal agencies that oversee employment taxes and social security taxes.

Summary

This chapter, discusses the many program modules that make up the entire DacEasy Accounting *system and how they interact to automatically calculate and record data to reflect change in other modules.*

DacEasy Graph + Mate

Chapter Goals
- *This chapter features one of the most powerful utilities for the* DacEasy *series.* DacEasy Graph + Mate *is an essential part of making the* DacEasy *series more effective and efficient. The program is considered essential by us, and will be an integral part of the discussions throughout the book.*

DacEasy Graph + Mate is an optional program—it is not necessary in order to use the accounting or payroll modules. It adds so much flexibility and power, however, that it should be considered essential in performing all the accounting and payroll tasks.

DacEasy Graph + Mate

DacEasy Graph + Mate is an ''up-front'' program—that is, it loads before the accounting and payroll programs and provides services as you use those programs. When either the accounting or payroll program is loaded, *DacEasy Graph + Mate* provides several features that would not, otherwise, be available. These features include:

(1) A menu where accounting, payroll, graphing, and report modules can be accessed without memorizing a set of commands in order to start a program.

(2) Files that contain information about accounts, customers, vendors, employees, and other items can be viewed on-screen at any time. Without this feature, paper copies of those files must be used when looking for specific records or special information.

(3) A ''pop-up'' calculator that can be displayed at any time for calculations needed for data entry. Answers can then be automatically ''pasted'' from the calculator into the current work screen.

(4) A " pop-up" note pad can be used to make notes as you work. The notes can be printed for later use. Information written on the note pad at one work screen can be kept on the pad until needed on another work screen and can then be "pasted" into the screen where it's needed.

(5) Data files can be backed up from within the accounting or payroll program. This is extremely useful when you begin an important posting process and would like to have a backup in case the power fails during the process. This backup feature is different from making a backup from the DOS command line, which is discussed in Chapter 2. When needed, the backup files can be restored from within the program.

(6) Printed reports can be viewed on-screen before they are printed to paper. This permits verification of data before reports are actually printed.

(7) A "macro" feature permits you to assign a number of keystrokes to only one key that, when pressed, will result in all the desired keystrokes being entered. ("Macro" is the opposite of "micro"—the latter indicates something smaller than normal such as "microcomputer" is a small computer, the former indicates something larger than normal, such as one key doing the work of several.)

Another important feature of *DacEasy Graph+Mate* is its Help facility. At any point in the use of *DacEasy Graph+Mate* you can press the <F1> key to get a list of keystrokes to be used for a current task. That list of keystrokes relates to the task you are currently trying to complete. When you move from one section of *DacEasy Graph+Mate* to another—such as from viewing files to using the calculator—the lists of keystrokes will be different, based on what you are trying to do.

The remainder of the chapter discusses two aspects of using *DacEasy Graph+Mate*. We will complete the installation process and how to use the program's features.

Completing the Installation

Chapter 2, discusses the installation of *DacEasy Graph+Mate* but we left out several of the installation options for later discussion. Installation procedures that were discussed in Chapter 2 included only those that were necessary for immediate use of the program. We will now discuss the other options that will allow you to take advantage of the program's special features, such as setting screen colors and defining report formats (in File Views).

Setting the Screen Colors for *DacEasy Graph+Mate*

As *DacEasy Graph+Mate* is used with the accounting and payroll modules, data are displayed in "windows" that open on your work screens. These windows can be displayed in various colors so to maximize readability. The Colors option on the Installation Menu (see Fig. 2-9) lets you define colors for each of the eight types of windows that can be opened on a screen. Each of these windows has four different areas, all of which can be colored differently.

There are eight types of windows that can be opened through *DacEasy Graph + Mate*:

(1) The Background Screen refers to the total screen displayed when *DacEasy Graph + Mate* is running.

(2) The Main Menu Window is the bordered window that contains the menu options from which you can select.

(3) After you select an option from the Main Menu Window, a Pull-Down Menu Window will be displayed. An example of a pull-down window can be seen in Fig. 2-9.

(4) The Selection/Pick Windows are displayed when you make a selection from a Pull-Down Menu Window. This window lets you select a final action or transaction.

(5) Processing Windows provide work screens or data screens where you can initiate or complete a transaction. An example of this screen is the list of account numbers from the general ledger chart of accounts.

(6) Message Windows prompt you about available options at specific steps in the accounting and payroll processes.

(7) Query Windows permit you to enter criteria so that *DacEasy* can find specific information. In effect, you can ask the software questions and it should give you appropriate answers. (Keep in mind that all software will do exactly what you ask it to do—whether or not that's what you want it to do.)

(8) Help Windows pop-up when you press the <F1> key at any point during your work session.

You can define the colors for four parts of each of the windows. Each window will have "normal" text, with a background color on which your text is written. You can also define an "inverse" color combination that will emphasize the text written to it. Usually (but not always), the inverse color combination will be the opposite of the normal combination—that is, the inverse of white letters on a blue screen will be blue letters on a white screen. Each screen will also have a border that can be colored to suit your personal preference. At times, special information will be displayed and you may want the colors to contrast with the other colors already displayed on a work screen. Those special color combinations can be defined by adjusting the "extra" colors provided in the colors window (see Fig. 6-1).

Figure 6-1 shows the color definition window for the Background Screen. A marker under the "normal" box indicates that colors for normal text can be defined by using the arrow keys. The left and right arrow keys change the background colors while the up and down arrow keys change the color of the text. Pressing <ENTER> will permanently store the changes so that you don't have to repeat it each time you start the program. The <ESC> key will cancel all color changes and reset the colors to the default values.

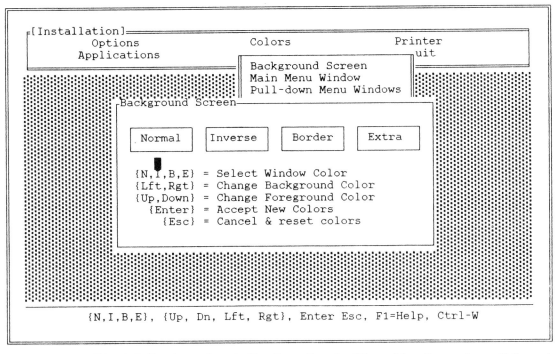

Fig. 6-1. Setting colors in DacEasy Graph + Mate. *Move the marker, roll through the color possibilities, and press <ENTER> to accept new colors.*

When you press N, I, B, or E the marker's location will change to correspond to the box for which the letter is an abbreviation. When the marker is moved to the "inverse" box, you can select background and foreground colors by using the arrow keys, again. The colors of the borders and the "extra" windows can be changed and stored in the same manner.

When all colors are set for each of the eight window types, press <ESC> to return to the Installation Menu.

Defining Fields for File Views

DacEasy Graph + Mate permits you to look into your accounting and payroll files without leaving your current task. For example, you might be working in the purchasing module and you need the inventory number of an item you want to put on your purchase order. You can press the <ALT+F10> key combination to display the *DacEasy Graph + Mate* Menu at the top of the work screen. From that menu, you will be able to select FILEVIEW to view the inventory file (see Fig. 6-2 to see the complete example).

The FILEVIEW option enables you to see several columns of information in a viewing window. You can choose the data you wish to be displayed by defining the fields to be included in the view format. To do this, just select the FILEVIEW options from the Installation Menu.

Figure 6-3 shows seven files that you can view while using *DacEasy Accounting*

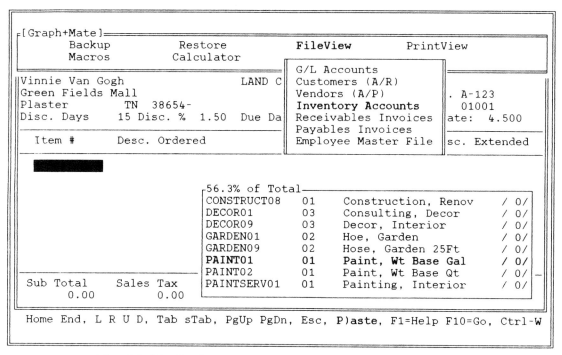

Fig. 6-2. The DacEasy Accounting work screen in the background as DacEasy
Graph+Mate is "popped up" over it. *The inventory accounts under FileView are
shown in the window at the lower right. User options are displayed at the bottom of
the screen.*

and *Payroll*. These are the same seven files listed in the window in Fig. 6-2, which displays
the FILEVIEW from within the purchasing module. Each of these files has a built-in set
of columns that can be used for viewing. This installation process, however, will allow
you to delete fields you don't want to view and insert other fields you wish to see.

Figure 6-4 shows the work screen for defining the view of the Inventory Accounts.
The screen is divided into three distinct parts. The top section of the screen shows the
names of the fields that will be displayed through FILEVIEW, if you elect to use the
default fields. The center section of the screen lists all possible fields that can be included
if you decide to change the default fields. The bottom section of the screen is used when
you want a calculation to be made and displayed as you view the file.

Each section of the screen uses a separate set of keys to move the highlight from
field to field. These keys are listed at the bottom of the screen. Press <F1> to see
a brief description of each of these keys.

In the top section of the screen, the <TAB> and <SHIFT+TAB> keys move
the highlight bar right and left, respectively. The <DEL> key will delete the highlighted
field from the viewed fields. The <ENTER> key will insert the field that is highlighted
in the middle section of the screen and push other fields to the right.

As you move from one field in the top section of the screen, to another field in the

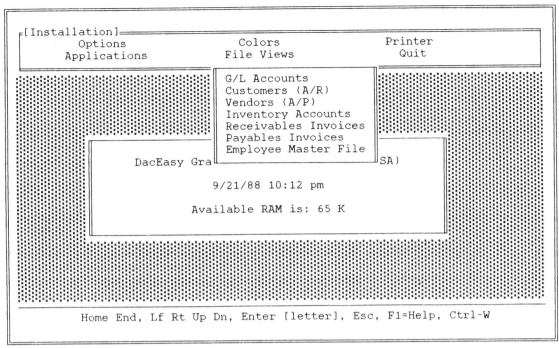

Fig. 6-3. Selecting a file to define a DacEasy Graph+Mate window.

section, a counter will move across the line separating the parts of the screen. The counter cannot be greater than 132, which is the number of characters a standard printer can print on one line—provided it prints in condensed print.

In Fig. 6-4, you will notice the letter "S" above the field name for ITEM NUMBER. That "S" indicates that the viewed file will be "sorted" by that field. If you want to sort by some other field, move the highlight to that field by using the <TAB> or <SHIFT + TAB> keys and pressing <CTRL + S>. The "S" will be moved from the current field and placed above the newly marked field.

If you want to include a calculation in the viewed information, <TAB> the highlight bar in the top section of the screen to where you want the calculation to be displayed. Press <CTRL + F> to move the cursor to the bottom section of the screen. Here you can create a formula using fields from the files or using constants with the fields in the file. Once the cursor is in the formula area, use the arrow keys to move the highlight to the middle section to the field you want included in the calculation and press <ENTER>. The field will be inserted into the formula. You must then press an operation key (addition, subtraction, division, or multiplication) to continue the formula. Once the operation key is entered, you can enter a constant value or select another field to add to the formula. When your formula is complete, press the < = > key to end it. You will be asked for a title for the column to be viewed and a width for the column. When all fields are set, press <F10> to finalize the view format.

In the middle of the screen, you can select fields for viewing or calculating. The highlight bar can be moved one field at a time by pressing the appropriate arrow keys.

```
┌F[Installation]════════════════════════════════════════════════╗
│┌FInventory Accounts═══════════════════════════════════════════┐│
││    [S]                                                        ││
││  Item         Product        Item          Last    On-hand   On-hand  ││
││  Number        Type       Description      Sale    Fractions  Dollars ││
││                                                              ││
││[1]══════════════════════════════════════════════════════[77]││
││ [Record Status    ]      Item Number          Item Type      ││
││  Item Description        Unit Measure         Unit Fraction  ││
││  Product Type            Bin Number           Vendor Number  ││
││  Sales Price             Taxable Y/N          Last Sale      ││
││  Minimum Quantity        Reorder Quantity     Last Purchase  ││
││  Last Price              Standard Cost        Average Cost   ││
││  On-hand Fractions       On-hand Dollars      Committed Fractions ││
││  On-order Fractions      YBL Purch-#          Last-YR Purch-# ││
││  YTD Purch-#             Forecast Purch-#     YBL Purch-$    ││
││  Last-YR Purch-$         YTD Purch-$          Forecast Purch-$ ││
││  YBL Sold-#              Last-Yr Sold-#       YTD Sold-#     ││
││═══════════════════════════[Formula]══════════════════════════││
││                                                              ││
││                                                              ││
││                                                              ││
│└──────────────────────────────────────────────────────────────┘│
│ Home End Lf Rt Up Dn, Tab sTab Ctrl-F,S, Enter Esc,F1=Help F10=Ok, Ctrl-W │
└────────────────────────────────────────────────────────────────┘
```

Fig. 6-4. Selecting the fields to show when the DacEasy Graph+Mate Main Menu FileView is selected.

The <HOME> key and the <END> key will move the highlight to the beginning or end of the list of fields. Pressing <ENTER> selects the highlighted field for placement in the top section of the screen or in the bottom section, depending on the location of the cursor.

(Figure 6-4 shows a sample work screen where a view file can be made. At the bottom of the screen is a list of usable keys. Our figure abbreviates the left arrow, right arrow, up arrow, and down arrow keys because the arrow symbols are not printable characters on most printers. Also, the <SHIFT+TAB> combination is abbreviated (with ''sTab'') because the <SHIFT> key was symbolized by an up arrow, which is not a printable character.)

Using this procedure, you can delete, add, or change the order fields displayed in your file views. Figure 6-5 shows a modified view made for the inventory file. Note the formula for the inserted field.

Go through the procedures described above for each of the seven types of files, so the viewed data will have meaning to you and your business. In the middle section of the screen, field names will be different for each of the seven file types.

After completing the view formats, you have completed the setup and installation of *DacEasy Graph+Mate*. You are now ready to start working with *DacEasy Accounting* and *Payroll* at the business level.

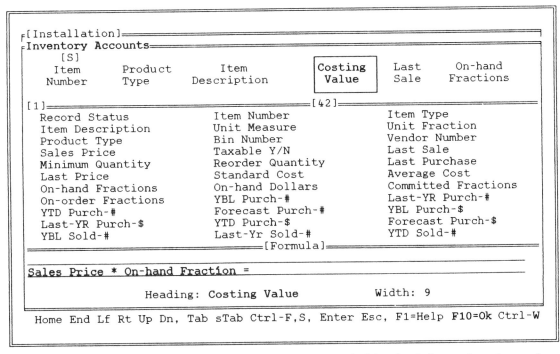

```
 ┌[Installation]════════════════════════════════════════════════════════════╗
 ┌Inventory Accounts════════════════════════════════════════════════════════
     [S]
    Item          Product        Item        │Costing │   Last     On-hand
   Number          Type       Description    │ Value  │   Sale    Fractions

 [1]═════════════════════════════════════[42]══════════════════════════════
   Record Status            Item Number            Item Type
   Item Description         Unit Measure           Unit Fraction
   Product Type             Bin Number             Vendor Number
   Sales Price              Taxable Y/N            Last Sale
   Minimum Quantity         Reorder Quantity       Last Purchase
   Last Price               Standard Cost          Average Cost
   On-hand Fractions        On-hand Dollars        Committed Fractions
   On-order Fractions       YBL Purch-#            Last-YR Purch-#
   YTD Purch-#              Forecast Purch-#       YBL Purch-$
   Last-YR Purch-$          YTD Purch-$            Forecast Purch-$
   YBL Sold-#               Last-Yr Sold-#         YTD Sold-#
 ═══════════════════════════════════════[Formula]══════════════════════════

 Sales Price * On-hand Fraction = _____

               Heading: Costing Value            Width: 9

 ══════════════════════════════════════════════════════════════════════════
  Home End Lf Rt Up Dn, Tab sTab Ctrl-F,S, Enter Esc, F1=Help F10=Ok Ctrl-W
```

Fig. 6-5. Defining a formula to be included in the information shown in a DacEasy Graph+Mate window.

Adding Programs to the Applications Menu

Chapter 2 discusses adding additional lists of programs you can run automatically from the applications menu (see Fig. 2-12 and Fig. 2-13). Figure 6-6 shows the actual menu that is displayed after setup and installation is completed.

We discussed the setup routine only in terms of the basic start-up for *DacEasy Accounting* and *Payroll*. Consequently, Fig. 6-6 shows only those items for actually using the programs. The installation of the applications menu, however, offers more power than the simple start-up process. Part of the power lies in using the installation to set up more than one company or department.

Figure 6-7 shows an applications menu displayed when *DacEasy Graph+Mate* is started after setting up two companies. That menu includes accounting and payroll access for Parts and Parcels (our sample company from the tutorial chapters) and for the Temple of Groom, a pet care center.

To work with the Parts and Parcels files, simply move the highlight bar to the appropriate application and press <ENTER>. With the Temple of Groom files you would select the appropriate application in a similar manner. Either choice will start the *DacEasy* program; however, the data files used by that program will be in a subdirectory separate from the data files for the other application.

During installation, you can elect to edit the applications menu, as shown in Fig. 6-8. Compare that figure to Fig. 2-13, where we made the original installation. Giving

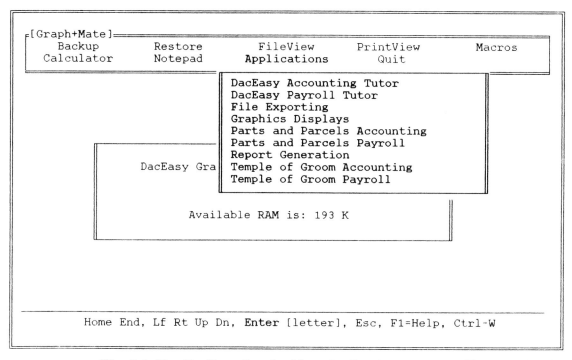

Fig. 6-6. The DacEasy Graph + Mate Applications window. You can select the DacEasy application you want to work with.

the name of the company as the application name and giving a data path to a separate subdirectory—C: \ DEP3 \ GROOM—allows *DacEasy* to use the appropriate data files. You can edit the application name for another company—Parts and Parcels—and give the path to the C: \ DEP3 \ PARTS. When that option is selected, *DacEasy* will use the appropriate data files.

Figure 6-9 shows the configuration required to display the applications menu in Fig. 6-7. Note that the program and path columns are the same for each payroll option. The same is true for each accounting option. The command/data directory column, however, shows that each program will look in different subdirectories for each company and application.

The applications menu shown in Fig. 6-7 and built in Fig. 6-9 includes several programs provided by *DacEasy Graph + Mate*. File exporting, graphics displays, and report generation are modules provided by *Graph + Mate* and are not available within the accounting or payroll programs alone. These modules will be discussed in the next section of this chapter.

In addition, the menu includes the two tutorial modules—one for accounting and one for payroll—that have been placed in a subdirectory called TUTOR3. *DacEasy Accounting* and *Payroll* tutorials will not be discussed in this book.

Using *DacEasy Graph + Mate*

After installing *DacEasy Graph + Mate* as described here and in Chapter 2, you can start either the accounting or payroll programs. Access the *DacEasy Graph + Mate* features by pressing <ALT + F10> at any time, for either program.

To start *Graph + Mate* and *DacEasy Accounting* from the DOS prompt:

CD ＼ GRAFMATE   (to change directory to the *Graph + Mate* subdirectory)

GM   (to run *DacEasy Graph + Mate*)

DacEasy Graph + Mate displays a top-line menu where you can select the APPLICATIONS menu to choose the department or company you wish to work with. Figure 6-7 shows a sample of that screen. When you make an application selection, the selected program—accounting or payroll—starts normally.

The *DacEasy Graph + Mate* Options

The *DacEasy Graph + Mate* menu gives you seven utility options to choose from. Each of these can be run simultaneously with *DacEasy Accounting* or *DacEasy Payroll*. The remainder of this chapter will describe how to use each of the options.

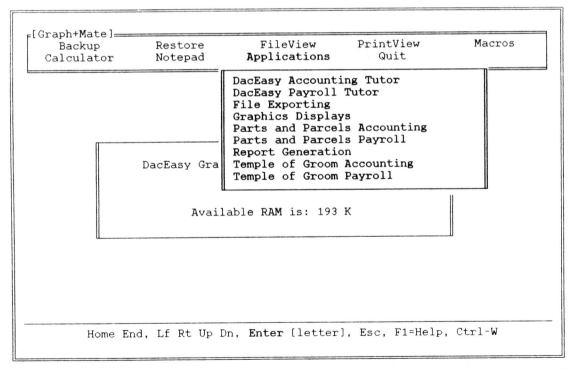

Fig. 6-7. The Applications window shows that accounting and payroll applications can be added for different companies or departments.

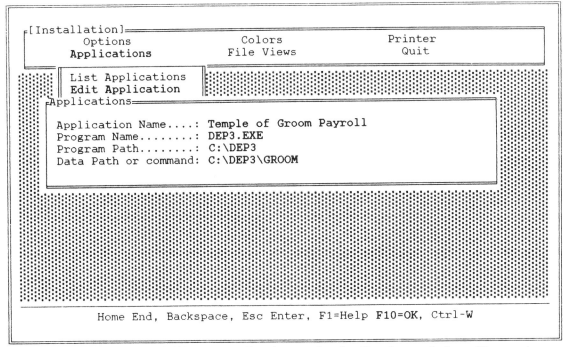

```
┌[Installation]═══════════════════════════════════════════════════
│       Options              Colors              Printer
│       Applications         File Views          Quit
│  ┌──────────────────────┐ ░░░░░░░░░░░░░░░░░░░░░░░░░░░░░░░░░░
│  │ List Applications    │ ░░░░░░░░░░░░░░░░░░░░░░░░░░░░░░░░░░
│  │ Edit Application     │ ░░░░░░░░░░░░░░░░░░░░░░░░░░░░░░░░░░
│ ┌Applications═════════════════════════════════════════════┐
│ │ Application Name....: Temple of Groom Payroll            │
│ │ Program Name.......: DEP3.EXE                            │
│ │ Program Path.......: C:\DEP3                             │
│ │ Data Path or command: C:\DEP3\GROOM                     │
│ │                                                         │
│ └─────────────────────────────────────────────────────────┘
│
│
│
│
│
│  ──────────────────────────────────────────────────────────
│   Home End, Backspace, Esc Enter, F1=Help F10=OK, Ctrl-W
└──────────────────────────────────────────────────────────────
```

Fig. 6-8. Adding an application to the Applications window. You must name the business, the program to run, and the paths to the program and the data. DacEasy allows you to use the same program path with different data paths for different companies or departments.

To activate *DacEasy Graph + Mate* while working within the accounting or payroll programs, hold down the <ALT> key and press the <F10> key. The *DacEasy Graph + Mate* menu will be displayed. (As you are using *DacEasy Graph + Mate*, note that *"Graph + Mate"* is printed in the upper left corner of the screen. While you were installing the program, the word "Installation" was displayed in that location.)

Pressing the <F1> key will provide help in selecting available options. The <ESC> key will remove the help window.

Backup/Restore

When the *DacEasy Graph + Mate* menu is displayed (press <ALT + F10>), the first option on the menu line is highlighted. This option allows you to make a quick backup copy of one or more of the *DacEasy* data files.

To use this option, you should have at least one newly-formatted disk on hand to make the backup copy. Once the backup is made, put it in a safe place until needed again.

Figure 6-10 shows the three-step process for backing up your files. From the *DacEasy Graph + Mate* menu, select Backup. A window will open and you will be asked whether you want to backup your accounting files or your payroll files (both should be done daily). Select one and provide the required information so the program can find

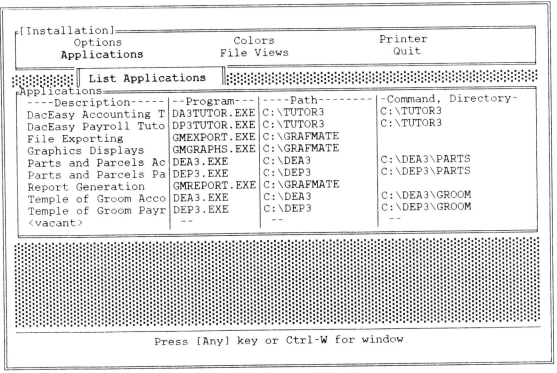

```
┌[Installation]═══════════════════════════════════════════════════════════
│      Options                 Colors              Printer
│      Applications            File Views          Quit
│
├─────────────────────────────────────────────────────────────────────────
│░░░░░░░░║ List Applications ║░░░░░░░░░░░░░░░░░░░░░░░░░░░░░░░░░░░░░░░░░░░░░░
┌Applications═══════════════════════════════════════════════════════════
│ ----Description----- │--Program---│----Path--------│-Command, Directory-
│ DacEasy Accounting T │DA3TUTOR.EXE│C:\TUTOR3       │C:\TUTOR3
│ DacEasy Payroll Tuto │DP3TUTOR.EXE│C:\TUTOR3       │C:\TUTOR3
│ File Exporting       │GMEXPORT.EXE│C:\GRAFMATE     │
│ Graphics Displays    │GMGRAPHS.EXE│C:\GRAFMATE     │
│ Parts and Parcels Ac │DEA3.EXE    │C:\DEA3         │C:\DEA3\PARTS
│ Parts and Parcels Pa │DEP3.EXE    │C:\DEP3         │C:\DEP3\PARTS
│ Report Generation    │GMREPORT.EXE│C:\GRAFMATE     │
│ Temple of Groom Acco │DEA3.EXE    │C:\DEA3         │C:\DEA3\GROOM
│ Temple of Groom Payr │DEP3.EXE    │C:\DEP3         │C:\DEP3\GROOM
│ <vacant>             │  --        │  --            │  --

            Press [Any] key or Ctrl-W for window
```

Fig. 6-9. Applications list after modifications.

the files you are to backup. Be sure to give the path to your data files. For our examples, the path would be the same as shown in Fig. 6-10.

The Backup Directory will be the name of the disk drive where you want the backup copies made. Place your empty, formatted disk in drive A: and then type the backup directory as shown in Fig. 6-10. If you are restoring files, you would give the name of the disk drive that contained the disk with your backup files.

When you press <ENTER> to confirm the Backup Directory, a window will open to remind you to place your first backup diskette into the designated drive. If the first diskette fills up, you will be prompted to remove it and insert a second diskette. This process continues until all of your files are copied.

Should you decide to stop the backup at any point, you can press <ESC>. To name the backup copies of data files, the system uses the file extension .D1 and the extension .K1 to name the backup copies of key files. To check your diskettes after copying your files, use the DIR command from the DOS prompt.

There are two important considerations when using this backup utility:

(1) A backup should always be made before you start a posting process, since the posting process changes your data files. If there is a power failure during the posting process, your files can be irreparably damaged.

(2) This backup procedure is best used for short-time purposes only. In addition

to doing the necessary backups using this utility, you should make regular backups using the DOS command level. This procedure is described in your DOS manual under the BACKUP command. The DOS RESTORE command is also important.

Restore

The Restore option does the opposite of the Backup option. If there is ever damage to your files, the Restore option will copy your backup files from your backup diskettes to the appropriate subdirectory so that you can continue with your work.

A very important consideration before using the Restore option is that files backed up from within *DacEasy Graph+Mate* must be restored from within *DacEasy Graph+Mate*. The DOS RESTORE command cannot restore these files.

FileView

The FileView option from the *DacEasy Graph+Mate* menu will be one of the most used features of the program. This option permits you to see, on-screen, any of the files in your accounting or payroll programs. Because you can call these files to the screen at any time, it is not necessary to keep printed copies of files near your work area.

Figure 6-11 shows how to open a FileView window. After selecting FileView from the menu line, select the name of the file to view. In the sample, we selected the Customer

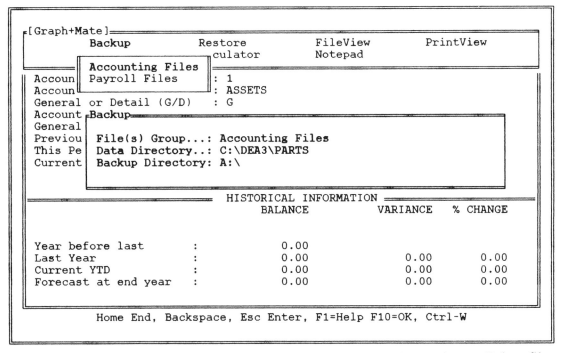

Fig. 6-10. Window where backup copies of accounting and payroll data files are made.

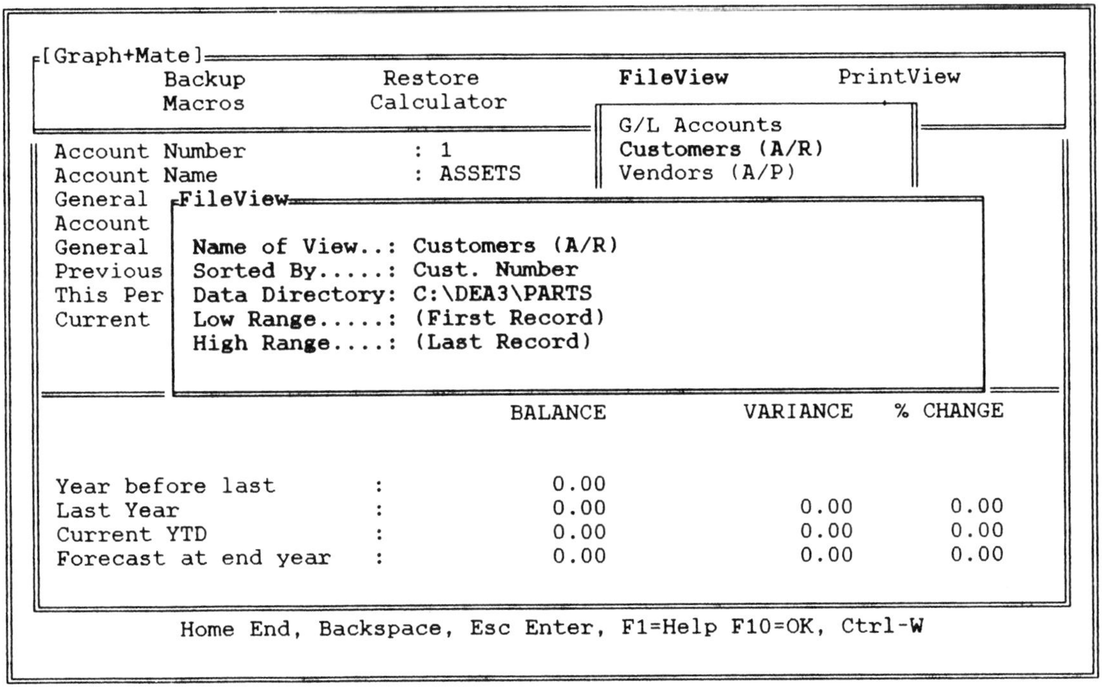

```
┌[Graph+Mate]════════════════════════════════════════════════════════════════
│        Backup         Restore       FileView        PrintView
│        Macros         Calculator   ┌──────────────────────┐
│════════════════════════════════════│ G/L Accounts
│  Account Number           : 1      │ Customers (A/R)
│  Account Name             : ASSETS │ Vendors (A/P)
│  General  ┌FileView═══════════════════════════════════════════════
│  Account  │
│  General  │  Name of View..: Customers (A/R)
│  Previous │  Sorted By.....: Cust. Number
│  This Per │  Data Directory: C:\DEA3\PARTS
│  Current  │  Low Range.....: (First Record)
│           │  High Range....: (Last Record)
│           │
│═══════════│
│                              BALANCE        VARIANCE    % CHANGE
│
│  Year before last    :         0.00
│  Last Year           :         0.00           0.00        0.00
│  Current YTD         :         0.00           0.00        0.00
│  Forecast at end year:         0.00           0.00        0.00
│
└──────────────────────────────────────────────────────────────────────────
       Home End, Backspace, Esc Enter, F1=Help F10=OK, Ctrl-W
```

Fig. 6-11. Selecting a file to view within a DacEasy Graph+Mate window.
You can define a range of records, or view all of the records in a particular file.

File (the A/R is an abbreviation for "accounts receivable"). The name of the file will appear in the FileView window. The window also displays the "sorted by" field and the path to the data directory (which can be edited). You can name a starting number and an ending number within the file so the computer knows which records to select. We chose to start at the first record and end at the last record, which are the default values. Figure 6-12 shows a list of customer records.

At the top of the window containing the customers list is the message "0.0% of Total." This represents the percentage of the file though which you have moved the cursor. As the cursor is moved through the file, the percentage changes to reflect the relative location of the cursor within the file.

At the bottom of the window, all of the options for operating FileView are listed. (Note that we used L, R, U, and D to designate the left, right, up, and down arrows. On screen, however, these arrows will actually be displayed.) One of the options is <CTRL+W>, which gives you access to the "window" commands. These commands let you shrink the window so you can see the screen behind it if necessary. You can also move the shrunken window using the arrow keys.

Another option, shown at the bottom of the screen in Fig. 6-12, is the "P)aste" command. When you press the <P> key, the customer number under the cursor will be "pasted" into the workscreen under the window. The window will then close so you can continue working on the customer's record.

```
┌────────────────────────────────────────────────────────────────────────────┐
│ ┌──────────────────────────────────────────────────────────────────────┐═══ │
│ │ ┌0.0% of Total───────────────────────────────────────────────────┐   │    │
│ │ Cust.              Customer         Area  Telephone     Credit    Current│  │
│ │ Number               Name           Code   Number       Limit     Balance│ │
│ │ ------  -------------------------   ---   --------      --------   --------│ │
│ │ BILD01 Bildah Supply, Inc.          803   555-2745      8000.00      0.00 ║  │
│ │ PAMS01 Pam's Spades/Garden Shop     803   555-9875      2000.00      0.00 ║  │
│ │ VOLT01 Volten, Rhea                 803   555-1578       500.00      0.00 ║  │
│ │ WEIR01 Weir Lighting Fixtures       803   555-3467      5000.00      0.00 ║  │
│ │ WEIR02 Weir, P. Annie               803   555-2086       500.00      0.00 ║  │
│ │                                                                          ║  │
│ │                                                                          ═  │
│ │                                                                          ═  │
│ │                                                                             │
│ │                                                                             │
│ └──────────────────────────────────────────────────────────────────────┘    │
│ Home End, L R U D, Tab sTab, PgUp PgDn, Esc, P)aste, F1=Help, F10=Go, Ctrl-W  │
└────────────────────────────────────────────────────────────────────────────┘
```

Fig. 6-12. DacEasy Graph+Mate window, showing a customer list. Viewing in a window means you need not keep printed lists from which to search for names or customer numbers.

The following is one example of when you might want to use the FileView option. Suppose you are creating a purchase order to buy items sold in your store and you do not remember the vendor's ID number. Press the <ALT+F10> keys combination to select FileView and choose Vendors (the A/P stands for ''accounts payable'') to see the ID numbers for each vendor. Move the highlight bar to the appropriate ID number, press <P> to ''paste'' the number straight onto your purchase order on the screen. Figure 6-12 shows an example of a FileView listing.

The same procedure is used to put inventory numbers on purchase orders. This allows *DacEasy* to keep track of what you are ordering.

The ability to find ID numbers is important to your efficiency in working with *DacEasy* programs.

PrintView

The PrintView option will most often be used when you are using the Reports module from the *DacEasy Accounting* Main Menu. It will permit you to view reports before they are printed.

Reports are written on the disk in ''capture'' mode and then viewed. After viewing the report, you can decide if additional information is needed or other adjustments, before it is actually printed.

Figure 6-13 shows how a report is viewed. From the *DacEasy Accounting* Main

```
┌─────────────────────────────────────────────────────────────────────────────┐
│ ┌───────────────────────────────────────────────────────────────────────┐   │
│ │ [Graph+Mate]════════════════════════════════════════════════════════    │
│ │    Backup          Restore          FileView       PrintView           │
│ │    Macros          Calculator       Notepa┌────────────────────────────┐ │
│ │ ═══════════════════════════════════════════│ Capture a Report          │ │
│ │ Account Number         : 1                  │ View a Captured Report    │ │
│ │ Account Name           : ASSETS             │ Print a Captured Report   │ │
│ │ General or Detail (G/D) : G                 │ Write/Append Report to File│ │
│ │ Account Level (1-5)    : 1                  └────────────────────────────┘ │
│ │ General Account        :                                                │
│ │ Previous Balance       :              0.00                              │
│ │ This Period Balance    :              0.00                              │
│ │ Current Balance        :              0.00                              │
│ │                                                                         │
│ │                         ═══ HISTORICAL INFORMATION ═══                  │
│ │                              BALANCE          VARIANCE    % CHANGE      │
│ │                                                                         │
│ │ Year before last   :         0.00                                       │
│ │ Last Year          :         0.00             0.00        0.00          │
│ │ Current YTD         :         0.00             0.00        0.00          │
│ │ Forecast at end year :       0.00             0.00        0.00          │
│ └───────────────────────────────────────────────────────────────────────┘   │
│        Home End, Lf Rt Up Dn, Enter [letter], Esc, F1=Help, Ctrl-W          │
└─────────────────────────────────────────────────────────────────────────────┘
```

Fig. 6-13. The PrintView window lets you preview your reports on-screen before you commit to printing them on paper. You must "capture" a report before it can be viewed or filed to disk.

Menu, select a report to print. The report will then be "captured" before it gets to the printer, viewed in the captured format, printed (if a printed copy is wanted), or written to a diskette for later use.

Choosing a Report

As a sample of the "capture" process, let's look at one of the financial reports available from the accounting module. When you select the Financials option from the *DacEasy Accounting* Main Menu, a list of available reports will be displayed. One of these reports is the "Changes in Financial Conditions" report. Move the highlight bar down to that option but do not press <ENTER> to select the report until after you have started the "capture" process.

Capturing a Report

To capture a report for viewing—instead of printing it straight to the printer—press <ALT + F10> to display the *DacEasy Graph + Mate* menu window. From the menu, select PrintView. Highlight the Capture a Report option and press <ENTER>. Name the path and file where the captured report can be printed. Once the path is named, you will be returned to the pull-down window listing the "Changes in Financial Conditions" report. Highlight it and press <ENTER>. Answer the questions about the levels of accounts to include, the first and last records to include, and the status of inactive records.

After the questions are answered, the report will be printed to disk and to the computer's memory.

Viewing a Captured Report

In order to view a report, first capture the report, press <ALT+F10> to start *DacEasy Graph+Mate* and select PrintView. The report will be displayed on the screen just as it would look if you had printed it to paper. Figure 6-14 shows a portion of the "Changes in Financial Conditions" report printed earlier.

If a report is wider than 80 columns—that is, if it is wider than your screen—use the <TAB> key to move the screen to the left so you can see what's to the right. Pressing <SHIFT+TAB> will move it back the other way. If the report is longer than your screen, use the <PgUp> and <PgDn> keys to move up or down.

A report cannot be edited at this stage. The only way to change data is to re-enter it in the appropriate *DacEasy* program and reprint the report.

Pressing <F1> will provide a list of keystrokes that can be used to print reports from your accounting and payroll data.

Macros

A macro is a set of keystrokes or commands assigned to one key so that when the key is pressed, the entire series of keystrokes or commands is entered—as if they had each been typed individually.

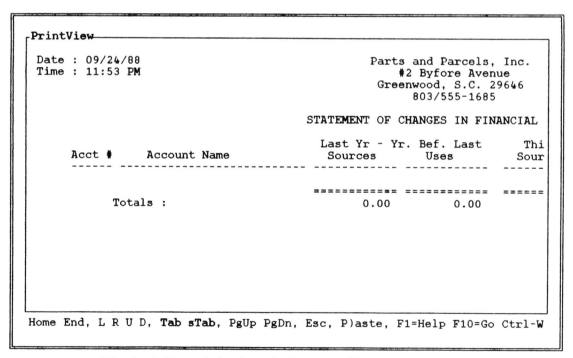

Fig. 6-14. Upper left edge of a "captured" report. *Because our data has not yet been placed in the accounting system, the report shows zero totals.*

Keyboard macros are common tools in many programs. In fact, there are several programs that do nothing but let you create and use macros.

DacEasy lets you build macros and use them in the *DacEasy Graph + Mate* Macros option. There are two ways to build a macro: (1) Write down the keystrokes the first time you use them; then call up the Macros option and enter the keystrokes one at a time; or (2) use the "learn" mode as you go through the keystrokes for the first time. *DacEasy* will learn the keystrokes and then let you assign them to one key—or you can assign the macro to a screen name that can be marked for use.

Regardless of how macros are created, all macros are assigned a name and saved in a list of macro names. You can save any macro you create or edit so it is available to you each time you use *DacEasy*.

To use a macro at any point in *DacEasy Accounting* or *Payroll*, press < ALT + F10 >, choose Macros, move the highlight to the macro name, press < Ctrl + P > to "paste" the macro into your work screen. All keystrokes assigned to that name will be handled as though you were typing them in. In effect, a lot of work can be done with only a few keystrokes.

As an example of the use of a macro, let's assume we want to "automate" printing our Chart of Accounts so it can be done by pressing a macro key instead of going through the 12 keystrokes required to do it manually.

Before we build the macro, consider the 12 keystrokes individually. At the *DacEasy Accounting Main Menu*, the highlight bar is on Files when the menu is first displayed. Press the < RIGHT ARROW > key five times to move the highlight bar to Financials, where the Chart of Accounts can be printed as a report. When Financials is highlighted, press < ENTER > to display the pull-down window with the financial reports listed. The first item on the list is the Chart of Accounts. Press < ENTER > to select it. A window opens and asks you to give the account levels to be included in the report. Five is the default value and it is accepted by pressing < ENTER > again. Select the range of accounts to print, to include all accounts, from the first to the last, press < ENTER > twice. Press < ENTER > one more time to tell the printing program to include the general accounts with the detailed accounts. A total of 12 keystrokes was required to print a list of your Chart of Accounts.

If these 12 keys were assigned to a macro, however, you would only have to select the macro and the 12 keys would be pressed for you automatically.

To create the Chart of Accounts macro, move the highlight bar to Files on the *DacEasy Accounting* main menu; press < ALT + F10 > to display the *DacEasy Graph + Mate* menu line. Press < M > to choose macros and < L > to instruct *DacEasy* to "learn" the macro. You will be asked to name the macro. Type "Print COA" (for "print Chart of Accounts") and press < ENTER >. The *DacEasy Graph + Mate* windows will immediately disappear and you will be returned to the beginning of the accounting menu. Type the 12 keystrokes as described above to print your Chart of Accounts.

Once the Chart of Accounts is printed, press < ALT + F10 >. A message indicating that the "learn" process is over will appear and the macro window will be displayed.

To see the macro you've just created, move the highlight bar to "edit" in the macro window and press < ENTER >. You will see a list of keystrokes like those shown in

```
┌[Graph+Mate]════════════════════════════════════════════════════════════════╗
│         Backup              Restore            FileView           PrintView  │
│         Macros              Calculator         Notepad                       │
╚┌[Insert][NUM]───────────────────────────────────────────────────────────────┐
 │<Right><Right><Right><Right><Right><Enter>                                    │
 │<Enter>                                                                       │
 │<Enter>                                                                       │
 │<Enter>                                                                       │
 │<Enter>                                                                       │
 │<Enter>                                                                       │
 │<Enter>                                                                       │
 │                                                                              │
 │                                                                              │
 │                                                                              │
 │                                                                              │
 │                                                                              │
 │                                                                              │
 │                                                                              │
 │                                                                              │
 │                                                                              │
 └──────────────────────────────────────────────────────────────────────────────
   Home End, Lf Rt Up Dn, {data} Ctrl-P Enter, Esc, F1=Help Ctrl-W
```

Fig. 6-15. A sample macro that automatically moves the cursor when a record is called to the screen.

Fig. 6-15. In Fig. 6-15 you can see the 12 keystrokes that were needed to print the Chart of Accounts.

Press <ESC> to return to the *DacEasy Accounting* Main Menu. To use the macro, move the cursor to the Files option on the main menu, press <ALT + F10> to display the *DacEasy Graph + Mate* menu line. Press <M> for macros, then <I> to "invoke" a macro. If you have more than one macro defined, you will see a list of macros, one of which will be "Print COA," see Fig. 6-16. Select the macro by moving the highlight bar and pressing <ENTER>. The Chart of Accounts will be automatically printed.

If you have only one macro defined, it will run automatically and you will not see a list containing only that macro name.

Macros offer much potential in reducing your repetitive work. If, for example, you were updating all your vendor and customer files because your state changed the tax rates, you could build a macro that would look up each vendor and customer record, move to the tax field, update it, and go on to the next record, repeating the process as many times as necessary.

Calculator

The "pop-up" calculator is another valuable utility *DacEasy Graph + Mate* provides. Any time you need a calculation, you can press <ALT + C>, and a calculator window will open.

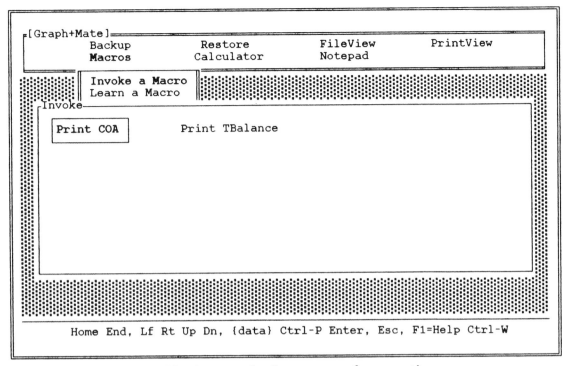

Fig. 6-16. Naming or selecting a macro for execution.

To adjust the calculator window to see data that is covered by the window, press <CTRL+W> to display the window commands and use the arrow keys to move the calculator to another part of the screen. You can also shrink the size of the calculator to see the screen behind it.

Figure 6-17 shows the calculator and its help window. In the background, you can see a workscreen from the Accounts File Maintenance module. To display the help window, press <F1> while the calculator is displayed. The help window defines the keys listed at the bottom of the screen when the calculator is being used.

The calculator functions as most hand-held calculators. It can be used to find answers to special problems, calculate the square root of any value, calculate exponential values, and change the sign of any number in the display area. Finally, calculations can then be "pasted" straight on the current work screen just by pressing <P>.

Notepad

The notepad utility can be used at any time and from any work screen within *DacEasy*. It can be "popped" up by pressing <ALT+N>. The notepad can keep notes about certain transactions, store questions about specific entries, hold information that may be needed in another module, and then paste it into that module when appropriate (see Fig. 6-18). (It can replace all those darned little yellow stick-ups that keep falling off the front of your monitor.)

When you decide to quit *DacEasy Accounting* or *Payroll*, your notes will be automatically saved in a file with an .NP extension. When you load *DacEasy Graph + Mate* again, these notes will be restored for you.

Special Features and Considerations

When Not to Use *DacEasy Graph + Mate*

DacEasy Graph + Mate can be used anytime you are in one of the *DacEasy Accounting* or *Payroll* modules—except when one of these programs is using one of your disk drives. Do not use *DacEasy Graph + Mate* at any time when it is writing or reading files on your disks. Using *Graph + Mate* at that time can stop the normal operations of the *DacEasy* program you are in and abort the feed to the disk drive. The file can be irreparably damaged.

Information Viewed in Files Window

Any information you see when viewing the data files from within *DacEasy Graph + Mate* can be changed. Instead of the default format, you can select the columns of data to be displayed. This is done during *DacEasy Graph + Mate* installation, and can be changed at any time by re-running the installation program.

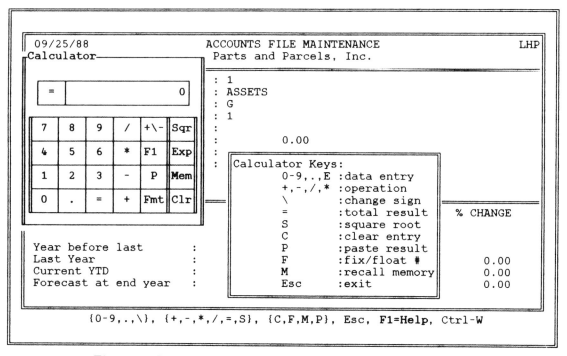

Fig. 6-17. The "pop-up" calculator, with its help window. *Calculated answers can be pasted directly to work screens.*

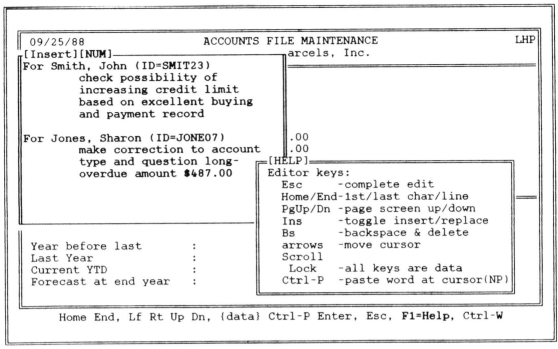

Fig. 6-18. The "pop-up" notepad, with its help window. Notes can be created as you work, saved, and printed when needed.

Help Windows

Some *DacEasy Graph + Mate* operations options are not displayed on-screen. In this case, press the <F1> key to display a list of options. Typically, a list of acceptable keystrokes will be displayed in a help window. Figure 6-18 shows a help window for use with the pop-up notepad.

Other Applications

There are three additional functions provided by *DacEasy Graph + Mate*. These are file exporting, report generation, and graphic displays. All three of these functions will be discussed in Chapter 15.

Summary

This chapter discusses DacEasy Graph + Mate *and its utilities, including backup and restore procedures, files viewing options, reports capture, macro definitions, the calculator, and the notepad. Examples of the utilities are provided. Finally, the importance of the <F1 key in listing helpful keystrokes is emphasized.*

Setting Up the Company Accounting System

Chapter Goals
- *In this chapter, we begin to work directly with* DacEasy Accounting. *We begin setting up the data files that you and the program will use as you keep your accounting records. We discuss the chart of accounts, something called the "general ledger interface table," methods for costing your inventory, internal messages file, messages for your customer statements, security procedures and passwords, and several setup procedures that must be completed. In the next chapter, the four major data files that* DacEasy *will use are discussed.*
- *Recommendations about organizing and structuring the data in the files you create are presented.*

Before starting this chapter, you should have completed all of the required installation procedures for *DacEasy Accounting, DacEasy Payroll,* and *DacEasy Graph + Mate*. You are now ready to set up our company's accounting system so you can put those programs to work.

Starting *DacEasy Accounting*

To start *DacEasy Accounting*, with *DacEasy Graph + Mate*, boot your computer, wait for the DOS prompt, and type the following series of commands:

```
CD \ GRAFMATE <ENTER>
GM <ENTER>
```

If you are not using *DacEasy Graph + Mate*, type the following commands:

```
CD \ DEA3 <ENTER>
DEA3 <ENTER>
```

Because this is the first time *DacEasy Accounting* is started, you will be asked a series of questions about the location of your data files, your choice of a chart of accounts, the numbers of customers, vendors, and other criteria.

Figure 7-1 shows the initial system-entry screen if you are using *DacEasy Graph + Mate*. Choose the Parts and Parcels Accounting file to work with. You will be asked to give the path to the data files for that company. This will happen each time you choose a company to work with. It is to ensure that you are working with the files that actually belong to the company you have selected.

When *Graph + Mate* passes control to the accounting module, it will follow up with a path confirmation to the data files (see Fig. 7-2). This would be the first screen you see if you are not using *DacEasy Graph + Mate*.

Note that the help available at the bottom of the screen explains some of your options. It recommends using the path, C: \ DEA3 \ FILES; however, we are going to create a company called "Parts and Parcels," which will be the basis of our examples throughout this book. Therefore, we will create a path called C: \ DEA3 \ PARTS, as shown in Fig. 7-2.

You will then be asked if you want to use the sample chart of accounts. For the examples in this book, use the sample that is built into *DacEasy Accounting*. Figure 7-3, which is several pages long, shows the chart of accounts. Figure 7-3 is discussed in greater detail after the setup procedures are completed.

```
┌[Graph+Mate]════════════════════════════════════════════════════════════════
│   Backup        Restore         FileView        PrintView        Macros
│   Calculator    Notepad         Applications     Quit
├──────────────────────┌──────────────────────────────────────────┐──────────
│                       │ DacEasy Accounting Tutor                  │
│                       │ DacEasy Payroll Tutor                     │
│                       │ File Exporting                            │
│                       │ Graphics Displays                         │
│                       │ Parts and Parcels Accounting              │
│                       │ Parts and Parcels Payroll                 │
│                       │ Report Generation                         │
┌[Response]─────────────└──────────────────────────────────────────┘──────────
│
│     Program Parameters/data:  C:\DEA3\PARTS
│
│
│
│
│    ─────────────────────────────────────────────────────────────────
│       Home End, Backspace, Esc Enter, F1=Help F10=OK, Ctrl-W
```

Fig. 7-1. When Parts and Parcels Accounting is selected from the DacEasy Graph + Mate Applications window, you are asked to confirm the path to the data files for Parts and Parcels.

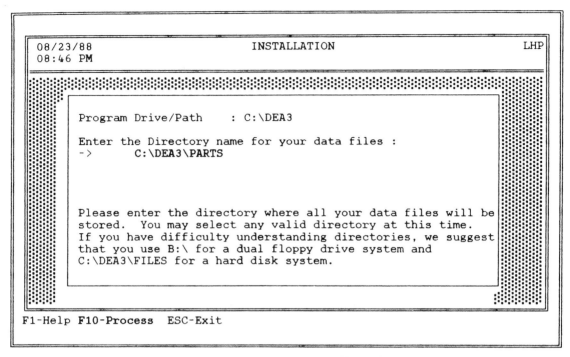

```
08/23/88                      INSTALLATION                        LHP
08:46 PM
```

```
   Program Drive/Path    : C:\DEA3

   Enter the Directory name for your data files :
   ->        C:\DEA3\PARTS




   Please enter the directory where all your data files will be
   stored.  You may select any valid directory at this time.
   If you have difficulty understanding directories, we suggest
   that you use B:\ for a dual floppy drive system and
   C:\DEA3\FILES for a hard disk system.
```

```
F1-Help  F10-Process   ESC-Exit
```

Fig. 7-2. The first time you install DacEasy Accounting, you will be asked to define the data path for your company's records.

If you decide to use the sample chart of accounts, place the *DacEasy Accounting* Disk 1—the "Install/Program" disk—into drive A: so *DacEasy* can copy the chart of accounts from the program disk to your fixed disk.

After copying the chart of accounts, *DacEasy Accounting* will ask a series of questions about the number of records you will need in each file. Figure 7-4 shows the entire series of questions that you must answer in order to set up your disk files. As shown in the help window on the screen, you should provide numbers that reflect your actual business situation, plus some room for growth.

You need not worry about outgrowing your *DacEasy Accounting* programs. If your business experiences an unanticipated growth, and you find that your files do not contain enough space for one or more types of records, you can easily increase your file size—without starting your company all over again.

For the examples in this book, we used the numbers shown in Fig. 7-4. The 275 records reserved for the chart of accounts are placed there automatically when we chose to use the sample chart of accounts. You must enter the numbers for the other types of records as they are needed.

Once you give *DacEasy* the appropriate numbers, it calculates the amount of disk space needed to store all of the records you will add. The program displays the total disk space required and compares that number to the total disk space available. If the

```
Date : 09/25/88              Parts and Parcels, Inc.           Page no. 1
Time : 12:55 PM                  #2 Byfore Avenue
                             Greenwood, S.C. 29646
                                 803/555-1685

                              CHART OF ACCOUNTS

                                        Acct.
         Acct. # Account Name           Type   Level  Type     General
         ------- -------------------------- -----  -----  -------  --------
         1       ASSETS                     ASSET    1   GENERAL
         11         CURRENT ASSETS          ASSET    2   GENERAL  1
         1101         Petty Cash            ASSET    3   DETAIL   11
         1102         CASH IN BANKS         ASSET    3   GENERAL  11
         11021          Checking Account    ASSET    4   DETAIL   1102
         11022          Payroll Account     ASSET    4   DETAIL   1102
         11023          Savings Account     ASSET    4   DETAIL   1102
         1103         CASH REGISTER FUND    ASSET    3   GENERAL  11
         11031          Cash Register # 1   ASSET    4   DETAIL   1103
         11032          Cash Register # 2   ASSET    4   DETAIL   1103
         1104         MKTABLE SECURITIES    ASSET    3   GENERAL  11
         11041          Cert. of Deposit    ASSET    4   DETAIL   1104
         11042          US Gover. Securities ASSET   4   DETAIL   1104
         11043          Other Securities    ASSET    4   DETAIL   1104
         1105         ACCOUNTS RECEIVABLE   ASSET    3   GENERAL  11
         11051          Accts Rec'ble Module ASSET   4   DETAIL   1105
         11052          Allow Doubtful Accts ASSET   4   DETAIL   1105
         1106         OTHER RECEIVABLE      ASSET    3   GENERAL  11
         11061          Affiliated Company  ASSET    4   DETAIL   1106
         11062          Employee Loans      ASSET    4   DETAIL   1106
         11063          Officers Loans      ASSET    4   DETAIL   1106
         11064          Other Receivable    ASSET    4   DETAIL   1106
         1107         INVENTORY             ASSET    3   GENERAL  11
         11071          Inventory - Module  ASSET    4   DETAIL   1107
         11072          Allow Damage/Obsol. ASSET    4   DETAIL   1107
         12        FIXED ASSETS             ASSET    2   GENERAL  1
         1201         AUTOS & TRUCKS NET    ASSET    3   GENERAL  12
         12011          Original Value      ASSET    4   DETAIL   1201
         12012          Accum. Depreciation ASSET    4   DETAIL   1201
         1202         FURNITURE & FIXT.NET  ASSET    3   GENERAL  12
         12021          Original Value      ASSET    4   DETAIL   1202
         12022          Accum. Depreciation ASSET    4   DETAIL   1202
         1203         OFFICE EQUIPMENT NET  ASSET    3   GENERAL  12
         12031          Original Value      ASSET    4   DETAIL   1203
         12032          Accum. Depreciation ASSET    4   DETAIL   1203
         1204         MACHINERY & EQ. NET   ASSET    3   GENERAL  12
         12041          Original Value      ASSET    4   DETAIL   1204
         12042          Accum. Depreciation ASSET    4   DETAIL   1204
         1205         BUILDING NET          ASSET    3   GENERAL  12
         12051          Original Value      ASSET    4   DETAIL   1205
         12052          Accum. Depreciation ASSET    4   DETAIL   1205
         1206         OTHER FIXED ASSETS    ASSET    3   GENERAL  12
         12061          Original Value      ASSET    4   DETAIL   1206
         12062          Accum. Depreciation ASSET    4   DETAIL   1206
         1207         Land-Original Value   ASSET    3   DETAIL   12
```

Fig. 7-3. The built-in Chart of Accounts. We will add several accounts to the Chart of Accounts as we work through our tutorials.

77

```
Date : 09/25/88          Parts and Parcels, Inc.          Page no. 2
Time : 12:55 PM              #2 Byfore Avenue
                          Greenwood, S.C. 29646
                             803/555-1685
```

```
                        CHART OF ACCOUNTS

                                   Acct.
Acct. #  Account Name              Type  Level  Type     General
-------  ----------------------    ----- -----  -------  --------
13          DEFERRED ASSETS        ASSET   2    GENERAL  1
1301          ORGANIZATION EXPENSE ASSET   3    GENERAL  13
13011           Original Value     ASSET   4    DETAIL   1301
13012           Accum. Amortization ASSET  4    DETAIL   1301
1302          LEASEHOLD IMPROV.NET  ASSET   3    GENERAL  13
13021           Original Value     ASSET   4    DETAIL   1302
13022           Accum. Amortization ASSET  4    DETAIL   1302
1303          PREPAID EXPENSES      ASSET   3    GENERAL  13
13031           Insurance          ASSET   4    DETAIL   1303
13032           Rent               ASSET   4    DETAIL   1303
13033           Interest           ASSET   4    DETAIL   1303
13034           Taxes              ASSET   4    DETAIL   1303
14          OTHER ASSETS           ASSET   2    GENERAL  1
1401          DEPOSITS             ASSET   3    GENERAL  14
14011           Rent               ASSET   4    DETAIL   1401
14012           Leases             ASSET   4    DETAIL   1401
14013           Utilities          ASSET   4    DETAIL   1401
14014           Security           ASSET   4    DETAIL   1401
1402          LONG TERM INVESTMENT ASSET   3    GENERAL  14
14021           Cert. of Deposit   ASSET   4    DETAIL   1402
14022           Other Long Term Inv. ASSET 4    DETAIL   1402
2        LIABILITIES               LIAB.   1    GENERAL
21          SHORT TERM LIABILITY   LIAB.   2    GENERAL  2
2101          Accts Payable-Module LIAB.   3    DETAIL   21
2102          Notes Payable        LIAB.   3    DETAIL   21
2103          Accrued Payable      LIAB.   3    DETAIL   21
2104          TAXES PAYABLE        LIAB.   3    GENERAL  21
21041           PAYROLL TAXES      LIAB.   4    GENERAL  2104
210411            Federal Income W/H LIAB. 5    DETAIL   21041
210412            FICA W/H Employee LIAB.   5    DETAIL   21041
210413            FICA W/H Employer LIAB.   5    DETAIL   21041
210414            FUTA             LIAB.   5    DETAIL   21041
210415            SUTA             LIAB.   5    DETAIL   21041
210416            State Income W/H LIAB.   5    DETAIL   21041
210417            City Income W/H  LIAB.   5    DETAIL   21041
210418            Disability Insurance LIAB. 5   DETAIL   21041
21042           Sales Tax Payable  LIAB.   4    DETAIL   2104
21043           Property Tax       LIAB.   4    DETAIL   2104
21044           Franchise Tax      LIAB.   4    DETAIL   2104
21045           Foreign Tax        LIAB.   4    DETAIL   2104
21046           INCOME TAX PAYABLE LIAB.   4    GENERAL  2104
210461            Federal Income Tax LIAB. 5    DETAIL   21046
210462            State Income Tax LIAB.   5    DETAIL   21046
210463            City Income Tax  LIAB.   5    DETAIL   21046
21047           Other Tax Payable  LIAB.   4    DETAIL   2104
```

Fig. 7-3. Continued.

```
Date : 09/25/88              Parts and Parcels, Inc.              Page no. 3
Time : 12:55 PM                 #2 Byfore Avenue
                              Greenwood, S.C. 29646
                                 803/555-1685

                               CHART OF ACCOUNTS

                                    Acct.
        Acct. # Account Name       Type   Level  Type     General
        ------- --------------------------------- -----  -----  -------  --------
        2105        OTHER PAYROLL PAYABLE      LIAB.   3    GENERAL  21
        21051          Union Dues              LIAB.   4    DETAIL   2105
        21052          Employee Charity        LIAB.   4    DETAIL   2105
        21053          X'mas Fund Accrued      LIAB.   4    DETAIL   2105
        2106          Dividends Payable        LIAB.   3    DETAIL   21
        2107          Other Payable            LIAB.   3    DETAIL   21
        22        LONG TERM LIABILITY          LIAB.   2    GENERAL  2
        2201          Mortgages Payable        LIAB.   3    DETAIL   22
        2202          Notes Payable            LIAB.   3    DETAIL   22
        2203          Current L/Term Liab.     LIAB.   3    DETAIL   22
        2204          Other Long Term Liab     LIAB.   3    DETAIL   22
        23        DEFERRED LIABILITY           LIAB.   2    GENERAL  2
        2301          Commit & Contingency     LIAB.   3    DETAIL   23
        2302          Deferred Income          LIAB.   3    DETAIL   23
        2303          Profit/Instalm.Sales     LIAB.   3    DETAIL   23
        2304          Unearned Interest        LIAB.   3    DETAIL   23
        3         STOCKHOLDERS EQUITY          CAP.    1    GENERAL
        31            CAPTIAL STOCK            CAP.    2    GENERAL  3
        3101          COMMON STOCK             CAP.    3    GENERAL  31
        31011          Par Value               CAP.    4    DETAIL   3101
        31012          Surplus                 CAP.    4    DETAIL   3101
        3102          PREFERRED STOCK          CAP.    3    GENERAL  31
        31021          Par Value               CAP.    4    DETAIL   3102
        31022          Surplus                 CAP.    4    DETAIL   3102
        3103          Treasury Stock           CAP.    3    DETAIL   31
        32        RETAINED EARNINGS            CAP.    2    GENERAL  3
        3283          1983 Profit/(Loss)       CAP.    3    DETAIL   32
        3284          1984 Profit/(Loss)       CAP.    3    DETAIL   32
        3285          1985 Profit/(Loss)       CAP.    3    DETAIL   32
        3286          1986 Profit/(Loss)       CAP.    3    DETAIL   32
        3287          1987 Profit/(Loss)       CAP.    3    DETAIL   32
        33            Current Earnings         CAP.    2    DETAIL   3
        4         REVENUES                     REV.    1    GENERAL
        41            SALES                    REV.    2    GENERAL  4
        4101          Sales Dept. 01           REV.    3    DETAIL   41
        4102          Sales Dept. 02           REV.    3    DETAIL   41
        42        SALES RETURNS                REV.    2    GENERAL  4
        4201          Returns Dept. 01         REV.    3    DETAIL   42
        4202          Returns Dept. 02         REV.    3    DETAIL   42
```

Fig. 7-3. Continued

```
Date : 09/25/88                Parts and Parcels, Inc.              Page no. 4
Time : 12:55 PM                    #2 Byfore Avenue
                                 Greenwood, S.C. 29646
                                    803/555-1685

                                 CHART OF ACCOUNTS

                                       Acct.
        Acct. # Account Name           Type   Level  Type     General
        ------- ----------------------- -----  -----  -------  --------
        43        SHIPPING              REV.    2     GENERAL   4
        4301        Freight             REV.    3     DETAIL   43
        4302        Insurance           REV.    3     DETAIL   43
        4303        Packaging           REV.    3     DETAIL   43
        4304        Surcharge           REV.    3     DETAIL   43
        44        FINANCIAL INCOME      REV.    2     GENERAL   4
        4401        Ints. Investments   REV.    3     DETAIL   44
        4402        Finance Charges     REV.    3     DETAIL   44
        4403        Dividends           REV.    3     DETAIL   44
        4404        Purchase Discounts  REV.    3     DETAIL   44
        45        OTHER REVENUES        REV.    2     GENERAL   4
        4501        Recovery Bad Debt   REV.    3     DETAIL   45
        4502        Gain in Sale/Assets REV.    3     DETAIL   45
        4503        Miscellaneous       REV.    3     DETAIL   45
        5       TOTAL EXPENSES          EXP.    1     GENERAL
        51        COST OF GOODS SOLD    EXP.    2     GENERAL   5
        5101        COGS Dept. 01       EXP.    3     DETAIL   51
        5102        COGS Dept. 02       EXP.    3     DETAIL   51
        52        GEN & ADMIN EXPENSES  EXP.    2     GENERAL   5
        5201        PAYROLL             EXP.    3     GENERAL  52
        52011         WAGES             EXP.    4     GENERAL  5201
        520111          Salaries        EXP.    5     DETAIL   52011
        520112          Hourly          EXP.    5     DETAIL   52011
        520113          Commissions     EXP.    5     DETAIL   52011
        520114          Overtime        EXP.    5     DETAIL   52011
        520115          Compensations   EXP.    5     DETAIL   52011
        520116          Bonuses         EXP.    5     DETAIL   52011
        520117          Other Wages     EXP.    5     DETAIL   52011
        520118          Contract Labor  EXP.    5     DETAIL   52011
        52012         BENEFITS          EXP.    4     GENERAL  5201
        520121          Health Insurance EXP.   5     DETAIL   52012
        520123          Dental Insurance EXP.   5     DETAIL   52012
        520124          401(k) Plan     EXP.    5     DETAIL   52012
        520125          Other Benefits  EXP.    5     DETAIL   52012
        52013         TAXES             EXP.    4     GENERAL  5201
        520131          FICA Employer   EXP.    5     DETAIL   52013
        520132          FUTA            EXP.    5     DETAIL   52013
        520133          SUTA            EXP.    5     DETAIL   52013
        520134          Disability Insurance EXP. 5   DETAIL   52013
        520135          Other Payroll Taxes  EXP.  5  DETAIL   52013
```

Fig. 7-3. Continued

Parts and Parcels, Inc.
#2 Byfore Avenue
Greenwood, S.C. 29646
803/555-1685

CHART OF ACCOUNTS

Acct. #	Account Name	Acct. Type	Level	Type	General
5202	MAINTENANCE	EXP.	3	GENERAL	52
52021	Autos & Trucks	EXP.	4	DETAIL	5202
52022	Furniture & Fixtures	EXP.	4	DETAIL	5202
52023	Office Equipment	EXP.	4	DETAIL	5202
52024	Machinery & Equip.	EXP.	4	DETAIL	5202
52025	Building	EXP.	4	DETAIL	5202
52026	Other Assets	EXP.	4	DETAIL	5202
5203	DEPRECIATION	EXP.	3	GENERAL	52
52031	Autos & Trucks	EXP.	4	DETAIL	5203
52032	Furniture & Fixtures	EXP.	4	DETAIL	5203
52033	Office Equipment	EXP.	4	DETAIL	5203
52034	Machinery & Equip.	EXP.	4	DETAIL	5203
52035	Building	EXP.	4	DETAIL	5203
52036	Other Assets	EXP.	4	DETAIL	5203
5204	AMORTIZATION	EXP.	3	GENERAL	52
52041	Organization Expense	EXP.	4	DETAIL	5204
52042	Leasehold Improv.	EXP.	4	DETAIL	5204
5205	RENTS AND LEASES	EXP.	3	GENERAL	52
52051	Autos & Trucks	EXP.	4	DETAIL	5205
52052	Furniture & Fixtures	EXP.	4	DETAIL	5205
52053	Office Equipment	EXP.	4	DETAIL	5205
52054	Machinery & Equip.	EXP.	4	DETAIL	5205
52055	Building	EXP.	4	DETAIL	5205
52056	Other Leases or Rent	EXP.	4	DETAIL	5205
5206	ASSETS INSURANCE	EXP.	3	GENERAL	52
52061	Autos & Trucks	EXP.	4	DETAIL	5206
52062	Furniture & Fixtures	EXP.	4	DETAIL	5206
52063	Office Equipment	EXP.	4	DETAIL	5206
52064	Machinery & Equip.	EXP.	4	DETAIL	5206
52065	Building	EXP.	4	DETAIL	5206
52066	Other Assets Insur.	EXP.	4	DETAIL	5206
5207	TRAVEL & ENTERTAIN	EXP.	3	GENERAL	52
52071	Lodging	EXP.	4	DETAIL	5207
52072	Transportation	EXP.	4	DETAIL	5207
52073	Meals	EXP.	4	DETAIL	5207
52074	Entertainment	EXP.	4	DETAIL	5207
52075	Other Travel Expense	EXP.	4	DETAIL	5207
5208	SHIPPING	EXP.	3	GENERAL	52
52081	Freight	EXP.	4	DETAIL	5208
52082	Insurance	EXP.	4	DETAIL	5208
52083	Packaging	EXP.	4	DETAIL	5208
52084	Duties	EXP.	4	DETAIL	5208
52085	Other Shipping Exp.	EXP.	4	DETAIL	5208

Fig. 7-3. Continued

```
Date : 09/25/88                 Parts and Parcels, Inc.              Page no.  6
Time : 12:55 PM                     #2 Byfore Avenue
                                  Greenwood, S.C. 29646
                                     803/555-1685
```

```
                                  CHART OF ACCOUNTS

                                          Acct.
          Acct. # Account Name             Type  Level   Type     General
          ------- --------------------------- ----- ----- ------- --------
            5209       TAXES (OTHER)          EXP.    3   GENERAL  52
            52091        Sales Tax/Purchases  EXP.    4   DETAIL   5209
            52092        Property Tax         EXP.    4   DETAIL   5209
            52093        Franchise Tax        EXP.    4   DETAIL   5209
            52094        Other Taxes          EXP.    4   DETAIL   5209
            5210       CONSULTING FEES        EXP.    3   GENERAL  52
            52101        Accountants          EXP.    4   DETAIL   5210
            52102        Legal                EXP.    4   DETAIL   5210
            52103        Other                EXP.    4   DETAIL   5210
            5211       Office Supplies        EXP.    3   DETAIL   52
            5212       Telephone & Telegrph   EXP.    3   DETAIL   52
            5213       Mail/Postage           EXP.    3   DETAIL   52
            5214       Utilities              EXP.    3   DETAIL   52
            5215       Alarms                 EXP.    3   DETAIL   52
            5216       Contribution/Donat.    EXP.    3   DETAIL   52
            5217       Licenses/Permits       EXP.    3   DETAIL   52
            5218       Memships./Dues/Subscr. EXP.    3   DETAIL   52
            5219       ADVERTISING            EXP.    3   GENERAL  52
            52191        Broadcast Advert.    EXP.    4   DETAIL   5219
            52192        Print Advertising    EXP.    4   DETAIL   5219
            5220       PROMOTION              EXP.    3   GENERAL  52
            52201        Catalogues           EXP.    4   DETAIL   5220
            52202        Brochures            EXP.    4   DETAIL   5220
            52203        Other Promotions     EXP.    4   DETAIL   5220
            5221       Public Relations       EXP.    3   DETAIL   52
            5222       Marketing Research     EXP.    3   DETAIL   52
            5223       Bad Debt Loss          EXP.    3   DETAIL   52
            5224       Inventory Losses       EXP.    3   DETAIL   52
            5299       Other Expenses         EXP.    3   DETAIL   52
            53       FINANCIAL EXPENSES       EXP.    2   GENERAL  5
            5301       Credit Card Discount   EXP.    3   DETAIL   53
            5302       Interest               EXP.    3   DETAIL   53
            5303       Bank Charges           EXP.    3   DETAIL   53
            5304       Sales Discounts        EXP.    3   DETAIL   53
            5305       Agents Commissions     EXP.    3   DETAIL   53
            5399       Other Financial Exp.   EXP.    3   DETAIL   53
            54       OTHER EXPENSES           EXP.    2   GENERAL  5
            5401       Cash Short             EXP.    3   DETAIL   54
            5402       Loss on Sale/Assets    EXP.    3   DETAIL   54
            5403       Miscellaneous Losses   EXP.    3   DETAIL   54
            55       INCOME TAX               EXP.    2   GENERAL  5
            5501       Federal Income Tax     EXP.    3   DETAIL   55
            5502       State Income Tax       EXP.    3   DETAIL   55
            5503       City Income Tax        EXP.    3   DETAIL   55
            D        Journal Difference       OTHER   1   DETAIL

            Number of Accounts printed 257
```

Fig. 7-3. Continued

```
┌──────────────────────────────────────────────────────────────────────┐
│ 08/23/88                    INSTALLATION                          LHP │
│ 08:53 PM                                                              │
├──────────────────────────────────────────────────────────────────────┤
│                                                                        │
│   Data Directory      : C:\DEA3\PARTS                                  │
│                                                                        │
│   Please answer the following questions:                               │
│                                                                        │
│   How many Accounts in your chart of Accounts? ............. 275       │
│   How many Customers do you have? .......................... 100       │
│   How many Vendors do you have? ............................ 25        │
│   How many Products and/or Services do you have? ........... 250       │
│   What is the maximum number of Invoices you have per day? . 100       │
│                                                                        │
│                                                                        │
│   Note: your answers to the questions  above are used to estimate the  │
│         size  of  your  Dac-Easy  Accounting  system files, and to     │
│         reserve space for them in your disk. It is not critical to be   │
│         100% accurate now since you will be able to change these file   │
│         sizes   later.   However,  we  recommend  that, if possible, you│
│         allow  enough  space  for your current files requirement plus   │
│         some expected growth.                                          │
│                                                                        │
├──────────────────────────────────────────────────────────────────────┤
│ F1-Help F10-Process  ESC-Exit                                          │
└──────────────────────────────────────────────────────────────────────┘
```

Fig. 7-4. "Sizing" files. You must give the number of records you might expect to work with in a normal business.

first is greater than the second, you must re-think your use of space because your records will not fit on the disk.

Once you tell *DacEasy* to start creating your files, it will display a progress report at the bottom of the screen. After the files have been created, you will be asked to give your company's name and address (see Fig. 7-5 for the appropriate information to be used for our sample company). As you enter your company's information, press <F2> to center each line. Then, when reports are printed, the information will be centered at the top of the reports.

The File Options

When the company's information is completed, the *DacEasy Accounting* Main Menu will be displayed (see Fig. 5-1 in Chapter 5). The highlight bar will be on the File option and can be moved to any of the other options on the menu line by pressing the left or right arrow keys. When you have highlighted the options you wish to work with, press <ENTER> to display the pull-down menu window where additional options are available.

The *DacEasy Accounting* Main Menu lists eight functions that can be performed within the accounting system. The File option provides the facility to build and maintain files containing the chart of accounts, customer information, vendor information, and product and service information. Figure 7-6 shows the selections available from the File option. The Options option provides additional setup procedures that must be completed before

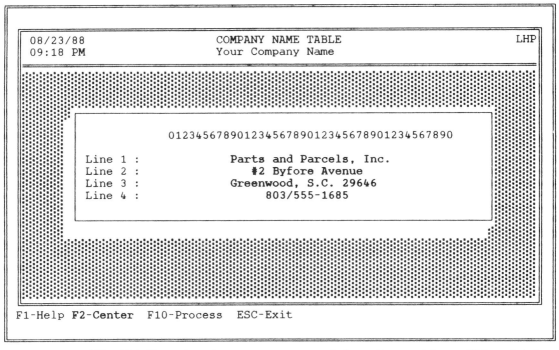

Fig. 7-5. Entering the company name. Information used here will be printed on reports and lists.

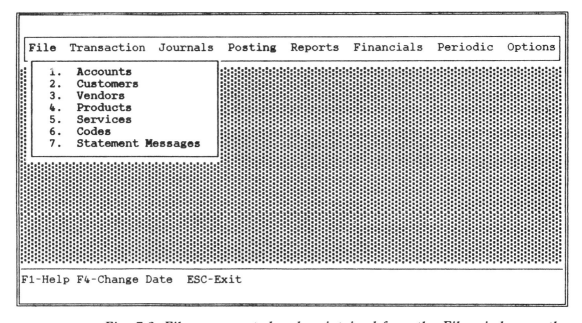

Fig. 7-6. Files are created and maintained from the File window on the DacEasy Accounting Main Menu.

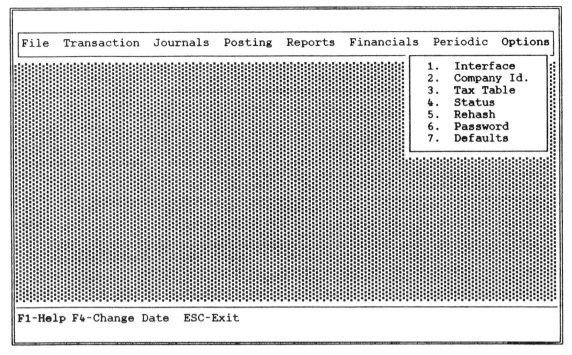

| File | Transaction | Journals | Posting | Reports | Financials | Periodic | Options |

```
                                                   1.   Interface
                                                   2.   Company Id.
                                                   3.   Tax Table
                                                   4.   Status
                                                   5.   Rehash
                                                   6.   Password
                                                   7.   Defaults
```

F1-Help F4-Change Date   ESC-Exit

Fig. 7-7. The DacEasy Accounting Main Menu Options window. Information must be provided here before we can use the system.

we can use the accounting system to our full advantage. Figure 7-7 shows the selection window for Options. The last part of this chapter will address options.

From the File option, we must perform several tasks. The first is to add an asset account for the current business year. We must do this because the Chart of Accounts (see Fig. 7-3) includes Profit/Loss accounts through 1987 only. We must add the accounts needed to bring the system up to the current year. Consequently, we will add one account for 1988. Subsequent yearly accounts would be added as needed.

The Chart of Accounts

To add an account to the Chart of Accounts, select File from the *DacEasy Accounting* Main Menu. Then select Accounts from the pull-down window for File. Once Accounts is highlighted, press <ENTER> to select the option. The Accounts File Maintenance screen will be displayed (Fig. 7-8).

The cursor will flash on the first entry line of the screen where you must enter the account number you wish to add or edit. If the number you enter already exists in the Chart of Accounts, all the information for that account will be displayed. If the number you enter does not exist in the Chart of Accounts, you will be able to create a new account for that number.

Figure 7-8 shows the information you need to enter for a new account. When the last piece of information is entered, press <F10> to tell *DacEasy* to process and save the account information. The next screen will be empty so you can enter additional accounts if you need them. To leave the empty chart of accounts screen, press <ESC> and the File selection window will be re-displayed. (If you press <ESC> after completing the information on the Accounts File Maintenance screen, the information will be lost.)

The Chart of Accounts is the backbone of any accounting system. If the Chart of Accounts is not designed and structured adequately, the accounting system can—and will—fall apart.

The following paragraphs explain the items to be completed on the Accounts File Maintenance screen.

Account Number

An account number can contain as many as six characters, either numerals or letters. In almost all cases, you will want to use numerals and not letters. Some letters are used for special accounts. The account number is related to the type of account discussed in Chapter 3. Account number 1 indicates assets, number 2 indicates liabilities, number 3 indicates owners' equity (also called capital accounts), number 4 indicates revenue, and number 5 indicates expenses.

Account number 21, for example, indicates the first account under liabilities. Account 22, then, indicates the second account under liabilities. Accounts 21 and 22 would be second level accounts, which are discussed more fully in the following section.

Figure 7-9 shows the significance of each account number in the Chart of Accounts listed in Fig. 7-3. Note that the two digits used for level 3 accounts can also be used as department numbers if you want to track revenue and expenditures for separate departments. Departments will be discussed in further detail in Chapter 10.

If you have an existing Chart of Accounts and do not wish to use the sample chart provided by *DacEasy Accounting*, you can create a chart that will be identical to yours—so long as you can adhere to the six-character limitation. If you create and use your own Chart of Accounts, you must also create a new "general ledger interface table," which is discussed later in this chapter.

Account Name

An account name should be descriptive. It can contain as many as 20 characters (either numeric or alphabetic). It is suggested that "general" account names be typed into *DacEasy* as all uppercase, and that "detail" account names be entered with the first character of each word capitalized, and all other characters in lowercase. By typing in the account names this way, your printed chart of accounts and the screen version (from *DacEasy Graph + Mate*) will be easy to read. If you are using the Chart of Accounts provided by *DacEasy*, you must edit the accounts you want to use all uppercase letters for. The Chart of Accounts shown in Fig. 7-3 illustrates the ease of reading reports when the general accounts are listed in uppercase.

General/Detail Status

The general/detail status tells *DacEasy* whether it is to use an account for accumulating totals (see the discussion below) or for direct entry from the keyboard, or from a program module.

A "general" account is typically any account that a lower-level account exists. A "detail" account is the lowest level account in a direct line from a higher account. Fig-

```
 09/25/88                ACCOUNTS FILE MAINTENANCE                  LHP
 06:12 PM                Parts and Parcels, Inc.

 Account Number          : 3288
 Account Name            : 1988 Profit/(Loss)
 General or Detail (G/D)  : D
 Account Level (1-5)     : 3
 General Account         : 32
 Previous Balance        :            0.00
 This Period Balance     :            0.00
 Current Balance         :            0.00


                        HISTORICAL INFORMATION
                            BALANCE          VARIANCE    % CHANGE


 Year before last     :            0.00
 Last Year            :            0.00       0.00        0.00
 Current YTD          :            0.00       0.00        0.00
 Forecast at end year :            0.00       0.00        0.00


 F1-Help  F6-Delete  F7-Update Balance  F10-Process  ESC-exit
```

Fig. 7-8. Adding an account number to the Chart of Accounts.

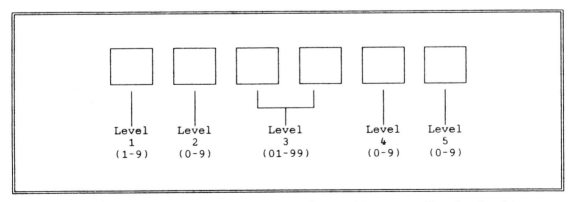

Fig. 7-9. Account numbers in the Chart of Accounts. Note that Level 3 accounts have two digits.

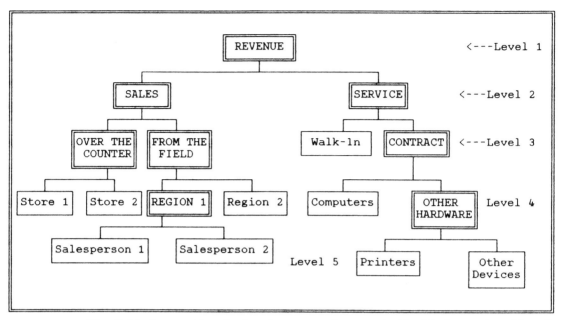

Fig. 7-10. Account levels showing general accounts (double frames) and detail accounts (single frames).

ure 7-10 illustrates the relationships between general and detail accounts. General accounts are named with uppercase letters and framed with double lines in Fig. 7-10; detail accounts are named with lowercase letters and have single-line frames. If you classify an account as "general," there must be at least one detail account that follows it in line.

Account Level

DacEasy Accounting permits five levels of accounts in your Chart of Accounts. As lower levels are used, the totals are automatically accumulated and placed in the levels above them.

Figure 7-10 also illustrates five levels of account relationships. At level 5, two salespersons are shown in Region 1. For each of those, an amount could be entered as "revenue," showing the source of income. Those amounts would be totaled and placed in the Region 1 account. Then the Region 1 and Region 2 amounts would be added together and that sum would be placed in the account called "From the field." "From the field" and "Over the counter" totals would be added and placed in the account called "Sales"; then "Sales" and "Service" amounts would be totaled in the overall "Revenue" account. All the totals are done automatically by *DacEasy Accounting* so you can see patterns of profitability in your business.

General Account

Except for level 1 accounts, every account will have a "general" account immediately in line above it in the file structure. When you are asked for the general account that goes with a particular account number, you should give the number of the account that totals will be accumulated. Note that every account, whether general or detail, will have a general account immediately above it (except level 1 accounts).

Previous Balance, This Period Balance, and Current Balance

These fields will contain information provided by the *DacEasy* programs. The Previous Balance field will contain the balance brought forward from the previous period. This Period Balance data will include all amounts posted during the current period. The Current Balance will be the total of the previous balance and this period's data. You will not be able to add or delete data in these fields.

Historical Information

You will probably want *DacEasy* to accumulate the historical data for you as you use the program over a period of years. At the end of each fiscal year, *DacEasy Accounting* will fill in the blanks for you. You can, however, enter information manually if you want to include such information from previous years immediately.

DacEasy automatically displays the actual variance and the percent change for each account, using data from the current year and from two previous years. In addition, it forecasts your end-of-year figures for each account based on previous patterns.

Journal Difference Account

In Fig. 7-3, you see that the last account number listed is not an account number but a letter. This level 1 detail-credit account is a special account that you might find very helpful at times.

DacEasy Accounting will not permit you to quit an entry unless the entry is properly balanced within the accounting system. By requiring your accounting to be in balance, the program ensures that your recordkeeping is accurate and absolutely up-to-date.

The journal difference account is used in those (rare) instances when something doesn't balance and you need time to look for the mistake—but you don't have the time at the moment. The amount of the error (the amount you are out of balance by) can be entered into the account so that your work will balance. Later, when you have found your mistake, you can come back to the system and post the correction to the proper account, balancing the correction by zeroing the journal difference account.

If the balance in the journal difference account is not zero, *DacEasy* will not let you run the end-of-period routines.

After adding the account shown in Fig. 7-8, there are two additional tasks to be done from the File window—before we begin to build customer, vendor, products, and services files (which will be discussed in detail in Chapter 8).

Billing and Purchasing Codes Table

When you bill a customer or make a purchase from a vendor, there may be one or more items that do not belong in your inventory or in your services files. These might include items such as freight, insurance on items shipped, packaging, and other items related to buying and selling. In addition, you may purchase services or fixed assets that would not be included in your inventory. You may also sell some of your fixed assets (such as a used delivery truck) that would not be in your product inventory file.

The proceeds from these purchases or sales must be accounted for in the normal accounting procedures used by your business. *DacEasy* permits you to set up two codes tables to handle items that would not be put in your product inventory file. Figures 7-11 and 7-12 show the *DacEasy* tables (if you are using *DacEasy*'s Chart of Accounts). Additional items can be added or existing items deleted from either table.

If you are using your own Chart of Accounts, you may include those items that are important to you. The account numbers must reference existing accounts in your chart and must reference the appropriate accounts.

To create or edit the billing and purchase order codes tables, select the Codes option from the File window. You will be given a choice of working with the billing codes or with the purchase order codes. Select the appropriate code by moving the highlight bar and pressing <ENTER>.

Let's start with the purchase order codes (Fig. 7-11).

For each item in the table, an account number relates the values to the general ledger Chart of Accounts so the amounts can be properly accounted for—although they are not in your inventory or service files (these files are discussed in Chapter 8). Each item is marked as taxable or non taxable so that the appropriate calculations can be made on the purchase order or the customer's bill.

You can switch between the billing codes table and the purchase order codes table

```
┌─────────────────────────────────────────────────────────────────────┐
│ ┌──────┬────────────────────────────────────────────────────┬──────┐ │
│ │ 09/  │      ****   PURCHASE ORDER CODES   ****            │ LHP  │ │
│ │ 08:  │                                                    │      │ │
│ │ ═══  │ Code No.    Description     Amount   Account No.  Taxable═══│ │
│ │ ░░░  │ --------    -----------     ------   -----------  ------- ░░│ │
│ │ ░░░  │    1     Freight             0.00     52081         N    ░░│ │
│ │ ░░░  │    2     Insurance           0.00     52082         N    ░░│ │
│ │ ░░░  │    3     Packaging           0.00     52083         N    ░░│ │
│ │ ░░░  │    4     Advertising Radio/TV 0.00    52191         Y    ░░│ │
│ │ ░░░  │    5     Advertising Print   0.00     52192         Y    ░░│ │
│ │ ░░░  │    6     Autos & Trucks      0.00     12011         Y    ░░│ │
│ │ ░░░  │    7     Furniture & Fixtures 0.00    12021         Y    ░░│ │
│ │ ░░░  │    8     Office Equipment    0.00     12031         Y    ░░│ │
│ │ ░░░  │    9     Machinery & Equip.  0.00     12041         Y    ░░│ │
│ │ ░░░  │   10     Other Fixed Assets  0.00     12061         Y    ░░│ │
│ │ ░░░  │   11     Office Supplies     0.00     5211          Y    ░░│ │
│ │ ░░░  │   12                         0.00                        ░░│ │
│ │ ░░░  │   13                         0.00                        ░░│ │
│ │ ░░░  │   14                         0.00                        ░░│ │
│ │ ░░░  │   15                         0.00                        ░░│ │
│ │ ░░░  │   16                         0.00                        ░░│ │
│ │ ░░░  │                                                          ░░│ │
│ └──────┴────────────────────────────────────────────────────┴──────┘ │
│ F1-Help   F2-Toggle PO/Billing   F10-Process   ALT D-Delete   ESC-Exit│
└─────────────────────────────────────────────────────────────────────┘
```

Fig. 7-11. Accounting for purchase order codes for non-inventory items in the Chart of Accounts.

```
┌──────────────────────────────────────────────────────────────────────────┐
│  ┌───────────────────────────────────────────────────────────────────┐   │
│  09/              ****  BILLING CODES   ****                    ┌LHP┐  │
│  09:                                                            │    │  │
│  ═══   Code No.    Description       Amount  Account No. Taxable│════│  │
│        --------  --------------------  ----------  -----------  -------  │
│           1      Freight                0.00     4301        N          │
│           2      Insurance              0.00     4302        Y          │
│           3      Packaging              0.00     4303        Y          │
│           4      Surcharge              0.00     4304        Y          │
│           5                             0.00                            │
│           6      Autos & Trucks         0.00    12011        Y          │
│           7      Furniture & Fixtures   0.00    12021        Y          │
│           8      Office Equipment       0.00    12031        Y          │
│           9      Machinery & Equip.     0.00    12041        Y          │
│          10      Other Fixed Assets     0.00    12061        Y          │
│          11                             0.00                            │
│          12                             0.00                            │
│          13                             0.00                            │
│          14                             0.00                            │
│          15                             0.00                            │
│          16                             0.00                            │
│                                                                         │
│  F1-Help  F2-Toggle PO/Billing  F10-Process  ALT D-Delete  ESC-Exit     │
└──────────────────────────────────────────────────────────────────────────┘
```

Fig. 7-12. Accounting for billing codes for non-inventory items in the Chart of Accounts.

by pressing the <F2> key, as indicated at the bottom of the screen (see Fig. 7-11).

Figure 7-12 shows the billing codes table. The account numbers listed in this table refer to the Chart of Accounts. These accounts are debited and credited whenever the listed items appear on a customer's bill or when operational assets are sold.

On both the purchase order codes screen and the billing codes screen, you can enter as many as 40 items. Items 17-40 can be seen simply by pressing the <DOWN ARROW> until they scroll onto the screen. In addition, you can add new items as you need them from within the purchase order and billing modules—that is, it is not necessary to come back to these setup screens in order to add items.

For our purposes, we will not add to either list at this time.

When you complete the information, press <F10> to tell *DacEasy* to process and store the data in the appropriate file. If you press <ESC> before pressing <F10>, all of your changes and additions will be lost.

Statement Messages

Pre-defined messages can be placed in a file and used when customer statements are printed. After you define these statements, *DacEasy* will select the appropriate message—without your intervention—based on the status of the customer's account at the time the statement is printed. Each message can contain one or two lines, and will be printed automatically on each statement you send to your customers.

The statements can be progressively more forceful as the number of days past due increases, as shown in Fig. 7-13.

We recommend strongly that you use proper grammar and punctuation techniques when defining statement text. Your image with your customers is at stake and the circumstances of sending late notices to customers places your image at risk, as is. Carelessly worded or poorly worded text will be taken as a sign that you don't care about that image. If you don't care about your business any more than your statement indicates, past due customers will not care about your business either—that is, they won't pay the amount due.

Except for building the customer, vendor, product, and services files from the File option, we have completed all the setup tasks within this window. We will build the four files in Chapter 8. There are, however, several other setup tasks that must be completed in the Options window.

The Options Window

Figure 7-7 shows the Options window from the *DacEasy Accounting* Main Menu. We will discuss five of the seven items, and briefly explain the other two at the end of the chapter.

The General Ledger Interface Table

The General Ledger Interface Table is, simply put, a list of account numbers that

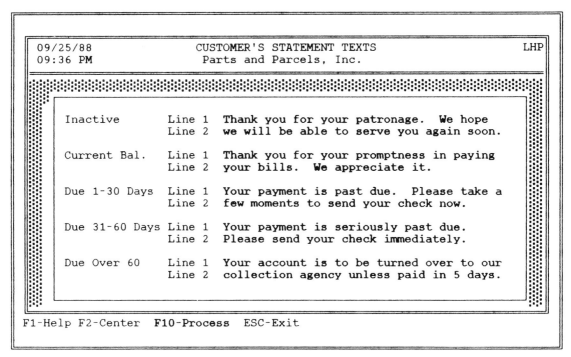

Fig. 7-13. Comments printed on customer statements. DacEasy Accounting selects an appropriate comment depending on the status of the account.

DacEasy uses as you enter your business information. The table tells the accounting module which accounts to update (with summary data) from the postings in the transactions journals.

As an example of how the table functions, consider the process of writing a check to pay one of your vendors. The check is written in the accounts payable module. When the accounting process for the check begins, *DacEasy* must know the account to debit the cash from (represented by your check). This account, in your Chart of Accounts, is the "bank checking" account. Figure 7-3 lists your Chart of Accounts and you can see that account number 11021 is the Checking Account under the CASH IN BANKS account.

Figure 7-14 shows the general ledger interface table that is used when you use the Chart of Accounts shown in Fig. 7-3. If you develop your own Chart of Accounts, you must complete an interface table that will include these accounts.

If you are using a Chart of Accounts different from the one provided by *DacEasy*, you must complete a new general ledger interface table so that it contains the account numbers that identify the proper accounts in your chart. It is not necessary to use the same names given in the interface table, but the accounts must perform the same functions indicated by the names in the interface table.

When you enter an account number in the interface table, the name of that account will be displayed near the bottom of the screen.

The screen shown in Fig. 7-14 also asks if you wish to set up departments from

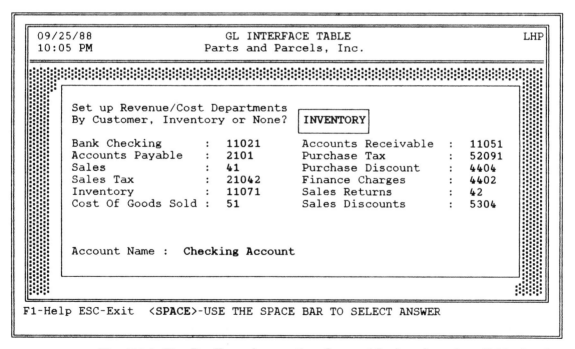

Fig. 7-14. The DacEasy Accounting General Ledger Interface Table for the Chart of Accounts. *Revenue/cost departments are also established here.*

93

which to determine revenue and cost information. You can choose to use your inventory file, your customer file, or no departments at all. The <SPACE BAR> will toggle your choices. Departments will be discussed in more detail in Chapter 10. For our purposes, we will use the inventory file as the foundation of our revenue and expense centers (departments).

The Company Name

From the Options window, we can enter our company's identification information. Press the number for that option, or the <DOWN ARROW> until the option is highlighted, and press <ENTER>. Figure 7-5 represents the Company Name Table screen that is displayed. We completed this information during the early part of the set up routines; thus, selecting this option will simply let us see our current information or edit the information (for example, if we moved to the mall, our address would change).

The Tax Table

By selecting item 3 from the Options window, you can enter up to 10 tax rates commonly used in your work with your customers and vendors. The percentages you place in this table are used in the customer and vendor files to help the accounting system to automatically calculate the sales tax you pay and the sales tax you collect. Figure 7-15 shows a sample table.

The sample tax table we've included lists the rates in sequence from low to high.

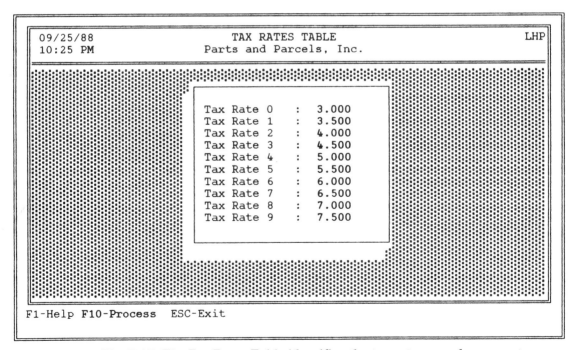

Fig. 7-15. The Tax Rates Table identifies the tax rates you charge customers, and vendors charge you.

Your tax table, however, should include those commonly-used rates for the states and territories in which you operate your business. It is not necessary to list the rates sequentially.

Security and Passwords

The sixth option in the Options window is Passwords. (We've skipped option four and five, for now.) Each module in *DacEasy Accounting* can be protected by a password system.

When you select the Passwords option, a small window will open in the middle of the menu screen and you will be able to enter up to five passwords (see Fig. 7-16). Each password represents one level of entry into your files, procedures, and reports.

When you start *DacEasy Accounting*, you must enter your password. Figure 7-17 shows the opening screen after you set passwords. You will be able to work in the accounting program only if your password is valid. Also, you will be locked out of some modules if your password is less than a Level 5.

People who know the Level 1 password will be able to access transaction entry, the transaction journal, and the cash receipts routines in accounts receivable. They will also have access to transaction entry, the transaction journal, and the payments journal in accounts payable. Level 1 people can enter the purchases and sales journals, as well as the purchase order and billing routines, but will be locked out of all other *DacEasy* functions.

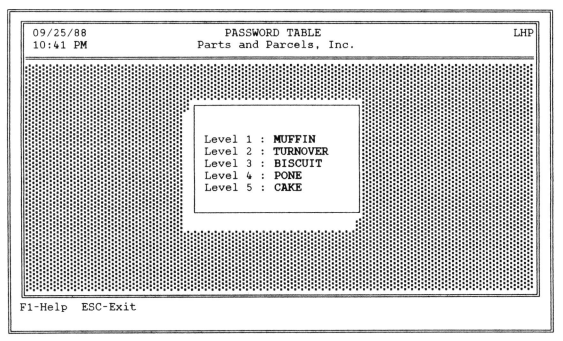

```
09/25/88                    PASSWORD TABLE                           LHP
10:41 PM                 Parts and Parcels, Inc.


                    Level 1 :  MUFFIN
                    Level 2 :  TURNOVER
                    Level 3 :  BISCUIT
                    Level 4 :  PONE
                    Level 5 :  CAKE




F1-Help   ESC-Exit
```

Fig. 7-16. The Password Table defines the levels of access available to employees. Level 5 gives access to all records and to the Password Table.

People who know the Level 2 password will be able to access all Level 1 modules plus the general ledger, accounts receivable, accounts payable, inventory, and file creation and maintenance. Reports from these files can be printed.

Level 3 passwords will admit people to Levels 1 and 2 and to the maintenance routines for the Chart of Accounts, vendors, customers, products, and services. In addition, Level 3 clearance permits modification of purchase order codes, price assignments, tax tables, and financial statements. Level 3 also permits the user to rehash files and post to the general ledger.

Level 4 access gives the user access to the general ledger interface table and the company identification information.

Anyone who has Level 5 access will be able to use all modules and procedures within *DacEasy*.

Level 5 offers the only access to the password table, as well. This has two important implications: (1) After passwords are set the first time, the program will permit only those with full clearance to see the list of passwords; and (2) if you don't assign a Level 5 password after assigning another level, you will not be able to change, delete, or add new passwords. If you elect to edit the password table, you must again give the Level 5 password. This prevents someone else from editing the password table if you've left your computer for a few minutes (although you should logout if you are to be away from your keyboard).

If you choose to use passwords—and you probably should—do not choose passwords that are the names of the people who have access. It's too easy for intruders to figure out. You should consider using nonsense words that are reasonably easy to remember

Fig. 7-17. The start-up screen that asks for the user's password.

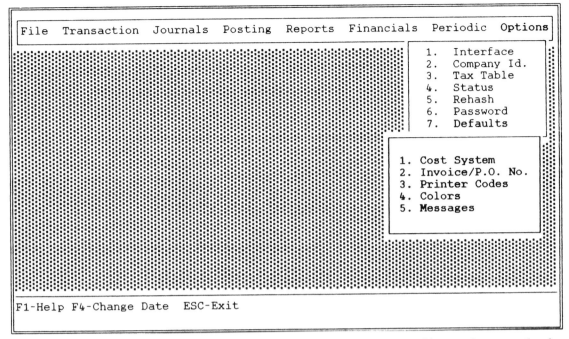

```
 ┌────────────────────────────────────────────────────────────────────────┐
 │┌──────────────────────────────────────────────────────────────────────┐│
 ││ File  Transaction  Journals  Posting  Reports  Financials  Periodic  Options││
 ││::::::::::::::::::::::::::::::::::::::::::::::::::::::::::::┌─────────────────────┐│
 ││::::::::::::::::::::::::::::::::::::::::::::::::::::::::::::│ 1.   Interface      │::│
 ││::::::::::::::::::::::::::::::::::::::::::::::::::::::::::::│ 2.   Company Id.    │::│
 ││::::::::::::::::::::::::::::::::::::::::::::::::::::::::::::│ 3.   Tax Table      │::│
 ││::::::::::::::::::::::::::::::::::::::::::::::::::::::::::::│ 4.   Status         │::│
 ││::::::::::::::::::::::::::::::::::::::::::::::::::::::::::::│ 5.   Rehash         │::│
 ││::::::::::::::::::::::::::::::::::::::::::::::::::::::::::::│ 6.   Password       │::│
 ││::::::::::::::::::::::::::::::::::::::::::::::::::::::::::::│ 7.   Defaults       │::│
 ││::::::::::::::::::::::::::::::::::::::::::::::::::::::::::::└─────────────┌─────────────────────────┐
 ││:::::::::::::::::::::::::::::::::::::::::::::::::::::::::::::::::::::::::::│ 1. Cost System          │
 ││:::::::::::::::::::::::::::::::::::::::::::::::::::::::::::::::::::::::::::│ 2. Invoice/P.O.  No.    │
 ││:::::::::::::::::::::::::::::::::::::::::::::::::::::::::::::::::::::::::::│ 3. Printer Codes        │
 ││:::::::::::::::::::::::::::::::::::::::::::::::::::::::::::::::::::::::::::│ 4. Colors               │
 ││:::::::::::::::::::::::::::::::::::::::::::::::::::::::::::::::::::::::::::│ 5. Messages             │
 ││:::::::::::::::::::::::::::::::::::::::::::::::::::::::::::::::::::::::::::└─────────────────────────┘
 ││:::::::::::::::::::::::::::::::::::::::::::::::::::::::::::::::::::::::::::::::::::::::::::
 ││ F1-Help  F4-Change Date   ESC-Exit                                     │
 │└──────────────────────────────────────────────────────────────────────┘│
 └────────────────────────────────────────────────────────────────────────┘
```

Fig. 7-18. The Options Default window shows several items that must be defined before the accounting system can be used.

but not easily guessed. Our Fig. 7-16 uses related words, and that is probably not a very good technique either.

After completing your assignment of passwords for your accounting system, you will be returned to the *DacEasy Accounting* Options window.

System Defaults

Selection 7 on the Options menu lets you assign several system default values that will be used for various purposes. Figure 7-18 shows the five system defaults you can define.

Define Cost System

You must define a costing method that *DacEasy* can use to assign value to your inventory and to assign value to the goods you sell.

The values assigned to your inventory items will be used in determining the value of your inventory so that that value can be placed in the appropriate account whenever posting is completed. In the Chart of Accounts shown in Fig. 7-3, the value would be written to account number 11071 and accumulated in account number 1107. The value is then included as an asset of your business.

In addition, the values assigned to your inventory items are used to determine your profit. The cost of each item sold is subtracted from the sales price and the result is entered on the screen for each item (see Fig. 8-3). The individual results are totaled and sent to the appropriate expense account. (For the Chart of Accounts in Fig. 7-3, that would be accounts under account number 51, as indicated in the general ledger interface table).

There are three options available to you when assigning values:

(1) Average Cost: The average cost for items in inventory is calculated by adding the current cost of newly-added items to the cost of existing items and dividing by the total number of items on-hand. This type of calculation is done on an item-by-item basis only. This is the default method.

(2) Last Purchase Price: The last purchase price is taken from the last purchase order and assigned to all on-hand items having the same inventory number. When an item is sold, the value is assigned as a cost to your business. This method is used by most retailers whose prices change frequently.

(3) Standard Cost: The standard cost is usually assigned to items that are manufactured, because the cost of goods sold must be calculated from the costs of the materials and resources used to manufacture the goods. This calculation is not done frequently, so a standard cost is calculated for use over a longer period of time.

Beginning Invoice and Purchase Order Numbers

You must give the beginning points for numbering your purchase orders, invoices, and the associated return forms. If you are setting up *DacEasy* in the middle of a business year, you might want to enter the numbers of the purchase orders, order return forms, invoices, and sales return forms that were last used. When these numbers are entered, *DacEasy* will start using the next numbers in sequence, so your forms are continuously recorded. If no numbers are given, *DacEasy* automatically will start each form at number 1.

Printer Codes

The next set up procedure you must complete is defining printer codes. These codes are important because they control the way your printer prints reports.

Types of Printers

There are two basic types of printers you can use with *DacEasy*: (1) A dot-matrix printer, which prints each character as a pattern of dots; and (2) a letter-quality printer, which uses a "daisy wheel", or a selectrictype ball to print in typewriter quality. Because *DacEasy* prints some reports in "condensed" print—132 characters per line instead of the normal 80 characters per line—it is recommended that you use a dot-matrix printer. Letter-quality printers, typically, cannot print condensed (sometimes called "compressed") characters.

If you are using a dot matrix printer you can instruct *DacEasy* to condense character size when small text is called for. *DacEasy* can automatically change between condensed and normal characters for some reports. Defining printer codes instructs *DacEasy Accounting* when to switch between normal and condensed text.

If you are using a "daisy wheel" printer—one that prints letters whole—you cannot adjust the character size. Therefore, some of your reports will not be complete. If your letter-quality printer has a wide carriage, however, you might be able to print your reports on wider paper. To do this, give the code for normal print in both the normal and condensed fields.

The following sections describe the importance and use of printer codes.

Printer Control Codes

For printers that can change the size of printed characters, there is a set of codes that give specific instructions to the printer about these size changes. These codes are typically given as a number, or a string of numbers, that the printer recognizes as control characters, which do not print.

DacEasy modules are pre-programmed to recognize standard IBM dot-matrix printer codes. These standard codes work with all models of the IBM Proprinter, the old IBM Graphics Printer, and other IBM-compatible printers, including most Epson models.

If you are using a printer that is not IBM-compatibile, you must run the routine to set the printer parameters (that is, you must type in the correct printer control codes so your printer will know when to condense print and when to use normal print sizes).

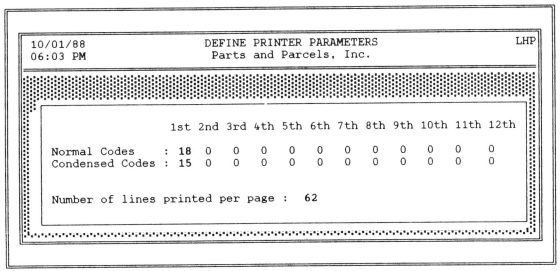

```
10/01/88                    DEFINE PRINTER PARAMETERS                   LHP
06:03 PM                      Parts and Parcels, Inc.


                 1st 2nd 3rd 4th 5th 6th 7th 8th 9th 10th 11th 12th

  Normal Codes    : 18  0   0   0   0   0   0   0   0   0    0    0
  Condensed Codes : 15  0   0   0   0   0   0   0   0   0    0    0


  Number of lines printed per page :   62
```

Fig. 7-19. Defining codes for normal-sized printer characters and for condensed printer characters. *The codes shown are for IBM/Epson compatible printers.*

The standard IBM and compatible printer codes for condensed print and normal print require only one code for each. For condensed print, the character code "15" is sent to the printer (see Fig. 7-19). To return to normal print, the character code "18" is sent. *DacEasy* recognizes these Printer Parameter numbers and automatically switches between the two.

Some non-compatible printers require "escape sequences" to switch from one style of print to another. These sequences require two codes for each style: (1) The code for the <ESC> key; and (2) the code for the printer command. (*DacEasy* does not accept codes that contain up to 12 numbers.)

Figure 7-20 gives an example of the "escape sequences" used for an old NEC portable printer that we regularly use. For condensed print, the *DacEasy* programs must send two codes to the printer: (1) Code 27, for <ESC>; and (2) code 81, for the uppercase letter "Q." For normal print, the codes are: (1) Code 27, for <ESC>, and code 78, for an uppercase "N."

When looking for the codes to use with your printer (if it is a "noncompatible"), you can check the index in the operator's manual that came with your printer. The first place to look is "Printer codes." If that is not a listing, you might try "ASCII codes" or "Control characters."

If your manual has no index (some of you recognized the reference in the previous paragraph as a joke), you should look through the manual for the table of control codes. But do not assume that a simple table has been included. Some manuals make you read

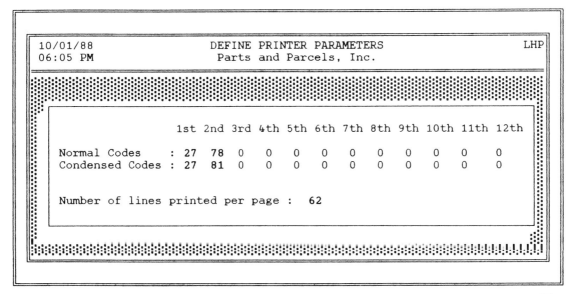

Fig. 7-20. Sample printer codes for non-IBM/Epson compatible printers. *The codes shown here are for our old NEC PC-8027A printer.*

through pages of coded information before you find the needed numbers.

A few manuals will use two-letter abbreviations to stand for codes. One of these abbreviations is "SI," which stands for "Shift In," a term used to describe the "shift into" condensed print. The matching abbreviation is "SO," for "shift out," the term used to indicate the "shift out" of condensed print to normal print. Each of these abbreviations is associated with a number code or sequence that is also given. You cannot use the letter abbreviations for *DacEasy's* printer parameters, only the associated numeric codes.

Other printer manuals give the codes in "hexadecimal" notation. The hexadecimal number system is based on 16 units rather than the base-ten number system we are accustomed to using. If you believe the codes are in "hex," refer to your DOS manual for a conversion to base-ten and use the base-ten equivalents in *DacEasy*.

To enter a printer code sequence, type the first number at the cursor's location on the original Printer Parameter screen. Once you press <ENTER>, the cursor will jump to the second column. Type the second number and press <ENTER> again. The cursor will continue to move across the line, letting you enter control characters. When the last character is entered, or the <ENTER> key is pressed 12 times, the cursor will move down to the next line, where you can repeat the process, using the codes for switching to condensed characters.

Once your printer codes are entered, press <F10> to process them. You will, then, be returned to the Options Defaults Menu.

Setting Screen Colors

During the installation of *DacEasy Graph + Mate*, we discussed setting the colors that would be used for the various windows that the program displays. The Defaults menu in *DacEasy Accounting* gives us the opportunity to set the screen colors for the screens used in the accounting program.

Figure 7-21 shows the workscreen where color default values can be set. This screen has three parts: (1) The top section lists each of the parts of a regular accounting screen; (2) the left side shows 128 possible color combinations (background with text in the foreground); and (3) the right side shows a sample of the colors you can select. The sample section is continuously updated as you try different color combinations. This lets you see what the screen will look like before you make a final decision.

The four arrow keys will move the highlight bar among the 12 items on the top section of the screen. When you have marked items you wish to set colors for, press <ENTER>. The default color combination will be shown in the sample section of the screen and markers will be placed in the left section so you can select other combinations if you wish. At that point, the arrow keys will move the marker among the 128 color combinations and the sample will change to reflect the marked combination. Once you have the combination you want, press <ENTER> and the default values will be saved. Move the highlight bar in the top section again and repeat for the next item.

After you have completed your color selections, press <F10> to process these selections. You will be returned to the Defaults menu.

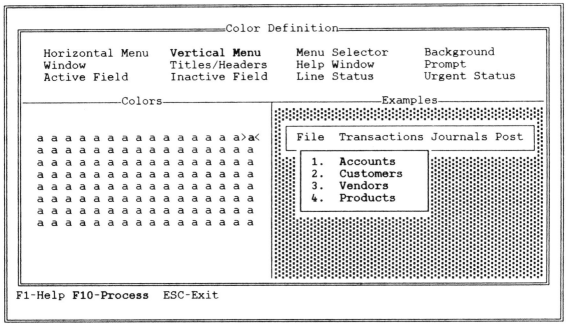

Fig. 7-21. Defining colors for various sections of your menus and work screens. *A sample changes colors on the right of the screen as you move the cursor from one color to another.*

Internal Messages File

A table of messages can be created and assigned to customers or vendors so that you can keep track of special considerations when dealing with them. The file can contain as many as 40 messages. Each of these messages is assigned a number that can be used in several ways.

When setting up a customer record or a vendor record, you can enter the number of a message you want to display every time you begin to work with that customer or vendor. When a transaction involving the customer or vendor is started, the message will be automatically displayed as a reminder to you or to the person entering data for you. The first three messages shown in Fig. 7-22 are examples.

In addition, when completing invoices or purchase orders, you can type an "M" (for message) in the Item Number column, followed by the number of the message you want to display. When that invoice or purchase order is printed, the message will be printed on the line where you entered the number. The fourth message shown in Fig. 7-22 is an example of such a message.

Be careful when placing messages on invoices or purchase orders. If a "check credit" message appears on an invoice to one of your best customers, feelings could be hurt enough to cause the loss of that account.

```
 09/04/88                    SPECIAL MESSAGES TABLE                  LHP
 11:49 PM                    Parts and Parcels, Inc.

     Msg. No.      Message
    ==========    ======================================================
         1         Check Credit Available.
         2         Ask P.O. Number.
         3         Check discount with manager.
         4         Thank you very much for your business.
         5
         6
         7
         8
         9
        10
        11
        12
        13
        14
        15
        16
```

Fig. 7-22. As many as 40 internal comments can be included to assist in managing your files.

Summary

This chapter presents overviews and details about the Chart of Accounts and several important procedures to complete during the set up process. All the procedures are accessed through the File or Options items from the Main Menu. The procedures include company identification, integration through the general ledger interface table, selecting an inventory costing method, defining internal messages for customers and vendors, listing statement messages for regular and overdue accounts, establishing codes for non-inventory items, password protection for all your files, and printer control codes that DacEasy will need to print reports.

8

Setting Up the Company
Accounting Files

Chapter Goals
- *This chapter discusses the information to be included in the customer file, the vendor file, the product/inventory file, and the service/services-rendered file. Specific suggestions are provided on the organization and structure of the information in these files.*

Before you begin entering data in *DacEasy Accounting* and *Payroll*, you should invest a little time in considering how the data is going to be used. Planning and organizing your data before you begin to build files will save you much time later. In addition, if your files can be referenced through an intuitive system of identification codes, you will reduce the difficulty of working in these files.

Part of our discussion in this chapter relates to planning and organizing data before it is entered. We make specific recommendations about structuring your files, however, you are not limited to the types of structures discussed. It is our intent to provide you with sufficient information so you can plan a structure that is best suited to your needs.

Accessing the Company Accounting Files

From the *DacEasy Accounting* Main Menu, you can access your company accounting files by selecting the File option. From this pull-down menu, you can access the five major files that your accounting system pulls information from (see Fig. 7-6 in Chapter 7). We discussed the Accounts File—the Chart of Accounts—in Chapter 7 and it is discussed further in later chapters.

The Customer File

It is important to create and maintain an accurate customer file so that *DacEasy Accounting* can assist you with serving and billing your customers. Your accounts receivable is tied directly to your customer file and your inventory control is linked to your customer file through the billing module.

If you do not use an accounts receivable system, you can use the customer file and the billing module as a point-of-sale recordkeeping system that can automatically handle your inventory, as well as your actual sales records (see Fig. 8-1).

The following information might be helpful to consider when creating a customer file.

Customer Code

A customer code can contain as many as six characters (either alphabetic or numeric). Codes should not be random, but are designed to give you easy access to a customer's record, because you must ask for a record by code rather than a customer's name. This also assists *DacEasy Accounting* in processing a customer's information efficiently. The code must be unique for each customer.

It is extremely important, for ease of use, that all customer codes follow the same pattern of identification. One way to do this that we have found particularly efficient is to use the first four characters of a customer's name followed by a two-digit number. The two digits are used to distinguish customers who might have the same four letters to start their names. This type of coding system allows you to have as many as 99 customers with the same four letters starting their name.

```
09/04/88              CUSTOMER FILE MAINTENANCE                LHP
11:59 PM                Parts and Parcels, Inc.

Customer Code :   WEIR01          Type (O=Open B=Balance):   O
Name          :   Weir Lighting Fixtures    Sales Person  :  WYNN
Contact       :   Sam Charger              G/L Department:   01
Address       :   4312 S. Socket Street    Discount %    :    3.00
City          :   Ninety Six      State :  SC  Discount Days :     10
Zip Code      :   29666-    Tel : (803)555-3467 Due days    :     30
Tax Id. Number:   15-1234567-2              Message Code  :   1
Credit Limit     :      5000.00   Previous Balance  :      0.00
Credit Available :      5000.00   This Period Bal.  :      0.00
                                  Current Balance   :      0.00
Last Sale Date   :   /  /         Last Payment Date :     /  /
Month Int. Rate  :   0.00         Sales Tax Code    :   4 Rate:  5.000
                      ═══ STATISTICAL INFORMATION ═══
                Yr.Bef.Lst Last Year This Year  Forecast  Variance    %

# Invoices :        ████        0         0         0         0      0.0
$ Sales    :          0         0         0         0         0      0.0
$ Costs    :          0         0         0         0         0      0.0
$ Profit   :          0         0         0         0         0      0.0

F1-Help  F2-Add Tax Rate  F6-DELETE  F7-Enter Invoice F10-Process  ESC-exit
```

Fig. 8-1. Work screen for entering information for the customer file in DacEasy Accounting. Sample data are included.

If a customer is an individual, rather than a company, use the first four letters of their last name. If a customer code contains letters, they must be uppercase.

With this method, you can call up a customer's record simply by entering the first four letters of the name and choosing digits until you find the right record. We have found that this method helps when we can't find our printed list of customers—which should be on the shelf above the computer but hasn't been since it was first printed. (With *DacEasy Graph + Mate*, you can look up customer codes and display them on-screen.)

When you enter a customer code and *DacEasy* cannot find it, you will be given an empty customer file maintenance screen where you can enter the appropriate information. If a record with that code already exists, the record will be displayed and you can edit it as needed—or you can give another code until you find the record you're looking for.

The customer code is the most important part of the customer record because it is used to access the records. You cannot recall a customer's record if you do not know the code.

Customer Name

The customer name can contain as many as 30 characters. It is important that all customer names follow the same pattern of identification. If your customer is a business, the customer name should be the name of the business. You can use the ''contact'' field to include the name of the business' representative who works with you. You can enter all company names just as they appear on each company's business materials (leaving off the word ''The,'' as in ''The Book Company''). Individual's names can be entered with the last name followed by a comma, a space, and first name. Organizing customer data this way provides for meaningful sorting and printouts.

Company Contact

The company contact is the name of the company's representative who serves you directly. You can use as many as 30 characters in this Field. Patterns of gathering contact names are not important because *DacEasy* does not use these names to sort or find information within the file. If the customer is an individual, and a contact is not relevant, you can leave this field blank by pressing <ENTER>.

Customer Address

The customer address should include the street address or postal service box where you regularly make mailings. The address can contain as many as 30 characters. It is not unusual to abbreviate part of the address. Be sure, however, that your abbreviations will be clear to the postal service person who will be trying to get your bills to your customers.

Customer City, State, and Zip Code

As many as 15 characters can be used for the customer's city. Within the United States, you should use the two-character abbreviations for states and the appropriate zip codes (the zip-plus-four format is supported).

When you are entering a series of customers, these fields will contain the information you entered in the previous customer screen. If the information is correct, simply confirm it by pressing <ENTER>. This can be very helpful if you plan the entry of customer records by city so you can take advantage of the default values. If the information is incorrect, type the new information into each of the fields.

Telephone Number

The customer's telephone number should be entered in a separate field. Type the area code in the displayed parentheses, press <ENTER>, and type the rest of the telephone number. You do not type the parentheses around the area code and you do not type the dash in the remainder of the number, these are provided by the system.

Account Type

You have two choices for choosing an account type. Either one determines how *DacEasy Accounting* handles outstanding balances for customers.

Balance Forward. This type of account itemizes purchases and payments and keeps them in *DacEasy* until the end-of-period routines are completed. At that time, only the net balance for the customer will be kept and printed on subsequent statements. The net balance will be labeled "Balance Forward."

To use this type of account, enter the letter "B" in the customers field.

Open Invoice. This type of account itemizes purchases and payments in *DacEasy* until the invoice is zero and the end-of-period routines are completed. Each subsequent statement will include all transactions until the invoice amount is fully paid.

We recommend the "open invoice" method because it provides the most information without additional work, although monthly statements will be longer when printed.

To use this type of account for a specific customer, leave the default letter "O" in the field.

Sales Person

The sales person might be identified with a code, created by you, that can contain as many as four characters. The code should be unique for each sales person. *DacEasy Accounting* can use these codes to print sales reports, or determine a performance measure (in dollars and cents) for each member of your sales staff.

G/L Department

You can create two-digit codes to designate departments if you use customer information to determine revenue and costs by department. Departmental controls are discussed fully in Chapter 10.

(When we discussed the general ledger interface table in Chapter 7, we selected Revenue/Cost Departments by inventory instead of by customer (see Fig. 7-14).

If you are not using customer information for department controls, you could use the codes to identify preferred customers, special discount customers, or provide other customer classifications. *DacEasy* can sort and print reports based on information stored in this field. For example, you can print mailing labels for preferred customers who are to be invited to a special sale event.

Special Discounts

If you give discounts to customers, companys or individuals, you can place the percent of discount and the number of days to qualify for the discount in these two fields. The percent is entered as the actual percent, instead of its decimal equivalent, for example: three-and-a-half percent would be entered as ''3.5,'' not at ''.035''. This information is used to calculate amounts to be included on customer invoices and statements.

Due Days

The number of days an invoice is actually due should be entered in this field. This information is used in aging reports based on overdue accounts. It is also used to determine the message (see Fig. 7-13) printed on your customer statements. As with discount information, this can be different for each customer.

Tax Identification Number

A tax identification number can be placed in each customer's record. This number can contain as many as 12 digits. This can be useful if some customers have tax exempt status that must be documented in reports to various tax agencies. You might also use this field to store federal tax identification numbers for companies to which you make sales.

Message Code

The most important thing to remember about message codes is that they are for internal use only. The customer will never see the codes, or the messages associated with them. The message code references a message that you have entered into a special messages file, which is discussed in Chapter 7. When an invoice or statement is being prepared for a customer who has a code in his record, the message will be displayed to remind you that special circumstances are to be considered for that customer. Figure 7-22 shows a partial list of available messages. This list can contain as many as 40 different messages, with one of these ''flagged'' in a customer record.

Credit Limit and Credit Available

You can set a different credit limit for each of your customers that can be placed in the credit limit field. *DacEasy Accounting* will calculate and display the credit available. The only way to change these two fields is to modify the credit limit field; you cannot directly modify the credit available field.

Previous Balance, This Period Balance, and Current Balance

The previous balance is automatically entered from the previous period. Activity in the current period will result in the automatic display of the balance for the current period. *DacEasy* will use these two values to calculate and display the current balance. These fields are calculated and displayed by the system and cannot be edited directly.

Last Sale Date and Last Payment Date

The date of the last invoice for each customer and the date of the last payment made by each customer are displayed in each record. These dates cannot be modified directly.

Monthly Interest Rate

If you charge a "finance charge" for late payment, enter the rate in this field. The rate should be given as a monthly percent instead of an annual percent (that is, the yearly rate should be divided by 12 and the result entered here). The rate should be written as the actual percent and not as its decimal equivalent (see the example given for "discount rate," in the Special Discounts section of this chapter). *DacEasy* will calculate finance charges based on the "due days" and the date of the last invoice. Whenever an invoice is printed for the customer, the actual finance charges (if there are any) will be automatically added.

Sales Tax Code and Rate

When the cursor is placed in the sales tax code field, a window opens on the screen and a tax table of rates is displayed. The tax rates table is the same table that is set up in Chapter 7 (see Fig. 7-15).

If you are required to collect federal, state, or local sales taxes on the items you sell, enter the tax rate number and press <ENTER>. The code number and its associated rate will be displayed. This rate will be used for calculating the sales tax to be automatically added to each customer invoice.

Statistical Information

DacEasy automatically accumulates statistical information for three years—you do not have to enter anything in these fields in order to use the information stored here.

When you start a new company, these fields are blank, but will be updated for the current year each time a transaction is posted for a customer. When you run the end-of-year procedures, all current yearly information will be moved to "last year" and all of last year's information will be moved to "year before last."

Starting in the Middle of a Business Year

If you have an existing company and are just starting to use *DacEasy* in the middle of an accounting year, you can bring each customer's record up-to-date in one of two ways. If you are using a "balance forward" type account, you can enter the current to-date data in the statistical information section at the bottom of the customer file maintenance screen. This data can be entered in the "This Year" column.

If you are using an "open invoice" type account, you can enter all open invoices by pressing <F7>. A window will open at the bottom of the screen (see Fig. 8-2) you can then key in the current year's open invoices for the displayed customer. You can enter as many invoices as necessary, although you can see only three at one time.

For each of the invoices you enter, you must provide several pieces of information. Figure 8-2 shows these column labels.

```
┌─────────────────────────────────────────────────────────────────────────┐
│ ┌───────────────────────────────────────────────────────────────────────┐ │
│ │ 10/02/88              CUSTOMER FILE MAINTENANCE                    LHP│ │
│ │ 09:30 AM              Parts and Parcels, Inc.                        │ │
│ │                                                                        │ │
│ │ Customer Code :   WEIR01              Type (O=Open B=Balance):    O   │ │
│ │ Name          :   Weir Lighting Fixtures      Sales Person   :   WYNN │ │
│ │ Contact       :   Sam Charger                 G/L Department:    01   │ │
│ │ Address       :   4312 S. Socket Street       Discount %     :    3.00│ │
│ │ City          :   Ninety Six       State :  SC  Discount Days :     10 │ │
│ │ Zip Code      :   29666-     Tel : (803)555-3467 Due days     :     30 │ │
│ │ Tax Id. Number:   15-1234567-2                Message Code   :   1    │ │
│ │ Credit Limit      :       5000.00   Previous Balance   :      0.00    │ │
│ │ Credit Available  :       5000.00   This Period Bal.   :      0.00    │ │
│ │                                     Current Balance    :      0.00    │ │
│ │ Last Sale Date    :                 Last Payment Date  :              │ │
│ │ ═══════════════════════════ ADDING OPEN INVOICES ═══════════════════  │ │
│ ├───────────────────────────────────────────────────────────────────────┤ │
│ │           Transaction:            Discount Available:  Due   Reference │ │
│ │ Invoice # Code Date    Amt. Balance  Date     Amount   Date   Number   │ │
│ │ --------- ---- ------  ------------ -------- ----------- ------ ------  │ │
│ │                          0.00                   0.00          NONE     │ │
│ │                          0.00                   0.00          NONE     │ │
│ │                          0.00                   0.00          NONE     │ │
│ └───────────────────────────────────────────────────────────────────────┘ │
│  F1-Help   F2-Add Tax Rate   F6-DELETE   F7-Enter Invoice F10-Process   ESC-exit │
└─────────────────────────────────────────────────────────────────────────┘
```

Fig. 8-2. Window at bottom of customer work screen lets you enter outstanding invoices if you are starting your accounting system in the middle of a business year.

Invoice Number. Enter the invoice number, using as many as eight characters.

Transaction Code and Date. The transaction code must be one of three letters. "I" indicates the transaction is, indeed, an invoice; "D" indicates the transaction is a miscellaneous debit to the customer record; and "C" indicates the transaction is a miscellaneous credit to the record. Once the code is entered, the current system date will be displayed; you can, however, change this to reflect the actual transaction date.

Transaction Amount Balance. Enter the invoice amount or the balance forward from this invoice. If the number is negative, enter the negative sign first.

Discount Date and Amount. The discount date and the calculated discount amount is entered automatically from the information in the customer record. You can override these calculations by typing in the appropriate data.

Due Date. The due date for each invoice will be calculated from the transaction date given above and the due date given in the customer record. This date can be changed in this window.

Reference Number. A reference number can be given for each invoice transaction. The number might be the customer's purchase order number, or some other reference, that will have meaning to the customer or to your accounting system.

When you have finished entering invoices for a customer, press <F10>. *DacEasy* will process the entered invoices and add new transactions as you use the program.

The <F7> option permits you only to enter data. After you've made the entries, you cannot edit the information on this screen. Instead, go to the appropriate journal to make correcting entries into the accounting system.

Editing an Existing Customer Record

If you must make changes in a customer's record, or if you want to delete a customer's record, you can enter the File routine and select option 2. When an empty customer screen is displayed, the cursor will flash in the customer code field. Type the code for the customer record you want to work with. Keep in mind that you can see a list of customers and their codes from within *DacEasy Graph+Mate*. When the record is displayed, make the changes.

If you want to delete the record from the file, press <F6> while the cursor is in the customer name field. You cannot, however, delete a customer with outstanding obligations.

When all information on the customer screen is correct, press <F10> to tell *DacEasy* to process the information. All of the displayed information will be saved to disk so it can be retrieved when it is needed later. Pressing <ESC> will eliminate any changes and will restore all the previous values.

The Vendor File

It is important to create and maintain an accurate vendor file in order for *DacEasy Accounting* to assist you with purchasing and paying your bills. Your account payables are tied directly to your vendor file, and your inventory control is linked to your vendor file through the purchase order module.

If you do not use an accounts payable system, you can use the vendor file and the purchasing module as a disbursements journal and recordkeeping system that can automatically handle your inventory as well as your purchasing records (see Fig. 8-3).

From the File option on the *DacEasy Accounting* Main Menu, you can select option 3 to create or edit vendor files. The following information might be helpful to consider when creating a vendor file.

Vendor Code

A vendor code can contain as many as six characters (either alphabetic or numeric). Codes should be designed to give you easy access to a vendor's record because you must ask for a record by code rather than a vendor's name. The code must be unique for each customer.

It is important, for ease of use, that all vendor codes follow the same pattern of

```
┌─────────────────────────────────────────────────────────────────────────┐
│ ┌───────────────────────────────────────────────────────────────────┐   │
│ │ 09/04/88            VENDOR FILE MAINTENANCE                    LHP  │   │
│ │ 01:00 AM              Parts and Parcels, Inc.                      │   │
│ ├───────────────────────────────────────────────────────────────────┤   │
│ │ Vendor Code    :   SHAD01          Type (O=Open B=Balance):   O    │   │
│ │ Name           :   Shady Vore Lumber Company   Territory   :  WEST  │   │
│ │ Contact        :   Bubba Vore, President       Type        :  WD    │   │
│ │ Address        :   543 Barron Hills Canyon   Discount %    :  2.00  │   │
│ │ City           :   St. Arbor      State :  AZ  Discount Days :  10  │   │
│ │ Zip Code       :   85899-    Tel : (602)555-1234 Due days  :   30  │   │
│ │ Tax Id. Number:    23-4561239-0              Message Code  :  2    │   │
│ │ Credit Limit      :     15000.00   Previous Balance :     0.00     │   │
│ │ Credit Available  :     15000.00   This Period Bal. :     0.00     │   │
│ │                                    Current Balance  :     0.00     │   │
│ │ Last Purch. Date :   /  /          Last Payment Date :    /  /     │   │
│ │                                    Sales Tax Code   :  0 Rate:  3.000 │ │
│ │ ══════════════════════ STATISTICAL INFORMATION ══════════════════ │   │
│ │           Yr.Bef.Lst Last Year This Year  Forecast  Variance    %  │   │
│ │                                                                    │   │
│ │ # Invoices :    ███████      0        0        0        0      0.0 │   │
│ │ $ Purchases:       0          0        0        0        0      0.0 │   │
│ │                                                                    │   │
│ └───────────────────────────────────────────────────────────────────┘   │
│                                                                           │
│ F1-Help  F2-Add Tax Rate  F6-DELETE  F7-Enter Invoice F10-Process  ESC-exit │
│                                                                           │
└─────────────────────────────────────────────────────────────────────────┘
```

Fig. 8-3. Work screen for entering information for the vendor file in DacEasy Accounting. *Sample data are included.*

identification. One particularly efficient way to do this is to use the first four characters of a vendor's name, followed by a two-digit number. The two digits are used to distinguish vendors who might have the same four letters to start their names. This type of coding system allows you to have as many as 99 vendors with the same four letters starting their name.

If a vendor is an individual, rather than a company, use the first four letters of their last name. If a vendor code contains letters, they must be uppercase.

Using this method, you can easily call up a vendor's record by simply entering the first four letters of the name and choosing digits until you find the right record.

If you enter the code for a vendor record that already exists, that record will be displayed so you can edit it. If a record for that code does not already exist, you will be given an empty record to add a vendor to the file.

Vendor Name

The vendor name may contain as many as 30 characters. It is important that all vendor names follow the same pattern of identification. If your vendor is a business, the name should be that of the business, dropping any "The," "A," or "An" that may appear as the first word of a vendors name. If your vendor is an individual, you should use the last name, a comma, a space, and the first name.

Company Contact

The company contact is the name of the company's representative who serves you directly. You can use as many as 30 characters, including punctuation and spaces in this field. Patterns of entering contact names are not important because *DacEasy* does not use these names to sort or find information within the file. If the vendor name is the same as the contact name, you may leave this field blank by pressing <ENTER>.

Vendor Address

The vendor address should include the vendor's mailing address. If you abbreviate, be sure your abbreviations will be clear to the postal service. This address will be printed on the checks that *DacEasy* prints to pay each vendor's invoices and will appear in the window of your mailing envelope.

Vendor City, State, and Zip Code

As many as 15 characters can be used for the vendor's city. Within the United States, you should use the two-character abbreviation for states. The zip-plus-four format is supported.

You can organize your entry of vendors by name of city and save time in the entry process. *DacEasy* retains the city, state, and zip code of the previous vendor and displays it in the new record each time new entry is begun. This way you do not have to re-enter these fields unless the city changes.

Telephone Number

Type the area code in the displayed parentheses, press <ENTER> and type the rest of the telephone number. The dash between numbers and the parentheses are provided by the system and do not need to be typed.

Account Type

There are two types of accounts. Either one determines how *DacEasy Accounting* handles outstanding balances due to vendors.

Balance Forward. This type of account itemizes invoices and keeps them in *DacEasy* until the end-of-period routines are completed. At that time, only the net balance for the vendor will be saved and printed on subsequent statements. You can print vendor statements for your own records. These provide a check against statements received from these vendors. To use this type of account, enter the letter "B" in the vendor field.

Open Invoice. This type of account itemizes invoices and keeps them in *DacEasy* until the invoices are zero and the end-of-period routines are completed. Each subsequent statement includes all transactions on non-zero invoices.

Territory

You can use as many as four alphabetic or numeric characters to identify a territory or some other purchasing factor for a particular vendor, or to identify a mailing zone so that shipping charges can be calculated for purchase orders.

Vendor Type

The vendor code can have up to two characters (alphabetic or numeric), and can be used for whatever purpose you want. There are no set standards for defining a vendor type.

If you contract for services from a vendor and the amount paid for those services must be reported to federal agencies through the Form 1099, you would enter ''1099'' in this field. From the Reports option on the *DacEasy Accounting* Main Menu, you can print information to be used in completing Form 1099 for each vendor. Specific report formats are discussed further in Chapter 15.

Special Discounts

If your vendor offers you a discount for paying your bills early, the percentage can be entered in this Field. The percent should be entered as the actual percent, instead of its decimal equivalent. For example, three-and-a-half percent would be entered as ''3.5,'' not as ''.035''. The discount days would be the number of days that the bill must be paid to qualify for the discount.

DacEasy Accounting can print, daily, a list of invoices with pending discounts so you can pay them within the given period. When you begin printing your vendor checks (through the accounts payable module), *DacEasy Accounting* will notify you of available discounts—if you first provide the information in the vendor's record.

Due Days

The due days field contains the number of days that indicate when a total payment is due. This number can be different for each vendor and will be used to notify you, through daily reports, of bills due.

Tax Identification Number

A tax identification number, of up to 12 characters, can be placed in each vendor's record. You might use this field to store federal tax identification numbers for companies that you make purchases from.

Message Code

The most important thing to remember about the message codes is that they are for internal use only. The vendor will never see the codes or the messages associated with them. The code refers to a message that you entered in the special messages file (see Fig. 7-22). When a purchase order or statement is being prepared for a vendor who has a code in his record, the message is displayed to remind you that special circumstances are to be considered for that vendor.

Credit Limit and Credit Available

You can enter a credit limit provided by your vendor. *DacEasy* will calculate and display the credit you have remaining with the vendor. The only way to modify the credit available field is to change the credit limit field.

Previous Balance, This Period Balance, and Current Balance

The previous balance is automatically entered from the previous period. Activity in the current period results in the automatic display of the balance for the current period. *DacEasy* will use these two values to calculate and display the current balance. These fields are calculated and displayed by the system and cannot be edited directly.

Last Purchase Date and Last Payment Date

The Last Purchase Date and the Last Payment Date are supplied by *DacEasy*, using information in the accounts payable and inventory files.

Sales Tax Code and Rate

When the cursor is placed in the sales tax code field, a window opens on the screen and the table of tax rates is displayed. This tax rates table is the same table that was set up in Chapter 7 (see Fig. 7-15).

If you are required to pay federal, state, or local sales taxes on the items you buy from a particular vendor, enter the tax rate number and press <ENTER>. The code number and its associated rate will be displayed. This rate will be used to automatically calculate the sales tax for each purchase order.

Statistical Information

DacEasy automatically accumulates statistical information for three years—you do not have to enter anything in these fields in order to use the information stored there. At anytime you can determine and include any statistical information for previous years.

When you start a new company, these fields will be blank but will be updated for the current year each time a transaction is posted for your vendor. When you run the end-of-year procedures, all current year's information will be moved to "last year" and all of last year's information will be moved to "year before last."

Starting in the Middle of a Business Year

If you are starting to use *DacEasy* in the middle of an accounting year, you can bring each vendors record up-to-date in one of two ways. If your vendor is using a "balance forward" type of account, you can enter the current to-date data in the statistical information section at the bottom of the vendor file maintenance screen. This data can be entered in the "This Year" column.

If your vendor is using an "open invoice" type of account, you can enter all open invoices by pressing <F7>. A window will open at the bottom of the screen (see Fig. 8-4) where you can key in the current year's open invoices for a particular vendor. You can enter as many invoices as necessary, although you can see only three at a time.

For each outstanding invoice you enter, you must provide several pieces of information. Figure 8-4 shows these column labels.

Invoice Number. You must enter the invoice number, using as many as eight characters.

```
┌─────────────────────────────────────────────────────────────────────────┐
│  10/02/88              VENDOR FILE MAINTENANCE                      LHP    │
│  01:05 PM              Parts and Parcels, Inc.                            │
│ ─────────────────────────────────────────────────────────────────────── │
│  Vendor Code    :  SHAD01              Type (O=Open B=Balance):   O       │
│  Name           :  Shady Vore Lumber Company    Territory     :  WEST     │
│  Contact        :  Bubba Vore, President        Type          :  WD       │
│  Address        :  543 Barron Hills Canyon      Discount %    :    2.00   │
│  City           :  St. Arbor       State :  AZ  Discount Days :      10   │
│  Zip Code       :  85899-    Tel : (602)555-1234 Due days     :      30   │
│  Tax Id. Number:  23-4561239-0                  Message Code  :   2       │
│  Credit Limit    :     15000.00    Previous Balance  :     0.00           │
│  Credit Available :    15000.00    This Period Bal.  :     0.00           │
│                                    Current Balance   :     0.00           │
│  Last Purch. Date :                Last Payment Date :                    │
│ ══════════════════════════ ADDING OPEN INVOICES ═══════════════════════  │
│ ┌─────────────────────────────────────────────────────────────────────┐ │
│ │        Transaction:          Discount Available:    Due   Reference  │ │
│ │ Invoice # Code Date   Amt. Balance  Date   Amount   Date   Number    │ │
│ │ --------- ---- ------ ------------  ----- --------- ------ --------   │ │
│ │                          0.00                 0.00         NONE       │ │
│ │                          0.00                 0.00         NONE       │ │
│ │                          0.00                 0.00         NONE       │ │
│ └─────────────────────────────────────────────────────────────────────┘ │
│ ═══════════════════════════════════════════════════════════════════════ │
│  F1-Help   F2-Add Tax Rate   F6-DELETE   F7-Enter Invoice F10-Process  ESC-exit │
└─────────────────────────────────────────────────────────────────────────┘
```

Fig. 8-4. Window at bottom of vendor work screen lets you enter outstanding invoices if you are starting your accounting system in the middle of a business year.

Transaction Code and Date. The transaction code must be one of three letters. "I" indicates the transaction is, indeed, an invoice; "D" indicates the transaction is a miscellaneous debit to the vendors record; and "C" indicates the transaction is a miscellaneous credit to the record. Once the code is entered, the current system date will be displayed; you can, however, change it to reflect the actual transaction date.

Transaction Amount Balance. You must enter the invoice amount or the balance forward from the invoice. If the number is negative, enter the negative sign first.

Discount Date and Amount. The discount date and the calculated discount amount is automatically entered from the information given in the vendor record. You can override these calculations by typing in the appropriate data.

Due Date. The due date for each invoice is calculated from the transaction date given and the due days given in the vendor record. This date can be changed in this window.

Reference Number. A reference number can be assigned for each invoice transaction. A reference number might be your purchase order number, or some other reference that has meaning to the vendor, or to your accounting system.

```
┌──────────────────────────────────────────────────────────────────────┐
│ 09/05/88                  PRODUCT FILE MAINTENANCE                 LHP │
│ 08:27 AM                  Parts and Parcels, Inc.                      │
│  Product Code   : PAINT01        Description : Paint, Wt Base Gal      │
│  Measure        : CASE           Fraction    :   4       Dept.  : 01   │
│  Bin            : P01            Vendor      : PAIN01                   │
│  Sales Price    :      75.800    Taxable(Y/N): Y                       │
│  Last Sale Date:   /  /          Minimum     :      25     Reorder :  10│
│  Last Purch. Date :  /  /   Lst.Purch.Price :     0.000                │
│  Std. Cost       :     0.000      Avg. Cost  :     0.000               │
│  On Hand   Units  :        0.000  Dollars    :        0.000            │
│  Committed Units  :        0.000                                       │
│  On Order  Units  :        0.000                                       │
│ ═══════════════════════ STATISTICAL INFORMATION ═══════════════════════│
│                   Yr.Bef.Lst Last Year This Year  Forecast  Variance  %│
│  Units Purch. :   ████████      0         0         0          0  0.0   │
│  $ Purchase   :          0      0         0         0          0  0.0   │
│  Units Sold   :          0      0         0         0          0  0.0   │
│  $ Sales      :          0      0         0         0          0  0.0   │
│  $ Cost       :          0      0         0         0          0  0.0   │
│  $ Profit     :          0      0         0         0          0  0.0   │
│  Times Turn   :        0.0    0.0       0.0       0.0        0.0  0.0   │
│  Gross Return :          0      0         0         0          0  0.0   │
│                                                                        │
│ F1-Help  F6-Delete  F7-Enter Stock  F10-Process  ESC-exit              │
└──────────────────────────────────────────────────────────────────────┘
```

Fig. 8-5. Work screen for entering information in the inventory/product file in DacEasy Accounting. Sample data are included.

Press <F10> to process the vendor invoices. *DacEasy* will add new transactions as you use the program.

The <F7> option permits you only to enter data. After you've made the entries, you cannot edit the information on this screen. Instead, you must go to the appropriate journal to correct entries in the accounting system.

Editing an Existing Vendor Record

If you need to make changes to a vendor's record, or you want to delete a vendor's record, enter the File routine and select option 3. An empty vendor screen is displayed and the cursor will flash in the vendor code field. Type the code for the vendor in whose record you want to work. Keep in mind that you can see a list of vendors and their codes from within *DacEasy Graph + Mate*. Once the record is displayed, make the changes.

To delete the record from the file, press <F6> while the cursor is in the vendor name field. You cannot delete a vendor if there is an account balance.

When all of the information on the vendor screen is correct, press <F10> to tell *DacEasy* to process the information. All the displayed information will be saved to disk and can be retrieved whenever it is needed. If you press <ESC> instead of <F10>, all changes will be ignored and previous values retained.

The Inventory/Product File

The product file is your inventory file. After you set up your inventory codes for the products you buy and sell, the purchase order module and the billing module will automatically update your items on-hand, committed-to-customer, and on-order figures. These figures are always immediately available simply by selecting the inventory file from the main menu and entering the inventory number of the item you want to check.

Also, from the inventory file, you can print a list of items that are below the minimum number you want to keep on-hand. If your vendor gives you a special price for ordering a certain number of items, the number can be entered as a "re-order" number and the program will alert you when you create a purchase order for those items.

In addition to inventory control, the inventory file will let you see which items are moving and which items are not, so you can eliminate any items that are simply taking up space in your inventory.

If you organize your inventory file well, it can be one of the most powerful tools you have in operating your business. Therefore, it is important that you prepare a good and logical structure for your files (see Fig. 8-5). The inventory number for each item should not be a "random" number, picked out of the air. The inventory number should let you know something about the item you're stocking.

To start defining your inventory/product items, select the File option from the *DacEasy Accounting* Main Menu, from the secondary menu, choose option 4 (see Fig. 7-6).

The following descriptions might be helpful as you plan your inventory numbers and enter them into the inventory/product file.

Inventory Number

The inventory number can contain as many as 13 characters (alphabetic or numeric) and can use standard UPC bar-coding conventions, adding another measure of control.

Inventory numbers are used on all purchase orders and customer invoices so that *DacEasy* can track the buying and selling of all inventory items.

DacEasy Graph + Mate makes using inventory codes simple. When you complete a purchase order, *DacEasy Graph + Mate* can open windows into the inventory file. Through these windows, you can point to the item you want to add to the purchase order and the number and description will be "pasted" directly to the current line of the purchase order. To complete customer invoices, the same windows can be opened to point to inventory numbers to be placed on those invoices.

Item Description

The item description can contain as many as 20 characters. Write inventory descriptions so they can be sorted meaningfully. For example, if you sell trash cans and list one type as "large round kitchen," you will find them under "L" in a sorted listing. If, however, you give the description as "kitchen, large round," they would be placed in one location under "K." Consequently your printed listing will be easier to use.

Unit of Measure

A unit of measure is typically the size of the unit you purchase. For example, tree bark might be purchased by the "bushel," loaves of bread might be purchased by "trays," or nails could be purchased by the "pound." You may use as many as four letters or numbers to give the unit of measure.

The four-character abbreviation you use for the unit of measure has no real arithmetic significance. It will be used by *DacEasy* to list items on purchase orders, customer invoices, and inventory reports. It is used strictly to benefit the persons who read it. For example, if you order two cases of paint thinner, you would enter the "2" on the purchase order. When *DacEasy* looks in the inventory file to find the paint thinner, it will find that it is ordered by the "case"—the unit of measure. Thus, the word "case" is printed on the purchase order beside the number "2." The "2" will be used for all arithmetic.

Fraction of the Unit of Measure

The fraction of a unit to be bought or sold provides a means to buy or sell parts of a unit of measure. For example, if you buy paint thinner by the case and each case contains four one-gallon cans, you might wish to sell the thinner by the can instead of the case. The "fraction" would be, in this case, 4—because there are four cans to a case. If you buy soft drink syrup by the canister, you may want to sell it by the cupful. If one canister contains enough syrup to make 500 10-ounce cups of soft drink, you would enter "500" as the fraction.

If you decide to order 10 cases of paint thinner plus two additional cans, you can enter the fraction on the purchase order as "10.2" and *DacEasy* will know that you want 10 full cases and "¾" of another case. The ".2" does not represent—to *DacEasy Accounting*—"two-tenths"; rather, it represents two of the fractional parts entered for that product. See the "Sales Price" paragraphs below, for further information on fractional units.

Department

If you have departmentalized your revenue and cost centers by inventory, you can assign a two-digit department code to each product. Departmentalization is discussed in Chapter 10.

Bin

The bin field is used to locate the item in your warehouse. You can use as many as four characters (alphabetical or numerical), to give the location. This four-character code can incorporate whatever system you use in your warehouse.

Primary Vendor

The vendor field is used for the identification code of the vendor from whom you normally purchase the given item. This code should be the same as the code in the vendor file. Entering a code here does not limit you to that vendor; it is simply a way to record information that can be useful to you when you purchase additional stock.

Sales Price

For every item in your inventory, you will give the selling price. You can use up to three decimal places (such as $1.875 per item) should you need to. *DacEasy* will use the sale price whenever you complete an invoice or a sales ticket from the billing module. You can change the sales price of any item, at any time, simply by returning to the inventory record and changing the field.

The sale price is for the "unit of measure" and not the "fraction" of that measure. For paint thinner, inventoried by the case, but sold by the gallon, you would enter the sales price for the entire case, which might contain four cans. If a customer purchased only one gallon can from that case, you would enter the fraction "0.1" on the customer's invoice. *DacEasy* would use that "0.1" and the "4" given in the fraction field to calculate "¼" of the cost of the case. That amount would then be placed on the invoice. The calculation is automatic, based on the information placed in the inventory file.

If you enter only the sales price of the fractional part, you will lose money.

Sales Tax

If you are required to collect sales taxes on a given item, you should place a "Y" (for "yes") in the Taxable field. If not, place a "N." When *DacEasy* finds a "Y" in this field, it will check the customer file to determine the tax rate for the customer and will automatically calculate and include the taxes on the customer's invoice or sales ticket.

Last Sale Date

DacEasy will supply the date of the last sale of a given item. That date will be obtained from the last invoice or sales ticket that included the inventory number.

Minimum

You can provide *DacEasy* with the minimum number of each item you wish to have on-hand. For example, you might want to always have no fewer than 50 pairs of sneakers in stock. You would, in that case, put the number "50" in this field. You can order more than 50 and, as the sneakers are sold, *DacEasy* will adjust your inventory count downward. Once the item reaches 50, *DacEasy* can print an "alert" to tell you that your stock is getting low.

Re-order

You might include, in this field, the number of items you would like to re-order whenever a new order is placed. This might be a number you chose or a quantity given by your vendor. If you use a number from a vendor, it usually represents the amount for which you can get a discount for ordering in multiples of that number. *DacEasy* automatically references this number when you make an order to the primary vendor.

Last Purchase Date

The date of your last order for a particular item is automatically supplied by *DacEasy*. This date comes from the purchasing module.

Last Purchase Price, Standard Cost, and Average Cost

The next three fields name the "costing methods" available for determining the costs of the goods you sell. *DacEasy* allows you to choose one of the three methods, and includes information about alternatives for each item you carry in inventory. More information on costing methods can be found in Chapter 7. Figure 7-14 and Fig. 7-18 show information relating to costing methods. The following information can be useful in your analysis of the costing methods that are displayed:

Last Purchase Price. The last price you paid for a given item will be automatically provided. This price comes from your last order for an item.

Standard Cost. If you are using the "standard cost" method for determining the costs of the items you sell, enter an amount here to represent the standard cost. After you have entered the amount, *DacEasy* will calculate your profit from each sale (by comparing this amount to the sales price).

Average Cost. *DacEasy* will calculate and display the average cost for each of your inventory items. If you choose this method of "costing" your inventory, this figure will be used to determine your profit from sales.

On-Hand Units and Dollars, Committed Units, and On-Order Units

DacEasy provides the number of items currently in stock and the value of that stock, calculated from your costing system. The number of committed units represents the number of units committed to customers. The on-order units represent the number of units currently ordered but not received from vendors.

Statistical Information

DacEasy automatically accumulates statistical information for three years—you do not have to enter anything in these fields in order to use the information stored here. You can determine and include any of the statistical information for previous years.

When you start a new company, these fields are blank but will be updated for the current year each time a transaction is posted for your inventory. When you run the end-of-year procedures, all current year's information will be moved to "last year" and all of last year's information will be moved to "year before last."

Starting in the Middle of a Business Year

If you have an existing company and are just starting to use *DacEasy* in the middle of an accounting year, you can bring each inventory record up-to-date by pressing <F7>. Key in the current year's total-to-date information for the displayed item. *DacEasy* will add new transactions to whatever you have keyed in. Figure 8-6 shows the window for entering these values.

The <F7> option permits you only to enter data. After you've made the entries, you cannot edit the information on this screen. Instead, you have to go to the appropriate journal or activity to make correcting entries into the accounting system.

```
10/02/88                    PRODUCT FILE MAINTENANCE                    LHP
03:39 PM                    Parts and Parcels, Inc.
 Product Code   : PAINT01       Description : Paint, Wt Base Gal
 Measure        : CASE          Fraction    :     4         Dept.  : 01
 Bin            : P01           Vendor      : PAIN01
 Sales Price    :      75.800   Taxable(Y/N): Y
 Last Sale Date:                Minimum     :     25     Reorder :   10
 Last Purch. Date :        Lst.Purch.Price :       0.000
 Std. Cost        :    0.000    Avg. Cost  :       0.000
 On Hand   Units  :        0.000  Dollars  :          0.000
 Committed Units  :        0.000
 On Order  Units  :        0.000 ┌─ Enter Additional Stock : ─────────┐
═══════════════════════════ STATISTI│                                    │
              Yr.Bef.Lst Last│ Units     :              .         │%
 Units Purch. :        0       │ Unit Cost :          0.000        │0.0
 $ Purchase   :        0       │ Dollars   :          0.00         │0.0
 Units Sold   :        0       └────────────────────────────────────┘0.0
 $ Sales      :        0         0         0         0          0  0.0
 $ Cost       :        0         0         0         0          0  0.0
 $ Profit     :        0         0         0         0          0  0.0
 Times Turn   :      0.0       0.0       0.0       0.0          0  0.0
 Gross Return :        0         0         0         0          0  0.0

 F1-Help   F6-Delete   F7-Enter Stock   F10-Process   ESC-exit
```

Fig. 8-6. Window in work screen lets you enter existing stock data if you are starting your accounting system in the middle of a business year.

Editing an Existing Inventory Record

If you must make changes in an inventory record or if you want to delete an item from inventory, enter the File routine and select option 4. When an empty inventory screen is displayed, the cursor will flash in the product code field. Type the code for the item you want to work with. Keep in mind that you can see a list of inventory items and their codes from within *DacEasy Graph + Mate*. When the record is displayed, make the changes.

To delete a record from the file, press <F6> while the cursor is in the description field. You cannot delete an item for which there is an account balance.

When all information on the product file maintenance screen is correct, press <F10> to tell *DacEasy* to process the information. All the displayed information will be saved to disk so it can be retrieved when it is needed later. If you press <ESC> instead of <F10>, all changes will be lost and previous values restored.

The Services File

In addition to your inventory—which could include the products you sell and the things you own that are not for sale—you might also sell services to your customers. Services differ from products in that services are intangibles—and in most states, services are not subject to sales taxes.

```
┌─────────────────────────────────────────────────────────────────────┐
│ ┌─────────────────────────────────────────────────────────────────┐ │
│ │                                                                   │ │
│ │  09/05/88              SERVICE FILE MAINTENANCE            LHP    │ │
│ │  09:11 AM              Parts and Parcels, Inc.                    │ │
│ │                                                                   │ │
│ │                                                                   │ │
│ │   Service Code  : SOILTEST01    Description : Soil, Prelim Test   │ │
│ │   Measure       : HOUR          Fraction    :   4    Dept.  : 02  │ │
│ │                                                                   │ │
│ │   Sales Price   :    30.000     Taxable(Y/N): Y                   │ │
│ │   Last Sale Date:   /  /                                          │ │
│ │                                                                   │ │
│ │ ════════════════════════ STATISTICAL INFORMATION ══════════════  │ │
│ │           Yr.Bef.Lst Last Year This Year  Forecast  Variance  %  │ │
│ │                                                                   │ │
│ │  Units Sold : ████████████    0       0       0       0     0.0  │ │
│ │  $ Sales    :            0     0       0       0       0     0.0  │ │
│ │                                                                   │ │
│ │                                                                   │ │
│ │                                                                   │ │
│ └─────────────────────────────────────────────────────────────────┘ │
│  F1-Help F6-Delete  F10-Process  ESC-Exit                           │
└─────────────────────────────────────────────────────────────────────┘
```

Fig. 8-7. Work screen for entering information in the services file in DacEasy Accounting. Sample data are included.

For the most part, *DacEasy* handles the services file in the same way it handles the products file. The same types of reports are available from both.

The services file can be created or edited from the File option of the *DacEasy Accounting* Main Menu. Figure 8-7 shows the types of information needed to complete the services file. The following may provide some guidance as you begin to organize your services file.

Service Code

You can use as many as 13 characters (alphabetic or numeric) for the service code. The field length is large enough to use the standard UPC bar-coding conventions. We recommend you use a code that easily identifies the service.

Service Description

The description of each service can contain as many as 20 characters and should be created so that they can be sorted meaningfully. For example, all services that deal with consulting should be described as ''Consulting, ...,'' where the three dots can be replaced with the type of consulting. This way, sorted listings of services will group similar services together.

Unit of Measure

The unit of measure for services is usually time—and that time is usually by the hour. Other appropriate measures can be used.

Fraction

The fractional measure should be the smallest portion of the unit of measure for which you will bill a customer. For example, if you bill a service by the hour, it can be cumbersome to use a minute as the fractional part for which you will bill. It might be more appropriate to bill by the quarter hour or the half hour.

If you do decide to bill by the minute, the fractional measure would be entered as "60"—because there are 60 minutes in an hour. If you decide to bill by the quarter hour, you would enter "4" as the fraction, since there are four quarters in each hour. When billing, an entry of "2.3" would be interpreted by *DacEasy* as "two hours and three fractional parts," as opposed to two and three-tenths of an hour.

Sales Price

The sales price is the amount you would charge for the unit of measure—not the fractional part. *DacEasy* will calculate the appropriate fractional cost when necessary.

Sales Tax

If you are required to collect sales tax for a particular service, you should place a "Y" (for "yes") in the Taxable field. If not, place a "N." When *DacEasy* finds a "Y" in this field, it will check the customer file to determine the tax rate and automatically calculate and include the taxes on the customer's invoice for services.

Last Sale Date

DacEasy will supply the date of the last sale of a particular service. This date is obtained from the last invoice that included the service rendered number.

Statistical Information

DacEasy automatically accumulates statistical information for three years—you do not have to enter anything in these fields in order to use the information stored here. You can determine and include any of the statistical information for previous years if you want.

When you start a new company, these fields will be blank but will be updated for the current year each time a transaction is posted for your services file. When you run the end-of-year procedures, all current year's information will be moved to "last year" and all of last year's information will be moved to "year before last."

Starting in the Middle of a Business Year

If you are just starting to use *DacEasy* in the middle of an accounting year, you can bring each service record up-to-date by entering the current totals in the statistical information fields. *DacEasy* will add new transactions to whatever you have keyed in.

Editing an Existing Inventory Record

If you need to make changes in a services record, or you want to delete an item from the file, enter the File routine and select option 5. An empty service file maintenance screen is displayed and the cursor will flash in the service code field. Type the code for the service with which you want to work. Keep in mind that you can see a list of services and their codes from within *DacEasy Graph + Mate*. When the record is displayed, make the changes.

To delete a record from the services file, press <F6> while the cursor is in the description field. You cannot delete a service item for which there is an account balance.

When all information on the service file maintenance screen is correct, press <F10> to tell *DacEasy* to process the information. All the displayed information will be saved to disk and can be retrieved if needed later. If you press <ESC> instead of <F10>, all changes will be lost and previous values restored.

Summary

This chapter discusses creating and maintaining the four major files used by DacEasy Accounting. *These include the customer file, vendor file, product/inventory file, and the services file. Each field is described and recommendations given regarding the structure of data to be entered in these fields.*

Setting Up the Company Payroll System and Files

Chapter Goals

• *This chapter adds the payroll module to your accounting system. We discuss the* DacEasy Payroll *set up information and creating an employee file. We assume that you will interface* DacEasy Payroll *with* DacEasy Accounting. *It is, however, possible to use the payroll module without using the accounting module which is discussed.*

We will take advantage of the things you learned setting up the accounting module of the *DacEasy Accounting* system. You should now be able to go through the entire payroll set up with very little difficulty, and in much less time than it took to go through the accounting module set up.

Starting *DacEasy* Payroll

To start *DacEasy Payroll* with *DacEasy Graph + Mate*, boot your computer to display the DOS prompt. Assuming the installation process was completed as described in Chapter 2, type the following commands:

```
CD \ GRAFMATE <ENTER>
GM <ENTER>
```

Then you can select payroll for the appropriate company or department from the *Graph + Mate* Applications options (see Fig. 6-7).

If you are not using *DacEasy Graph + Mate*, type the following commands:

```
CD \ DEP3 <ENTER>
DEP3 <ENTER>
```

Because this will be the first time *DacEasy Payroll* is started, you will be asked questions about the location of your data files and the number of employees you expect to have in your employee file.

Figure 9-1 shows the first installation screen. You are asked to give the directory for your data files. The screen will provide explanations for some of your options. It recommends using a path of C: \ DEP3 \ FILES. We will continue, however, to work with our company named "Parts and Parcels" throughout the book. Therefore, we named a subdirectory C: \ DEP3 \ PARTS, as shown in Fig. 9-1. If you are using *DacEasy Payroll* for more than one company, you can assign a different subdirectory for each company.

DacEasy Payroll will then ask for the maximum number of employees to be included in your payroll files. Don't worry about giving a number that could later be too small. You can easily increase the file sizes if your company experiences an unanticipated growth period. (This is discussed in a later chapter.)

Figure 9-2 displays the screen where the number of employees are entered. The examples throughout this book use 15, which is the number given in the figure. The number is greater than the actual number of employees we will use in our examples, but it is intended to provide room for growth.

After you have provided *DacEasy* with the number of employees, it calculates the amount of disk space needed and compares, on-screen, the amount of available space

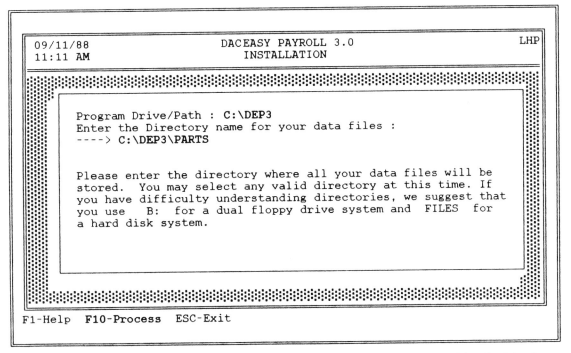

Fig. 9-1. Naming the directory (path) to your payroll files. Give the drive letter, the payroll directory, and the data file subdirectory.

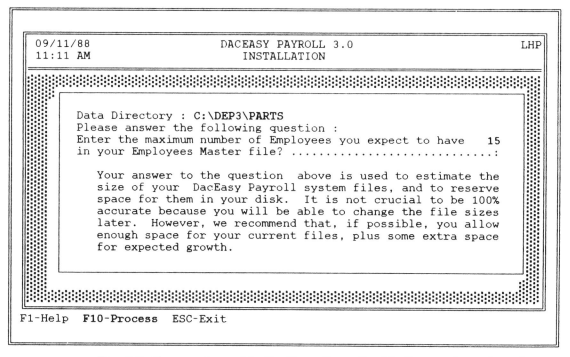

Fig. 9-2. You must provide DacEasy Payroll with the number of employees you expect to pay. You can later change the number if you need to.

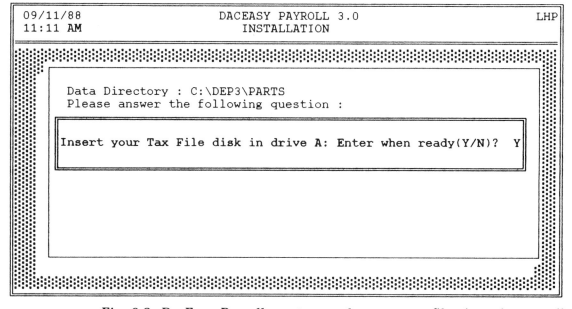

Fig. 9-3. DacEasy Payroll must copy the state tax files into the payroll directory to use the data to calculate deductions.

on your disk. If the available spacc is less than the space actually needed, you must re-consider the number of employees you've given or use a larger fixed disk.

You will then tell *DacEasy* to create your files, which it will do as it displays a series of file names at the bottom of the screen. During the process, you will be asked to insert your "Tax File" disk in drive A: (see Fig. 9-3). One data file will be copied from this disk, and additional files will be created, to accommodate the numbers you gave *DacEasy Payroll*.

The Payroll Control File

Press <F10> to finalize the number of employees and display the Payroll Control File screen (see Fig. 9-4). Some of the information on this screen is similar to the information provided in Chapter 7 for the accounting module. The information must be provided here again because the payroll module is designed to run independently of the accounting module.

The employer identification number is the federal number that is used on all government income reports, quarterly reports.

The name and address to be provided on the Payroll Control Screen is for the employer and will appear on all payroll module reports. It is particularly important that the name and address be correct if you are doing payroll records for more than one company.

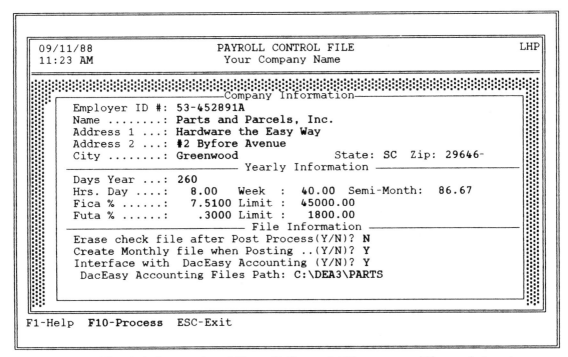

Fig. 9-4. A completed Payroll Control File screen. *The work days in a year amount are used for determining partial payment for some employees.*

Next, give the number of days in the normal working year—usually 260 (52 weeks multiplied by 5 days per week). This will be used for various calculations, including vacation and sick leave and the amount of salary to be deducted from an employee's wages when an employee is absent without official leave. More important, it is used to determine an employee's wages when using the automatic payroll generation process.

It is extremely important that the number of days in the working year be accurate.

Enter the number of hours in a regular working day (usually 8), the number of hours in a regular working week (usually 40), and the number of hours in a semi-monthly period (usually 86.67) in the system. (The typical semi-monthly hours are calculated by dividing 260 days by 12 months to find the number of days in a typical month; dividing it by 2 to find the number of days in one-half month; and multiplying it by 8 hours per day to find the number of hours in a half month). Values can differ depending on your particular type of business.

The FICA percentage and limit is given so DacEasy can determine the amounts to deduct for Social Security. These numbers can change periodically.

On January 1, 1988, the FICA percentage increased to 7.5 percent. On that same date, the FICA limit increased from $43,800 to $45,000. It is your responsibility to ensure that these numbers are correct, so that amounts withheld are accurate and quarterly reports and deposits are accurate.

The FUTA (Federal Unemployment Tax) percentage and limit must be monitored and updated as they are changed by federal law. It is also your responsibility to know current values, so that your contributions records are accurate. (SUTA—State Unemployment Tax Act—information will be entered elsewhere.)

Four additional *DacEasy* questions must be answered to process your payroll records. These include:

Erase Check File after Post Process? Your answer to this question will determine whether or not you maintain a check register after periodic reconciliation of your checking account. If you answer "Y" (for "yes"), records of checks that have cleared the bank will be erased after the amounts are posted for each pay period. There will be no check register that includes checks that clear the bank. If you answer "N" (for "no"), *DacEasy* will not erase the check file and your check register will be available at any time during the business year. In effect, a "Y" answer will automatically purge your check file rather than requiring that you do it manually.

Create Monthly file when Posting? Your answer to this question will determine whether *DacEasy* creates a file into which it writes monthly payroll reports when the posting process is run each month. If you answer "Y" (for "yes"), a file will be created on your fixed disk and you can use that file for monthly payroll reports. If you answer "N" (for "no"), a file will not be created although payroll values will be posted to the proper accounts.

Interface with *DacEasy Accounting*? Answering "Y" (for "yes") to this question will mean that all payroll data is automatically sent to the proper accounts in *DacEasy Accounting*. The *DacEasy* chart of accounts contains all of the necessary accounts to track payroll amounts, deductions, and contributions. These accounts are addressed automatically when you elect to interface with the accounting module. (If you are using

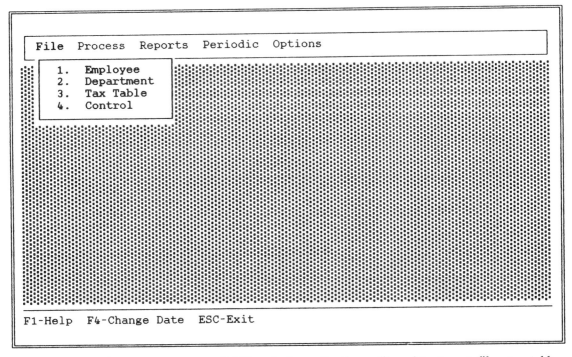

```
 File  Process  Reports  Periodic  Options

    1.  Employee
    2.  Department
    3.  Tax Table
    4.  Control




 F1-Help  F4-Change Date  ESC-Exit
```

Fig. 9-5. The Payroll File window. *Employee files, department files, tax tables, and the Payroll Control File can be created and maintained in this window.*

your own chart of accounts in *DacEasy Accounting*, you must be sure that the proper payroll accounts are included.)

DacEasy Accounting Files Path. If you answer ''Y'' to interface with *DacEasy Accounting*, you will be asked to give the directory path to the accounting files. This path permits *DacEasy Payroll* to find the appropriate files within the accounting files. Our example for Parts and Parcels uses the C:\DEA3\PARTS path.

Once the last response is given on the Payroll Control File screen, the *DacEasy Payroll* Main Menu (Fig. 5-3) will be displayed. Your company's name is also displayed as a result of completing the control file. If you ever need to change any of the information in the Payroll Control File, you can do so from the File option on the *DacEasy Payroll* Main Menu, using the Control selection in the pull-down window (see Fig. 9-5).

Setting Up the Payroll System

As with *DacEasy Accounting*, there are a few tasks to complete and a few concepts to understand before you actually start using the payroll program. Most of these tasks are done once and never modified again. A couple, however, require that you update information as tax laws change.

To begin the set-up process for *DacEasy Payroll*, look at the File options available from the main menu.

Figure 9-5 shows the File pull-down window menu. In this menu, you can set up departments, create and modify state tax tables, and modify the payroll control file (Fig. 9-4). You can also create or modify the employee file.

Departments and Codes

From the File option, select option 2 to enter the departments and codes for *DacEasy Payroll*.

DacEasy Payroll departments are not the same as *DacEasy Accounting* departments. The function of payroll departments are described in this chapter; accounting departments are discussed in Chapter 10.

Each payroll department has a set of codes describing how to handle the payroll data. Each set of codes is referred to as a "department general ledger interface table," because they include information about the accounts that are assigned payroll data as *DacEasy* moves these data to the general ledger.

We have chosen to use only one department to explain the purpose and function of the "department general ledger interface table." (You can complete tables for as many as 1,000 departments.) Completing a table for a department actually creates that payroll department within *DacEasy*.

The cursor is displayed in the Department # field, where you must enter the department number for which information is to be entered. The number must be at least one, but not greater than 1,000. You cannot skip department numbers; that is, your departments must be sequentially numbered. If one or more departments have already been created, a window will display the departments so you can select an existing one, or add a new department to the list.

When entering the department number, you can duplicate data stored for an existing department, if it will help to set up a new department. A small window will open where you can give the number of an existing department that you want to duplicate. Because we have no other departments defined, our only choice is to press <ENTER>, to not duplicate anything.

If you did choose to duplicate an existing department, give the number, press <ENTER>, and then edit any differences. Once you have provided the duplication information, you can name the new department using up to 20 characters. Because we are using only one department, simply enter the name of the business as the department name.

The first account number you must give is checking account number. Figure 7-3 shows that we have three bank accounts. One of these is a savings account, and we would, of course, not pay personnel from this account. The "Checking Account" account would not be used either, because it is the regular checking account. We know this only because the third bank account is called "Payroll Account." It is the account that all payroll will be written from. Enter the account number 11022 on the Departments File screen.

If you are using your own chart of accounts, rather than the chart shown in Fig. 7-3, select the appropriate checking account and enter the number on the Departments File screen. Keep in mind that all your accounts can be displayed from within *DacEasy Graph+Mate*, if you are using it.

If you are not interfacing with *DacEasy Accounting*, you must still provide account numbers when requested on this screen, although they would not relate to a *DacEasy* chart of accounts. They should, however, relate to the chart of accounts you are using because they will be printed on all reports. You can then manually relate them to your regular accounting system, posting the payroll amounts to the proper general ledger accounts as part of your paper-and-pencil accounting system.

The bottom line is to organize the accounts you place on this screen so the system will work for you.

After you have entered your checking account number, you must provide two account numbers for the FICA, FUTA, and SUTA employer expenses. One of these is the expense account, to which each amount will be debited. The other is the liability account, to which these amounts will be accrued (credited) until paid.

The accrual accounts are necessary because *DacEasy* posts the proper amounts when end-of-period routines are completed. These amounts, however, are paid only quarterly; so they must be accumulated until actual payment is made. Once these expenses are paid, the accrual accounts is debited and the checking account is credited.

Figure 9-6 provides examples of the accounts used in a department general ledger interface table (from the chart of accounts in Fig. 7-3). For the employer's FICA, FUTA, and SUTA obligations, expense and liability accounts are listed and correspond to those given in the chart of accounts.

DacEasy does not require a base amount, percentage, or a limit on the FICA, FUTA, or SUTA accounts because they are listed in the Payroll Control File (see Fig. 9-4).

In addition to the FICA, FUTA, and SUTA accounts, *DacEasy* provides you with up to three additional liabilities for which an employer may keep records. These might be used to record an employer's shares for union dues, insurance benefits, retirement plans, or other amounts to be accounted for. For each liability listed here, a balancing expense and liability account must be provided, just as they were for FICA, FUTA, and SUTA expenses.

Figure 9-6 shows that Parts and Parcels provides disability insurance for their employees. The expense account is given as 520134, which is described as "Disability Insurance." The liability account is given as 210418, which is also labeled "Disability Insurance" in the chart of accounts (Fig. 7-3).

After providing the proper account numbers, you must instruct *DacEasy* to calculate the amount to post to these accounts. This is done by providing three pieces of information:

Base Calculation. There are six options for inclusion in the "Base Calculation" column. These are displayed in a window when the cursor is moved to this column. You can toggle among these by pressing the <SPACE BAR> until the highlight is on the one you need. Figure 9-6 shows the Base Calculations window with the six options available.

The options are "$" for a fixed amount for each pay period, "G" for a percentage of the net gross pay, "T" for a percentage of the total gross pay, "W" for a percentage of the federal withholdings, "F" for a percentage of the FICA withholdings, and "S" for a percentage of the state withholdings. For the Disability Insurance in our example,

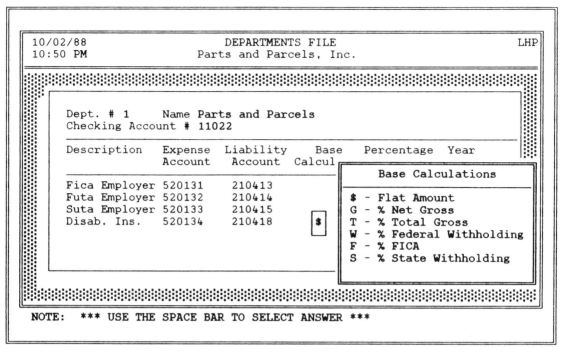

```
Dept. # 1      Name Parts and Parcels
Checking Account # 11022

Description    Expense    Liability    Base     Percentage   Year
               Account    Account      Calcul
                                                  Base Calculations
Fica Employer  520131     210413
Futa Employer  520132     210414         $ - Flat Amount
Suta Employer  520133     210415         G - % Net Gross
Disab. Ins.    520134     210418    [$]  T - % Total Gross
                                         W - % Federal Withholding
                                         F - % FICA
                                         S - % State Withholding
```

NOTE: *** USE THE SPACE BAR TO SELECT ANSWER ***

Fig. 9-6. Defining accounts that departmental payroll information is posted.

there is a fixed amount for each pay period; thus, the ''$'' is entered in the Base column.

Percentage or Amount. If you select a base indicator or ''$,'' you must enter the amount of liability. If you select any of the other options for the Base Calculation column, you must enter the percent amount to be multiplied by that base. The percent must be entered as the actual percent and not as its decimal equivalent (that is, three and one-half percent would be entered as ''3.5'' and not as ''0.035'').

Year Limit. You would enter an amount in this column if there was a limit to the amount to be paid. For example, if the maximum disability insurance to be paid by the employer, in any year, was $1,500, you would put that amount in this column. When that amount was reached, *DacEasy* would stop calculating for the rest of the year. You must enter some amount in this column. If there is no actual limit, enter a very large number so that *DacEasy* will always calculate the liability. (Gross salary would be a good value to enter in this case.) Figure 9-7 shows the figures we will use for our company.

When all of your accounts are entered, press <F10> so that *DacEasy* can process the information. *DacEasy* will store the information in a file and refer to it whenever payroll is done.

It is important to note that this discussion deals with amounts for which the employer is responsible. This discussion does not relate to withholdings taken from employees' paychecks.

There are three screens where you must provide department information. Once

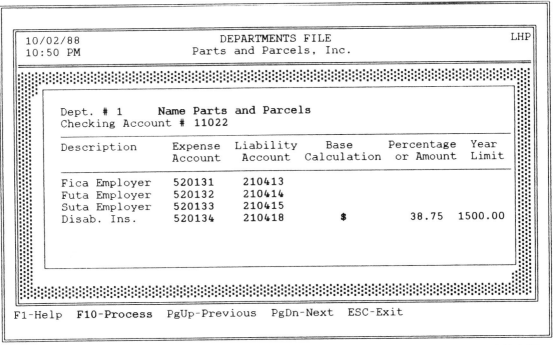

```
10/02/88                    DEPARTMENTS FILE                         LHP
10:50 PM                 Parts and Parcels, Inc.


   Dept. # 1      Name Parts and Parcels
   Checking Account # 11022

   Description        Expense   Liability    Base     Percentage  Year
                      Account    Account   Calculation or Amount  Limit

   Fica Employer      520131     210413
   Futa Employer      520132     210414
   Suta Employer      520133     210415
   Disab. Ins.        520134     210418        $           38.75  1500.00




F1-Help  F10-Process  PgUp-Previous  PgDn-Next  ESC-Exit
```

Fig. 9-7. Screen 1 of the Departments File shows the expense and liability accounts for specific deductions. It also shows the calculations for some of those deductions.

all employer liabilities are accounted for on the first screen, proceed to the next screen by pressing the <PgDn> key (as indicated at the bottom of the *DacEasy* screen).

The Departments File: Screen 2

The second screen allows you to identify the types of earnings your employees might have. *DacEasy Payroll* lets you identify as many as 15 sources of earnings for employees. These can be different for each department. Eight of the 15 are pre-defined by the program and cannot be changed.

On the eight, pre-defined earnings lines, give the expense account numbers found in your chart of accounts, where earnings will be posted. Samples are given in Fig. 9-8. Account numbers are taken from the chart of accounts in Fig. 7-3.

Note that the E.I.C.—Earned Income Credit—account is not listed as an expense account. It is a liability account because the employer is actually paying the equivalent of an advance tax refund. This amount offsets the liability account and reduces the employer's liability for federal withholdings accrued.

For three of the eight types of earnings—hourly wages and the two overtime wages—the cursor will stop in the Amount/Rate column so you can enter the prevalent amounts. The numbers entered here will be the default values in the employee file. These can, however, be edited to reflect differing rates of wages and overtime payments. Editing

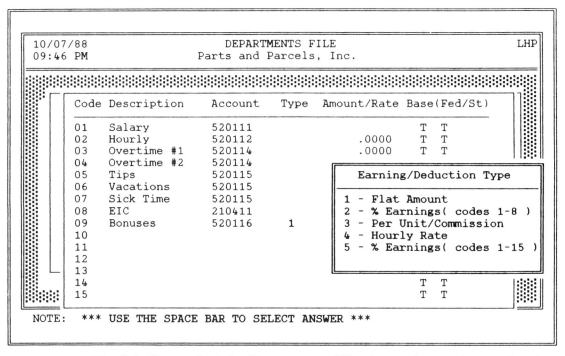

```
  10/07/88                      DEPARTMENTS FILE                        LHP
  09:46 PM                   Parts and Parcels, Inc.
::::::::::::::::::::::::::::::::::::::::::::::::::::::::::::::::::::::::::::::::::::
    Code Description    Account   Type  Amount/Rate Base(Fed/St)
    01   Salary         520111                        T   T
    02   Hourly         520112           .0000        T   T
    03   Overtime #1    520114           .0000        T   T
    04   Overtime #2    520114          ┌──────────────────────────────┐
    05   Tips           520115          │     Earning/Deduction Type    │
    06   Vacations      520115          │                               │
    07   Sick Time      520115          │  1 - Flat Amount              │
    08   EIC            210411          │  2 - % Earnings( codes 1-8 )  │
    09   Bonuses        520116     1     │  3 - Per Unit/Commission      │
    10                                  │  4 - Hourly Rate              │
    11                                  │  5 - % Earnings( codes 1-15 ) │
    12                                  │                               │
    13                                  └──────────────────────────────┘
    14                                                      T   T
    15                                                      T   T

  NOTE:   *** USE THE SPACE BAR TO SELECT ANSWER ***
```

Fig. 9-8. Screen 2 of the Departments File shows the earnings codes that must be used to report exceptions to the payroll program.

is done in each employee's record in the employee file.

Next, you must indicate whether the earnings are taxable. Two columns are provided for you to give the federal base (the first column) and the state base (the second column). There are three possible entries for each column and these are shown in a small window each time you move the cursor into one of the tax base columns.

Tax Table. Place a "T" in either, or both columns, to indicate that *DacEasy* should use the appropriate tax tables for the tax base.

Supplemental Earnings Percentage. Place an "S" in either, or both columns, to indicate that *DacEasy* should use the percentage for supplemental earnings. The percentage will be entered for the specific state or locale once you complete the SUTA and Supplemental information in the next step of our set up procedure.

Not Taxable. If the earnings are not taxable, delete the displayed letter and press <ENTER>.

Other earnings can be entered on lines 9 through 15. Keep in mind that the tax base must be entered for each entry. In addition to including the tax base, you must indicate the "Type" of earning so *DacEasy* will know how to calculate the tax liability. There are five additional types of earnings. These are displayed in a small window when you add earnings types.

Type 1. Enter a "1" in the Type column if the earnings are a fixed amount. The cursor will stop in the Amount/Rate column, where you can enter the amount.

Type 2. Enter a "2" if the earnings represent a percentage of other gross earnings. The cursor will stop in the Amount/Rate column, where you can enter the percentage.

Type 3. Enter a "3" if the earnings represent a commission percentage, or an amount paid for piece-work. The cursor will stop in the Amount/Rate column, where you can enter the percentage. Any additional information, such as the unit for which a commission is to be paid, will be given in the individual employee record in the employee file.

Type 4. Enter a "4" if the earnings represent a fixed amount based on time worked. This amount will be applied only to regular wages and not to overtime wages. Additional information will be required in the individuals employee record.

Type 5. Enter a "5" if the earnings represent an hourly rate for special or supplementary earnings. The cursor will stop in the Amount/Rate column where you can enter the hourly rate. Additional information will be required in the individuals employee record.

For each type of income beyond the eighth type, any amount or percentage given in the Amount/Rate column will be the default value and will be displayed in the appropriate employee records. In the employee file, however, these amounts and rates can be changed to reflect different pay values. The amount or rate given in the individual employee record will over-ride the values set in this table.

In our sample screen (Fig. 9-8), the Bonus amount would be $100.

For all 15 types of earnings, the column labeled "Code" is the code entered in each employee's record as payroll information is processed. A printed list of these codes is essential to work with employee payroll records.

The third screen of the department general ledger interface table list the types of withholdings the employer is required to take and keep records for. To display the withholdings table, press <PgDn>.

Figure 9-9 shows the withholding categories that *DacEasy* automatically includes in its recordkeeping. The account numbers must be keyed in, and must be based, on the appropriate liability accounts in your chart of accounts. The numbers in Fig. 9-9 correspond to the chart of accounts shown in Fig. 7-3.

If you do not interface with *DacEasy Accounting*, you must still provide account numbers. These should correspond to the actual account numbers in your regular accounting system, whether you are using a pencil-and-paper system or another computer-based system.

Liability accounts are provided here because all withholdings are accrued until paid to the appropriate agency. Figure 4-1 summarizes the accounting procedures for a typical payroll system. Withholdings are credited to liability accounts, and debited to wages, and salaries, when payroll is done. When these liabilities are debited, at the time of deposit with the appropriate agencies, the checking account is credited for the same amount.

The checking account and the earnings accounts have been identified on previous

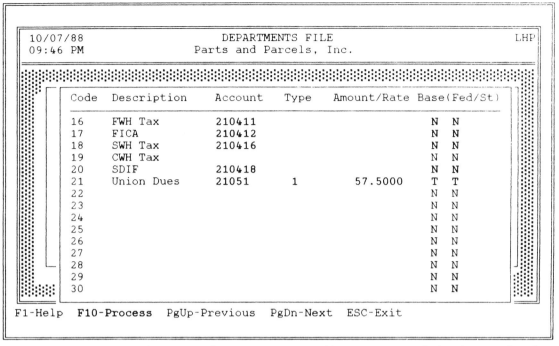

Code	Description	Account	Type	Amount/Rate	Base(Fed/St)	
16	FWH Tax	210411			N	N
17	FICA	210412			N	N
18	SWH Tax	210416			N	N
19	CWH Tax				N	N
20	SDIF	210418			N	N
21	Union Dues	21051	1	57.5000	T	T
22					N	N
23					N	N
24					N	N
25					N	N
26					N	N
27					N	N
28					N	N
29					N	N
30					N	N

F1-Help   **F10-Process**   PgUp-Previous   PgDn-Next   ESC-Exit

Fig. 9-9. Screen 3 of the Departments File shows the deductions codes that must be used to report exceptions to the payroll program.

screens. The purpose of completing the screen shown in Fig. 9-9 is to identify the liability accounts where withholdings are kept between collection and deposit. These accounts are credited when payroll is completed each period; and debited when deposits are made to government agencies each quarter.

In our example, there is no city/county income tax (line 19) and that line has been left empty. We added the deduction for Union Dues, using the "Type" definitions that are discussed earlier in the chapter.

When you are satisfied with your withholding interface information, press <F10> to save it to a file so *DacEasy* can refer to it whenever you do payroll.

If you wish to keep records for payroll by department, you must set up each department before entering any information into the employee records. Each department would be set up exactly as described here, using the next number and a descriptive department name.

If you set up employee records before setting up departments, references to specific departments will be rejected because the department does not already exist. The employee's record will be rejected any time you attempt to use a department number that has not been previously defined.

When the Departments process is completed, your department general ledger interface table is ready to use. *DacEasy Payroll* knows all the account numbers to which payroll data are to be automatically assigned.

Tax Tables

There are several other pieces of information that *DacEasy Payroll* needs in order to perform state tax and withholding calculations. This data is entered using option 3 in the File window (see Fig. 9-5).

Figure 9-10 shows the Tax Table screen and the window that lists several states and their tax options. We moved through the list of states to show the code for South Carolina, the location of the fictitious Parts and Parcels Company. The tax table selected from the list will be placed on the screen where it is used by *DacEasy Payroll* as it calculates tax withholdings and employer liabilities for Parts and Parcels. Figure 9-11 shows the actual tax table for South Carolina, which is displayed when the table number 58 is entered.

If you have employees who live and work in states other than the state in which the home office is located, you must complete screens such as the one shown in Fig. 9-11 for each of these states. In each employee's record, indicate the tax table to be used in determining withholdings and employer liabilities.

The data in the top section of the Tax Table screen must be completed for each of the states in which you pay employees. The bottom section of the screen contains the tables used for withholdings in each of these states. These tables are updated each year by *DacEasy* (for a small fee, of course).

The Tax Table screen permits you to edit tax tables if the law changes during the course of the business year.

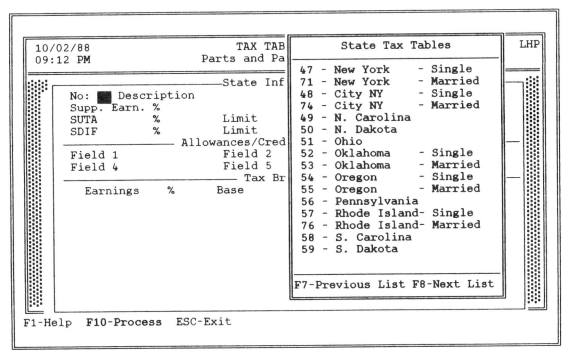

Fig. 9-10. Selecting the state where basic payroll deductions are calculated.

```
┌──────────────────────────────────────────────────────────────────────┐
│ 10/02/88                    TAX TABLE FILE                         LHP │
│ 09:12 PM                 Parts and Parcels, Inc.                       │
│ ┌────────────────────────State Information────────────────────────┐   │
│ │ No:58  Description SOUTH CAROLINA      ID # 1-23409-A Code SC     │   │
│ │ Supp. Earn. %     0.000                                          │   │
│ │ SUTA        %     0.015  Limit        1500.00                    │   │
│ │ SDIF        %     0.015  Limit         750.00                    │   │
│ │ ─────────────── Allowances/Credits/Exemptions ───────────────    │   │
│ │ Field 1      800.000 Field 2       0.100 Field 3     500.000     │   │
│ │ Field 4     1000.000 Field 5    0.000000 Field 6       0.000     │   │
│ │ ───────────────────── Tax Brackets ──────────────────────        │   │
│ │    Earnings      %      Base     Earnings     %        Base      │   │
│ │        0.01   2.00       0.00       0.00   0.00        0.00      │   │
│ │     2000.00   3.00      40.00       0.00   0.00        0.00      │   │
│ │     4000.00   4.00     100.00       0.00   0.00        0.00      │   │
│ │     6000.00   5.00     180.00       0.00   0.00        0.00      │   │
│ │     8000.00   6.00     280.00       0.00   0.00        0.00      │   │
│ │    10000.00   7.00     400.00       0.00   0.00        0.00      │   │
│ │        0.00   0.00       0.00       0.00   0.00        0.00      │   │
│ │        0.00   0.00       0.00       0.00   0.00        0.00      │   │
│ │        0.00   0.00       0.00                                    │   │
│ └──────────────────────────────────────────────────────────────────┘  │
│ F1-Help   F10-Process   ESC-Exit                                       │
└──────────────────────────────────────────────────────────────────────┘
```

Fig. 9-11. The Tax Table for South Carolina. *The company's state ID number, employer liability percentages, and the state's tax tables for deductions are included in this table.*

Appendix C contains a complete list of states and the appropriate tax information to be used by *DacEasy*. The table also contains all the known 1988 tax law revisions for individual states. You might need to refer to Appendix C as you complete the information for the Tax Table screen.

The following information might assist you as you complete the state tax table screens for states where you pay wages.

Table Number. This field contains the number for the state tax table you will use. You will find the number for each state in the window that opens each time you access the Tax Table screen. For some states, you may have to create more than one screen because more than one table is indicated. For example, Alabama has one tax structure for unmarried taxpayers and another structure for everyone else. Single tax payers' exemptions and rates would come from Table #3 while all other exemptions and rates would come from Table #4 (see the window or Appendix C). Consequently, if you pay employees in Alabama, you must create at least two Tax Table screens so *DacEasy* can find the appropriate information. Finally, indicate the table to be used in each employee's record.

Description. Once you enter the Table Number, this field is completed by *DacEasy*. It will contain the name of the state to which the Table Number refers. It may also contain the District of Columbia or New York City, which are the only two non-states included in *DacEasy*'s tax tables.

ID Number. Enter your state employer ID number in this field. That number can have as many as 10 characters, and will be used on all reports to the appropriate state agencies.

Code. *DacEasy* will automatically enter the code for the state you've indicated, usually the two-character abbreviation used by the postal service.

Supplemental Earnings Percentage. Some states tax supplemental earnings—such as commissions, tips, royalties, and others—at a different rate than the rate used for regular income. The Supplemental Earnings Percentage field is used to record the percentage used by these states. (Most states do not have a different supplemental tax rate.) The percentage should be entered as the actual percentage and not as its decimal equivalent. For example, if the percentage for your state is two percent, it should be entered as "2" and not as ".02."

One special factor about supplemental earnings should be noted: If the supplemental earnings are paid at the same time as regular earnings are paid, *DacEasy* will treat both as regular earnings. In this case, there could be a significant difference in the tax rates applied. Be sure to pay supplemental earnings separately from regular wages and salaries. Also, be sure to place a different code in the earnings tables (see Fig. 9-8).

SUTA Percentage and Limit. The percent used to calculate the State Unemployment Tax, which is an employer liability, must be entered here. This percentage is used to determine your liability. *DacEasy* will post the liability to the appropriate account. The limit amount is the cumulative payroll amount at which SUTA is no longer calculated. In Fig. 9-11, the limit is given as $1,500. This means that no SUTA will be calculated for wages or salaries over $1,500. In this case, the employer's liability for an individual ends as soon as that individual makes more than $1,500.

SDIF Percentage and Limit. Some states require the employer to pay a Disability Insurance Fund tax that is used when an employee becomes disabled as a result of work-related injuries. Most states do not have such funds. In those states that do, the percentage and limit must be provided. The procedure for SUTA percentage and limit (next page) is appropriate.

Fields 1 - 6. Fields 1 through 6 contain special information used to calculate employee tax obligations in a given state. Each field can have a different meaning as you move from state to state—and some states might not have any value in these fields. Appendix C contains a complete listing of states based on the values placed in these fields.

State Tax Calculation Tables. The bottom half of the Tax Table screen contains the table used for the actual calculation of state income taxes to be withheld. These tables vary from state-to-state. Appendix C contains an explanation of these tables. Techniques for editing these tables is also included.

Complete the screens for each state in which you pay employees. Press <F10> between screens to save the information. Press <ESC> to return to the *DacEasy Payroll* Main Menu. Be sure to press <F10> at the last screen before you press <ESC> to return to the main menu.

The fourth option in the File window is used to edit the Payroll Control File, which was discussed earlier (see Fig. 9-4).

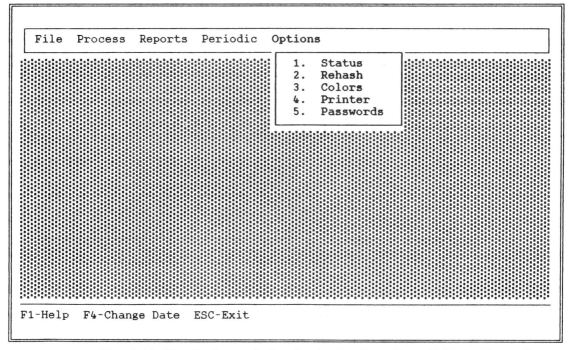

```
        File    Process    Reports    Periodic    Options

                                          1.    Status
                                          2.    Rehash
                                          3.    Colors
                                          4.    Printer
                                          5.    Passwords




        F1-Help    F4-Change Date    ESC-Exit
```

Fig. 9-12. The Options window in the DacEasy Payroll Main Menu. Options must be defined before the system can be used.

The Payroll Options

There are three additional set up routines that must be completed before creating the employee file. These are found in the Options window of the *DacEasy Payroll* Main Menu (see Fig. 9-12).

The three required routines set up the screen colors, the printer parameters, and the password security system. All three of these routines can be completed as described in Chapter 7 for the accounting system. Refer to that chapter before completing the payroll set up procedures. When these are completed, continue with creating your employee payroll files, described in the remainder of this chapter.

Creating the Employee Master File

At this point, you should have completed the payroll interface information, which includes the federal information required for your recordkeeping, and you should have completed the state information for payroll. The only information we need, now, in order to begin working with the payroll program, is contained in the Employee Master File. This file can be accessed by selecting option 1 from the File window on the *DacEasy Payroll* Main menu.

The Employee Master File uses three screens to accumulate and display data for each employee. Figures 9-13, 9-14, and 9-15 show samples of these screens. You can

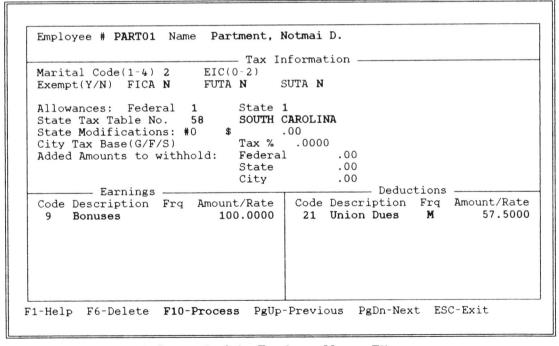

```
                     ── Employee Data ──────────
No.PART01
Name ..:Partment, Notmai D.
Address:"C" Next Isle
City ..:Abbeville        State  SC   Zip 29620-
Phone  (803)555-3409     Social Security 222-33-4444
Sex(M/F) F Marital(S/M) M  Origin
Memo
                       ── Dates ──────────
  Birth      Hire      Raise     Review     Promotion    Termination
  01/21/63   01/01/87  06/01/87   /  /        /  /          /  /
                   ── Payment Information ──────────
 Dept  1    Parts and Parcels      │ Vacation: Date   06/01/87   Freq W
 Title Sales Clerk                 │ Hrs     1.540
                                   │ Acrd     .000
 Pay Suspended(Y/N) N              │ Paid     .000
 Freq(W/B/S/M) W                   │
 Type(H/S/C) H                     │ Sick Time: Date   /  /      Freq
 Amount     5.75                   │ Hrs      .000
 Ovt1       8.63                   │ Acrd     .000
 Ovt2      11.50                   │ Paid      .

 F1-Help   F6-Delete   F10-Process   PgUp-Previous   PgDn-Next   ESC-Exit
```

Fig. 9-13. Screen 1 of the Employee Master File.

```
 Employee # PART01  Name  Partment, Notmai D.

                     ── Tax Information ──────────
 Marital Code(1-4) 2      EIC(0-2)
 Exempt(Y/N)  FICA N     FUTA N     SUTA N

 Allowances:  Federal   1     State 1
 State Tax Table No.    58    SOUTH CAROLINA
 State Modifications: #0    $      .00
 City Tax Base(G/F/S)     Tax %   .0000
 Added Amounts to withhold:   Federal      .00
                              State        .00
                              City         .00
     ── Earnings ──────────           ── Deductions ──────
 Code Description  Frq  Amount/Rate   Code Description  Frq  Amount/Rate
  9   Bonuses           100.0000       21  Union Dues    M      57.5000




 F1-Help   F6-Delete   F10-Process   PgUp-Previous   PgDn-Next   ESC-Exit
```

Fig. 9-14. Screen 2 of the Employee Master File.

```
┌──────────────────────────────────────────────────────────────────────────────┐
│ ┌────────────────────────────────────────────────────────────────────────────┐ │
│ │  Employee # PART01  Name  Partment, Notmai D.                               │ │
│ │  ─────────── Earnings ───────────────────────── Deductions───────────      │ │
│ │  Description Qtr.to Date Yr.to Date  Description Qtr.to Date Yr. to Date     │ │
│ │  Gross FWH        0.00       0.00    Fed. W/H        0.00        0.00        │ │
│ │  Gross FICA       0.00       0.00    FICA W/H        0.00        0.00        │ │
│ │  Gross FUTA       0.00       0.00    State W/H       0.00        0.00        │ │
│ │  Gross SUTA       0.00       0.00    City  W/H       0.00        0.00        │ │
│ │  Tips             0.00       0.00    SDIF            0.00        0.00        │ │
│ │  EIC              0.00       0.00     Union Dues     0.00        0.00        │ │
│ │  Bonuses          0.00       0.00                                           │ │
│ │                                                                            │ │
│ │                                                                            │ │
│ │  Net Paid         0.00       0.00                                           │ │
│ │  Days Paid        0.00       0.00                                           │ │
│ │  Hours Paid       0.00       0.00                                           │ │
│ │  Ovt.Hrs. Paid    0.00       0.00                                           │ │
│ │  ───────────────────────────── Liabilities ─────────────                   │ │
│ │  Description  Qtr.to Date Yr. to Date Description  Qtr.to Date Yr. to Date  │ │
│ │  FICA             0.00       0.00    Disab. Ins.     0.00        0.00       │ │
│ │  FUTA             0.00       0.00                                           │ │
│ │  SUTA             0.00       0.00                                           │ │
│ └────────────────────────────────────────────────────────────────────────────┘ │
│   F1-Help   F6-Delete   F10-Process   PgUp-Previous   PgDn-Next   ESC-Exit    │
└──────────────────────────────────────────────────────────────────────────────┘
```

Fig. 9-15. Screen 3 of the Employee Master File. Data on this screen are provided by the payroll and accounting system.

toggle among the screen by pressing <PgDn> or <PgUp> as indicated at the bottom of the screen.

Employee Master File—Screen 1

Screen 1 of the Employee Master File is used to store individual data used in determining pay, vacation, sick leave, and other factors directly related to each employee.

When you elect to work in the Employee Master file, an empty screen will be displayed, with the cursor in the Number field. Enter the employee ID number—as many as six characters (letters and numbers)—for the existing employee whose record you want to view or edit, or enter the ID number for a new employee whose record is to be added to the file.

The following information might be helpful as you complete Screen 1 for each of your employees.

ID Number. As you create your employee ID numbers, we suggest you use the same type of pattern used to create ID numbers and codes for customers and vendors. By using the same pattern for all of your files, you need only remember that one pattern to search for records. If your files use different codes, you must be familiar with each of the different codes in order to find a record.

As with the customer and vendor files we created in Chapter 8, we recommend that you use the first four letters of an individual or companys name and a two-digit code as your employee ID number. This pattern simplifies finding employee records. In addition, if you are using *DacEasy Graph + Mate*, the employee list displayed in the open window will be alphabetized so that finding the employee will be easier there, as well.

Name. Each employee's name should be entered as last name, comma, first name, space, and middle name or initial. Note that there is not a space between the comma and the first name. The check printing routine uses the comma to find the end of the last name and the first letter of the first name. Then, when checks are printed, that routine re-writes each name as first name, space, middle name or initial, space, and last name. If there is a space between the comma and the first name on Screen 1, the employee's name on his check will appear to be indented one space, while the address lines will print at the proper margins.

Address, City, State, and Zip. Enter the complete address for each employee. This information is printed on each check and will show through the address window on mailing envelopes. If you abbreviate parts of the address, be sure the abbreviations can be understood by the postal service.

Phone. Enter the area code and telephone number for each employee. Unlike entering telephone numbers in the customer and vendor files, you should not press <ENTER> after the area code. In this field, the cursor will move to the appropriate location for proper entry. To correct a mistake, press <BACKSPACE> and re-type.

Social Security Number. Accurately enter each employee's Social Security number. Note that you do not have the dashes—the cursor will move automatically to the proper entry locations.

Sex, Marital Status, and Ethnic Origin. Enter the sex of each employee. Only male and female (''M'' or ''F'') are acceptable. Marital status may be entered as married or single (''M'' or ''S''). You can use as many as four characters to identify the ethnic origin of each employee. These codes can be defined by you and are not restricted except in length.

Memo. A short note relating to the calculation of payroll data, or other type of reminder can be included in this field.

Dates. Enter the dates for the employee's birth, hiring, next scheduled raise or last raise, and next scheduled review. You can also enter the date of the next promotion or the last promotion, and the date of termination if the employee is no longer with your company. Each date will be entered in a MM/DD/YY format (MM = month, DD = day, and YY = year). The cursor will automatically skip the slashes; so you will enter only the numbers that represent each part of the date.

Department. Each employee must be assigned to a department and each department must be set up in the Departments routine (see Figs. 9-6 and 9-7 for samples). A window will be displayed that lists all previously defined departments when you place the cursor in the Department field. You can select from this list. When the department number is entered, the department name will be automatically displayed.

Title. You can use as many as 30 characters for the employee title. You should standardize your list of positions before setting up your employee file so that all employees having similar positions in your company have exactly the same title listed in the payroll file.

Pay Suspended (Y/N). For employees who are on leave without pay or whose pay has been suspended for another reason, you would enter "Y" in the Pay Suspended field. *DacEasy* will stop pay until you change the "Y" to "N" to indicate the employee has been re-instated.

Frequency of Pay. (W/B/S/M). You can pay your employees weekly (W), every two weeks (B for biweekly), every half month (S for semimonthly), or monthly (M). Different classes of employees might be paid differently and individuals within departments might be paid on different schedules. You are not limited to one choice for any group of employees.

Type of Pay. You can enter "H" for employees who are paid an hourly wage, an "S" for employees who are salaried, or a "C" for contracted services.

Amount. If the employee is salaried, you must enter the annual salary. Do not enter a monthly, weekly, or other amount. If the employee is paid an hourly rate, enter that rate here. For contracted employees, do not enter an amount here.

Overtime Amounts. The Ovt1 and Ovt2 fields are used to enter the amounts to be paid for overtime hours. Note that you must enter the dollars-and-cents amounts for each of the three fields. If your company pays time-and-a-half for overtime, you must enter the amount that that would equal; you cannot enter the percentage.

Vacation Information. Enter, in a MM/DD/YY format, the date on which the employee qualifies for vacation time. Then enter the Frequency at which the employee will accumulate vacation time. In the Hours field, enter the vacation time the employee can earn for each period entered in the Frequency field. For example, you might offer two weeks' vacation after a year's employment and another two weeks after each continuing year. You could enter "80" hours in the Hours field and a "Y" (for "year") in the frequency field. In the sample shown in Fig. 9-13, the employee can accumulate 1.54 hours of vacation time each week she works after June 1, 1987. That would amount to two weeks per year for a 52-week working year.

The Accrued (Acrd) field is updated each time payroll is posted. The Paid field is updated when vacation time is processed.

Sick Time Information. Sick leave is handled exactly as described in the Vacation Information section above. If you do not provide sick leave, press <ENTER> as many times as needed to skip through these fields.

When you are sure that everything on Screen 1 is correct and complete, press <F10> to tell *DacEasy* to process the data. Then press the <PgDn> key to go to Screen 2.

Employee Master File—Screen 2

Marital Code (1-4). This code and the other data to be placed in the tax information section of Screen 2 are related to the tax status of the employee. Most of this information comes from the federal W-4 Form.

The marital code relates to the four tax classifications: "1" is used for single persons, "2" is used for married persons filing separate returns, "3" is used for married persons filing joint returns, and "4" is used for those people classified as heads of households.

These codes determine the amount of the federal deduction for income taxes, based on information provided in the tax table built into *DacEasy Payroll*.

EIC. EIC is an abbreviation for "earned income credit" which is discussed in Chapter 4 and earlier in this chapter. Each employee has the right to request the EIC if his or her salary is below certain levels. If an employee has not requested the EIC, leave the field blank by pressing <ENTER>. If the employee has requested the EIC, enter a "1"; if the employee and spouse qualify, you can enter a "2." The employee must file Form W-5 in order to qualify for the EIC. While the cursor is in this field, a window will display the options available for entry.

Exemptions. For FICA, FUTA, and SUTA taxes, enter a "Y" for each employee who is exempt. If the employee is not exempt from these taxes, enter "N." This field determines the employee's liability for paying the taxes indicated as percentages of eligible employees' earnings.

Allowances. Enter the number of allowances reported by the employee on the current federal W-4 form. Most states also use the W-4 data.

State Tax Table. For each employee, enter the tax table number *DacEasy* will use to calculate taxes to withhold. When the cursor is in this field, a window display that list the states and the corresponding tax table numbers. The window indicates the keys to press to scroll through the list of states. A complete list of states and their appropriate tax tables can be found in Appendix C.

Note that two employees who live and work in the same state may require different tax tables. Consider the example given earlier in this chapter for the State of Alabama, which has different tax structures for single and married persons.

State Modifications. You have two options for your state's tax modifications and exemptions. If your state permits the employee to claim a number of exemptions, that number is entered in the number field. If the exemption is an amount, the amount should be placed in the dollar field. At this time, only 12 states permitted modifications to the number of exemptions reported for federal tax purposes. The tax tables in Appendix C list the exemptions permitted by each state. Press <ENTER> in each field if you are not in one of the states that permit modifications.

City Tax Base (G/F/S). If you have no city/local income tax, press <ENTER> to skip this field and the next. If you must pay a city/local income tax, you must instruct *DacEasy* how it is to be calculated. Enter "G" if it is calculated as a percentage of the gross earnings. Enter "F" if it is calculated as a percentage of the federal withholdings. Enter "S" if it is calculated as a percentage of the state withholdings. While the cursor is in this field, a window will list the possible choices.

Tax Percentage. Enter the percentage to be used in calculating city/local income taxes. This percent is entered as the actual percent and not as the decimal equivalent of the percent. For example, three-and-a-half percent should be entered as "3.5" and not as ".035." If your employees do not pay a city/local income tax, press <ENTER> to pass this field.

Added Amounts to Withhold. If your employee would like to have additional amounts deducted each pay period, you can enter the amounts for federal, state, and city taxes. Do not enter percentages.

Earnings. Figure 9-8 lists all the possible types of special earnings your company can use (actually, the list is for the fictitious Parts and Parcels Company). If an employee qualifies for one of the special earnings categories (Codes 09 through 15), that code can be entered here. When the automatic payroll generation routine is run for a payroll period, the special pay categories are added in.

If the special earnings are to be paid periodically, the Frequency column can include the letter for the appropriate period (W = weekly, B = bi-weekly, S = semi-monthly, and M = monthly). While the cursor is in this field, a window will list the acceptable responses. If the field is left blank, the special earnings will not be calculated until specifically activated. This is useful for such items as annual bonuses or seasonal supplements.

The Amount/Rate column lets you enter the periodic rate or the total amount to be paid. The default value from the Earnings table (Fig. 9-8) will be displayed but can be overridden.

Deductions. Figure 9-9 lists all the possible types of deductions your company can take from an employee's check (again, these are for Parts and Parcels; you are able to add any you need). If an employee must have one of the special deductions (codes 21 through 30) taken from his or her check, the code can be entered here. When the automatic payroll generation routine is run for a payroll period, the special deductions categories will be accounted for.

As with the special earnings categories, you can indicate the frequency with which the deductions are to be made. If the Frequency field is left blank, the deduction will not be calculated. The Amount/Rate to be deducted can be entered into the last column.

For the special deductions and the special earnings categories, you must remember to create the codes and categories in the Departments File (Figs. 9-8 and 9-9) before you can use them in the employee file.

When the last piece of information has been entered on Screen 2 of the Employee Master File, press <F10> to process data. Then press <PgDn> to go to Screen 3.

Employee Master File—Screen 3

Screen 3 of the Employee Master File is used by *DacEasy Payroll* to accumulate totals for withholdings, earnings, and employer liabilities for each employee. Totals are automatically updated each time the payroll is posted to the accounting system.

If you are starting to use *DacEasy Payroll* in the middle of a business year, you can enter cumulative amounts in each field for each employee and *DacEasy* will update these figures each time you generate your payroll from *DacEasy*.

Note that the specific items we listed for earnings, deductions, and liabilities are listed on this screen. *DacEasy* obtains this information from the Departments File (see Figs. 9-8 and 9-9).

Summary

The DacEasy Payroll *module requires a series of set up procedures that must be completed before the module can be used. The procedure includes providing data for the payroll control file, which identifies the company and establishes the interface between the payroll module and the accounting module. FICA and FUTA percentages are also defined.*

In the Files routine, you can create departments for your payroll. You can also identify your payroll liabilities and your employees' earnings and deductions. Information needed for state withholdings are also identified.

Finally, the Employee Master File is created, including an example of the information needed to compete the file. One record must be created for each employee.

10

Setting Up Departments

Chapter Goals
- *This chapter discusses using departments to track revenue and expenses within DacEasy Accounting. The discussion centers on adding to the chart of accounts to identify the departments and entries in the customer file, the inventory and services files, and the income statement in the Reports module. The impact of departmentalization on the general ledger interface table is also discussed.*

- *We also briefly discuss the process for keeping records for more than one business.*

DacEasy Accounting and *DacEasy Payroll* permit you to establish departments within your business. You can then monitor your costs and income within these departments, giving you a detailed picture of each operating area.

Departments

Departments in the accounting module are different from departments in the payroll module and set up procedures are different as well. Each module is discussed separately, however, we discuss ways to pull the results together so you can use information from both modules as you make decisions about your daily operations.

Types of Departments

You can build your accounting departments based on one of two bases. You can use your customer file as the basis of income and costs, or you can use your inventory as the basis. The following explains the benefits of each.

Customer-Based Departments. You can use your customer file to track revenues and expenditures for sales territories, or for other criteria that is customer-based.

Inventory-Based Departments. You can use your inventory file to track revenues and expenditures for products and services, or for other criteria that is related to inventory.

Be sure to choose a type of department you can live with. After you select a department and enter your customers and vendors in their respective files, you cannot change the department bases—without throwing away all your work and starting over.

For our sample company, Parts and Parcels, we use inventory-based departments. For your purposes, select the option that provides the best cost/income information.

Effects of Departments

Once you departmentalize your recordkeeping, you must make corresponding entries in the customer, inventory, and services files. In addition, new accounts have to be added to your chart of accounts and the income statement in the Reports module must be modified. We discuss these entries, in some detail, in the remainder of the chapter.

DacEasy uses departments to keep records for three types of accounts: (1) Sales accounts are departmentalized so you can see revenues for individual departments; (2) Sales Returns are departmentalized so you can see decreases in revenues related to those returns; and (3) the Costs of Goods Sold are departmentalized so you can see the expenses related to each department. When you decide to departmentalize your accounting system, you must modify the accounts for each of these areas. If you do not add accounts in all three areas, the system will not permit entry of inventory items.

In the payroll module, each department general ledger interface can contain a different set of accounts to which payroll data are sent. These accounts would permit you to see your payroll and the accompanying liabilities based on individual departments.

All of these departmental effects are recorded in the general ledger's chart of accounts, provided you have the individual accounts set up to receive the appropriate amounts through the general ledger interface tables.

We will modify our recordkeeping for Parts and Parcels so that we have three departments. As indicated earlier, these departments will be based on the inventory file. The departments are listed below.

Department 01. Department 01 will be used to keep records for the products and services sold through basic hardware and building supplies.

Department 02. Department 02 will be used to keep records for the products and services sold through the gardening section.

Department 03. Department 03 will be used to keep records for the products and services sold through the housewares section.

The Chart of Accounts

Figure 10-1 shows portions of our chart of accounts (see Fig. 7-3 for the complete chart). We have added three accounts.

Sales 4103, Dept. 03. The general ledger interface table will send all inventory records regarding sales for items designated for Department 03 to this detail account. Sales for items designated for the other two departments will be sent to those existing accounts.

Sales 4203, Returns Dept. 03. The general ledger interface table will send all returned items recorded for Department 03 to this detail account. Returns for items designated

```
                        CHART OF ACCOUNTS

  Account  Account                                            General
  Number   Type     Level   Account Name          Type        Account

  1        Asset    1       ASSETS                General
  11       Asset    2       CURRENT ASSETS        General      1
  .        .        .       .                     .           .
  .        .        .       .                     .           .
  .        .        .       .                     .           .
  4        Rev      1       REVENUES              General
  41       Rev      2       SALES                 General      4
  4101     Rev      3       Sales Dept. 01        Detail       41
  4102     Rev      3       Sales Dept. 02        Detail       41
  4103     Rev      3       Sales Dept. 03        Detail       41      <==
  42       Rev      2       SALES RETURNS         General      4
  4201     Rev      3       Returns Dept. 01      Detail       42
  4202     Rev      3       Returns Dept. 02      Detail       42
  4203     Rev      3       Returns Dept. 03      Detail       42      <==
  43       Rev      2       SHIPPING              General      4
  4301     Rev      3       Freight               Detail       43
  .        .        .       .                     .           .
  .        .        .       .                     .           .
  .        .        .       .                     .           .
  5        Exp      1       TOTAL EXPENSES        General
  51       Exp      2       COST OF GOODS SOLD    General      5
  5101     Exp      3       COGS Dept. 01         Detail       51
  5102     Exp      3       COGS Dept. 02         Detail       51
  5203     Exp      3       COGS Dept. 03         Detail       51      <==
  52       Exp      2       GEN & ADMIN EXPENSES  General      5
  .        .        .       .                     .           .
  .        .        .       .                     .           .
  .        .        .       .                     .           .
```

Fig. 10-1. Accounts added to the Chart of Accounts to accommodate Department 03. *Each new account is marked with an arrow at the right of the list. Sales, Sales Returns, and Cost of Goods Sold must all be added. One account cannot be added without the other two.*

for the other two departments will be sent to those existing accounts.

Cost of Goods Sold 5103, Dept. 03. The general ledger interface table will send the costs of all inventory items sold to the appropriate detail accounts under the general account for cost of goods sold.

There are two very important considerations in adding these three accounts. First, all three must be added for each department. It is not possible to add only two of the three or only one of the three. The accounting system will not let you add inventory items if all three accounts for each department do not exist.

The second consideration is that the general ledger interface table (see Fig. 7-14), shows only the Level 2 accounts for sales, sales returns, and cost of goods sold. *DacEasy Accounting*, however, knows to add the appropriate department to the Level 2 account number. For example, the general ledger interface table includes only account 41 as the sales account. When you define departments within your inventory, *DacEasy Accounting* automatically adds the "01," the "02," or the "03" to the account number in order to send transaction amounts to the general ledger. The same is true for account 51 and account 42 in the general ledger interface table (Fig. 7-14).

To add the three accounts, select the Files option from the *DacEasy Accounting* Main Menu. Select option 1, to modify the chart of accounts (see Fig. 7-6). When the empty Accounts File Maintenance screen is displayed, enter the information as listed in Fig. 10-1.

Once the new accounts have been added, enter records in the Products file and the Services file. When you enter these items (an example is shown in Fig. 8-5), enter the department number in which you want each item accounted for. Each end-of-period routine will then post values to the designated departments through the appropriate account numbers.

The General Ledger Interface Table

The general ledger interface table directs the flow of information from the individual modules of *DacEasy Accounting* back to the general ledger chart of accounts. You are required to include 12 accounts that provide this direction.

If you do not departmentalize, all 12 accounts named in the general ledger interface table will be detail accounts. This means that *DacEasy Accounting* will post information from its modules directly to the accounts given in the interface table.

If you define departments to track revenues and expenditures, three of the accounts in the general ledger interface table will be general accounts. This means that *DacEasy Accounting* will assign information to the detail accounts for each department and that detail information will be totaled and placed in the general account designated in the interface table.

Figure 7-14 shows the general ledger interface table that we accepted for use during the set up procedures in Chapter 7. Compare the accounts listed in this table with the chart of accounts and you will see that 9 of the 12 accounts are detail accounts. The other three are general accounts: Sales, Sales Returns, and Cost of Goods Sold.

Each general account in the general ledger interface table accumulates detail from accounts that record individual department information; using the department number as an addition to the general account number. For example, the Sales account in the general ledger interface table is 41. The department accounts for Sales are 4101, 4102, and 4103.

The next section, The Inventory File, describes the process used to place the appropriate amounts in the appropriate accounts.

The Inventory File

Information placed on the Product File Maintenance screen is used to send the sales, returns, and cost figures to the appropriate accounts in the general ledger. Figure 8-5 shows a sample screen.

For each item in your inventory file, and for each service in your services file, you must indicate the department to which you want costs and income assigned when the item is bought and sold.

For our samples, we are using two-digit numbers to designate departments. In the chart of accounts, the numbers 4103, 4203, and 5103 were added and assigned to general accounts 41, 42, and 51, respectively. The two-digit "03" identifies Department 03. The "01" and "02" for Department 01 and Department 02 mean the same thing.

When you enter the department number in the "Dept." field on the Product File Maintenance screen or the Service File Maintenance screen, *DacEasy* checks to see that the 41, 42, and 51 general accounts have detail accounts that correspond to the given department number. If any of these accounts do not exist, you will be given the opportunity to create it.

If you enter a "1" instead of a "01" *DacEasy* would warn you that that account does not exist (at least it does not exist in our chart of accounts).

(A note for your consideration: *DacEasy* checks to see that accounts 41, 42, and 51 exist only because they are identified in the general ledger interface table for sales, returns, and cost of goods sold. If you are using your own chart of accounts, your general ledger interface might include different numbers for the three accounts and, consequently, *DacEasy* would check for these numbers.

The Services File

All services offered by your company can be stored in the Services File. Part of the information in each services record is the department that costs and revenues are assigned to. *DacEasy Accounting* treats the Services File as an extension of the inventory file when you choose to use the inventory as your department base. Figure 8-7 shows a sample of the Service File Maintenance screen, which includes a field for department numbers.

The Customer File

If you are using the customer file as your departmental base, *DacEasy* would use the same process as described for the inventory file. Each Customer Maintenance File screen has a field called "G/L Department" where you would put the department number where you want revenues and costs assigned. Figure 8-2 shows the Customer File Maintenance screen and the general ledger department field.

The Financial Statements File

One of the options on the *DacEasy Accounting* Main Menu (Fig. 10-2) is "Financials." This option provides access to four pre-defined report formats. The fifth item in the Financials window permits you to create new report formats, or to edit any of the existing report formats available through the Financial Statements Generator.

The financial reports include a financial balance sheet and income statement, a report for changes in financial condition, and printing the chart of accounts and trial balances. The formats for these four reports is pre-defined in the program and cannot be modified. The significance of these reports will be discussed in Chapter 15.

In the Financial Statements Generator, however, there are two report formats, one

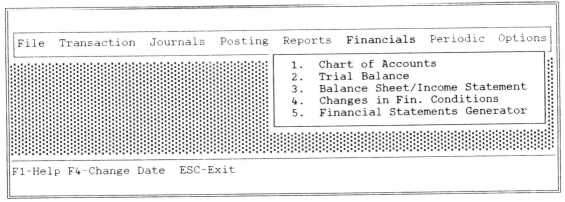

Fig. 10-2. The Financials window of the DacEasy Accounting Main Menu.
The Chart of Accounts can be printed from this window.

for a balance sheet, the other for an income statement. Both are summary reports for the detailed reports described above. Detailed reports cannot be modified and will automatically include new account numbers added to your chart of accounts. The summary reports listed in the Financial Statements Generator, however, are not automatically updated to include new account numbers as they are added.

For now, you need to know that using departments might require you to modify the balance sheet and the income statement in the Financial Statements Generator File. Figure 10-3 shows a portion of the original income statement provided by *DacEasy Accounting*.

Although the statement format looks a little strange to you right now, you can see that it includes only two departments—those included in the original chart of accounts shown in Fig. 7-3. Because we are adding a third department, we must modify the report format to include the new department.

Figure 10-4 shows a section of the report format after the lines have been added to include the third department. At this point, it is not necessary that you understand the coding of the format. It is, however, important that you know not to use the report until the adjustments have been made. The process of modifying the income statement is discussed in depth in Chapter 16.

Payroll Departments

DacEasy Payroll handles departments different from the way *DacEasy Accounting* does. For the payroll module, each department has its own general ledger interface table, as opposed to the one the accounting module maintains.

Because of the way our chart of accounts is set up, we cannot include different payroll departments as separate accounts. It would, however, be a simple matter to adapt the chart of accounts to include separate payroll departments.

Figures 9-7, 9-8, and 9-9 show the account numbers *DacEasy Payroll* uses for Department 1, which we set up for Parts and Parcels. We could, in our Chart of Accounts, include other account numbers that we could put into a similar set of screens for other

```
10/14/88                                                              LHP
12:44 PM                    Parts and Parcels, Inc.

   Enter Report Name :  INC2
═══════════════════════════════════════════════════════════════════════
   Print                            Amount  Amount To        Lines
   (Y/N)  Acct.#  Description        From    1   2   3    %  99=pg.
─────────────────────────────────────────────────────────────────────────
     Y             *  Income  Statement  *  0                       C
     Y                                      0
     N       4     Revenues                99                   +
     Y               GROSS MARGIN:          0                       C
     Y                                      0
     Y               Department 01          0                       C
     Y                                      0
     Y     4101    Sales                   99    +
     Y     4201    Returns                 99    +               -
     Y            Net Sales                 1                       1
     Y     5101    Cost of Goods  Sold     99    -               -
     Y            Gross Margin Dept.01      1                       1
     Y               Department 02          0                       C
     Y                                      0
     Y     4102    Sales                   99        +
     Y     4202    Returns                 99        +           -
     Y            Net Sales                 2                       1
     Y     5102    Cost of Goods  Sold     99        -           -
     Y            Gross Margin Dept.02      2    +   0             1
     Y            GROSS MARGIN:             1                       =
     Y                                      0                      99
─────────────────────────────────────────────────────────────────────────
F1-Help ALT I-Insert ALT D-Delete ALT P-Print F10-Process ESC-exit
```

Fig. 10-3. A section of the original Income Statement, with lines only for Departments 01 and 02. Sales, Sales Returns, and Costs of Goods Sold are included.

payroll departments. By giving each payroll department a different set of account numbers, you can have payroll data sent to the general ledger by department. Keep in mind, however, that you must have the appropriate numbers built into your chart of accounts before they can be assigned to departments.

(Another note for your consideration: At this time we are unable to add payroll departments to our chart of accounts, because many of the payroll liability accounts (numbered between 210411 and 210463) and many of the payroll expense accounts (numbered between 520111 and 520135) are Level 5 accounts. In order to add departments to payroll, we would need to add a sixth level to list the departments. *DacEasy Accounting* gives us only five levels of accounts. You can, however, develop a chart of accounts in which the department level would be the fifth level. This can be easily accomplished within *DacEasy*. Figure 10-5 illustrates a portion of such a chart of accounts.)

Accounting For More Than One Company

Keeping records for multiple companies is quite different from keeping records for multiple departments within one company. For different departments, all accounting is done within one chart of accounts; for different companies, a different chart of accounts may be used for each.

DacEasy Accounting and *DacEasy Payroll* permit you to keep records for more than one company using only one copy of the accounting and payroll programs, while maintaining many different sets of accounts and files.

```
10/14/88                                                              LHP
12:44 PM                  Parts and Parcels, Inc.

  Enter Report Name : INC2

  Print                            Amount Amount To        Lines
  (Y/N) Acct.# Description         From   1    2    3   %  99=pg.

    Y            * Income Statement * 0                        C
    Y                                 0
    N     4      Revenues            99                     +
    Y              GROSS MARGIN:      0                        C
    Y                                 0
    Y            Department 01        0                        C
    Y                                 0
    Y    4101   Sales               99    +
    Y    4201   Returns             99    +                    -
    Y           Net Sales            1                         1
    Y    5101   Cost of Goods Sold  99    -                    -
    Y           Gross Margin Dept.01 1                         1
    Y           Department 02        0                        C
    Y                                 0
    Y    4102   Sales               99         +
    Y    4202   Returns             99         +               -
    Y           Net Sales            2                         1
    Y    5102   Cost of Goods Sold  99         -               -
    Y           Gross Margin Dept.02 2         +    0          1
    Y           Department 03        0                        C
    Y                                 0
    Y    4103   Sales               99         +
    Y    4203   Returns             99         +               -
    Y           Net Sales            2                         1
    Y    5103   Cost of Goods Sold  99         -               -
    Y           Gross Margin Dept.03 2         +    0          1
    Y           GROSS MARGIN:        1                         =
    Y                                 0                        99

 F1-Help ALT I-Insert ALT D-Delete ALT P-Print F10-Process ESC-exit
```

Fig. 10-4. A section of the Income Statement showing lines added for Department 03. Sales, Sales Returns, and Costs of Goods Sold must be included together.

```
┌─────────────────────────────────────────────────────────────────┐
│ ┌─────────────────────────────────────────────────────────────┐ │
│ │                     CHART OF ACCOUNTS                        │ │
│ ├─────────────────────────────────────────────────────────────┤ │
│ │  New        Acct                                        New  │ │
│ │  Number     Type   Lv   Account Name        Type    Gen Acct │ │
│ │                                                              │ │
│ │   521       Exp     3   PAYROLL             General    52    │ │
│ │   5211      Exp     4   SALARIES            General    521   │ │
│ │   521101    Exp     5   Salaries:  Dept. 01 Detail     5211  │ │
│ │   521102    Exp     5   Salaries:  Dept. 02 Detail     5211  │ │
│ │   521103    Exp     5   Salaries:  Dept. 03 Detail     5211  │ │
│ │   5212      Exp     4   WAGES              General     521   │ │
│ │   521201    Exp     5   Hourly:    Dept. 01 Detail     5212  │ │
│ │   521202    Exp     5   Hourly:    Dept. 02 Detail     5212  │ │
│ │   521203    Exp     5   Hourly:    Dept. 03 Detail     5212  │ │
│ │   5213      Exp     4   OVERTIME           General     521   │ │
│ │   521301    Exp     5   Overtime:  Dept. 01 Detail     5213  │ │
│ │   521302    Exp     5   Overtime:  Dept. 02 Detail     5213  │ │
│ │   521303    Exp     5   Overtime:  Dept. 03 Detail     5213  │ │
│ │   522       Exp     3   TAXES              General     52    │ │
│ │   5221      Exp     4   FICA EMPLOYER      General     522   │ │
│ │   522101    Exp     5   FICA Empl.: Dept. 01 Detail    5221  │ │
│ │   522102    Exp     5   FICA Empl.: Dept. 02 Detail    5221  │ │
│ │   522103    Exp     5   FICA Empl.: Dept. 03 Detail    5221  │ │
│ │   5222      Exp     4   FUTA EMPLOYER      General     522   │ │
│ │   522201    Exp     5   FUTA Empl.: Dept. 01 Detail    5222  │ │
│ │   522202    Exp     5   FUTA Empl.: Dept. 02 Detail    5222  │ │
│ │   522203    Exp     5   FUTA Empl.: Dept. 03 Detail    5222  │ │
│ └─────────────────────────────────────────────────────────────┘ │
└─────────────────────────────────────────────────────────────────┘
```

Fig. 10-5. A sample Chart of Accounts to include payroll departments. These accounts would be listed in the Departmental General Ledger Interface Table.

On a fixed disk, each company's records would be placed in a subdirectory of the accounting/payroll directory. One example is the way we set up the records for Parts and Parcels. We created a directory called C:\DEA3 where we placed all of our accounting and payroll PROGRAMS. We then created a subdirectory called C:\DEA3\PARTS in where *DacEasy* placed our data.

To begin record-keeping for another company (for example: The Temple of Groom, an animal care and maintenance shop), simply create—or have *DacEasy* create—another subdirectory. We could name the new subdirectory C:\DEA3\GROOM so it would be easily identified. Note that the subdirectory name includes the ''path'' through the C.\DEA3 directory so the computer can find the PROGRAM files as well as the DATA files (see Fig. 6-7 for an example).

If you are using *DacEasy Graph + Mate*, selecting a company is as easy as moving the cursor and pressing the <ENTER> key.

To add another company to your *DacEasy Graph + Mate* selection menu, run the program called INSTALL as described in Chapter 2.

If you are not using *DacEasy Graph + Mate*, boot your system and follow your normal procedures to reach the DOS prompt. At the prompt, type the following series of commands:

```
CD\DEA3 <ENTER>
DEA3 GROOM <ENTER>
```

If the subdirectory named GROOM does not already exist, *DacEasy Accounting* creates it for you and then starts you through the procedures for setting up the files for that company. If the subdirectory already exists, *DacEasy Accounting* will start up using the data it finds in that subdirectory.

The same process will start *DacEasy Payroll*:

```
CD\DEP3 <ENTER>
DEP3 GROOM <ENTER>
```

In each of the above series of commands, you can substitute any valid subdirectory for GROOM so *DacEasy* will start the program with the appropriate data files.

At the beginning of this section on record keeping for different companies, we emphasized that departments are handled differently from companies. However, that is not entirely true. If two departments are to use different charts of accounts, each of these departments can be treated as though it were a company. The major drawback to using this method is that there is no way to consolidate department records into one company report.

Summary

We discussed using departments to track revenue and expenses within DacEasy Accounting *and* DacEasy Payroll. *The discussion concentrates on additions to the chart of accounts to identify the departments and entries in the customer file, the inventory and services files, and the income statement in the Financial Reports module. The impact of departmentalization on the general ledger interface table is also discussed.*

The process of keeping records for more than one business is also covered.

11

Daily Accounting
and Payroll Tasks

Chapter Goals
- *This chapter reviews the daily activities of accounting and payroll. This chapter will help you develop a structure for working on a day-to-day basis with* DacEasy. *References to appropriate menu selections and work screens help build an understanding of the programs' structure as it relates to the day-to-day operations of your business.*
- *Each of the routines and procedures discussed in this chapter begin and end with the* DacEasy Accounting *Main Menu or the* DacEasy Payroll *Main Menu. The sample screens and reports in this chapter are used later as we go through the tutorial chapters with Parts and Parcels.*

This chapter is meant to be a summary of daily tasks. We are not asking you to enter any of the items discussed here. You will have plenty of time for practice when we begin the tutorials in Chapter 17. For now, we are trying to show you some of the answers before you have to work the problems (that's the only way we made it through high school algebra).

We assume, for the purpose of our discussion, that all the set up procedures have been completed.

Buying

One of the continuing daily tasks you and your business will face is purchasing products to re-sell, or to use in the operation of your business. When this is done within the Purchasing module of *DacEasy Accounting*, more than just your purchasing is taken care of. As discussed in Chapter 5, *DacEasy Accounting* relates one completed task to several others, so you are not required to do repetitive recordkeeping. You should seriously consider doing all of your purchasing through the Purchasing module.

On most working days, you will place at least one order with someone for something that you will later sell. This purchasing process must be completed before the selling process can begin.

From the *DacEasy Accounting* Main Menu, select the Transactions option for entering purchase orders. Figure 11-1 shows the Purchasing window. From the menu in that window, use the first three items to enter information about purchases you make, and items 4 through 6 will print the forms containing the information you enter.

Before purchasing items to re-sell, consider the Reports module on the Main Menu. The Product Alert Report, available from the Inventory option in the Reports window (see Fig. 11-2), should be printed each evening or morning. It lists all of the products in your inventory for which on-hand counts have fallen below the minimum count you specified when you created the product record in the inventory file. This alert report can be the basis of your purchasing tasks each day.

To create a purchase order, select option 1 from the Purchasing window. Figure 11-3 shows a purchase order screen with sample data. (We discuss creating purchase orders in Chapter 15.) For now, simply point out that the vendor is referenced by the vendor code, which is created in the vendor file. When items are added to the purchase order, they are selected from your inventory once you provide the inventory number.

Once the vendor code is entered at the top of the purchase order, a window will open in the middle of the screen that displays your current credit limit with the vendor,

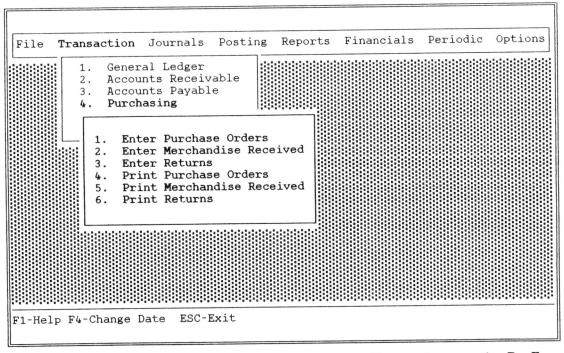

Fig. 11-1. The Purchasing window from Transactions on the DacEasy Accounting Main Menu.

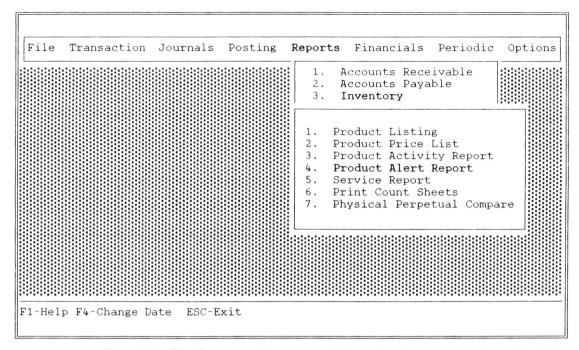

```
┌─────────────────────────────────────────────────────────────────┐
│ ╔═══════════════════════════════════════════════════════════════╗ │
│ ║                                                               ║ │
│ ║  File  Transaction  Journals  Posting  Reports  Financials  Periodic  Options ║ │
│ ║ ┌───────────────────────────────┐┌──────────────────────────┐ ║ │
│ ║ ::::::::::::::::::::::::::::::::::::│ 1.   Accounts Receivable  │::::::::: ║ │
│ ║ ::::::::::::::::::::::::::::::::::::│ 2.   Accounts Payable     │::::::::: ║ │
│ ║ ::::::::::::::::::::::::::::::::::::│ 3.   Inventory            │::::::::: ║ │
│ ║ :::::::::::::::::::::::::::::::┌────┴──────────────────────────┴─┐:::::: ║ │
│ ║ ::::::::::::::::::::::::::::::::│ 1.  Product Listing            │:::::: ║ │
│ ║ ::::::::::::::::::::::::::::::::│ 2.  Product Price List         │:::::: ║ │
│ ║ ::::::::::::::::::::::::::::::::│ 3.  Product Activity Report    │:::::: ║ │
│ ║ ::::::::::::::::::::::::::::::::│ 4.  Product Alert Report       │:::::: ║ │
│ ║ ::::::::::::::::::::::::::::::::│ 5.  Service Report             │:::::: ║ │
│ ║ ::::::::::::::::::::::::::::::::│ 6.  Print Count Sheets         │:::::: ║ │
│ ║ ::::::::::::::::::::::::::::::::│ 7.  Physical Perpetual Compare │:::::: ║ │
│ ║ ::::::::::::::::::::::::::::::::└────────────────────────────────┘:::::: ║ │
│ ║                                                               ║ │
│ ║ F1-Help F4-Change Date   ESC-Exit                             ║ │
│ ╚═══════════════════════════════════════════════════════════════╝ │
└─────────────────────────────────────────────────────────────────┘
```

Fig. 11-2. The Inventory Reports window showing reports that should be printed regularly and frequently.

the current balance owed the vendor, and the credit available to you for the current purchase. When you press a key to close the window, the vendor's name, address, and other relevant information are displayed on the purchase order.

If the vendor code or inventory number is not already in the files when entered on the purchase order, you will be asked if you want to add these and, a window will permit you to create the appropriate records. Your password, however, might restrict your ability to add vendor or inventory records in this way.

When the order is completed, you can print it, using option 4 from the Purchasing window. Once you have a printed copy, you can mail it and wait for the good stuff to arrive. Figure 11-4 shows the print options available when you are ready to print the purchase order. These options include four form types from which you can select the form to use. We have chosen type 3, plain paper. You can purchase forms from several vendors, including Dac Software, if you want to use pre-printed forms.

At the same time you print the purchase order to mail to the vendor, you can print a "packing list" without costs. This copy can be retained for the receiving department to use when the items arrive.

Once the ordered items are received, you will let *DacEasy* know by selecting option 2 from the Purchasing window (see Fig. 11-1). Figure 11-5 shows a sample screen for recording items that have been received. Notice that only 25 cases of item PAINT01 were received although 30 were ordered. *DacEasy* automatically marks the remaining

```
┌─────────────────────────────────────────────────────────────────────────┐
│                      Purchase Order  #      01001                          │
│  Vendor Code:     PAIN01         Remark:                                   │
│  Paint By the Numbers, Inc.      Ship Overnight      Via Land Express      │
│  Vinnie Van Gogh                 Land Carrier Only   FOB                   │
│  Green Fields Mall                                   Your Ref. A-123       │
│  Plaster            TN  38654-                       Our Ref.   01001      │
│  Disc. Days       15 Disc. %   1.50  Due Days    30 Tax Code: 3 Rate:  4.500│
│  ─────────────────────────────────────────────────────────────────────   │
│     Item #        Desc. Ordered                Price    Disc. Extended     │
│                                                                           │
│    PAINT01        Paint, Wt Base Gal                                       │
│                      30.000                    51.850   0.00    1555.50    │
│    PAINT02        Paint, Wt Base Qt                                        │
│                      10.000                    51.000   0.00     510.00    │
│    PIGMENT99      Pigment, Asst Pt                                         │
│                       4.000                    51.600   0.00     206.40    │
│                                                                           │
│                                                                           │
│  ─────────────────────────────────────────────────────────────────────   │
│    Sub Total      Sales Tax      Total                                     │
│      2271.90        102.24      2374.14                                    │
│                                                                           │
│  F1-Help  F6-CANCEL   F10-Process   ALT D-Delete Line                      │
└─────────────────────────────────────────────────────────────────────────┘
```

Fig. 11-3. Completing a purchase order on-screen. You enter only the Vendor
Code, Item Number from Inventory, Quantity, and Price. DacEasy does the rest.

items as back ordered. To enter merchandise received, you must type in the number
of the purchase order and the number of items received. *DacEasy* provides all remaining
information, allowing you to edit much of that. For example, if the price of one or more
of the items on your original purchase order changed, you can enter the new price. A
new extended price would be calculated, a new subtotal would be displayed, and the
new sales tax amount would be added—all done automatically.

You can add, to the merchandise received screen, non-inventory items charged to
you that the vendor may have included, such as shipping charges. Before you can add
these types of charges, however, they must be listed in your purchase order and billing
codes (see Figs. 7-11 and 7-12). In our sample, the "C 1" in the Item Number column
tells *DacEasy Accounting* to use the item with Purchase Order Code 1 (from Fig. 7-11).
We typed in the amount.

You can also add messages from the messages list that was created during the set
up process for *DacEasy Accounting* (see Fig. 7-22). To place one of your messages
on the purchase order, use "M x" in the Item Number column (where "x" is the message
number you want to use. Examples are used during the tutorial section on creating
purchase orders in Chapter 15.

If you want to add a message that is not included in your "canned" messages, you
can type the letter "D" (for description message) in the Item Number column. When

163

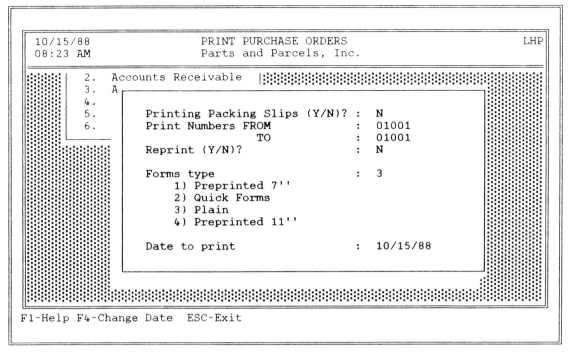

```
  10/15/88                PRINT PURCHASE ORDERS                        LHP
  08:23 AM                Parts and Parcels, Inc.
 ┌──────────────────────────────────────────────────────────────────────┐
 │  2.  Accounts Receivable  │                                           │
 │  3.  A                                                                 │
 │  4.  ┌─────────────────────────────────────────────────────────┐      │
 │  5.  │      Printing Packing Slips (Y/N)? :   N                 │      │
 │  6.  │      Print Numbers FROM            :   01001             │      │
 │      │                        TO          :   01001             │      │
 │      │      Reprint (Y/N)?                :   N                 │      │
 │      │                                                          │      │
 │      │      Forms type                    :   3                 │      │
 │      │          1) Preprinted 7''                               │      │
 │      │          2) Quick Forms                                  │      │
 │      │          3) Plain                                        │      │
 │      │          4) Preprinted 11''                              │      │
 │      │                                                          │      │
 │      │      Date to print                 :   10/15/88          │      │
 │      │                                                          │      │
 │      └─────────────────────────────────────────────────────────┘      │
 └──────────────────────────────────────────────────────────────────────┘
  F1-Help  F4-Change Date   ESC-Exit
```

Fig. 11-4. Options for printing purchase orders. Everything is automatic.

you press <ENTER> after that "D," a space is provided to write the message you want to include. See Fig. 11-7 to see a sample message on a customer invoice.

Sometimes (always accidentally; never intentionally), you receive items you did not order or you receive unacceptable items that were substituted for items you ordered or, finally, you receive items that are simply not what you thought they were when you ordered them. If you have such items to be returned to vendors, enter them using option 3 on the Purchasing window and printed using option 6 (see Fig. 11-1).

We discuss printing of purchase journals, the posting process, and the purchase order status report when we discuss the end-of-day routines and posting later in this chapter.

Selling

After placing your orders and receiving the merchandise from your vendors, the next step is to put price stickers on everything and to sell as much as you can to the next person who comes into the store.

When you sell something to a person or a business that pays only after you bill them, the billing process becomes the lifeblood of your business. You can't expect to collect if you can't bill these customers. In addition, you might have customers who pay cash for their purchases. Your accounting system must be able to accomodate these cash sales as well.

You should seriously consider recording all of your selling through the Billing module.

```
┌──────────────────────────────────────────────────────────────────────────┐
│  ┌────────────────────────────────────────────────────────────────────┐   │
│  │     Merchandise Received from Purchase Order #     01001            │   │
│  │  Vendor Code:    PAIN01          Remark:                            │   │
│  │  Paint By the Numbers, Inc.      Ship Overnight      Via Land Express│  │
│  │  Vinnie Van Gogh                 Land Carrier Only   FOB            │   │
│  │  Green Fields Mall                                   Your Ref. A-123│   │
│  │  Plaster          TN  38654-                         Our Ref.  01001│   │
│  │  Disc. Days      15 Disc. %  1.50  Due Days    30  Tax Code: 3 Rate:  4.500│
│  │  ────────────────────────────────────────────────────────────────  │   │
│  │   Item #      Desc. Ordered    Received Back Ord.   Price    Disc. Extended│
│  │                                                                    │   │
│  │  PAINT01        Paint, Wt Base Gal                                  │   │
│  │                   30.000     25.000     5.000     51.850  0.00  1296.25│
│  │  PAINT02        Paint, Wt Base Qt                                   │   │
│  │                   10.000     10.000     0.000     51.000  0.00   510.00│
│  │  PIGMENT99      Pigment, Asst Pt                                    │   │
│  │                    4.000      4.000     0.000     51.600  0.00   206.40│
│  │  C 1            Freight                                             │   │
│  │                                                                76.80│   │
│  │  ────────────────────────────────────────────────────────────────  │   │
│  │    Sub Total      Sales Tax    Total                  Net to Pay   │   │
│  │     2089.45          90.57     2180.02                  2180.02    │   │
│  │  ────────────────────────────────────────────────────────────────  │   │
│  │  F1-Help   F6-CANCEL   F10-Process   ALT D-Delete Line             │   │
│  └────────────────────────────────────────────────────────────────────┘   │
└──────────────────────────────────────────────────────────────────────────┘
```

Fig. 11-5. When merchandise is received, it should be entered immediately.
Note that DacEasy also tracks your back orders (see PAINT101).

As with the Purchasing module, the Billing module takes care of more than just billing. It helps control your recordkeeping and your inventory.

On most working days, you will sell something. To record the sale, choose the Billing module from the *DacEasy Accounting* Transactions window (Fig. 11-6).

When your customer places an order using a purchase order, you enter the items on an invoice similar to the one shown in Fig. 11-7. If you operate a shipping department or a warehouse, you can elect to print a ''packing list'' which can also be used as a ''picking list'' by those who gather and prepare your merchandise for shipping.

When your customer is a cash-and-carry account, there are several ways the sale can be handled. Some of these techniques are discussed in greater detail in Chapter 14, where we discuss using *DacEasy Accounting* as a point-of-sale accounting system. For now, let us say that you should create a sales ticket for that customer, listing all the items purchased on an invoice similar to the one shown in Fig. 11-7. When the sale is completed, you would enter the ''payment reference'' (a check number or the word ''Cash'') and the payment amount at the bottom of the screen. You would then print the invoice to give to the customer. When the end-of-day routines are completed, all affected accounts are updated automatically.

When you create an invoice, press the <ENTER> key while the cursor is in the invoice number field and the next available invoice number will be entered for you. When you enter a customer code, a window opens in the middle of the screen to show the

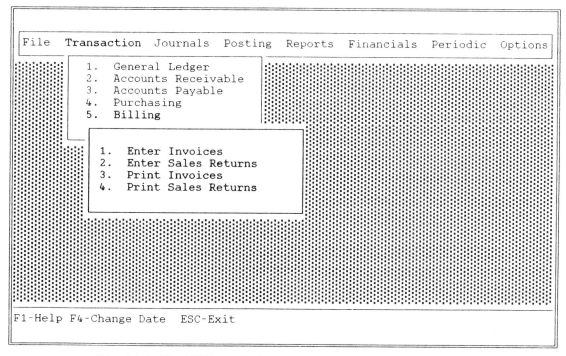

```
┌──────────────────────────────────────────────────────────────────────┐
│┌──────────────────────────────────────────────────────────────────────┐│
││ File  Transaction  Journals  Posting  Reports  Financials  Periodic  Options │
│├──────────────────────────────────────────────────────────────────────┤│
││            1.  General Ledger                                          ││
││            2.  Accounts Receivable                                     ││
││            3.  Accounts Payable                                        ││
││            4.  Purchasing                                              ││
││            5.  Billing                                                 ││
││            ┌──────────────────────────────────┐                       ││
││            │  1.   Enter Invoices             │                       ││
││            │  2.   Enter Sales Returns        │                       ││
││            │  3.   Print Invoices             │                       ││
││            │  4.   Print Sales Returns        │                       ││
││            └──────────────────────────────────┘                       ││
││                                                                        ││
││                                                                        ││
│├──────────────────────────────────────────────────────────────────────┤│
││ F1-Help  F4-Change Date   ESC-Exit                                     ││
│└──────────────────────────────────────────────────────────────────────┘│
└──────────────────────────────────────────────────────────────────────┘
```

Fig. 11-6. The Billing window from the Transactions option on the DacEasy Accounting Main Menu. The Billing module takes care of more than just billing. It contributes to inventory control and helps control recordkeeping.

current account status for that customer. This status check shows the customer's credit limit, current balance due, and credit available. When you press a key to close the window, the remainder of the customer's record is printed automatically on the invoice.

We've used the sample invoice in Fig. 11-7 to show examples of several transactions.

Fractional Parts. On this invoice, we have billed the customer for "5.001" units of PAINT01. The decimal part of the quantity represents a fractional part of the unit of measure, which was discussed in Chapter 8. Figure 8-5 shows that PAINT01 comes in a "case" and that the case is divided into four fractional parts (that is, there are four cans of paint in each case). The "5.001" indicates the customer bought 5 cases and 1 can of paint. The extended price has been adjusted automatically to show the corresponding price.

Out-of-Stock Items. On the customer invoice shown in Fig. 11-7, we have included an order for three 16-foot sections of aluminum conduit. When *DacEasy* checked our inventory, however, it found that we did not have that conduit in stock. It automatically marked it as back ordered on the customer's invoice. The extended price is zero because we will not bill that item to the customer until it is actually shipped.

Descriptive Message. By placing a "D" in the Item Number column of the invoice, we can enter a message to print on the invoice. The "D" will not be printed. This can be done on purchase orders as well. (Note that this message is typed in at the time

```
                          Invoice #   01001
Customer Code: WEIR01        Remark:
Weir Lighting Fixtures       Ship to address      Via Truck
Sam Charger                  at left.             FOB
4312 S. Socket Street                             Your Ref. PO4531
Ninety Six      SC  29666-                        Our Ref.   01001
Disc. Days      10 Disc. %  3.00  Due Days    30  Tax Code: 4 Rate:   5.000
────────────────────────────────────────────────────────────────────────
Inv. #        Desc. Ordered     Shipped  Back Ord.   Price   Disc. Extended
────────────────────────────────────────────────────────────────────────
 PAINT01       Paint, Wt Base Gal
                   5.001       5.001     0.000      75.800  0.00   397.95
 CONDUIT01     Conduit, Alum 16Ft
                   3.000       0.000     3.000       8.590  0.00     0.00
 D             Conduit will be shipped in 3 days.




────────────────────────────────────────────────────────────────────────
Sub Total     Sales Tax     Total     Pmt.Ref.  Payment $   Net to Pay
   397.95        19.90      417.85                   0.00      417.85
────────────────────────────────────────────────────────────────────────
F1-Help   F6-CANCEL   F10-Process   ALT D-Delete Line
```

Fig. 11-7. Completing a customer invoice on-screen. *You enter only the Customer Code, the Inventory Number, and Quantity. DacEasy does the rest.*

the invoice is created. This is not related to the "canned" messages that were placed in a message table when we went through the set up procedures (Fig. 7-22), nor is it related to the statement messages shown in Fig. 7-13.

Sometimes a customer will return an item that he bought. If you have items returned, select the appropriate option within the Billing window and enter the inventory codes. This will update inventory records as well as your accounts receivable records.

Printing sales journals and posting sales transactions are discussed later in the chapter.

Other Transactions

In addition to the daily buying and selling of products and services, you will enter other information that is essential to your recordkeeping. These tasks can be divided into three basic types of entries: (1) entries directly to the general ledger, (2) entry of cash receipts, and (3) entry of cash disbursements. We will take a quick look at these three entries. (Keep in mind that these are discussed more fully in the tutorial chapters.)

General Ledger Transactions: Transferring Cash

Most of the entries made to the general ledger will come from the other modules of *DacEasy*. There are, however, times when you must make a direct entry to the general ledger. Such entries are usually associated with transfers of cash from one account to another.

```
┌─────────────────────────────────────────────────────────────────┐
│ ┌─────────────────────────────────────────────────────────────┐ │
│ │             GENERAL LEDGER TRANSACTION ENTRY                  │ │
│ │ Journal.. :CA          Transaction #..:0001      Date..:10/15/88│ │
│ │                                                               │ │
│ │ Acct.#   Account Name      Description      Debit     Credit  │ │
│ │ ───────────────────────────────────────────────────────────  │ │
│ │ 11021  Checking Account  Personal Investment  25000.00        │ │
│ │ 31011  Par Value         Personal Investment           25000.00│ │
│ │ 11021  Checking Account  Loan Proceeds        50000.00        │ │
│ │ 2202   Notes Payable     Loan Proceeds                 50000.00│ │
│ │                                                               │ │
│ │                                                               │ │
│ │                                                               │ │
│ │                                                               │ │
│ │                                                               │ │
│ │ ─────────────────────────────────────────────────────────── │ │
│ │ Total Debits :    75000.00   │ Total Credits :    75000.00   │ │
│ └─────────────────────────────────────────────────────────────┘ │
│ F1-Help F2-Difference F6-Delete F9-Auto Entry F10-Process ALT D-Delete line │
└─────────────────────────────────────────────────────────────────┘
```

Fig. 11-8. A sample General Ledger Transaction. Start-up cash is entered into the accounting system.

Figure 11-8 illustrates a direct entry to the general ledger. This work screen is displayed when you select the General Ledger option from the Transactions window on the *DacEasy Accounting* Main Menu. The given sample is for Parts and Parcels and is explained in detail in Chapter 17 (as we start the tutorial section). The entry has been made to the ''cash journal'' (abbreviated CA) because it details the personal investment of the owner and the inclusion of a loan to be used for operating expenses.

To make an entry of this type, you simply name the journal, enter the account numbers to be affected, type a description to explain the transaction, and give the amounts in the proper column. *DacEasy* keeps totals for debits and credits and will not let you process your entry (with <F10>) until the entry is in balance—that is, until the total debits equal the total credits.

Cash Receipts: Receiving Payments

One of the most important day-to-day tasks you will have is recording cash receipts. The accounting system must be able to accomodate the receipt of checks, cash, and credit card amounts. Cash receipts can be entered from the Accounts Receivable option in the Transactions window of the *DacEasy Accounting* Main Menu.

For each check you receive, you will make an entry into the accounting system, using option 2 from the Accounts Receivable window. Figure 11-9 shows a sample entry for a payment received during the discount period that Parts and Parcels offered its customer.

To complete the transaction, enter the customer code and the transaction type (either a payment or an adjustment, shown in a window when the cursor stops at this field). Give the amount of the check you received. *DacEasy* will list all the invoices for that customer and you will be able to give instructions about the invoices to which the payment should apply—or you can press <F9> and *DacEasy* will apply the check as it sees need. If there are several invoices on the customer's screen, *DacEasy* will keep track of the amounts as you apply them, letting you know the amount you have left to apply (see the upper right corner of Fig. 11-9). *DacEasy* also supplies the amounts available for discounts and displays these amounts for each invoice.

When the transaction is completed, all accounting procedures are automatically updated. You will have no other entries to make regarding the purchase of, and payment for, the items listed on a customers' invoices.

This accounting procedure is also used for cash received from sources that did not originate in the billing process.

Cash Disbursements: Making Payments

When you are ready to pay for merchandise you have received, select the Accounts Payable option from the Transactions window of the *DacEasy Accounting* Main Menu.

For each check you write, make an entry in the accounting system, using option

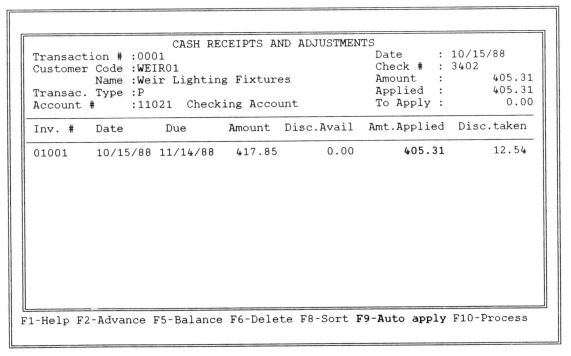

Fig. 11-9. A sample cash receipt. *Accounting for the money your customers pay you.*

```
                    PAYMENTS AND ADJUSTMENTS
Transaction # :0001                         Date    : 10/15/88
Vendor   Code :PAIN01                       Check # :
         Name :Paint By the Numbers, Inc.   Amount  :    2147.32
Transac. Type :K                            Applied :    2147.32
Account #     :                             To Apply:       0.00
─────────────────────────────────────────────────────────────────
Inv. #    Date      Due       Amount  Disc.Avail  Amt.Applied  Disc.taken
─────────────────────────────────────────────────────────────────
A-123   10/15/88 11/14/88   2180.02       0.00      2147.32       32.70




F1-Help F2-Advance F5-Balance F6-Delete F8-Sort F9-Auto apply F10-Process
```

Fig. 11-10. A sample entry screen for recording a payment to a vendor.
Discounts are automatically calculated based on data in vendor file.

2 from the Accounts Payable window. Figure 11-10 shows a sample entry for a payment made during the discount period offered by the vendor.

To complete the transaction, enter the vendor code and the transaction type (options are listed in a window when the cursor stops in this field). *DacEasy* will list all the invoices for that vendor and you will be able to give instructions about the invoices to which the payment is to apply—or you can press <F9> and *DacEasy* will apply the appropriate amount as it sees need. *DacEasy* also supplies the amounts available for discounts, and displays them for each invoice.

When the transaction is completed, all accounting procedures are automatically updated. You will have no other entries to make regarding the purchase of, and payment for, items listed on the invoices from your vendors.

This accounting procedure is also used for cash disbursed for items that did not originate in the purchasing process.

Payroll

Fortunately, payroll is not really a day-to-day task. The Payroll module stays fairly stable after the set up process is completed. There are, however, always adjustments to be made at one time or another.

Figure 11-11 shows the Payroll Processing window, which is accessed from the

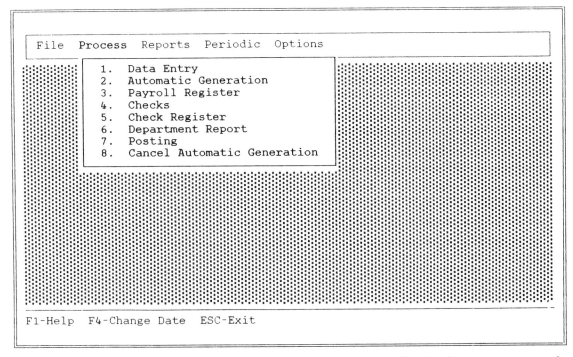

```
┌─────────────────────────────────────────────────────────────────────┐
│┌───────────────────────────────────────────────────────────────────┐│
││                                                                   ││
││ │ File   Process   Reports   Periodic   Options              │    ││
││ └───────────────────────────────────────────────────────────┘    ││
││ :::::::┌───────────────────────────────────────────┐:::::::::::  ││
││ :::::::│  1.   Data Entry                           │:::::::::::  ││
││ :::::::│  2.   Automatic Generation                 │:::::::::::  ││
││ :::::::│  3.   Payroll Register                     │:::::::::::  ││
││ :::::::│  4.   Checks                               │:::::::::::  ││
││ :::::::│  5.   Check Register                       │:::::::::::  ││
││ :::::::│  6.   Department Report                    │:::::::::::  ││
││ :::::::│  7.   Posting                              │:::::::::::  ││
││ :::::::│  8.   Cancel Automatic Generation          │:::::::::::  ││
││ :::::::└───────────────────────────────────────────┘:::::::::::  ││
││ ::::::::::::::::::::::::::::::::::::::::::::::::::::::::::::::::::  ││
││                                                                   ││
││ F1-Help   F4-Change Date   ESC-Exit                               ││
│└───────────────────────────────────────────────────────────────────┘│
└─────────────────────────────────────────────────────────────────────┘
```

Fig. 11-11. The Payroll Process window. *Accounting for the payments you make to your employees.*

Payroll Main Menu. Except for option 1, all the items on that processing menu are "output" procedures. Only the first option requires "input."

Figure 11-12 shows the work screen for the payroll processing. This screen permits you to approve non-scheduled bonuses (as in the example we have given), to record days that pay is to be withheld, or to enter other data that affects the current paycheck for a given employee.

Figure 11-12 shows the results of paying a non-scheduled bonus. The code for that bonus must exist in the department general ledger interface table (see Fig. 9-8). You can enter deductions that are not automatically deducted, but the codes for these must also be in the interface table. There are some additional codes that can be used on this screen and they are discussed in our tutorial for the payroll module.

Adjustments made this way should be exceptions to the information provided in the employee files and the set up procedures. If there are no exceptions to the normal payroll, you will have no adjustments to make.

End-of-Day Routines

At the end of each business day, there are several routines that should be completed before posting the day's records to the accounting system. The following might assist in organizing these routines for you.

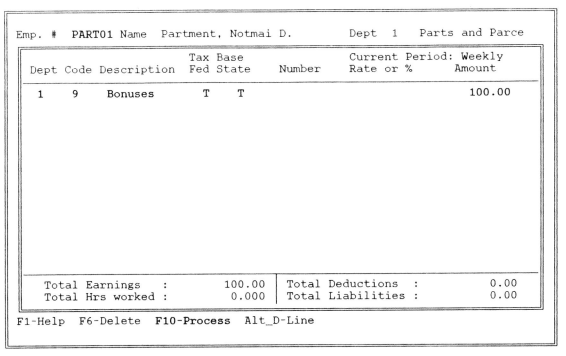

```
Emp.  #   PART01 Name   Partment, Notmai D.           Dept  1    Parts and Parce

                          Tax Base                    Current Period: Weekly
   Dept Code Description  Fed State      Number        Rate or %      Amount

    1   9     Bonuses      T    T                                     100.00








   Total Earnings   :      100.00   Total Deductions  :        0.00
   Total Hrs worked :       0.000   Total Liabilities :        0.00

 F1-Help   F6-Delete   F10-Process   Alt_D-Line
```

Fig. 11-12. A sample entry screen for recording payroll information that is different from the setup in the employee's file.

Purchasing Module Routines

After printing all of your purchase orders, your merchandise received forms, and your merchandise returned forms, print the Purchase Journal, which provides a list of purchases made during the day. The amounts in the Purchase Journal are posted to the General Ledger when the posting routine is run.

Billing Module Routines

After printing all invoices and sales return forms, print the Sales Journal, which lists all the sales for the day. The amounts in the Sales Journal are posted to the General Ledger when the posting routine is run.

General Ledger Routines

When all your direct entries have been made to the general ledger, print the general ledger journals to which you have made entries. Then you can print the Accounts Activity Detail Report, which will list all activity for each account in the chart of accounts. Amounts that have been entered directly into the general ledger will be formally posted when the posting process is run, which is not necessarily a daily task.

Accounts Receivable Module Routines

When you are ready to close the books for the day, generate finance charges so

Daily Routines DacEasy Accounting		
Daily Routines	DacEasy Accounting Transactions Option	Mod ule
Enter Purchase Orders for New Merchandise Enter Merchandise Received from Previous Orders Enter Merchandise Returned to Vendor Print Purchase Orders and Mail to Vendors	Purchasing Purchasing Purchasing Purchasing	# 1 # 2 # 3 # 4
Enter Invoice and Sales Tickets for Cash Sales Enter Invoice for Credit Account Sales Enter Sales Returns Print Invoices and Sales Tickets	Billing Billing Billing Billing	# 1 # 1 # 2 # 3
General Ledger Entries Enter Cash Receipts Enter Payments from Customers Enter Bills That Have No Invoice Enter Payments to Vendors	General Ledger Accounts Receivable Accounts Receivable Accounts Payable Accounts Payable	– # 1 # 2 # 1 # 2
End-of-Day Routines	DacEasy Accounting Main Menu Option	Mod ule
Print Merchandise Received Print Merchandise Returned Print Purchases Journal Print Sales Returned Print Sales Journal Generate Finance Charges Print Accounts Receivable Journal Print Checks to Vendors Print Accounts Payable Journal Print Inventory Activity Report Print Inventory Alert Report Print Services Report Print General Ledger Journals Print Account Activity Report	Trans:Purchasing Trans:Purchasing Journals Billing Journals Periodic:A/R Journals Trans:A/P Journals Reports:Inventory Reports:Inventory Reports:Inventory Journals Journals	# 5 # 6 # 7 # 4 # 9 # 4 # 3 # 4 # 5 # 3 # 4 # 5 # 1 # 2
End-of-Day Posting	DacEasy Accounting Main Menu Option	Mod ule
Post Purchases and Purchase Returns Print Purchase Order Status Report Post Sales and Sales Returns Post Accounts Payable Transactions Print Payments Report Post Accounts Receivable Transactions Post Physical Inventory Adjustments Post General Ledger Transactions Print Trial Balances Print Financial Statements	Posting Journals Posting Posting Journals Posting Posting Posting Financials Financials	# 4 # 8 # 5 # 3 # 6 # 2 # 6 # 1 # 2 # 3

Fig. 11-13. Daily routines, end-of-day routines, and end-of-day posting.

that they will be automatically added to accounts that are past due. Then print the accounts receivable journals. The amounts in these journals are posted to the general ledger when the posting process is run.

Accounts Payable Module Routines

After entering the amounts you wish to pay each of your vendors, print the vendor checks. After the checks are printed, print the accounts payable journals. The amounts in these journals are posted to the general ledger when the posting process is run.

Special Consideration for Payroll

Although payroll is not, typically, a daily task, there are several end-of-period routines that are important. These will be discussed more in Chapter 12, where we discuss periodic tasks that must be completed within *DacEasy*.

End-of-Day Posting

At the end of each business day, you will "post" your journal totals to the general ledger. This is done from the Posting option on the *DacEasy Accounting* Main Menu and from the Process option on the *DacEasy Payroll* Main Menu.

In addition to running the posting process for Purchasing, you will print a "Purchase Order Status Report," which lists all purchase orders for merchandise that has not been received. This list will also include purchase orders for which only partial orders have been received.

For Accounts Payable, print the "Payments Report" after posting the accounts payable to the general ledger. This report summarizes all payments to vendors for the day.

For the General Ledger, post your transactions and then print trial balances and financial statements. Financial statements include a balance sheet and an income statement, as well as other reports you might design yourself. (We discuss designing additional reports in Chapter 16.) If you have added accounts to your chart of accounts, re-print the chart.

Figure 11-13 outlines the daily tasks to be completed in the accounting and payroll modules. In addition, Fig. 11-13 presents, in outline form, a summary of the topics discussed in this chapter.

Summary

This chapter presents a summary of the daily accounting and payroll tasks that must be completed in the DacEasy *system. The tasks include daily entry in the purchasing and billing modules. Other tasks relate to paying the company's bills and being paid by the company's customers.*

End-of-day routines and posting tasks are also discussed in general terms.

This chapter is meant to be an overview of daily routines required to make DacEasy work for you. The specific procedures needed to complete these tasks are presented in the tutorial section, beginning with Chapter 17.

12

Periodic Accounting and Payroll Tasks

Chapter Goals
- *This chapter, reviews the periodic activities—those that are performed regularly but not necessarily daily—performed for accounting and payroll purposes. As in the last chapter, emphasis is on the structure and relationship of tasks that must be completed, rather than specific, in-depth steps to completing the tasks. Specifics are discussed in the tutorial chapters. The sample screens and reports in this chapter are used later in the tutorial chapters.*
- *We discuss periodic options from both the accounting and payroll modules. In addition, we discuss periodic data generated from the Reports module and the Financials module.*

  Routines that are specifically used at the end of an accounting year are discussed in Chapter 13.

This chapter is a summary of periodic accounting and payroll tasks. Do not enter any of the information printed here; this will be done in the tutorials.

Periodic Routines

There are several routines that should, or must, be completed regularly. One of the options from the *DacEasy Accounting* and *DacEasy Payroll* menus is "Periodic" routines. These routines permit you to perform most of the regularly scheduled routines for the end of each month, quarter, and year. There are also other routines that can provide valuable information if they are run periodically.

Periodic Financial Routines

The Financials options permits you to print several financial reports that are essential to the operation of your business (see Fig. 10-2). These include a balance sheet and income statement, as well as a report detailing the changes in your business' financial condition. These reports are automatic and can be printed at any time without having

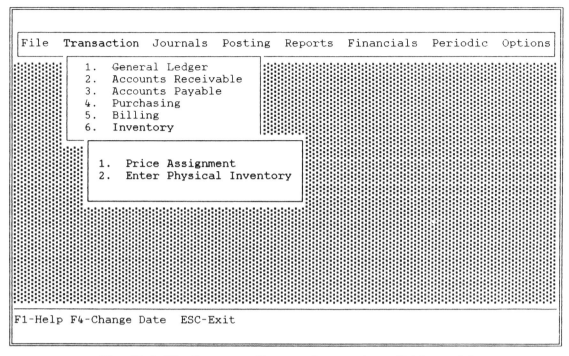

```
┌─────────────────────────────────────────────────────────────────────┐
│╔═══════════════════════════════════════════════════════════════════╗│
│║                                                                   ║│
│║ File  Transaction  Journals  Posting  Reports  Financials  Periodic  Options║│
│║ ┌──────────────────────────┐                                      ║│
│║ ░│ 1.   General Ledger      │░░░░░░░░░░░░░░░░░░░░░░░░░░░░░░░░░░░░░░░║│
│║ ░│ 2.   Accounts Receivable │░░░░░░░░░░░░░░░░░░░░░░░░░░░░░░░░░░░░░░░║│
│║ ░│ 3.   Accounts Payable    │░░░░░░░░░░░░░░░░░░░░░░░░░░░░░░░░░░░░░░░║│
│║ ░│ 4.   Purchasing          │░░░░░░░░░░░░░░░░░░░░░░░░░░░░░░░░░░░░░░░║│
│║ ░│ 5.   Billing             │░░░░░░░░░░░░░░░░░░░░░░░░░░░░░░░░░░░░░░░║│
│║ ░│ 6.   Inventory           │░░░░░░░░░░░░░░░░░░░░░░░░░░░░░░░░░░░░░░░║│
│║ ░└──┌──────────────────────────────────┐░░░░░░░░░░░░░░░░░░░░░░░░░░░║│
│║ ░░░░│ 1.   Price Assignment             │░░░░░░░░░░░░░░░░░░░░░░░░░░░║│
│║ ░░░░│ 2.   Enter Physical Inventory     │░░░░░░░░░░░░░░░░░░░░░░░░░░░║│
│║ ░░░░└──────────────────────────────────┘░░░░░░░░░░░░░░░░░░░░░░░░░░░║│
│║                                                                   ║│
│║ F1-Help  F4-Change Date   ESC-Exit                                ║│
│╚═══════════════════════════════════════════════════════════════════╝│
└─────────────────────────────────────────────────────────────────────┘
```

Fig. 12-1. The Inventory Transactions options. Pricing and inventory are two important procedures.

to design them, except to include new accounts (described in Chapter 10).

You can select the Financials option from the *DacEasy Accounting* Main Menu. Note that the window menu allows you to print the chart of accounts. You should do this periodically just to have a printed copy of the complete chart. During everyday operations, you might add new accounts and these will be listed on your newest printout.

Periodic Inventory Routines

From the *DacEasy Accounting* Main Menu, there are several options that permit you to update, or print, periodic data from your inventory. The Transactions options provides two such routines. The main function of these options is to allow you to periodically adjust your pricing (based on the percentage of profit, or on an absolute profit you want to make on each inventory item) and inventory counts so they will match the counts automatically updated through the Purchase Order and Billing modules.

Figure 12-1 shows the Inventory items from the Transaction module. Option 1 provides a work screen with a list of items from your inventory. The list will show your last price and give you the opportunity to set a percent mark-up, or a set amount of mark-up, for each item. The resulting price is displayed and, upon processing, the new price is sent to the inventory file where it becomes your new sales price. This is a very powerful tool to control your inventory and it should be used with care. Figure 12-2 shows the screen where you can set the inventory pricing.

```
 10/27/88                     PRICE ASSIGNMENT                      LHP
 02:34 PM                  Parts and Parcels, Inc.



 Product #     Description      Price    Last Cost    % OR $  New Price
 -----------   --------------   -------  ----------   ------- ---------
 BOARD01       2x4, Pine Stud     0.170      0.000 ▮
 BOARD51       Plywood, 3/4 4x   32.950      0.000
 CONDUIT01     Conduit, Alum 1    8.590      0.000
 CONDUIT07     Conduit, Plas 5   21.500      0.000
 GARDEN01      Hoe, Garden       19.950      0.000
 GARDEN09      Hose, Garden 25   11.880      0.000
 PAINT01       Paint, Wt Base    75.800      0.000
 PAINT02       Paint, Wt Base    83.400      0.000
 PIGMENT99     Pigment, Asst P  102.000      0.000
 WARES17       Oven, Toaster M   29.950      0.000




 F1-Help ALT P-Print   ESC-Exit
```

Fig. 12-2. Defining a mark-up as a percentage or a fixed amount. *The new price is automatically calculated and displayed.*

Option 2 from the inventory transactions window is where the actual inventory counts are entered once you have completed a physical inventory—one of those periodic processes that everyone who works in your business loves. *DacEasy* refers to your actual on-hand count as your "physical" inventory—that which you can physically lay hands on—and refers to the *DacEasy* count as the "perpetual" count—that which is going on automatically, from buying and selling.

Ideally, your physical count should always equal your perpetual count. There are, however, those taken-for-granted, mystical and magical forces in the universe that intervene, reducing physical inventory so it never quite matches up to what we thought we had.

Periodically, you will print "count sheets," and count the physical inventory in your warehouse or stockroom, writing down the actual counts. Figure 12-3 shows a sample of a count sheet, on which actual counts are recorded. These can be printed by department, bin, or other criteria so the counts can be completed more efficiently. Count sheets are printed from the Reports option on the *DacEasy Accounting* Main Menu.

Once the counts are completed and all the count sheets have been returned to the administrative office (or your desk, whichever comes first), they are entered into *DacEasy* through option 2 of the inventory transactions window (see Fig. 12-1). This work screen lists inventory items—sorted the same way your count sheets were sorted and printed—

```
Date : 10/27/88              Parts and Parcels, Inc.              Page no.  1
Time : 02:53 PM                 #2 Byfore Avenue
                             Greenwood, S.C. 29646
                               803/555-1685

Sorted by: Inventory #           Count Sheets            Ranked by: Inventory

Inventory # Description         Unit Frac Dept  Bin Vendor Units Frac Remarks
----------- -------------------- ---- ---- ----- --- ------ ----- ---- -------
BOARD01     2x4, Pine Stud 8Ft  BDFT 1    01    W01 SHAD01 _____.____ _____
BOARD51     Plywood, 3/4 4x8    SHET 1    01    W07 SHAD01 _____.____ _____
CONDUIT01   Conduit, Alum 16Ft  UNIT 1    01    E05 SINK01 _____.____ _____
CONDUIT07   Conduit, Plas 50Ft  COIL 1    01    E23 SINK01 _____.____ _____
GARDEN01    Hoe, Garden         UNIT 1    02    G01 SHOV01 _____.____ _____
GARDEN09    Hose, Garden 25Ft   UNIT 1    02    G03 SHOV01 _____.____ _____
PAINT01     Paint, Wt Base Gal  CASE 4    01    P01 PAIN01 _____.____ _____
PAINT02     Paint, Wt Base Qt   CASE 12   01    P02 PAIN01 _____.____ _____
PIGMENT99   Pigment, Asst Pt    CASE 24   01    P03 PAIN01 _____.____ _____
WARES17     Oven, Toaster M1203 UNIT 1    03    H41 NUTS01 _____.____ _____

            Total Products : 10 records
```

Fig. 12-3. A sample count sheet from the Inventory Reports options.

and you can enter the actual physical counts from the count sheets.

If you enter the counts by department, or some other method that might provide several different complementary counts, the counts are automatically added together to give you a running total.

When all the data from your count sheets are entered, print the ''Physical-Perpetual Comparison Report,'' which will list all inventory items, showing the physical count, the perpetual count, and the differences.

Using the comparison results, you can confirm your physical counts. Once counts are confirmed, you can post them to your accounting system (option 6 from the Posting option). Your inventory figures will be adjusted automatically to match the physical counts. Future perpetual counts are taken from the adjusted counts.

(Note that *DacEasy* also updates other accounting records that relate to any inventory adjustments.)

Periodic Reports Routines

The Reports module, which is accessed from the *DacEasy Accounting* Main Menu, provides 17 different sources of information. Several of these are not related to management decisions, but can reduce the time required to implement some of these decisions.

Figure 12-4 shows all the options available from the Reports module, overlapping each of the three sub-menus. The options in the Reports windows are divided into three categories: accounts receivable, accounts payable, and inventory.

Whenever you start a report from one of the Reports windows, you will be asked

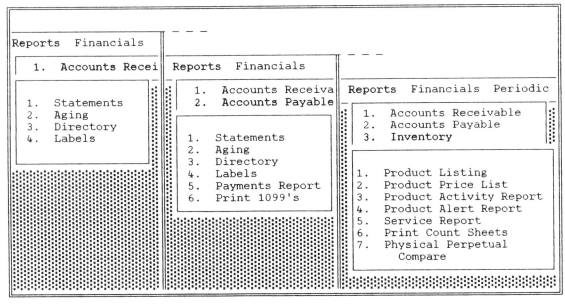

Fig. 12-4. Composite of Reports windows for Accounts Receivable, Accounts Payable, and Inventory.

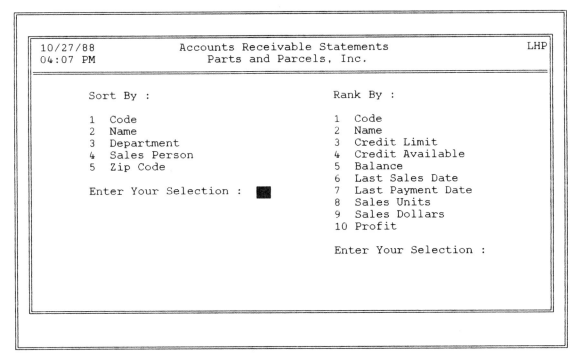

Fig. 12-5. Sorting and ranking options for reports from the Customer File.
The Rank By data generates subtotals based on the field you choose.

to name a "Sort By" field and a "Rank By" field. Figure 12-5 shows the sorting and ranking options available to you as you request information from *DacEasy Accounting*. The sorting field is the main division for sub-totals within your report. The ranking field indicates the rank of items listed within each sub-totaled group. For example, if you sort by Department and rank by Last Sales Date, your report will list and print items from the most recent sales date to the most remote sales date, and sub-totaled by department.

In accounts receivable, the "Statements" option prints statements for customers who have outstanding balances. It also can print statements for vendors with whom you have outstanding balances for accounts payable.

In the accounts receivable and accounts payable windows, you can print an "Aging Report." These reports give you an analysis tool for determining cash flow needs. These should be printed periodically to assist in your buying and expansion decisions.

Two other options under accounts receivable and accounts payable—-the "Directory"

```
Date : 10/27/88              Parts and Parcels, Inc.             Page no.  1
Time : 06:21 PM                 #2 Byfore Avenue
                             Greenwood, S.C. 29646
                                803/555-1685

Sorted by: Department        Product Price Listing     Ranked by: Inventory #

Inventory # Description        Unit  Fr  Dept Bin Vendor Tax Sales Pr  Code
---------- -------------------  ----  --  ---- --- ------ --- --------  ------
BOARD01     2x4, Pine Stud 8Ft  BDFT  1    01   W01 SHAD01  Y     0.170   P.POT
BOARD51     Plywood, 3/4 4x8    SHET  1    01   W07 SHAD01  Y    32.950  WQ.OTP
CONDUIT01   Conduit, Alum 16Ft  UNIT  1    01   E05 SINK01  Y     8.590   T.IOP
CONDUIT07   Conduit, Plas 50Ft  COIL  1    01   E23 SINK01  Y    21.500  QU.EWW
PAINT01     Paint, Wt Base Gal  CASE  4    01   P01 PAIN01  Y    75.800  TQ.ITP
PAINT02     Paint, Wt Base Qt   CASE  12   01   P02 PAIN01  Y    83.400  TQ.PPP
PIGMENT99   Pigment, Asst Pt    CASE  24   01   P03 PAIN01  Y   102.000  TQ.YPP

            Subtotal 01    :    7

GARDEN01    Hoe, Garden         UNIT  1    02   G01 SHOV01  Y    19.950  QW.WTP
GARDEN09    Hose, Garden 25Ft   UNIT  1    02   G03 SHOV01  Y    11.880   U.TPP

            Subtotal 02    :    2

WARES17     Oven, Toaster M1203 UNIT  1    03   H41 NUTS01  Y    29.950  QR.TYP

            Subtotal 03    :    1

            Total Products :    10 records


                 S A M P L E     1 2 3 4 5 6 7 8 9 0
                   C O D E
                 T A B L E       Q W E R T Y U I O P
```

Fig. 12-6. Encoding your costs. *You can assign alphabetic codes to the costs of your products, so your pricing formulas remain secret.*

and "Labels"—provide lists of customers and vendors and mailing labels from these two files.

In the inventory reports window, two of the options listed were discussed in Chapter 11 because they should be done on a daily basis. The last option, the "Product Listing" is just that—it lists all the products in your inventory, or it can list products within specified ranges of codes. This list serves the same purpose as the directories for accounts receivable and accounts payable—it gives you a printed reference of data in your files.

The "Product Price List" in the inventory reports options window is shown in Fig. 12-6. It lists your sale prices and your costs for each item in your inventory. You can code your cost figures, as we did in Fig. 12-6, by providing a 10-character code that *DacEasy* can use to replace the digits in the cost amounts. A sample code is given in Fig. 12-6, but the code does not print on the report.

Periodic Forecasting Routines

The Periodic module offers instant data for analysis in making decisions about the direction your business should take. It provides four different ways to look at data from your four major accounting areas. You can get forecasts from the general ledger, accounts receivable, accounts payable, and inventory and services as shown in Fig. 12-7.

In each of these four areas, *DacEasy* can perform the automatic calculations needed to make the predictions for analysis, print the forecast based on the calculations, and print the statistical year-to-date (YTD) data.

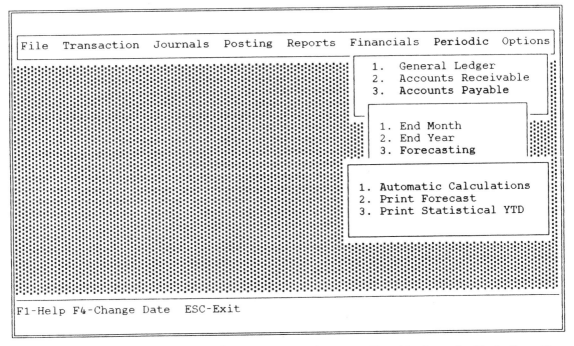

Fig. 12-7. Forecasting window for Accounts Payable from the Periodic option on the DacEasy Accounting Main Menu.

```
 10/29/88                  AP Forecast Calculation                      LHP
 09:14 AM                  Parts and Parcels, Inc.


    Calculation Method :                    Sort By :

    1  Previous Year                        1  Code
    2  Previous Year +/- Pct                2  Type
    3  Previous Year + Trend                3  Territory
    4  Trend Line Analysis
                                            Enter Your Selection :
    Enter Your Selection : █
```

Fig. 12-8. Calculation methods for forecasting with DacEasy Accounting. Data from previous years help to forecast the future.

Figure 12-8 shows the methods for calculating data for analysis. Data can be sorted by items included on the screens for each file. Figure 12-8 shows the sorting options for accounts payable (vendor code, type, and territory). Figure 8-3, the Vendor File Maintenance screen, includes this data. For the general ledger, calculation reports are sorted only by account number. For accounts receivable, calculations can be sorted by customer code, department, and sales person. From the inventory file, calculations can be sorted by inventory number, department, bin (warehouse location), and primary vendor. In services, reports can be sorted by inventory number and department.

Calculations can be based on one of four methods of analysis and forecasting. The first method uses the previous year's data, showing a comparison of current transactions. The second method calculates a percentage of the previous year's activity and either adds or subtracts this from the previous year's totals. The current year's activity is then compared to the anticipated growth or loss. The third method of calculation uses data that indicates natural trends in growth, based on the previous year's patterns. The fourth method is a statistical adjustment to the third, providing another level of analysis. All calculation methods are compared to the data for the current year.

The "Statistical YTD" option from the Forecasting windows prints the data at the bottom of each of the File Maintenance screens. From these reports, you can determine the value of customers, vendors, and products when planning future operations.

Periodic Payroll Routines

The most important periodic process in payroll is printing employee payroll checks. This can be done in any one or in all of the four periods, for which *DacEasy* keeps records.

Before printing payroll checks, however, there are a few recordkeeping and security measures that should be completed.

During each payroll period, you enter the exceptions to the regular payroll information (see Fig. 11-12). That is done in the Process option from the Payroll Main Menu. After any exceptions are entered, run the automatic payroll generator, which will create your payroll files for the current period. The payroll generator calculates and records all earnings, deductions, and employer taxes for each employee.

Once the payroll information has been organized by *DacEasy*, you need to print the Payroll Register, which is a summary of the payroll you are about to print. The Payroll Register allows you to catch any errors before actually printing the payroll checks.

After payroll checks are printed, print the check register, which lists all the checks that were printed. This is your official payroll report. In addition, you can print payroll reports by department as well as by special code, giving you several ways to analyze your payroll data.

The next step is to post the payroll data to the accounting system, a process that moves the appropriate amounts into the general ledger accounts. At this point, your payroll tasks are over until the next pay period.

DacEasy Accounting End-of-Month Routines

For each of the major accounting components (see Fig. 12-7) listed in the Periodic reports window in the *DacEasy Accounting* Main Menu, you can run end-of-month routines. These routines clear data that is no longer needed in the accounting system.

In the accounts receivable end-of-month process, all paid invoices are cleared out of the system. If you use the "open invoice" system (as we have done in all our examples), all invoices with zero balances are deleted from the system while all non-zero invoices are retained. In the "balance forward" system, all invoices with zero balances are deleted while all non-zero balances are totaled, which are carried forward into the next month.

You should run the accounts receivable end-of-month routine immediately after calculating finance charges and printing your customer statements. This prepares your files for the coming month, with your statements serving as a record for the previous month.

In the accounts payable end-of-month process, all invoices you have paid are cleared out of the system. If you are an "open invoice" customer, all invoices with zero balances are deleted and all non-zero invoices kept. If you are a "balance forward" customer, all zero invoices are deleted and all others are totaled, and a balance forwarded for the next month.

In the general ledger, all data for a given period comes together to give you the overall picture of your business. When you run the end-of-month posting, you will be asked to give the date of the last day in that month. Only transactions completed before this date will be posted.

Once all transactions are posted to the general ledger—accounts receivable and accounts payable, purchasing and billing, and inventory and services—your books are current.

One last word about the end-of-month routines before we go on to payroll. You can leave one or more months open—that is, unposted—if you need to wait for important information to include in your financial statements. Once that information is finally posted, you can close the month by giving the end-of-month date. Other items will not be posted at that time.

DacEasy Payroll End-of-Period Routines

Select the Periodic options shown in Fig. 12-9 from the *DacEasy Payroll* Main Menu to reconcile your payroll checks. This is done by instructing *DacEasy* which checks have cleared the bank or have been voided. This should be done every month.

After reconciling your checking records, return to the Payroll Main Menu and select the Payroll Processing option shown in Fig. 11-11 in the Process window. From this window, print your check register, requesting that only checks that have cleared the bank be included. This report will be your official record of checks that have been cashed.

Once your check register is printed, return to the Periodic window to purge the check file. Purging the file deletes all checks that have cleared the bank, leaving only those that you will keep records for. Now you can return to the Payroll Process window and print a check register of only the unpaid checks.

After these two routines have been done, you can run the end-of-period routines

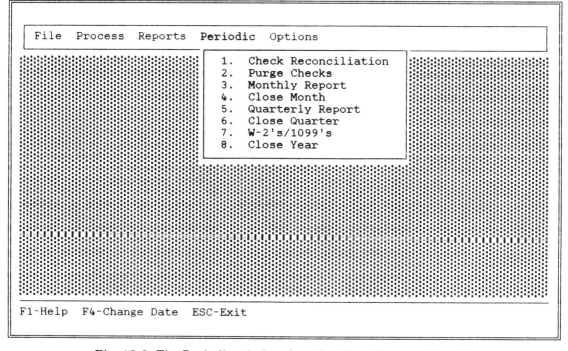

Fig. 12-9. The Periodic window from DacEasy Payroll. *Monthly, quarterly, and yearly reports are available.*

for *DacEasy Payroll* shown in Fig. 12-9. Although there are six routines, only four are discussed at this time. The other two options are discussed in Chapter 13.

The Monthly Report and the close-month options are run at the end of each month. The Monthly Report provides a list of all employees, payroll check patterns and areas in need of attention. The close-month routine clears the payroll files of unnecessary data but retains all information needed for quarterly reports and end-of-year forms.

The Quarterly Report provides information about your employees and the amounts of earnings that are subject to several taxes. This report is your official quarterly report and can be submitted to the appropriate state and federal agencies.

After printing your Quarterly Report—and only after printing it—run the close-quarter process, which moves all current quarter information to the previous quarter fields and clears the current quarter fields for new information of the new quarter. Summary data is maintained by the system in order to run end-of-year routines.

In addition to the procedures and reports discussed above for the payroll module, you can print a list of employees, including mailing labels with employee names and addresses. These items can be printed from the Reports window on the Payroll Main Menu.

Summary

In this chapter, all of the routines and reports that can be of value to you as you close out each week, month, or quarter within your accounting period are discussed. The discussion is of a general nature and is intended to give you an overall picture of the structure of the accounting and payroll modules.

13

End-of-Year Accounting
and Payroll Tasks

Chapter Goals
- *This chapter discusses the end-of-year procedures that must be completed to end each calendar year for payroll and each fiscal year for everything else. This is a general overview of these procedures, rather than in-depth instructions. Specifics are discussed in further detail in the tutorial chapters.*

The end-of-year procedures are designed to close out the current year and to make room for the new year's accounting information. All expense accounts and revenue accounts are accumulated into a capital account to indicate the current year's earnings. The expense and revenue accounts are then set to zero, so the new year can start anew. Asset accounts and liability accounts are retained and carried forward into the new year.

Preparing For the End

Before choosing the end-of-period options from the *DacEasy Accounting* Periodic windows (see Fig. 12-7 for an example), there are several small tasks that must be completed. These might have been completed in your end-of-month processing for the last month in the year and, if so, do not need to be duplicated in the end-of-year procedures.

In the Reports module, print any of the customized reports you have designed for analyzing your business' growth and needs. Also print all the Financial reports that apply to your business operations. If you don't print these before running the end-of-year processes, some of the data might be cleared to other accounts and would not be available for printing after the processes are completed.

From the Reports module, you can also print year-end listings of your customers and vendors. You might need your product listing and services report, which lists all available services. These lists can be valuable references during the next accounting year.

Your files of customers, vendors, inventory items, and services will be carried over into the next year and can be printed at any time during the next year.

From the Forecasting routines in the Periods windows, print statistical year-to-date reports from the general ledger, accounts receivable, accounts payable, and inventory. These reports provide important data for analysis and management decisions.

From the Financials window (see Fig. 10-2), print your trial balances (if you did not already do this at the end of the last month), balance sheet, income statement, and changes in financial conditions reports.

In the Payroll module, post your last payroll entries, print all your last quarter reports, and print your federal W-2 Forms and all Form 1099's. If you created and stored special report formats, you should print these as well. (We discuss creating and printing special report formats in Chapters 15 and 16.)

Once these preliminary steps are completed, you are almost ready to run the end-of-year procedures for all the modules in the *DacEasy* system. There is one other important task to be completed—you must make a backup copy of all your files and the programs that created them. If you are using *DacEasy Graph + Mate*, this can be done by pressing <ALT + F10> and selecting the Backup option. If you are not using *DacEasy Graph + Mate*, you must make backups from the DOS command level, using the BACKUP command. Consult your DOS manual for further information on using the BACKUP command. Also see the RESTORE command, which is used to put data back onto your fixed disk, should you need to.

End-of-Year Procedures

Figure 12-7 shows a sample window with the End Year option from *DacEasy Accounting*. This is the same menu from which you would run the end-of-month routines during the accounting year. For the general ledger, accounts receivable, accounts payable, and inventory files, there are specific end-of-year processes that must be run. In addition, there are specific end-of-year routines for payroll (see Fig. 12-9). We will take a brief look at these.

One important thing to keep in mind before starting the end-of-year process: The end-of-year process for the general ledger should be the last procedure run because the general ledger receives information from the other modules as they close the year.

Accounts Receivable

The end-of-year process for accounts receivable updates your customer file. It moves all current year's data to "last year," all of last year's data to the "year before last," and deletes all your year before last data. The "this year" fields are then set to zero so you can start the new year with new data. You can see the changes by viewing the work screens in the Files option from the main menu.

Accounts Payable

The end-of-year process for accounts payable does for the vendor file, what the end-of-year process for accounts receivable does for the customer file.

Inventory and Services

The end-of-year process for the inventory and services files moves all your statistical data back one year (as in accounts receivable and accounts payable).

After running the end-of-year procedures for the accounts payable, accounts receivable, and inventory and service, you are ready to leave the accounting module and run the payroll module.

Payroll

From the *DacEasy Payroll* Main Menu, select the Periodic option to access the close-year process.

The close-year process for payroll deletes all quarter-to-date and year-to-date data after the proper accounts have been updated through the department general ledger interface tables. Once these files are empty, you are ready to start the new payroll year.

General Ledger

The end-of-year process for the general ledger closes out the current fiscal year, accumulates all appropriate data from other modules, and posts them to the proper accounts. All revenue accounts and all expense accounts are emptied, and the balances placed in a capital account to determine any gain or loss for the year.

In Fig. 7-3, you can see the "Retained Earnings" account for 1987 (account number 3287). Figure 7-8 shows the screen used to add a "Retained Earnings" account for 1988 (account number 3288). For subsequent years, new "Retained Earnings" accounts would have to be added. As you start the end-of-year process, you will be asked for the account into which retained earnings are to be accumulated.

Summary

This chapter previewed the end-of-year procedures for DacEasy Accounting *and* DacEasy Payroll. *The overall procedures for using the* DacEasy *system—the structure and logic of the complete system—is explained throughout the last three chapters, providing you with a clearer picture of how* DacEasy *organizes and disseminates day-to-day operations, as well as end-of-month and end-of-year procedures.*

14

Point-of-Sale Accounting

Chapter Goals
- *This chapter discusses using* DacEasy Accounting *as a cash sales tool—that is, using the accounting system as the record-keeper for sales you make as they happen. This is called "point-of-sale" accounting. This process, when used as part of the overall accounting system, can save hours of time each week and greatly reduce the effort required to keep accurate sales records.*

One of the most time-consuming tasks in accounting is the daily recording of cash sales. You might use cash tickets or cash register tapes to track sales, however, these totals must be carried into the accounting system in some way—most often, manually.

Manually recording cash sales is probably the single most important factor in a poor inventory system in most small businesses. To manually maintain a perpetual inventory, not only must you account for the amounts placed in the general ledger accounts, you must also reduce the inventory count as items are sold.

Using *DacEasy Accounting* as a point-of-sale tool, you can maintain an up-to-the-minute accounting and inventory system without requiring any manual labor to update these files at the end of the day (as though that was done daily, anyway).

Point-of-Sale Accounting Essentials

In order to keep records for your walk-in cash-and-carry customers, you must have a means of recording the items they buy (so your inventory will be automatically updated) and a means of recording the amounts they pay (so your bank account can be automatically updated). These are the essentials.

In addition to the essentials, you can keep records concerning the type of payment (cash, credit card, etc.), the department in which the sale took place, and anything else that would be recorded if you were using the regular accounting features of *DacEasy*.

The Point-of-Sale Process

To record sales in *DacEasy Accounting*, you must have a customer file, an inventory file, and a customer invoice for the sale. In addition, you must have a purchasing system to maintain your inventory records. We assume the purchasing system is in place and your inventory file is complete. At this point, we will discuss using the customer file to record sales and the customer invoice to record inventory activity.

The Customer File

Some of your walk-in customers will have records in your customer file and you can continue to use these as customers come in. For point-of-sale accounting, which will probably involve many customers for whom you do not keep active records, you need several special "customer" records.

One of these "customers" will be called "Cash Sales" and will serve as the catch-all account for cash sales. When a walk-in customer makes a purchase and pays with cash, you can create an invoice for "Cash Sales" and fill in the items purchased, and the amount paid by the customer. Figure 14-1 gives an example of the "Cash Sales" record in the customer file.

If you use your customers as the basis of your departmentalization, you can create several "Cash Sales" customers, as illustrated in Fig. 14-1. For Department 02, the customer code could be CASH02. If your department basis is inventory (instead of

```
 10/29/88              CUSTOMER FILE MAINTENANCE               LHP
 11:33 AM              Parts and Parcels, Inc.

 Customer Code :   CASH01           Type (O=Open B=Balance):    O
 Name          :   Cash Sales                  Sales Person :  CASH
 Contact       :                            G/L Department:    01
 Address       :                            Discount %     :   0.00
 City          :                   State :  Discount Days :       0
 Zip Code      :           -    Tel : (   )   -   Due days  :       0
 Tax Id. Number:                            Message Code   :
 Credit Limit     :        0.00   Previous Balance  :       0.00
 Credit Available :        0.00   This Period Bal.  :       0.00
                                  Current Balance   :       0.00
 Last Sale Date   :   /  /        Last Payment Date :     /  /
 Month Int. Rate  :   0.00        Sales Tax Code    :   4 Rate:  5.000
 ═══════════════════ STATISTICAL INFORMATION ═══════════════════
           Yr.Bef.Lst Last Year This Year  Forecast  Variance    %

 # Invoices :      0         0         0         0        0       0.0
 $ Sales    :      0         0         0         0        0       0.0
 $ Costs    :      0         0         0         0        0       0.0
 $ Profit   :      0         0         0         0        0       0.0

 F1-Help  F2-Add Tax Rate  F6-DELETE  F7-Enter Invoice F10-Process  ESC-exit
```

Fig. 14-1. A sample cash "customer" for Department 01. A similar record can be created for Department 02, using CASH02 as the code.

customer), then having several "Cash Sales" customers might be of little, or no, value.

If you accept credit cards as payment, you might want to create a separate "customer" for each of the credit cards you accept. Each card could be represented by a code that is an abbreviation of the card name. By keeping credit card records, you are able to analyze data based on walk-in credit sales. The account records can also provide an audit trail to the actual credit card receipts. The summary of the account records should equal the total of the receipts filed with your bank.

Records similar to the "Cash Sales" customer can be set up for each credit card (see Fig. 14-1). The customer code might be CARD01, CARD02, or some other code that would provide information about the "customer." You might also enter the customer's name from the credit card in the Contact field and the card number in the address field (or vice versa).

The Invoice Procedure

When customer records are completed, you can treat every cash sale as an invoice process. When a cash customer enters the store and makes a purchase, you can go to your keyboard and enter the option for the Billing window in the Transactions module. When a blank invoice is displayed, press <ENTER> so that *DacEasy* can give you the next available invoice number.

```
                             Invoice #   01054
   Customer Code: CASH01      Remark:
   Cash Sales                                   Via
                                                FOB
                                                Your Ref. CK4567
                                -               Our Ref.  01054
   Disc. Days     0 Disc. % 0.00  Due Days    0  Tax Code: 4 Rate:  5.000

   Inv. #        Desc. Ordered   Shipped  Back Ord.   Price  Disc. Extended

   PAINT01       Paint, Wt Base Gal
                    2.002         2.002     0.000    75.800  0.00    189.50
   CONDUIT01     Conduit, Alum 16Ft
                    3.000         3.000     0.000     8.590  0.00     25.77




   Sub Total    Sales Tax    Total    Pmt.Ref.  Payment $   Net to Pay
     215.27        10.76    226.03    CASH        226.03        0.00

 F1-Help   F6-CANCEL   F10-Process   ALT D-Delete Line
```

Fig. 14-2. Completing a customer invoice for a cash sale. Customer codes are for cash customers, payment is entered at the bottom.

Figure 14-2 illustrates how the invoice is used when making a cash sale. A similar invoice can be used for credit card sales if you set up customer records for each of the credit cards you accept.

Sales Returns

As hard as you might work to please your customers, there will always be a few returns. There are two ways to deal with sales returns.

Negative Invoices. When an item for which cash was paid is returned, instruct *DacEasy* to give you the next invoice number and create a new invoice, using negative numbers to enter the number purchased and the purchase price. Inventory and sales will be adjusted when the day's posting is completed. (Oh, yes. Remember to give back the customer's money.)

Sales Return Routine. Instead of creating a negative invoice, you can use the Sales Return routine from the Billing transaction module. This is probably the best way to account for returned merchandise because the Sales Return form allows you to enter the original invoice number in the ''Our Reference'' field and will match the return to that invoice. (The negative invoice does not do this, thus you will have two invoices—the original and the negative—for which you must make special accounting considerations.)

The Results

If you use *DacEasy* for your cash sales, you will not have to enter cash sales data into the accounting system later. *DacEasy* can maintain all your accounting records and be ready to accept purchase orders and other customer orders whenever you have time to enter them.

If your inventory is the basis of your departmentalization, the invoicing process can maintain departmental sales for cash and credit cards as though they had gone through the accounting system as regularly-billed purchases.

Summary

DacEasy Accounting *can be used as a point-of-sale tool that generates sales tickets on the spot, automatically updates inventory, and lets you keep records for all cash and credit card sales.*

15

The Basics of Reporting

Chapter Goals
- *This chapter discusses the second most important aspect of an accounting system: Getting information out of the system after data has been entered. (And, of course, the most important aspect is entering good data.) We discuss the reports built into each* DacEasy Accounting *module, the reports included in the Reports and Financial modules, and reports available in the Payroll modules.*

In any decision-making process, valid information is needed. Making decisions without sound supportive data means that you have a very good chance of going out of business. It is worse, however, to make decisions based on bad data than to make decisions with no data at all.

We have discussed how you can collect, within *DacEasy Accounting* and *DacEasy Payroll*, good data to manage your business. After data is stored, the next task is to get it back out of the system in a format—or in several formats—that are most useful in helping you to make decisions about managing your business. This is the function of "reporting."

DacEasy Accounting and *DacEasy Payroll* provide a large number of built-in reports that are designed to help you make informative decisions about your business. In addition to the built-in reports, both *DacEasy* modules allow you to custom design reports that can give you specific information you might need to help make those decisions. *DacEasy* allows you great flexibility in designing reports. You can determine which information is included and the format in which it is displayed and printed. (Designing specialized reports is discussed in Chapter 16.)

We will begin with the *DacEasy Accounting* Main Menu and look at reports that are printed from the Journals option, the Reports option, and the Financials option. Then we discuss the reports that are built into the Payroll module.

Journals

Figure 15-1 shows the Journals window in the *DacEasy Accounting* Main Menu. All nine options in the window provide some type of report.

The General Ledger Journal Report

The General Ledger Journal Report includes summary information posted from all the modules in *DacEasy Accounting* and from direct entries into the general ledger. Figure 15-2 shows a sample journal report, containing summary information from the Cash Journal (abbreviated CA) and from the Purchase Journal (abbreviated PO).

The Cash Journal summarizes entries that were made directly into the general ledger (see the sample entry in Fig. 11-8). The description indicates the purpose of each entry. The Purchase Journal entries were made by *DacEasy Accounting*, using information from the Purchase Order module, consequently, the descriptions indicate that the data are summaries from this module.

If you keep in mind that the general ledger is the official record of your company's financial transactions, you can see that the General Ledger Journal Report is one of the most important reports you can print and analyze. It summarizes everything that has gone on in your business.

The General Ledger Account Activity Detail Report

The General Ledger Account Activity Detail Report prints a list of monthly activity in each account in your chart of accounts. Accounts in which there was no activity are not included in the report.

This report provides information about each account which your business had one, or more, transaction during the current month. You can check, for example, the status

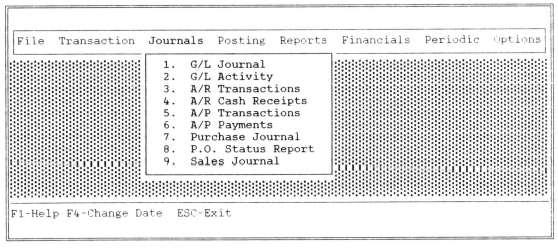

Fig. 15-1. The Journals window from the DacEasy Accounting Main Menu.

```
Date: 10/29/88                  Parts and Parcels, Inc.              Page No.  1
Time: 07:28 PM                      #2 Byfore Street
                                  Greenwood, SC 29646
                                    803/555-1685

                            General Ledger Journal Report

Journal                                                                    Post
Trans.#   Date    Acct #  Acct Name    Description      Debits    Credits   ed?
-------  -------- ------  ------------ ----------------- --------  --------  ----
CA 0001 10/29/88 11021   Checking Acc Personal Investme 25000.00            NO
                 11021   Checking Acc Loan Proceeds     50000.00            NO
                 2202    Notes Payabl Loan Proceeds               50000.00  NO
                 31011   Par Value    Personal Investme           25000.00  NO

                         TOTAL TRANSACTION:            75000.00 75000.00

PO 1223 10/29/88 11071   Inventory-Mo PO Summary        5636.53            NO
                 52091   Sales Tax/PO PO Summary         225.98            NO
                 2101    Accts Payabl PO Summary                   5862.51 NO

                         TOTAL TRANSACTION:             5862.51  5862.51

                         TOTAL TRANSACTION:            80862.51 80862.51

# OF ENTRIES PRINTED:   7
```

*Fig. 15-2. A sample General Ledger Journal Report. This report summarizes
all posted transactions from other modules, and from direct entries.*

of your accounts payable and accounts receivable as you analyze your cash flow for that
period. Figure 15-3 is a sample of the General Ledger Account Activity Detail Report.

The information presented in the Account Activity Detail Report is the same as that
printed in the General Ledger Journal Report, except the information is sorted by account
numbers, rather than journal names.

The General Ledger Journal Report and the General Ledger Account Activity Detail
Report should be printed every day. They must be printed before posting the day's
transactions to the general ledger because posting clears the transaction files, leaving
you with only the summary information that is posted. The printed copies of both those
reports are your official audit trail for transactions.

The Accounts Receivable Transactions Journal

The Accounts Receivable Transactions Journal lists all outstanding invoices that are
not entered through the Billing module. This journal also includes all adjusting transactions
entered directly into accounts receivable.

The list is sorted by transaction and gives each account number affected by the
transaction. The amounts posted to each account are itemized and then summarized in
the second part of the journal, titled "General Ledger Transfer Summary." This summary
is printed immediately after the detail report is printed.

195

```
Date: 10/29/88                    Parts and Parcels, Inc.                    Page No.  1
Time: 07:31 PM                        #2 Byfore Street
                                    Greenwood, SC 29646
                                        803/555-1685

                                G/L Account Activity Detail Report
                                    Complete Monthly Activity

Journal                                                                              Post
Trans.#   Date      Acct #  Acct Name    Description          Debits    Credits    ed?
-------   --------   ------  ------------ ------------------   --------  --------   ----
                     11021   Checking Acc BEGINNING BALANCE       0.00
CA 0001 10/29/88                          Personal Investme  25000.00               NO
CA 0001 10/29/88                          Loan Proceeds       50000.00               NO
                                          CURRENT BALANCE     75000.00

                     11071   Inventory-Mo BEGINNING BALANCE       0.00
PO 1223 10/29/88                           PO Summary          5636.53               NO
                                          CURRENT BALANCE      5636.53

                     2101    Accts Payabl BEGINNING BALANCE                 0.00
PO 1223 10/29/88                           PO Summary                    5862.51   NO
                                          CURRENT BALANCE               5862.51

                     2202    Notes Payabl BEGINNING BALANCE                 0.00
CA 0001 10/29/88                          Loan Proceeds                 50000.00   NO
                                          CURRENT BALANCE              50000.00

                     31011   Par Value    BEGINNING BALANCE                 0.00
CA 0001 10/29/88                          Personal Investme            25000.00   NO
                                          CURRENT BALANCE              25000.00

                     52091   Sales Tax/PO BEGINNING BALANCE       0.00
PO 1223 10/29/88                           PO Summary            225.98             NO
                                          CURRENT BALANCE        225.98

                      TOTAL TRANSACTIONS:                     80862.51 80862.51

# OF ENTRIES PRINTED:   7
```

Fig. 15-3. The General Ledger Account Activity Detail Report. *This report summarizes all posted transactions and lists them by account number.*

The Accounts Receivable Cash Receipts Journal

The Accounts Receivable Cash Receipts Journal (Fig. 15-4) is a summary of the money collected during the working day. The information provided in this report, and in the accounts payable journals allows you to evaluate your cash flow and gross earnings for a given day.

The Cash Receipts Journal is also your audit trail for cash deposits made to your bank accounts.

196

```
Date: 10/29/88              Parts and Parcels, Inc.              Page No.  1
Time: 10:03 PM                 #2 Byfore Street
                            Greenwood, SC 29646
                               803/555-1685

                 ACCOUNTS RECEIVABLE CASH RECEIPTS JOURNAL

Tran                                              Invoice  Discount    Check
No.   Acct #  Cust #  Invoice#    Date    Chk #  Type  Amount    Taken   Amount
----  ------  ------  --------  --------  ------  ----  -------  --------  -------
0001  11021   WEIR01  00001     10/29/88  3402   PMT.  426.22    12.79    413.43
              Acct. Total:                             426.22    12.79    413.43


   Grand Total:    # of Invoices     1                 426.22    12.79    413.43
```

*Fig. 15-4. A sample Accounts Receivable Cash Receipts Journal. Discounts
are automatically calculated and totals are given by account number.*

Both journals should be printed every day and both must be printed before posting
the accounts receivable file. Posting clears the accounts receivable transactions file and
posts only summary information for use in the general ledger.

The Accounts Payable Transactions Journal

The Accounts Payable Transactions Journal includes all outstanding bills owed by
your business that are not entered through the Purchase Order module. These amounts
are entered through the transactions entry option on the Accounts Payable transactions
window.

The list is sorted by transaction and gives each account number affected by the
transaction. The amounts posted to each account are itemized and then summarized in
the second part of the journal, titled "General Ledger Transfer Summary." This summary
is printed immediately after the detail report is printed.

The Accounts Payable Payments Journal

The Accounts Payable Payments Journal lists all the checks written the day the journal
is printed. Actually, the list includes all check transactions, including voided checks and
hand-written checks, as well as those printed through the Accounts Payable module.
The report can help reconcile your checking accounts because it is sorted by checking
account number and listed by check number under each account.

In addition to check information, the journal includes information about the amount
of each invoice and the effect of taking available discounts. The list includes each invoice
rather than summaries of the totals paid to every vendor.

Other accounts payable transactions are detailed in the journal as well. Consequently,
it is a concrete record of all cash disbursements for a given period.

The Purchase Journal

The Purchase Journal is really two reports in one. The first part is the Purchase Journal Report, the second part, the Purchase Journal Report Summary, by Inventory and Code. Figure 15-5 gives a sample of each.

The Purchase Journal Report—the first part—provides a clear audit trail for tax expenses and the amounts that will be posted to accounts payable. The totals for inventoried items will be posted to inventory assets. The information provided in this journal gives you a clear picture of a very important aspect of managing your business.

The Summary by Inventory and Code—the second part of the Purchase Journal—reflects the day's merchandise received. The number of items received, the gross

```
Date: 10/30/88                Parts and Parcels, Inc.              Page No. 1
Time: 08:03 AM                    #2 Byfore Street
                                Greenwood, SC 29646
                                   803/555-1685

                            PURCHASE JOURNAL REPORT

        Vend P.O.   Vender
Type    Dept Number Code    Vender Name      Date       Gross      Tax     Total
-----   ---- ------ ------  --------------   --------   --------   ------  --------
PURCH PT     00006  PAIN01 Paint By The N 10/30/88     1037.00    49.78   1086.78
                    Purchase Total :                   1037.00    49.78   1086.78
                    Department Total :                 1037.00    49.78   1086.78

                    Grand Totals :                     1037.00    49.78   1086.78
```

```
Date: 10/30/88                Parts and Parcels, Inc.              Page No. 2
Time: 08:03 AM                    #2 Byfore Street
                                Greenwood, SC 29646
                                   803/555-1685

                            PURCHASE JOURNAL REPORT
                         SUMMARY BY INVENTORY AND CODE
                                                        Avg./    Last    %
Dept Type  Item/Acct#  Description      Units    Amount Unit   P.Price Var.
---- ----- ----------  ---------------  ------- -------- ------ ------- ----
01   PROD  PAINT01     Paint, Wt Base   20.000  1037.00 51.85   0.00  0.00
                       Code Total :             1037.00

                       Department Total :       1037.00

                       Grand Total :            1037.00
```

Fig. 15-5. A sample Purchase Journal Report. Part 1 gives details by activity type; part 2 gives details by inventory item.

purchase price, and other information. The average unit cost is given and compared to the last purchase price. The report indicates the percent difference between the average cost for this purchase and the last purchase.

If your purchases include non-inventoried items, these are also listed in the summary and are categorized by the code set up in the purchasing and billing codes routines (see Figs. 7-11 and 7-12).

The report also includes information about items that are returned to vendors. This information could be useful when making decisions about future purchases, especially if the vendor's quality control seems suspect.

The Purchase Order Status Report

The Purchase Order Status Report should be printed after end-of-day posting is completed in the Purchase Order module. Posting clears purchase orders that were fulfilled during the day, leaving only purchase orders for which merchandise has not yet been received. Unfulfilled purchase orders are listed in the Purchase Order Status Report, as well as purchase orders for which there are back orders.

The Sales Journal

The Sales Journal is as important to the Billing module as the Purchase Journal is to the Purchasing module. When you compare Fig. 15-6 to Fig. 15-5, you can see the similarities in the reports.

The Sales Journal provides a clear audit trail for tax liabilities and amounts that are to be posted to accounts receivable. The totals for inventoried items are deleted from inventory assets (since they are no longer in your inventory). You can see that the information provided in this journal gives you a clear picture of a very important aspect of managing your business.

The Summary by Inventory and Code—the second part of the Sales Journal—reflects the day's merchandise sold. The number of items sold, the gross sales price, and other information is given. The average unit price is given and compared to the purchase price in the inventory file. The report indicates the percent difference between the average price for the item and the official sale price.

If your sales include non-inventoried items, they are also listed in this summary and are categorized by the code set up in the purchasing and billing code routines (see Fig. 7-11).

This report also includes information about items that are returned by customers. This information might be useful in deciding whether to follow up with customer about why they returned the merchandise. It can also help you decide on merchandise purchased from certain vendors.

In Chapter 14, we discussed using *DacEasy Accounting* for point-of-sale operations. The Purchase Journal and the Sales Journal make point-of-sale process even more important in updating and maintaining your inventory records. All of these summaries can provide specific information about inventory movement on a daily basis—if you include information in the accounting system as you make sales and process purchases. The alternative is to update manually from written records used at the point-of-sale or the purchase.

```
Date: 10/30/88              Parts and Parcels, Inc.              Page No.  1
Time: 08:15 AM                  #2 Byfore Street
                             Greenwood, SC 29646
                                803/555-1685

                             SALES JOURNAL REPORT

       Cust Inv/Rt Cust
Type   Dept Number Code   Customer Name     Date      Gross     Tax    Total
-----  ---- ------ ------ --------------- --------- --------- ------- --------
INV    01   00001  WEIR01 Weir Lighting   10/30/88   404.77   21.45   426.22
                          Invoice Total  :           404.77   21.45   426.22
                          Department Total :         404.77   21.45   426.22

                          Grand Totals :            404.77   21.45   426.22
```

```
Date: 10/30/88              Parts and Parcels, Inc.              Page No.  2
Time: 08:15 AM                  #2 Byfore Street
                             Greenwood, SC 29646
                                803/555-1685

                             SALES JOURNAL REPORT
                         SUMMARY BY INVENTORY AND CODE
                                                      Avg./     Sale   %
Dept Type   Item/Acct# Description     Units  Amount  Unit     Price  Var.
---- ------ ---------- --------------- ------ ------- ------  ------- ----
01   PROD   CONDUIT01  Conduit, Alum   3.000   25.77   8.59    8.59  0.00
01   PROD   PAINT01    Paint, Wt Base  5.000  379.00  75.80   75.80  0.00
                       Code Total :           404.77

                       Department Total :     404.77

                       Grand Total :          404.77
```

*Fig. 15-6. A sample Sales Journal Report. Part 1 gives details by activity type;
part 2 gives details by inventory item or service.*

Other Important Reports from Accounts Payable

Two additional reports that are important in the accounts payable module are printed
from other options windows.

The Accounts Payable Checks-to-Print Journal

The Accounts Payable Checks-to-Print Journal is printed from the Transactions
window for accounts payable. The Checks-to-Print Journal list transactions for which
checks are to be printed. From this list, you can decide which checks to print, as well
as·checks not to print. The list can also be used to consider discounts offered by your

```
Date: 10/30/88                  Parts and Parcels, Inc.              Page No.  1
Time: 08:35 AM                       #2 Byfore Street
                                  Greenwood, SC 29646
                                     803/555-1685

                   ACCOUNTS PAYABLE CHECKS TO PRINT JOURNAL

Tran                                            Invoice   Discount    Amount
No.   Vendor      Vendor Name          Invoice#  Amount     Taken     To Pay
----  ------ -------------------------  -------- -------  --------   ------
0001  PAIN01 Paint By The Numbers, Inc  A23409  2109.26     31.64   2077.62
      Check Total:  # of Invoices          1    2109.26     31.64   2077.62


      Grand Total:  # of Invoices          1    2109.26     31.64   2077.62
```

Fig. 15-7. A sample Accounts Payable Checks-to-Print Journal. This includes all payables from purchasing and direct entries.

vendors, and can help you take advantage of discounts before the period ends. Figure 15-7 contains a sample Accounts Payable Checks-to-Print Journal.

The Accounts Payable Payments Report

The Accounts Payable Payments Report should not be confused with the Accounts Payable Payments Journal. The Journal is discussed above. The Payments Report is printed from the Reports window for accounts payable. It provides a list of invoices sorted by the discount date. The available discount is given, as well as the discounted amounts due and the regular amounts due. You can analyze the impact of paying before the discount days, making comparisons to other information that will detail your available cash.

The Payments Report should be analyzed before deciding which checks to pay, while the Accounts Payable Payments Journal should be analyzed after checks are printed for payment.

The Financials

There are three pre-defined reports available from the Financials option on the *DacEasy Accounting* Main Menu (see Fig. 10-2). The Trial Balance Report, the Balance Sheet and Income Statement, and the Statement of Changes in Financial Conditions provide important information regarding the financial status of your business.

The Trial Balances

After posting all transactions to the general ledger, you can print the trial balances from your chart of accounts. The Trial Balance Report shows the month's beginning balance, the month's activity, and the month's ending balance (called the ''current balance'' on the report). The ending balances are, of course, the beginning balances for the new month and accumulate so that the last report for a year summarizes the year.

From the trial balances, you can determine the accounts in which your business had activity and make decisions about efforts for the coming period. It also lets you examine your accounting summaries in case there are errors which can be found and corrected. The trial balances are also useful to your accountant or independent auditors who work with your books. In fact, independent auditors create a system of trial balances at the beginning of their work in your recordkeeping system.

The Balance Sheet and Income Statement

The Balance Sheet provides a look at all levels of your accounting system. Account levels are printed, in the detail that you request, and level one accounts for assets are balanced against liabilities and equity account totals (thus supporting the oldest known mathematical formula in the world—assets equal liabilities plus equity). By printing all five levels of accounts you can see the major activities contributing to your assets and liabilities. The equity accounts will include current earnings, which *DacEasy* calculates from the revenue and expense accounts.

The Income Statement is sometimes called the "profit-and-loss statement" and includes the values for the revenue and expense accounts. The difference between the two types of accounts is equal to the net income—that is, the profit (or loss)—for your company. That net income is posted to the current earnings account (which is an equity account) and is then included in the Balance Sheet. You can trace this amount back to the Balance Sheet, taking the net income from the Income Statement to the Retained Earnings account on the Balance Sheet.

In effect, the Balance Sheet summarizes your assets, liabilities, and equity in the company. The assets must be equal to the sum of the liabilities and equity. The Income Statement includes the balances from the revenue and expense accounts and indicates your net profit or loss for the current year.

The Changes in Financial Condition Statement

The Statement of Changes in Financial Condition is sometimes called the "Statement of Changes in Sources and Uses of Finances." This report summarizes the changes represented by three years of business operations. If you haven't used *DacEasy* that long, it will set previous years' values to zero and calculate changes from those.

The Changes in Financial Condition Statement tells you where your money is coming from and where it is going by pinpointing accounts where changes have occurred. Account amounts will indicate amounts that have gone toward certain uses and amounts that came from certain sources.

You can request that the report include all accounts, a range of accounts, or only accounts in which there has been activity that relates to changes in financial condition. *DacEasy* summarizes the appropriate accounts automatically as it prepares the report for printing.

Figure 15-8 shows the headings for the columns of information included in the Statement of Changes in Financial Condition. You can see that this report shows the differences in consecutive years' activity, detailing the sources and uses of funds.

The Financial Statements Generator Reports

There are four special financial statements that are built into the Financials module.

```
┌─────────────────────────────────────────────────────────────────────────┐
│ Date: 10/30/88            Parts and Parcels, Inc.         Page No.  1     │
│ Time: 09:11 AM               #2 Byfore Street                             │
│                             Greenwood, SC 29646                           │
│                               803/555-1685                                │
│                                                                           │
│              STATEMENT OF CHANGES IN FINANCIAL CONDITIONS                 │
│                                                                           │
│              Last Yr-Yr Bef.Last This Yr  Last Yr  Current   Period       │
│ Acct # Account Name  Sources  Uses   Sources   Uses    Sources   Uses     │
│ ------ -------------- --------- --------- -------- ------- ------- --------- │
│    .        ..          ..        ..        ..       ..      ..       ..   │
│    .        ..          ..        ..        ..       ..      ..       ..   │
│    .        ..          ..        ..        ..       ..      ..       ..   │
│    .        ..          ..        ..        ..       ..      ..       ..   │
│    .        ..          ..        ..        ..       ..      ..       ..   │
│    .        ..          ..        ..        ..       ..      ..       ..   │
└─────────────────────────────────────────────────────────────────────────┘
```

Fig. 15-8. The columns of information contained in the Changes of Financial Conditions Statement. This is a powerful management report.

These built-in financial statements are available from the Financial Statements Generator option in the Financials window on the *DacEasy Accounting* Main Menu (see Fig. 10-2).

The built-in reports are named BAL (for "Balance Sheet"), INC (for "Income Statement"), RA1 (for "Ratio Analysis Report Number 1"), and RA2 (for "Ratio Analysis Report Number 2").

The Balance Sheet and Income Statement printed from option 3 in the Financials window is more detailed than the two reports included in the Generator. The report formats available through the Generator contain summary data for the original report formats described above. While the Balance Sheet and Income Statement cannot be modified, the "BAL" and "INC" files listed in the Generator can be modified in the Generator (as discussed in Chapter 10 and shown in Figs. 10-3 and 10-4).

The first Ratio Analysis Report offers comparative data about cash availability, current assets, and short-term liability. These ratios are used by banks and other financial institutions to determine your capability to pay short-term debts and are considered in the approval of credit.

The second Ratio Analysis Report offers comparative data about your ability to pay the interest on liabilities, the number of times you "turnover" your inventory, the percentage of net sales that is tied up in accounts receivable, fixed assets, and total assets. These are all measures of your ability to make a profit. To further provide information about your "profitability," the report includes ratios relating your after-tax profits to total revenues, total assets, and equity before profit.

The financial statements printed from this routine are used more by financial institutions than by you. They provide further information on your ability to deal with your liabilities and debts.

Other report formats can be created in this module. The names that you give these formats are added to the list of formats that are displayed in the Financial Statements Generator option. Creating specialized reports is discussed in Chapter 16.

The Reports

Figure 12-4 shows a composite of the Reports option windows. It is divided into three sections: listing reports for accounts receivable, accounts payable, and inventory and services.

The Accounts Receivable and Accounts Payable Reports

The four receivable accounts are similar to the four accounts payable reports in that they have the same basic format and purpose—the difference being the source of the data included in the reports. The accounts receivable reports collect data from the billing and customer files; the accounts payable reports collect data from the purchasing and vendor files.

Statements. For your accounts receivable, statements are an integral part of your business operation. Statements can be mailed to customers who have past due accounts. For accounts payable, statements are simply records of invoices your business has not paid. These would almost never be mailed to the vendor but would be used for internal purposes.

Aging Reports. Aging Reports for accounts receivable and accounts payable are one of the most valuable tools for predicting and planning cash flow. You can choose to sort and rank by any of the criteria offered in the Reports module (see Fig. 12-5).

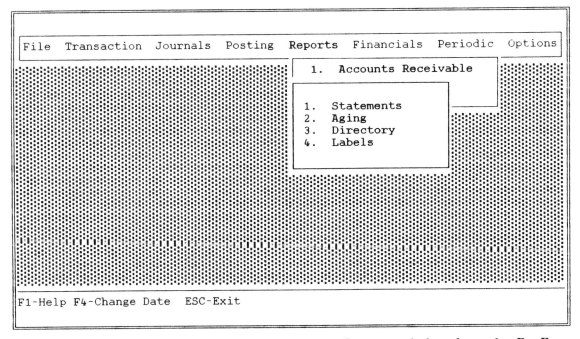

Fig. 15-9. The Accounts Receivable Reports window from the DacEasy Accounting Main Menu. *The Aging Reports provide data for analysis of cash flow and financial conditions.*

You can choose to sort and print particular ranges as well as define the number of days in each aging period. Figure 15-10 shows the set up screen for the Aging Reports. Figure 15-11 shows a sample Aging Report for accounts receivable.

In the sample Aging Report in Fig. 15-11, we sorted by department. In the Accounts Receivable Aging Report, the department is determined by the G/L Department field in each customer's record (see Fig. 8-1). For accounts payable, the department is determined by the vendor Type field in each vendor's record (see Fig. 8-3).

The aging period is pre-set to 30 days each period (except on the two ends, where the limits are 9999 and −9999, which will encompass any delinquent amounts). If you need more precise information for short-term cash flow, you can change the length of these seven aging periods. Whenever you start to print the aging report, a small window will open and ask if you want to edit the aging periods. Simply answer ''Yes'' and change the ''From'' and ''To'' columns appropriately. The seven ranges of days that you define in the set up screen become the columns printed in the actual Aging Report (compare Figs. 15-10 and 15-11).

Directories. You can print lists of your customers (from the accounts receivable side) or vendors (from the accounts payable side) by selecting the appropriate Directory option. These list include names, addresses, current status of account, and several other pieces of information. If you use ID numbers or codes that are not easily remembered, you will want to print these directories and keep them near your work area.

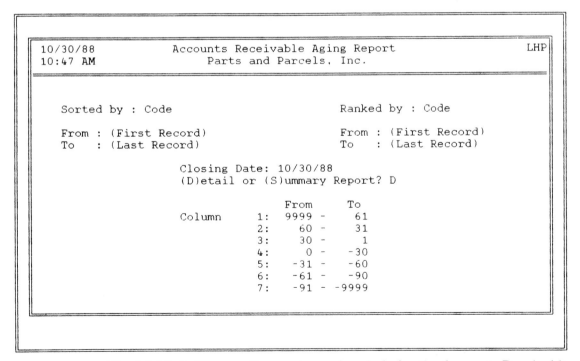

Fig. 15-10. Setting up the ranges and periods for the Accounts Receivable Aging Report. *''From'' and ''To'' indicate periods of days.*

```
Date: 10/30/88              Parts and Parcels, Inc.              Page No.  1
Time: 09:56 AM                 #2 Byfore Street
                              Greenwood, SC 29646
                                 803/555-1685

Closing Date: 10/30/88                              Codes:
Sorted by...: Department        AGING REPORT        1 Invoice   4 Payment
Ranked by...: Code          ACCOUNTS RECEIVABLE     2 Debit     5 Credit
*  Not posted                                       3 Fin Chg   6 Discount

                            9999/    60/    30/     0/    -31/    -61/    -91/
Invoice Date     Code Amount  61     31      1    -30     -60     -90   -9999
------- -------- ---- ------ ------ ------ ------ ------ ------ ------ ------
WEIR01  Weir Lighting Fixtures
------- -------------------- ------
00001   12/23/87  1*  426.22   0.00   0.00   0.00 426.22   0.00   0.00   0.00
                             ------ ------ ------ ------ ------ ------ ------
        Total         426.22   0.00   0.00   0.00 426.22   0.00   0.00   0.00

        Total         426.22   0.00   0.00   0.00 426.22   0.00   0.00   0.00

        Total         426.22   0.00   0.00   0.00 426.22   0.00   0.00   0.00
```

Fig. 15-11. A sample aging report for Accounts Receivable. *This shows $426.22 due within 30 days; compare it with the Payables Aging Report.*

Labels. You can print mailing labels for some, or all, of your customers or vendors when you select the appropriate Labels option. If you have defined your territories, departments, types, and other information in a useful and appropriate manner, you can select subsets of your files when printing labels.

Additional Accounts Payable Reports. The Reports window for accounts payable includes two reports that are not included in the accounts receivable window. The first of these is the Payments Report, which is discussed earlier in the chapter. The second option in the window, prints information used in completing the Form 1099 for contracted services. This report summarizes information for all vendors that have "1099" in the Type field in the Vendor File Maintenance screen (see Fig. 8-3).

The Inventory Reports

Figure 12-4 shows that there are seven separate reports for inventory and services available from the Reports inventory window.

Product Listing. The Product Listing is to inventory as the Directory is to accounts receivable or accounts payable. It provides a list of some, or all, of the items that have been assigned to inventory. The listing includes product codes, descriptions, and the current inventory status. This listing does not include services.

Product Price List. The Product Price List is discussed in Chapter 12 and Fig. 12-6 shows a sample list.

Product Activity Report. The Product Activity Report lists items in inventory including summaries of prices, costs, purchases, numbers on-hand, sales, profit, turns, and gross return on investment (abbreviated "G.R.O.I." on the report format). This list lets you see which items need to go on sale, which you need to change minimums for, which are money-makers (and which are not), and other types of information. At a glance, you can see the value of your inventory as well as the total profits, by department.

Product Alert Report. The Product Alert Report, which should be printed daily, includes all items that have current counts below the minimum you set for them in the product file (see Fig. 8-5). This report is the basis for orders placed the next day.

Service Report. The Service Report is a list of services you've included in your services file. It includes codes, descriptions, departments, and prices. It's purpose is the same as the Product Inventory List.

Count Sheets. Printing count sheets does not provide specific information about your inventory. Instead, it provides, a form on which you can take actual inventory counts

```
Date: 10/30/88           Parts and Parcels, Inc.            Page No.  1
Time: 10:51 AM              #2 Byfore Street
                         Greenwood, SC 29646
                           803/555-1685

Sorted by: Department     Physical-Perpetual      Ranked by: Inventory #
                          Comparison Report


                                           Perpetual Physical Difference
Inventory #  Description     Unit Fr Dept Bin Unit Frac Unit Fra Unit Frac
-----------  -------------   ---- -- ---- --- ----- --- ---- --- ----- ---
BOARD01      2X4, Pine Stud 8F BDFT 1   01  W01  6000.000 6000.000    0.000
BOARD51      Plywood, 3/4 4x8 SHET 1   01  W07    75.000   75.000     0.000
CONDUIT01    Conduit, Alum 16F UNIT 1   01  E05   122.000  122.000    0.000
CONDUIT07    Conduit, Plas 50F COIL 1   01  E23    25.000   25.000    0.000
PAINT01      Paint, Wt Base Ga CASE 4   01  P01    20.000   20.000    0.000
PAINT02      Paint, Wt Base Qt CASE 12  01  P02    10.000   10.000    0.000
PIGMENT99    Pigment, Asst. Pt CASE 24  01  P03     4.000    4.000    0.000

             Subtotal 01       :   7

GARDEN01     Hoe, Garden      UNIT 1   02  G01     6.000    6.000     0.000
GARDEN09     Hose, Garden 25Ft UNIT 1   02  G03     6.000    6.000    0.000

             Subtotal 02       :   2

WARES17      Oven, Toaster M12 UNIT 1   03  H41    12.000   12.000    0.000

             Subtotal 03       :   1

             Total Products    :   10 records
```

Fig. 15-12. A sample inventory report comparing "perpetual" inventory (counts kept in the accounting system) to "physical" inventory (counts made on the floor). This report is balanced by adjusting costs of goods sold.

from your warehouse or stockroom. Count sheets are discussed in Chapter 12 and Fig. 12-3 includes a sample form.

Physical/Perpetual Comparison Report. After you determine the actual count of inventory items you have on your shelves and in the warehouse, enter them into the inventory module from within the Transactions inventory window (see Fig. 12-1). *DacEasy* compares the actual counts with the "perpetual" counts it has been keeping as you purchased and sold inventory items. The Physical/Perpetual Comparison Report lists discrepancies between the two counts (see Fig. 15-12). This report is the audit trail for adjustments made in your inventory. After printing the report, you can instruct *DacEasy* to adjust its perpetual counts to match the physical counts so that the value of your inventory is more accurate. If large differences exist, or consistently show up in the report, you might want to evaluate your security system and the habits of some of your employees.

Periodic Forecasting

The Forecasting modules built into the Periodic procedures windows permit you to print forecasts based on as many as three years' data. In addition to the forecasts, you can print statistical year-to-date information that summarizes the information shown on customer, vendor, inventory and services, and the chart of accounts work screens. These reports can be printed from the general ledger, accounts receivable, accounts payable, and inventory and services reports.

Reports are discussed in Chapter 12. Figures 12-7 and 12-8 illustrate some factors to consider when printing these reports.

Payroll Reports

Reports from the Payroll module are important in the operation of your business. The Payroll module offers several pre-defined report formats and the capability to create original formats that you can design and use as your business grows.

The Payroll Reports

Figure 15-13 shows the Payroll Reports window and the options available.

The first option in the Payroll Reports window permits you to create specialized report formats, using the Report Generator that can be saved and recalled whenever they are needed. Creating specialized payroll reports are discussed in Chapter 16.

The employee directory, unlike the vendor and customer directories, is not a list of employees. Instead, the employee directory prints one page for each employee that includes everything placed on the work screen in the employee's file (see Figs. 9-13, 9-14, and 9-15).

The employee labels option lets you print two types of labels: mailing labels which include names and addresses; and time card labels which include name, department, classification, and ID code. Each type of label must be printed "one-up" and be at least 3-5 inches wide and six lines long. The number of lines can be adjusted up to a maximum of 66.

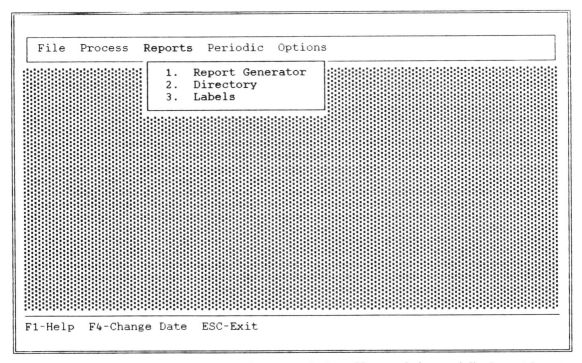

```
┌─────────────────────────────────────────────────────────────────────────────┐
║                                                                             ║
║  ┌───────────────────────────────────────────────────────────────────────┐ ║
║  │  File   Process   Reports   Periodic   Options                         │ ║
║  └──┬────────────────┬─────────────────────────────────────────────────┬──┘ ║
║     :::::::::::::::::│  1.   Report Generator  │:::::::::::::::::::::::::::::: ║
║     :::::::::::::::::│  2.   Directory         │:::::::::::::::::::::::::::::: ║
║     :::::::::::::::::│  3.   Labels            │:::::::::::::::::::::::::::::: ║
║     ::::::::::::::::└───────────────────────────┘:::::::::::::::::::::::::::: ║
║     :::::::::::::::::::::::::::::::::::::::::::::::::::::::::::::::::::::::::::: ║
║                                                                             ║
║   F1-Help   F4-Change Date   ESC-Exit                                       ║
║                                                                             ║
└─────────────────────────────────────────────────────────────────────────────┘
```

Fig. 15-13. The Payroll Reports window. *You can design specialized report formats, print lists of employees, and print mailing labels or time card labels.*

The Periodic Payroll Reports

Two reports are available from the Periodic window on the Payroll Main Menu (see Fig. 12-9)—the Monthly Report and the Quarterly Report. The Monthly Report summarizes payroll activity for the month and the Quarterly Report is designed to report FICA and income tax information to appropriate government agencies. Both can be used to analyze payroll liabilities and expenses. Both reports are discussed in Chapter 12.

The Payroll Process Reports

From the Payroll Process window (Fig. 11-11), you can print several important reports. These include the Payroll Register (a list of checks to be printed), the Checks Register (a list of checks that have been printed), and the Department Report (a payroll summary by department and special code). These reports are discussed in Chapter 12 as part of the periodic procedures required in the payroll process.

Summary

This chapter discusses most of the reports that are built into DacEasy Accounting and DacEasy Payroll. The purpose of these reports is included as an aid to using them for making decisions about the way you run your business.

16

Creating Specialized Reports

Chapter Goals
- *This chapter describes three ways you can create specialized reports for* DacEasy *files. We discuss creating and editing financial reports that can be printed from the accounting module; creating and editing reports that can be printed from the payroll files; and creating and editing files that can be printed from* DacEasy Graph + Mate.

Despite the abundance of report formats built into the *DacEasy* system, there is always the need to get data out of files in a format that might not be built-in. For example, you might need a list of customers ranked in order of "profitability" to the business—that is, you might want to stage a special sale for customers who have contributed the most to your profits for the last year. There is not a built-in report that provides this information.

  DacEasy Accounting can create specialized reports that give you a variety of views of your accounts and their relationship with other accounts. In *DacEasy Payroll*, you can create specialized reports that provide information about your employees, your payroll liabilities, and other information. With *DacEasy Graph + Mate*, you can expand reporting capabilities to include information from files other than the chart of accounts.

  One difficulty creating specialized reports using *DacEasy* software is that all three modules—Accounting, Payroll, and Graph + Mate—have different techniques for producing reports, however, none of the report techniques are difficult to master.

DacEasy Accounting Reports

  In *DacEasy* accounting, you can create original reports only from the general ledger chart of accounts. You cannot create reports that include customer, vendor, or inventory information. (*DacEasy Graph + Mate* permits you to create specialized reports using these files. This is discussed later in the chapter.) Figure 16-1 shows the Financial Statements Generator window where reports in the accounting module can be created or edited.

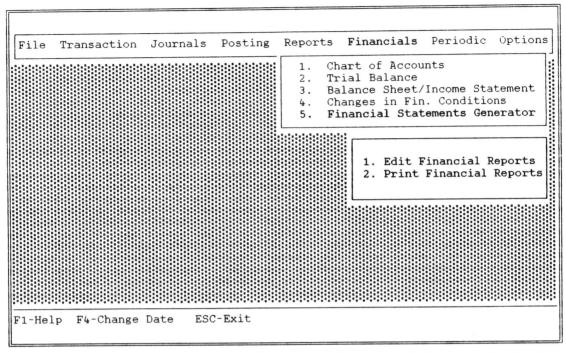

```
┌───────────────────────────────────────────────────────────────────────┐
│┌─────────────────────────────────────────────────────────────────────┐│
││ File  Transaction  Journals  Posting  Reports  Financials  Periodic  Options ││
││:::::::::::::::::::::::::::::::::::::::┌────────────────────────────────┐   ││
││:::::::::::::::::::::::::::::::::::::::│ 1.  Chart of Accounts          │:  ││
││:::::::::::::::::::::::::::::::::::::::│ 2.  Trial Balance              │:  ││
││:::::::::::::::::::::::::::::::::::::::│ 3.  Balance Sheet/Income Statement│: ││
││:::::::::::::::::::::::::::::::::::::::│ 4.  Changes in Fin. Conditions │:  ││
││:::::::::::::::::::::::::::::::::::::::│ 5.  Financial Statements Generator│: ││
││:::::::::::::::::::::::::::::::::::::::└──────────────┬─────────────────┘:  ││
││::::::::::::::::::::::::::::::::::::::::::::::::::::::::┌────────────────────────┐│
││:::::::::::::::::::::::::::::::::::::::::::::::::::::::::│ 1. Edit Financial Reports│││
││:::::::::::::::::::::::::::::::::::::::::::::::::::::::::│ 2. Print Financial Reports│││
││:::::::::::::::::::::::::::::::::::::::::::::::::::::::::└────────────────────────┘│
││::::::::::::::::::::::::::::::::::::::::::::::::::::::::::::::::::::::::::::::::::   ││
│└─────────────────────────────────────────────────────────────────────┘│
││ F1-Help   F4-Change Date     ESC-Exit                                   ││
└───────────────────────────────────────────────────────────────────────┘
```

Fig. 16-1. The Financial Statements Generator window from the DacEasy Accounting Main Menu. You can create new formats or print existing ones.

A Sample Report

The best way to understand a *DacEasy Accounting* report is by example. Figure 16-2 shows a portion of a report we can create to show our profits and losses. The report shows that we have two departments. This is similar to a report we discussed in Chapter 10 when we added the lines for a third department.

The portion of the report shown in Fig. 16-2 shows the year-to-date comparison to last year. It is the income part of the profit and loss statement. The other part—the expenses—is not presented here so that our example remains a manageable size. Our example does, however, provide an adequate model for discussing creating reports in *DacEasy Accounting*.

Standard report formats that can be created in *DacEasy Accounting* have pre-defined columns. The column headings cannot be changed within the financial statements generator—that is, all the reports you generate from this module will contain only the pre-defined columns. You can, however, instruct the program where to include account numbers on the lines printed in each of your reports. You can also instruct *DacEasy* to perform some basic calculations using the information you include. This gives you control of the level of specific information you want to include.

From a specific report format, you can request three separate reports. One of these will include only year-to-date information, the second will include a comparison of the

```
Date: 10/30/88                   Parts and Parcels, Inc.            Page No.  1
Time: 06:35 PM                      #2 Byfore Street
                                  Greenwood, SC 29646
                                     803/555-1685

                                FINANCIAL STATEMENTS

                         This          Year
Acct # Description       Period   %    to Date   %  Last Year    %  Variance     %
------ -----------       -------  ---- -------  ---- ---------  ---- --------  ----
PROFIT AND LOSS STATEMENT

Gross Margin

                                    Department 01

4101   Sales      01      45768 61.2   398946 60.9  1765432 57.8 -1366486 -77.4
4201   Returns    01       -932 -1.3    -5467 -0.8   -12765 -0.4     7298 -57.2
                         ------- ----  ------- ---- --------  ---- --------  ----
       Net Sales  01      44836 60.8   393479 60.2  1752667 57.1 -1359188 -77.6

5101   COGS       01      14433 19.3   153945 23.5   815520 26.7  -661575 -81.1
                         ------- ----  ------- ---- --------  ---- --------  ----
       Margin     01      30403 40.7   239534 36.6   937147 30.7  -697613 -74.4

                                    Department 02

4102   Sales      02      28528 38.2   251866 38.5  1269034 41.6 -1017168 -80.2
4202   Returns    02       -104 -0.1    -2314 -0.3   -11012 -0.4     8698 -79.0
                         ------- ----  ------- ---- --------  ---- --------  ----
       Net Sales  02      28424 38.0   249552 38.1  1258022 41.2 -1008470 -80.2

5102   COGS       02      16004 21.4   125776 19.2   751378 24.6  -625602 -83.3
                         ------- ----  ------- ---- --------  ---- --------  ----
       Margin     02      12420 16.6   123776 18.9   506644 16.6  -382868 -75.6

       GROSS MARGIN       42823 57.3   363310 55.5  1443791 47.3 -1080481 -74.8
                         ======= ====  ======= ==== ========  ==== ========  ====
       COGS=Cost of Goods Sold
```

Fig. 16-2. A sample portion of the Profit/Loss Statement created with the Financial Statements Generator. Percentages are from the total revenue.

current year to last year, and the third will provide a comparison of the current year's totals to the current year's budget. You can select the appropriate format when you print a report (after creating it, of course).

In the reports you create, the "Account Number" and the "Description" columns indicate the accounts from the general ledger chart of accounts. The other columns are paired, showing the amount assigned or calculated by *DacEasy* and the percentage of some criteria represented by the actual amount. These pairs of numbers represent the current period, the year-to-date, last year, and the variance between last year and the year-to-date amounts. All these columns are included in the reports for year-to-date/last year and year-to-date/budget comparisons. In the year-to-date format, only two columns of data are printed.

After we discuss the type of report we have created, we will discuss the process for creating it.

It appears that the amounts shown in Fig. 16-2 were gathered early in the business year since the year-to-date amounts are much smaller than last year's amounts (note the variance for each line).

The dollar amounts on the lines labeled Sales, Returns, and COGS (Cost of Goods Sold) come directly from the appropriate *DacEasy* accounts. *DacEasy* knows where to find the values because the account numbers are given in the left column.

Other dollar amounts and percentages are calculated by *DacEasy* as it prints the report. The amounts on the Net Sales line is the difference between Sales and Returns. The amounts on the Margin line are the Net Sales minus the Cost of Goods Sold (COGS). The amounts on the Gross Margin line are calculated by adding the margins for each department.

The Variance column is calculated by subtracting Last Year from Year-to-Date. The Variance Percentage column is calculated by dividing the Variance by the Last Year amount. The other percent columns are calculated by dividing the amount by the gross revenue (which is not printed on the report).

For example, Sales for Department 01 equal $45,768 for the current period, $398,946 for the year-to-date, and $1,765,432 for last year. The Variance (– $1,366,486) is found by subtracting Last Year from Year-to-Date ($398,946 – $1,765,432 = – $1,366,486). The sales for Department 01 in the current period ($45,768) represent 61.2 percent of all revenue taken in by the entire company during that same period. The same interpretation applies to the amounts and percentages for Year-to-Date and Last Year.

The percentage of Variance is a comparison of last year's sales to this year's—that is, to the variance.

In summary, this is what the report details. Let us remind you one more time that the columns are fixed and cannot be changed. The information included in the columns, however, can be selected by you as you create reports for your special needs.

Creating the Sample Report

Figure 16-3 shows the work required to create the report shown in Fig. 16-2. Before we go any further, note that the columns in Fig. 16-3 are not related to the columns you see in the report. Once you understand this, creating reports will be greatly simplified.

To build a specialized report in *DacEasy Accounting*, select the Financial Statement Generator option from the Financials window on the Main Menu for *DacEasy Accounting* (see Fig. 16-1). Here you can create a new report format, or edit an existing one. Figure 16-4 shows the screen that lists existing report formats (the four built-in reports). The menu line at the bottom of the screen shows the options available in this window.

Let us assume that we are creating the profit-and-loss statement from scratch. First, select <F3> to add a new format. An empty Financial Reports Statements Design screen will be displayed. The screen will look like the one shown in Fig. 16-3 except that it will have no detail lines on it. At this point, you need to name the report format. Type in "P&L". After you enter the format name, the cursor will appear in the work area where you can enter lines similar to those shown in Fig. 16-3.

```
┌─────────────────────────────────────────────────────────────────────────────┐
│ 11/05/88                                                              LHP     │
│ 11:22 AM                  Parts and Parcels, Inc.                            │
├─────────────────────────────────────────────────────────────────────────────┤
│   Enter Report Name : P&L                                                    │
├─────────────────────────────────────────────────────────────────────────────┤
│   Print                            Amount Amount To              Lines       │
│   (Y/N) Acct.# Description         From    1   2   3     %      99=pg.        │
│ ──────────────────────────────────────────────────────────────────────────   │
│     Y          PROFIT AND LOSS       0                            1          │
│     N    4     Revenues             99                      +                │
│     Y          Gross Margin          0                            1          │
│     Y          Department 01         0                            C          │
│     Y                                0                                       │
│     Y   4101   Sales Dept. 01       99     +                                 │
│     Y   4102   Sales Dept. 02       99     +                      -          │
│     Y          Net Sales Dept. 01    1                            1          │
│     Y   5101   COGS Dept. 01        99     -                      -          │
│     Y          Margin Dept. 01       1                            1          │
│     Y          Department 02         0                            C          │
│     Y                                0                                       │
│     Y   4102   Sales Dept. 02       99         +                            │
│     Y   4202   Returns Dept. 02     99         +                  -          │
│     Y          Net Sales Dept. 02    2                            1          │
│     Y   5102   COGS Dept. 02        99         -                  -          │
│     Y          Margin Dept. 02       2     +   0                  1          │
│     Y          GROSS MARGIN:         1                            =          │
│     Y                                0                            99         │
├─────────────────────────────────────────────────────────────────────────────┤
│ F1-Help ALT I-Insert ALT D-Delete ALT P-Print F10-Process ESC-exit           │
└─────────────────────────────────────────────────────────────────────────────┘
```

Fig. 16-3. A portion of the report design for the Profit/Loss Statement in Fig. 16-2. *Note the line that is not to be printed.*

Each column in the design screen has a specific purpose, and there are specific codes that must be entered for each as you create the format. It is important to check the bottom line of the screen as the cursor moves from one column to another. This line displays information about specific options. Sometimes it will indicate you are to press the <SPACEBAR> to cycle among the options for a particular column. These options are discussed below.

There are four columns, labeled "1," "2," "3," and "%," that are classified as "Amount To" columns. These four columns tell *DacEasy* where to put any amount used in the report. (Again, these columns do not correspond to the columns you see in the printed report.) These four columns act as additional memories for *DacEasy* to use as it gathers data to print. Numbers that are collected from your data files or calculated using the data files, are stored in these columns until they are used in the report. These four columns are discussed as we explain creating a specialized profit-and-loss statement.

The other columns provide additional information that *DacEasy* uses as it prints customized reports. Actually, you provide the information—in the form of codes—and *DacEasy* simply uses it as it prints.

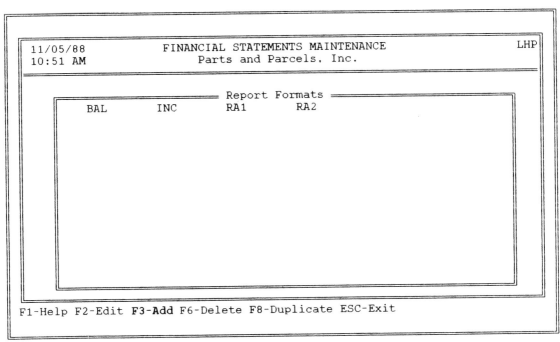

```
 11/05/88              FINANCIAL STATEMENTS MAINTENANCE           LHP
 10:51 AM                   Parts and Parcels, Inc.

                      ════════ Report Formats ════════
         BAL          INC        RA1        RA2




 F1-Help F2-Edit F3-Add F6-Delete F8-Duplicate ESC-Exit
```

Fig. 16-4. A list of reports available from the Financial Statements Generator.
These reports are built-in reports that are similar, but not as detailed, as the actual
reports available from another window.

Print (Y/N). If the line entered is to be printed in the report, enter a "Y" to include it in the printed report. If you enter a "N," the line will not print.

The purpose of unprinted lines is to allow for pieces of information that are used in a calculation. For example, the second line in Fig. 16-3 is marked with a "N" to indicate that it will not be printed. The plus sign in the "%" column indicates that this amount—total revenue—is to be used in calculating the percentages that are included in the rest of the report. We don't want the line printed, however—we simply want it to provide information to be used in calculations. We will discuss the function of the plus sign when we discuss the "%" column.

Note in the printed sample (Fig. 16-2), that a line named "Revenue" is not printed on the report. All other lines are printed.

The account number from the chart of accounts is given on each line that *DacEasy* includes information directly from the general ledger. Whenever *DacEasy* sees an account number in this column, it will go to the general ledger and retrieve the amount to be placed on this line. In fact, it retrieves three amounts—one for the current period, one for the year-to-date, and one for last year (even if it's zero)—and places them in the appropriate columns when the report is printed.

Amounts from the general ledger are printed on the line when an account number is included if the "Amount From" column is "99." This is further explained when the Amount From column is discussed later in the chapter.

Do not put an account number in this column if you want the report to include only a label at this point. If you will not be using an account number in this column, simply press <ENTER> and the cursor will move on to the next column.

Description. If you enter an account number in the Amount From column, the name of that account is automatically entered here. You can change the description if re-wording would make the report more meaningful to anticipated readers. If you do not use an account number in the previous column, you can enter whatever description you'd like (using as many as 20 characters).

Amount From. The Amount From column is used to tell *DacEasy* where the amounts for each line are to come from (readers with degrees in English are asked to ignore all dangling prepositions). There are six possible codes that can be entered in this column. To see the codes, press the <SPACEBAR>. Any non-zero code indicates that *DacEasy* is supposed to print something. The "Amount To" columns (which are discussed later) tell *DacEasy* where the data is to be printed.

(a)   "99" is displayed whenever an account number is entered in the left-most column. Once you accept the "99," *DacEasy* goes to the general ledger to get the amounts to be printed on this line. The amounts are then printed in the appropriate columns on the report.

(b)   Press the <SPACEBAR> to enter "0" if you want only the description printed. This tells *DacEasy* that no information will be placed in the columns on this line. Only the description entered in the previous column will be printed (as a label).

(c)   Select "1" if you want the report to print the amount from the column labeled "1." As you might expect, you would enter "2" to use the amount from the column labeled "2" and a "3" for the amount from column "3." (We will explain, in the next section, about putting values into these columns.)

(d)   Select "/" (slash, not backslash) if you want *DacEasy* to use two of the numbered columns to calculate ratios to be placed in this line. (You must, then, designate the columns to be used in that ratio. Those columns will be discussed in the next section.) The slash is the computer's symbol for division and ratios are calculated by division. Thus, the slash sign is used for this purpose.

Be sure to use numbers and not letters when selecting columns.

Amount to. The codes described in (c) and (d) indicate that *DacEasy* is to use information it finds in the three-numbered memory columns. There are two ways to put information in these memories. One way is to clear these memories, and the other is put in codes for use in calculations. To enter codes, press the <SPACEBAR> until the desired code is displayed, then press <ENTER>.

Consider the line in Fig. 16-3 that uses the account number 4101. The account number holds the amounts for Sales in Department 01. The Amount From column contains the code "99", which tells *DacEasy* to go to the general ledger and get the amount in the given account (4101). Once it has the amount, *DacEasy* must then be told what to do with it. The plus sign in the 1 column tells *DacEasy* to add the value to whatever is in the memory column. If there is some other amount already in the memory, the new number will be added to it.

In addition to the plus sign, you can include a minus sign if you want the account amount subtracted from the memory column. An example is the line with account number 5101, where instructions were given to subtract the cost of goods sold from whatever was already accumulated in memory column 1. Above the minus sign, there are two plus signs in memory column "1," indicating that two things have already been added to the column's memory.

If you place a zero in one of the three-numbered memory columns, the total in the column will be reset at zero, thus erasing any value that might have been accumulated. If the Amount From column was given instructions to print the value from the memory column, it will print before being erased.

An example is shown in the Margin Dept. 02 line (gross margin for Department 02). The Amount From column has a "2", which tells *DacEasy* to print the value it finds in memory column 2. It does this task, adds the amount to the value in memory column 1 (so it will be added to the margin value for Department 01), and then sets the memory in column 2 to zero. (The "1" in the last column will be explained in the next section.)

In addition to the plus, minus, and zero codes for the three-numbered memory columns, you can also enter "N" and "D"—if you used the "/" code in the Amount From column. The "/" indicates that a ratio, or division, is to be calculated using values stored in the memory columns. A ratio is usually written as a fraction and the slash sign designates the fraction symbol that separates the numerator from the denominator.

Place the "N" in the memory column that is to be the "numerator" in your ratio and the "D" in the memory column that is to be the "denominator." *DacEasy* will then divide the denominator into the numerator to get a decimal percent to indicate the ratio.

The fourth Amount To column is the percent column. This column is used to store the base number (the denominator) on which all the standard percentages are calculated. Figure 16-2 shows that each pair of information items contains an amount and a percentage. The percentage is always calculated from the base stored in the percent column.

The second line in Fig. 16-3 illustrates this calculation. The line is not to be printed but is to contain the total revenues available from account number 4. The "99" in the Amount From column tells *DacEasy* that the amount is to be printed somewhere. The plus sign in the percent column tells *DacEasy* that it is to be printed to this column and saved for later use.

The total revenues amount stored in the memory column is then used to automatically calculate all the other percentages you see in the report in Fig. 16-2. For example: The 61.2 percent for "this period sales" was calculated by dividing the sales amount ($45,768) by the value in the percent column. That value came from account 4 in the general ledger chart of accounts.

The Lines column tells *DacEasy* how to format the printed page. There are six codes that can be entered in this column. Of the six codes that can be placed in this column, five relate to what will happen with the next printed line in the report. The sixth code tells *DacEasy* to center the current line. It is important to note that the Lines column provides instruction about the "next" line in the report (except in the one case mentioned).

Acceptable numeric codes are "1," "2," and "99." The "1" and "2" indicate the number of lines following the current one that are to be skipped before the next line is printed. The "99" indicates that the printer is to skip the rest of the current page and proceed to the top of the next page to print the rest of the report. If this column is left blank, the report generator will move the next line and will print on that line instead of skipping it.

This column can also contain a "-" (dash/minus sign) or an " = " (equal sign). When *DacEasy* finds one of those two symbols in this column, it prints that type of underscore beneath each column on the report on the line after the symbol is found. Compare the location of the codes in the format in Fig. 16-3 with the report in Fig. 16-2 to see how underlines work.

The sixth symbol that can be placed in the Lines column is the letter "C". When this code is found in a specific label line, the label is centered within the report margins. Again, a quick comparison of Fig. 16-2 and Fig. 16-3 will show you how the code works.

Previously we discussed that you can skip a line in the report placing a "1" or a "2" in the Lines column. However, if you place a "C," a "-," or an " = " in that column, you cannot place a number there. If you want to skip the next line (that is, if you want to leave the next line blank in your report) after centering a line or after printing underlines in a line, you must insert a blank line in your report format. An example of a blank line can be seen in line five (following the Department 01 line) in Fig. 16-3.

Printing a Report from the Financial Statements Generator

Once the report format is designed, you can save it to your disk by pressing <F10>. The format will be saved and its name added to the list of reports that are displayed when you enter the generator (see Fig. 16-4). After processing our P&L format, the name "P&L" will appear on the list of available reports.

To print the report, return to the Financial Statements Generator window (Fig. 16-1) and select the printing option. A screen similar to that in Fig. 16-4 is displayed. Move the cursor to the report to be printed and press <F2> to mark the report. Mark any other reports you wish to print. When all reports have been marked, press <F10> to begin printing. You will be asked to select from the three possible reports (use the <SPACEBAR> to cycle among them) and decide whether to include account numbers in the report. The report will be printed at this point. (Be sure you have set your printer parameters. All three reports require wide paper or condensed characters.)

Summary of *DacEasy Accounting* Reports

Specialized reports from within *DacEasy Accounting* can be an important part of management and decision-making procedures. Creating specialized reports can be cumbersome the first couple of times you try it. It is not difficult to master, however, if you follow the examples given in this chapter. A little practice will certainly help.

DacEasy Payroll Reports

The report generator used in *DacEasy Payroll* provides a little more flexibility and is a little less trouble to design than the report formats in *DacEasy Accounting*.

To create a specialized report in *DacEasy Payroll*, select the Payroll Reports option window from the *DacEasy Payroll* Main Menu (see Fig. 16-5). The first option on the menu will start the payroll report generator.

The first screen in the Report Generator displays a list of reports that you might have already created. The first time you enter the generator, however, that list will be empty.

To define a new report format, press <F3> to add a new format to the list. A report creation work screen is displayed where you can create a new report which can include as many as 27 fields from the payroll file. Figure 16-6 shows a sample report printed from the payroll report generator. This report was printed from the report format shown in Fig. 16-7.

A Sample Report

As we did in the discussion of accounting reports, we will examine the printed payroll

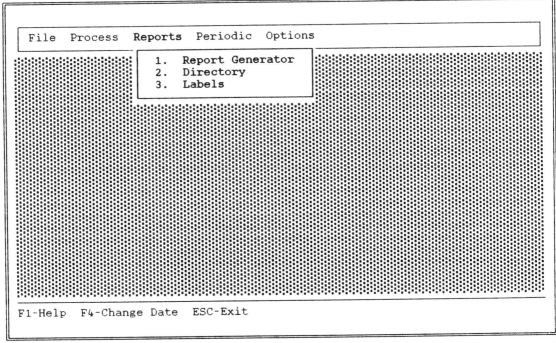

Fig. 16-5. The Payroll Reports window. The report generator is easy to use and will access all fields in the file.

```
Date: 11/04/88              Parts and Parcels, Inc.           Page No. 1
Time: 12:07 PM                 #2 Byfore Street
                             Greenwood, SC 29646
                               803/555-1685

                      Roster of Employees' Payroll Data
                         (Listed by Department)

Sorted By:   Department                              Ranked By: Name

Emp #   Name                        SS #          Hire Date  Base Pay
        Address                     Area Code     Department Hr Rate
        Ci, St Zip                  Phone         Pay Type
------  --------------------------  ----------    ---------- ----------
COAR02  Coard, Stension             666-00-9090   01/05/87         0.00
        10 Payne Lane                     803              1       4.19
        Greenwood, SC   29646       555-3409      H
COAR01  Coard, Wynn Doe             888-11-5555   01/01/87     18575.00
        10 Payne Lane                     803              1       0.00
        Greenwood, SC   29646       555-5454      S
PART01  Partment, Notmai D.         222-33-4444   01/01/87         0.00
        "C" Next Isle                     803              1       5.75
        Abbeville, SC   29620       555-3409      H
REAL01  Real, Rod N.                999-88-2222   01/04/87         0.00
        Fish Lakes Drive                  803              1       4.00
        Chappells, SC   29037       555-1209      H
ROUT01  Router, Bitsy               987-65-4321   01/01/87         0.00
        234 Drillman Road                 803              1       4.19
        Hodges, SC   29653          555-8741      H
        Total Dept 1    # Employees 5                         18575.00
        Grand Totals    # Employees 5                         18575.00
```

Fig. 16-6. A ROSTER report created in the Payroll Report Generator. *Compare this to Fig. 16-7 to understand report creation methods.*

report (Fig. 16-6) before looking at the format that is used to create the report.

The first thing to note about the report is that each person's record has three lines of information. In addition, each column label has three lines. The column label defines each of the lines in the employee's records.

The column that contains the name, address, city, state, and zip code is labeled in exactly that way. The next column contains the Social Security number, the area code, and the telephone number for each of the listed employees. The other two columns are labeled appropriately as well.

The information printed for each employee comes directly from the employee files and the payroll files that are maintained by *DacEasy Payroll.*

Note that totals are given at the bottom of the report. These totals are automatically included for each field that contains numeric data that can be added. The Hourly Rate field is not totaled because it does not mean anything. The Base Pay field is totaled because it can be used for analysis.

The report also automatically counts the number of records printed.

220

```
Name: ROSTER
Head 1 :      Roster of Employees' Payroll Data
Head 2 :         (Listed by Department)
           == Col 1 ============  == Col 2 === Col 3 === Col 4 ==
Line 1  ║ Name                      SS #          Hire Date  Base Pay
Line 2  ║ Address                   Area Code     Department Hr Rate
Line 3  ║ Ci, St Zip                Phone         Pay Type

  ┌General Data============Salary Data Tax Data    =========Vac/Sick==
  │ Code               Hire Date    Marital Cd  FICA Exem   Vac Date
  │ Name               Raise Date   EIC code    FUTA Exem   Vac Hrs
  │ Address            Rev Date     #Fed Allw   SUTA Exem   Vac Freq
  │ City               Prom Date    #St Allw    #St Exem    Vac Acrd
  │ State              Term Date    Tax Table#  $St Exem    Vac Paid
  │ Zip                Pay Susp                             Sick Date
  │ Memo               Department   Cty Tax Bs  FWH Added   Sick Hrs
  │ Area Code          Title        Cty Tax %   SWH Added   Sick Freq
  │ Phone              Pay Type                 CWH Added   Sick Acrd
  │ SS #               Frequency                            Sick Paid
  │ Sex                Base Pay
  │ Marital St         Hr Rate
  │ Origin             Ovt Rate 1
  │ Birth Date         Ovt Rate 2

 F1-Help  F10-Process  ALT_D-Field  ESC-Exit
```

Fig. 16-7. Creating a specialized payroll report format. *This format creates a report named ROSTER with three lines for each record.*

Creating the Sample Report

Figure 16-7 is the work screen on which the report was designed. The work screen has three major areas, but only one of those contains the actual report format. The other two contain information that helps *DacEasy* know how to find the format, or helps you build the format for *DacEasy* to use.

The first line of the work screen asks you to name the report format. This name will be added to the list of available formats when you are ready to use the report generator. A sample list can be seen in Fig. 16-8.

The next two lines (Head 1 and Head 2) ask you to give a two-line description that identifies the report. These two lines will be printed as the report title and should contain information that lets the reader know what the report is about.

The next three lines, labeled Line 1, Line 2, and Line 3, contain the real report format. You can place field names in each column so *DacEasy* will know which information to include in the report. The screen shows only columns 1 through 4, but you can have as many as nine columns in your report. We will discuss placing fields in these columns, but before we do that, let us explain the purpose of the last box on the screen.

The third section of the screen contains some of the fields you can place in the columns of your report. Those listed on the initial screen are but a few of the total fields that are available. You can use up to 27 fields in your report (that's three in each of the nine columns). You can select those 27 fields from a total of 140 available in the employee

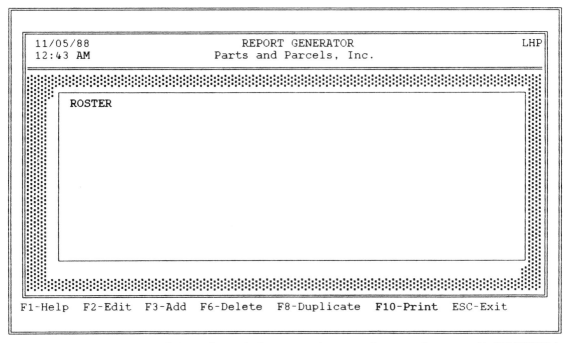

ROSTER

F1-Help   F2-Edit   F3-Add   F6-Delete   F8-Duplicate   **F10-Print**   ESC-Exit

Fig. 16-8. A list of specially-created report formats for payroll. ROSTER is the only format at this point.

file and the payroll files. Note that this box is loosely divided into four columns of information. General Data is in the first column; Salary Data is in the second column; Tax Data is in the third column; and Vacation/Sick Leave data is in the fourth column. Additional fields can be added when the cursor is in the third section of the screen.

Now that you know about the parts of the screen and the purpose of each, we can discuss the process of creating a new report. Select the report generator as described in the beginning of this section and add a new report format by pressing <F3>. An empty work screen similar to that in Fig. 16-7 is displayed.

Type the name of the report format. This name will appear in your report lists later, so to use a name that is reasonably descriptive of the purpose of the report. We used ROSTER to name the format shown in Fig. 16-7. Press <ENTER> after typing the name.

Once you press <ENTER>, the cursor will move to the "Head 1" field. In this field, and the next, you can type up to two lines for the report of title. Keep in mind that the title should be descriptive because it is given so the reader will have some idea about the nature of the report.

(In Fig. 16-7, notice that lines are not started immediately after the Head 1 and Head 2 labels. This is done because we wanted the title lines centered on the report—so we had to center them within the field. To center a line within a field: Type the line for Head 1. When that line is completed, do not press <ENTER>. Instead, press

<HOME> and the cursor will move back to the beginning of the field. With the cursor at the beginning of the field, press <INS>—the "insert" key. The shape and size of the cursor changes (to let you know you are in the "insert" mode). Then press the <SPACE BAR>—inserting spaces at the beginning of the field—until the line looks centered. Then press <ENTER>. The cursor then moves on to the next header line, where the process can be repeated. Figure 16-6 shows that the two title lines are centered—sort of.)

Once the two "header" lines are entered, the cursor moves to Line 1/Column 1 in the second part of the work screen. It will highlight the word "Name," indicating that each employee's name will appear in the first column of the first line of every report format. You cannot change this. In addition, when the report is printed, the employee's ID number will be printed immediately to the left of the name (see Fig. 16-6 for an example). Press <Down Arrow> to move to Line 2/Column 1.

Let us assume that you want to put each employee's address, city, state, and zip code on this line and the next (as in our sample in Fig. 16-6). With the cursor in Line 2/Column 1, press the <ENTER> key. The cursor moves immediately into the lower part of the screen. Use the arrow keys to move the cursor to the word "Address". Note that while the cursor is in the lower section of the screen, the <PgDn> and <PgUp> keys display additional fields that are currently not on the screen. The status line at the bottom of the screen gives information about these keys and others. When "Address" is highlighted, press <ENTER> and "Address" immediately moves into Line 2/Column 1.

Next, move the cursor to Line 3/Column 1 and press <ENTER>. The cursor will again move into the bottom section of the screen. Move it to the word "City" and press <ENTER>. An abbreviation for city will be moved to Line 3/Column 1, along with an abbreviation for state and zip code. (Note that "State" and "Zip" are separate options in the list of fields and can be selected individually if necessary.)

Except for one more small "trick," this is all there is to creating a report in *DacEasy Payroll*. Just name the format, type in two lines of title for the report and place the cursor in the line and column in which you want the information to be printed and press <ENTER>. Select the field that data is retrieved from for the report and press <ENTER>. The field name is placed in the marked line and column. You can use the <Right Arrow> key to move the cursor beyond the fourth column and include as many as nine columns of information in your report. Each column can contain three pieces of information for each employee (thus, the 27 limit on the number of fields that can be placed in one report). Keep in mind that the employee ID number and name are automatically included and cannot be changed.

The "trick," involves the availability of 140 different fields for use in report formats. Obviously, there are not 140 fields listed in the bottom section of the work screen (see Fig. 16-7). (There are only 53 fields on this screen.) When the cursor is in the bottom part of the screen, press <PgUp> or <PgDn> to see a total of four separate "pages" of field names that can be included in your report. After finding the page you want, move the cursor to the appropriate field and press <ENTER> to put that field into your report.

Printing a Report from the Payroll Reports Generator

After creating a payroll report format, save it to your disk by pressing <F10> to instruct *DacEasy* to process the format. It will be saved and added to the list of formats available to you when you enter the report generator.

To print your newly-created report, select the report generator to see the list of formats. Figure 16-8 shows the list after we created the ROSTER format as shown in Fig. 16-7. To print the report, move the highlight bar to the format name and press <F10>, as indicated at the bottom of the screen. You can then instruct the report generator the order in which to print your records and the sorting order for records within each sub-division of the report. Figure 16-9 shows our choices. In this screen, we chose to print the report to paper, however, we could have printed it to the screen for a quick preview.

Summary of *DacEasy Payroll* Reports

Specialized payroll reports can provide valuable information about one of your most valuable assets—your employees. Reports can include several types of information which can be included simply by highlighting choices and pressing <ENTER>.

DacEasy Graph+Mate Reports

If you are using *DacEasy Graph+Mate*, you have a third source of specialized

```
  Name: ROSTER

  Sort by: Dept                        Sort field: Name
     From: (First)                        From: (First)
     To..: (Last)                         To..: (Last)

  Print to [Paper]
  Include terminated employees(Y/N)? N
  ┌─General Data═══════════Salary Data Tax Data ═══════════════Vac/Sick═══
  │  Code               Hire Date   Marital Cd  FICA Exem   Vac Date
  │  Name               Raise Date  EIC code    FUTA Exem   Vac Hrs
  │  Address            Rev Date    #Fed Allw   SUTA Exem   Vac Freq
  │  City               Prom Date   #St Allw    #St Exem    Vac Acrd
  │  State              Term Date   Tax Table#  $St Exem    Vac Paid
  │  Zip                Pay Susp                            Sick Date
  │  Memo               Department  Cty Tax Bs  FWH Added   Sick Hrs
  │  Area Code          Title       Cty Tax %   SWH Added   Sick Freq
  │  Phone              Pay Type                CWH Added   Sick Acrd
  │  SS #               Frequency                           Sick Paid
  │  Sex                Base Pay
  │  Marital St         Hr Rate
  │  Origin             Ovt Rate 1
  │  Birth Date         Ovt Rate 2

  F1-Help  ESC-Exit  <SPACE BAR>-Use to change list
```

Fig. 16-9. When a specialized report is to be printed, all printer parameters must be set to fit the specific format.

reports. Specialized reports can be created using data found in the general ledger, the customer file, the vendor file, the inventory file, the services file, the employee file, and the files that contain unpaid invoices for your customers and your vendors. *DacEasy Graph + Mate* greatly expands the base of data you can access for analysis.

As with the other specialized reporting procedures discussed in this chapter, *DacEasy Graph + Mate* lets you design a report format and, then uses it to read data from your *DacEasy* files, and include them in reports for you to analyze. It is important that you distinguish between the report format and the report, itself. In *DacEasy Graph + Mate*, you create the format, *DacEasy Graph + Mate* creates the report.

Starting *DacEasy Graph + Mate*

DacEasy Graph + Mate is a separate utility that is not part of the original *DacEasy Accounting* or *DacEasy Payroll* programs. It is, however, written specifically to read data files created by these programs and place pieces of this data into special reports.

In Chapter 2, we discussed the process for installing *DacEasy Graph + Mate*. Provided you have completed that process, you can start *DacEasy Graph + Mate* by typing in the following commands:

CD \ GRAFMATE <ENTER>
GM <ENTER>

The Graph + Mate Main Menu will be displayed. Select the Applications option from the menu to access the reports generator. Figure 16-10 shows a sample Applications

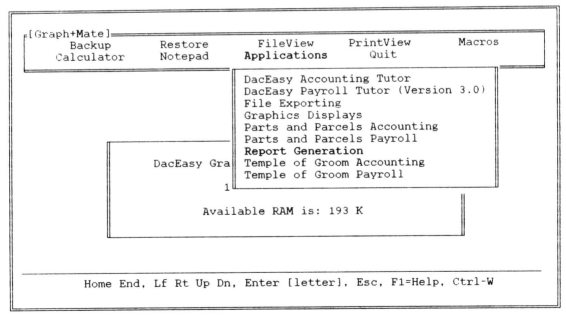

Fig. 16-10. The DacEasy Graph + Mate Applications window showing Report Generation as one of the built-in options.

window. In this window, three applications are listed that are part of the *DacEasy Graph + Mate* utilities. These utilities are File Exporting, Graphics Displays, and Report Generation. Note that the window also displays our companies, including Parts and Parcels and the Temple of Groom.

To create new reports or edit existing report formats, select the Report Generation option from the Applications window.

Creating a Report Format

If you have already created one or more report formats and saved them to your disk, they will appear on a list of existing formats. In this case, you can begin a new report format by moving the highlight bar to a location that does not already have a report name. Once the highlight is empty, press <ENTER> to start a new report format.

If you do not already have formats saved, you will be asked for a descriptive name for the format you will create. In our example, we entered "Big Customers" as the format name. The name that is typed, at this point, will be displayed in the list of saved formats.

When you select a report format or name a new format, you will be asked to provide specific information about the report (see Fig. 16-11). You can give up to two title lines, each of which can contain as many as 40 characters. The page width can be given to

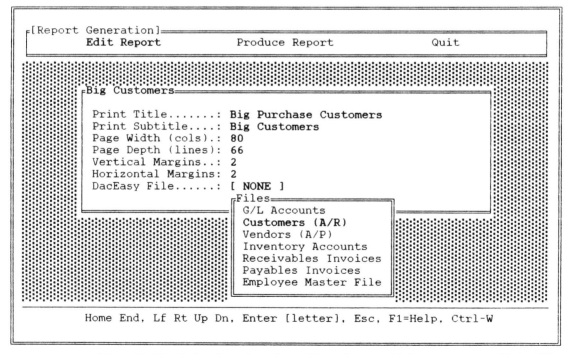

Fig. 16-11. Selecting the data files from which a report called "Big Customers" will be printed. *This screen lets you format the report to fit your printer and paper.*

accommodate the width of the report. The maximum width is 132 columns (characters). The page length can also be set to meet your reporting needs. Margins at the top and bottom (vertical), and at the left and right (horizontal), can be defined in terms of number of characters.

When you move the cursor to the *DacEasy* Files line of the definition screen, a window opens to display the available files from which data can be pulled (see Fig. 16-11). For our example, we selected the Customer file.

Figure 16-12 displays a completed report format. When you first enter this work screen, the top and bottom sections are empty. The middle section lists all the fields for the file you have named (notice that the customer file is named at the top of the screen; if you had selected Vendors from the file window, this screen would list the fields available from the vendor file and that file would be named at the top of the screen).

Let's identify the three parts of this screen before we go on. The top part of the screen is used to list the field names that are to be included. These field names identify the information to be printed in each column. You should note, at this point, that you can place only one piece of information in each column for each record (unlike the payroll report, which lets you put as many as three lines in each column for each record). The middle section lists all the fields available for use in your report. The bottom section is used when you want *DacEasy* to calculate information to be included in your report. (In our sample, we told *DacEasy* to divide Forecast Sales by Last-Year Sales to give

```
F[Report Generation]══════════════════════════════════════════════════
 Customers (A/R)══════════════════════════════════════════════════════
  S                                   G
 Cust.            Customer           YTD       Forecast    ┌─────────┐
 Number            Name              Sales      Sales      │Forecast │
                                                           │Increase │
                                                           └─────────┘
 [1]════════════════════════════════════════════════════════[65]══════
   Customer Contact      Street Address      City
   State                 Zip Code            Area Code
   Telephone Number      Message Code        Sales Person
   Cust. Type            Discount Rate       Discount Days
   Due Days              Account Type        Credit Limit
   Previous Balance      Current Balance     Last Sale
   Last Payment          Finance Charge      Tax Code
   YBL Invoices          Last-Yr Invoices    YTD Invoices
   Forecast Invoices     YBL Sales           Last-Yr Sales
   YTD Sales             Forecast Sales      YBL Costs
   Last-Yr Costs         YTD Costs           Forecast Costs
  ══════════════════════════════[Formula]═══════════════════════════════
  ┌─────────────────────────────────────────────────────────────────┐
  │ Forecast Sales / Last-Yr Sales =                                  │
  └─────────────────────────────────────────────────────────────────┘
         Heading: Forecast Increase       Width: 12

 Home End, L R U D, Tab STab Ctrl-F,S,B,G, Enter Esc, F1=Help F10=Ok,Ctrl-W
```

Fig. 16-12. A DacEasy Graph + Mate report format showing a calculated field, with the formula displayed at the bottom of the screen.

us an idea of continuing loyalty for each customer.)

When you first see this screen, the cursor is on the field name "Account Number" in the middle section of the screen. To move the highlight, use the arrow keys and the <Home> and <End> keys. If the list of fields is too long to fit in the middle section, additional fields can be displayed by pressing <PgUp> and <PgDn>.

As in our sample in Fig. 16-12, let's assume you want the account number (the customer ID number) to be printed first on each line of our report. With the highlight on that field, press <ENTER>. The field name will be copied to the top section of the screen, indicating that it is the first column of your report.

Above the field name an "S" is also displayed. This signifies that this field is a "sort field"—that is, the records in your report will be sorted by this field unless you designate another field before you start printing.

DacEasy Graph + Mate automatically selects the first column of your report format as the "sort by" field. If you wish to change this, at any time, simply press the <TAB> key (to select a column heading to the right) or <SHIFT + TAB> (to select a column heading to the left). When the appropriate column heading is highlighted, press <CTRL + S> and the column is designated as the "sort by" field. For our report, we should move the highlight to the year-to-date sales column and press <CTRL + S> because we want our list to be ranked by the current total sales.

Note that a number in brackets is also imbedded in the double line that separates the top of the screen from the middle section. This number tells you the column where your next field will begin. Let's assume that you want to place the account name (customer name) in the second column. Move the highlight in the middle section of the field name and press <ENTER>. The field name is added to the top of the screen. The location of the next field is imbedded in the double line, but the sort indicator remains on the first field.

Follow this process to add year-to-date sales and forecast sales to the report format. Now you are ready to create your first formula. We would, at this time, like to know how forecast sales compare to last year's sales for each customer who is included in the list. Because this is not one of the fields in the middle section of the screen, we must create the formula to tell *DacEasy* to calculate that value for each record and to print that in the report.

To build a formula, press <CTRL + F>, instead of selecting a field from the middle part of the screen. An empty field is displayed in the bottom section of the screen. The highlight is still displayed in the middle section. Move the highlight to the field to be used in the first part of the calculation. For our example, we selected year-to-date sales and pressed <ENTER>. The field name was moved to that empty field in the formula section.

After selecting the first field, enter the appropriate operation to be performed in the calculation. Your choices include addition (press the plus sign), subtraction (press the minus sign—the dash), multiplication (press the asterisk), and division (press the slash). When the operation is entered, another empty field is displayed. Move the highlight in the middle section to the appropriate field name and press <ENTER> again. This field name will be entered in the empty field. Continue the process until your calculation formula is complete.

Once your formula is the way you want it, press the equal sign to tell *DacEasy*. An empty field labeled "Heading" is displayed. Type in the heading you want added to the top part of the screen (and printed as the column title) to identify the calculation. In our sample, we typed in "Forecast Increase" and pressed <ENTER>. We were then asked to give the width we wanted for that column. The width is given in number of characters, and 12 is the default value. You can change that.

Once you press <ENTER> to confirm the column width, the heading is placed in the top section and you can continue adding columns if you want.

If you want any column totaled and the totals printed at the end of the report, move the highlight (with <TAB> or <SHIFT+TAB>) to the appropriate column and press <CTRL+G>. The letter "G" is displayed above the column title and, when the report prints, totals (actually, grand totals—thus the "G") are printed for that column.

Note that <TAB>, <SHIFT+TAB>, and <CTRL+S> affect only the top part of the screen. Also note that your formula is displayed in the bottom section of the screen only when that column heading is highlighted.

If you need a quick reminder about keys to use while you are working on this screen, press <F1> and a window will open, listing those keys.

To finalize your report, press <F10>. You will be returned to the Reports Generator menu.

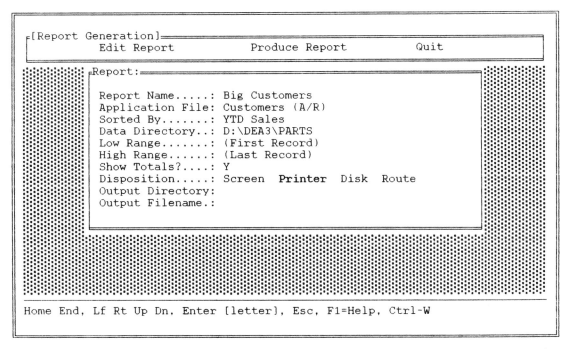

Fig. 16-13. A DacEasy Graph+Mate report setup will print a report to the screen, to the printer, to a disk, or into space.

Printing a Report from *DacEasy Graph+Mate*

After you have created a report format, you can print the report by selecting the Produce Report option from the Reports Generator Menu. This option lets you print a report to paper, to screen, or to disk.

Once you choose to "produce" a report, you are given a list of available report formats. To select a format, move the highlight and press <ENTER>.

The Produce Report screen (Fig. 16-13) is displayed. It includes the name of the report you selected and the order records will be sorted, as the report prints. You will be asked to confirm the path to the data files from where the report will be written.

You can select a range of records to be printed or, you can press <ENTER> in both the "From" and "To" lines to print from the first record to the last record. You also can choose whether to print the totals for the columns marked for grand totals or for subtotals.

The "Disposition" line will list three devices to which you can print your report—the screen, the printer, or a disk file. If you choose "file," the report is printed to the disk, subdirectory, and filename given below. If you choose "screen," the report is printed on your screen. If you choose "printer," the cursor will move to the Route field and ask you to identify the printer port that you want the report sent. Most of the time, your choices are "LPT1:", if you are using a parallel printer, or "COM1:" if you are using a serial printer. Check your printer set up to confirm the output route.

If you decide to print to a disk file, a default report directory is displayed. If the default is not what you want, you can change it. In this case, you want to name the disk and subdirectory to which the report is to be printed. The next line permits you to enter the name of the file the report is to be printed. A default filename is also given but can be changed. Figure 16-14 shows the report we defined.

```
11/05/88 11:14 pm          Parts and Parcels, Inc.              Page: 1
                                Big Customers

Cust.              Customer              YTD          Forecast      Forecast
Number               Name              Sales           Sales        Increase
------ -------------------------------  ------------  ------------  ------------
WEIR01 Weir Lighting Fixtures            765890.23     798564.00         0.86
BILD01 Bildah Supply, Inc.               345671.23     376543.00         1.26
PAMS01 Pam's Spades/Garden Shop           37654.56      87980.00         7.09
WEIR02 Weir, P. Annie                      1092.45       2019.00         3.55
VOLT01 Volten, Rhea                         234.17        568.00         5.57
                                         ------------
Grand Totals:                           1150542.64
```

Fig. 16-14. A sample report printed using "Big Customers" format.

Summary of *DacEasy Graph + Mate* Reports

DacEasy Graph + Mate provides access to information in all the files in the *DacEasy* series—accounting and payroll. Reports can be built by "pointing-and-shooting"—moving the highlight and pressing <ENTER> and printed to the screen, to a printer, or to a disk file.

Summary

This chapter presents procedures for printing specialized reports from DacEasy Accounting, DacEasy Payroll, *and* DacEasy Graph + Mate. *Specialized reports must be designed and created by the user and can supplement the reports that are built-in DacEasy accounting and payroll modules. The discussion details how to create and print specialized report formats.*

17

Tutorial 1: Setup and Start-up

Chapter Goals
- *In this chapter and the next four chapters, we present tutorial lessons using a sample business and fictional data.*
- *The tutorial lesson in this chapter involves two distinct phases of starting a new business with* DacEasy Accounting *and* Payroll:

  (1) Sample data that must be entered in the appropriate files and routines is provided.

  (2) Sample accounting entries are provided, illustrating the setup of accounts for the general ledger. The samples include direct entries to be made to the general ledger for start-up revenues and expenses.

- *When you complete this tutorial chapter, you will understand more of the setup routines and the use of the general ledger.*
- *This chapter must be completed before anything in the next four chapters can be attempted*

If you plan to work through the tutorial chapters (and we certainly recommend that you do), the information presented in the figures in this chapter must first be entered into the appropriate *DacEasy* modules. Explanations accompany the information and detail the process for using *DacEasy* with the given information.

In the preceding chapters, we have spent a great deal of time with the setup procedures for *DacEasy Accounting* and *DacEasy Payroll*. We contended, from the start, that proper setup—in the form of proper data collection and organization—was the single most important part of making *DacEasy* work for you. In fact, that is the most important step in making any piece of computer software work.

We have tried to stress the importance of coding information so that it is easy to recall and use after it is entered into the computer. It is much easier to remember a code that is related to the information you want to retrieve than to find information that has been assigned an unrelated code.

Start-Up

The start-up process for *DacEasy Accounting* includes three distinct steps. First, the software must be installed on your hard disk. Second, file sizes must be given. Third, the company information must be given. After these steps are completed, the accounting main menu is displayed.

Installing *DacEasy Accounting*

To set up our new company—Parts and Parcels, Inc. (which we have been discussing throughout the book—we will have *DacEasy* create a sub-directory of our **DEA3** directory. This sub-directory is called **C:\DEA3\PARTS** and the setup process is described in Chapter 2. If you have not installed your software and created subdirectories, as described in Chapter 2, please do so before proceeding.

Once the installation process is complete, you are ready to continue the chapter.

File Sizes

For our tutorials, we use the built-in chart of accounts provided by *DacEasy Accounting*. During installation, you need to indicate this. The size of the file for these accounts is automatically determined by the program.

Chapters 7 and 8 discuss the procedures for starting a company's recordkeeping system with *DacEasy Accounting*. Starting in Chapter 7 follow these procedures, using the basic setup information given there. Figure 7-4 includes the number of accounts to use for customers, vendors, products, and services. These file sizes must be entered when you start the *DacEasy* program.

Company Identification and Information

Figure 17-1 displays the results of filling out all the state and federal forms necessary to operate our business and to pay our employees. Some of the information in this figure

```
Company Name:            Parts and Parcels, Inc.
Company Address:         #2 Byfore Avenue
                         Greenwood, SC 29646
Company Telephone:       803/555-1685

Company Ad Line:         Hardware the Easy Way

Federal Employer Number: 53-452891A
State Employer Number:   1-23409-A

Type of Business:        Sole Proprietorship
```

Fig. 17-1. Identification information for Parts and Parcels. *This is needed for various reports.*

must be entered through the "Company ID" routine in the Options module of the *DacEasy Accounting* Main Menu. Some of the information is needed in the Payroll module, as well. Figures 9-4 and 9-11 show the screens where employer identification numbers are entered.

Start-up Information in the Files Window

Several pieces of information must be given in routines that are accessed from the Files window on the main menu. The following items must be completed before proceeding with the tutorials.

The Chart of Accounts

As stated earlier in this chapter, we decided to use the built-in chart of accounts shown in Fig. 7-3. Several accounts, however, must be added to the chart so the hardware store can maintain records for three departments (instead of the given two). Figure 17-2 list the accounts that must be added.

Keep in mind that three of the accounts listed in Fig. 17-2 must be added to the chart of accounts together. That is, if a Sales account is added, you must add the corresponding Returns account and the corresponding Cost of Goods Sold account. If you do not, you will not be allowed to enter items in your inventory or services files (when your department system is set up on inventory, as ours is).

These additional accounts are discussed in Chapter 10 and Fig. 10-1 illustrates the location of the accounts within the full chart of accounts.

To add these accounts, select the Accounts routine in the Files window of *DacEasy Accounting* (see Fig. 7-6).

The Billing and Purchasing Codes Table

When we selected the built-in chart of accounts, *DacEasy* automatically created tables of billing and purchasing codes for items that would not normally be included in our inventory (see Figs. 7-11 and 7-12). Chapter 7 discusses the importance of tables of billing, and purchasing codes. Later in this chapter, we discuss these codes as we purchase fixed assets for Parts and Parcels.

```
ADDITIONS TO THE CHART OF ACCOUNTS
```

Account Number	Account Type	Level	Account Name	Type	General Account
11033	Asset	4	Cash Register # 3	Detail	1103
3288	Cap	3	1988 Profit/(Loss)	Detail	32
4103	Rev	3	Sales Dept. 03	Detail	41
4203	Rev	3	Returns Dept. 03	Detail	42
5103	Exp	3	COGS Dept. 03	Detail	51

COGS=Cost of Goods Sold

Fig. 17-2. Accounts that must be added to your Chart of Accounts. Use the Files options from the DacEasy Accounting Main Menu.

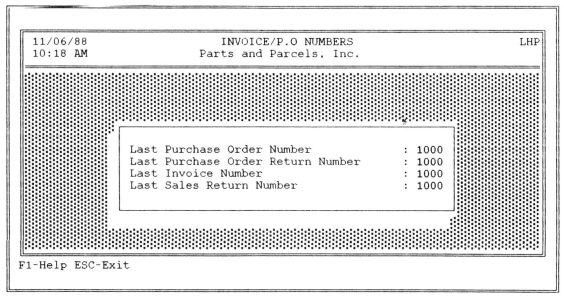

```
 11/06/88                    INVOICE/P.O NUMBERS                        LHP
 10:18 AM                   Parts and Parcels, Inc.



            Last Purchase Order Number           : 1000
            Last Purchase Order Return Number    : 1000
            Last Invoice Number                  : 1000
            Last Sales Return Number             : 1000




 F1-Help ESC-Exit
```

Fig. 17-3. Entering the numbers of the last-used forms. *The next printed form will use the next number after the number you enter here.*

For now, take a look at these tables by entering the Codes routine from the Files window. When you are sure that it closely approximates Figs. 7-11 and 7-12, return to the previous menu.

Statement Messages

There are two types of message files you can build for *DacEasy Accounting*. The first can be created from the Statement Messages option in the Files window. Figure 7-13 includes the five messages that appear on statements mailed to customers of Parts and Parcels. The appropriate message is automatically selected by *DacEasy* whenever statements are printed. The selection message is based on the number of days the account is past due.

Enter these messages before continuing.

The second type of message can be created from the Messages option on the Defaults window under the Options selection of the main menu. These messages are discussed later in the chapter.

Start-Up Information in the Options Window

Several pieces of information must be given in routines that are accessed from the Options window of the main menu. The following items must be completed before proceding with the tutorials.

The General Ledger Interface Table

Because we chose to use the built-in chart of accounts, *DacEasy Accounting* automatically creates the appropriate general ledger interface table (see Fig. 7-14). Do not change any of the account numbers in this table. You can trace these accounts back to the chart of accounts, so you can better understand the purpose of the interface table.

You should, however, be sure that the departments option is "Inventory" before going any further in the chapter. This can be checked—and changed, if needed—by entering the Interface routine from the Options window on the accounting main menu. This window is shown in Fig. 7-6.

The general ledger interface table is discussed in Chapters 7 and 10.

Company Identification Updates

During the installation process (described earlier in the chapter), you were asked to key in your company's identification information (see Fig. 7-5 and Fig. 17-1). If any of the information changes, it can be recorded in the Company Identification routine from the Options window.

Sales Tax Rates Tables

The Tax Table routine in the Options window lets you set up as many as 10 tax rates that are used in your customer and vendor files, and in the transactions involving these files. Figure 7-15 shows one such table. You can set up a table that actually reflects the different sales tax rates that you encounter in your regular business operation. It is not necessary that the table be sequential in value, although our example is set up with the rates given in ascending order of value.

Complete the tax table before going on to the next section.

Password Security and Protection

Figure 7-16 shows the passwords we discussed earlier, and Chapter 7 contains a detailed discussion of the implications of passwording. If you choose not to use passwords, your system will go directly to the main menu each time you start the accounting program. If you use passwords, you will be asked to enter your password before the main menu is displayed (see Fig. 7-17).

As stated in Chapter 7, we recommend that you use passwords so that your records are protected from unauthorized (and usually casual) prying. There are, however, some concerns about using passwords. You should review Chapter 7 before assigning passwords to your accounting system.

At this point in our tutorial, you can opt to use, or not to use, passwords.

Setting System Defaults

The last option in the Options window is Defaults. When you select this option, another window opens, listing five default options that must be specified before continuing. Typically, after setting these defaults one time, you do not have to change them again. If you upgrade your hardware, however, you might need to re-define the printer codes or the color options to fit the new hardware.

The Costing System

Earlier in this chapter, we looked at the general ledger interface table and designated "Inventory" as our departmental costing system. Now we must define the manner in which the value of the inventory is to be calculated. From the Defaults window, select the option that permits you to define your inventory costing system. Once the work screen is displayed, select the "Average Cost" option.

Chapter 7 contains a complete discussion of costing your inventory. After you have made a choice (for example, "Average Cost"), you cannot change the choice during the current year. Make the decision for your business after considering all the relevant information presented in Chapter 7.

Beginning Invoice and Purchase Order Numbers

If we were setting up *DacEasy* for use with a company that was already in operation, we probably would want to start using invoice and purchase order numbers that continued from the last number we used in our old system. *DacEasy* permits us to do this, however, we are starting a new company and we will start with beginning numbers of "01000" for invoices, purchase orders, purchase return forms, and sales return forms.

Select the "Invoice/P.O. Numbers" option from the Defaults window and enter numbers for each of the four form types. Figure 17-3 shows the screen where these numbers are entered.

Printer Codes and Screen Colors

You should set your printer codes before going any further. This is done from the Printer Codes routine in the Defaults window. Printer codes are discussed, in detail, in Chapter 7. Figures 7-19 and 7-20 show sample codes.

If you are using a color system you should set your screen colors. Select the option and follow the on-screen instructions if you'd like to add a little color to your accounting life. Again, Chapter 7 contains a detailed discussion on setting screen colors (Fig. 7-21 gives an example).

If you are using a composite monochrome monitor, you might want to set colors so that the program will display only in black-and-white. Some color patterns do not display well when used on composite monochrome monitors.

Help in Your Files Messages

When you entered the Statement Messages earlier in the chapter, we indicated that *DacEasy Accounting* used a second set of messages for working in your files. These messages are created and maintained in the Messages option from the Defaults window.

The message file includes messages that display when you access a customer or a vendor for whom the message code was entered for. Chapter 7 discusses the purpose of these messages and the setup procedures for this file. Figure 7-22 contains samples.

Building the Company Accounting Files

From the Files window of the *DacEasy Accounting* Main Menu, you can create and maintain five different company files (see Fig. 7-6). These files include your chart of accounts, customers, vendors, inventory (products), and services.

We discussed earlier in the chapter adding account numbers to the chart of accounts. Use the following information to create and maintain the other four files.

The Customer File

Several customers came in the first day to take advantage of the "grand opening" specials. Some of them made cash-and-carry purchases, and some used purchase orders from local contractors. Figure 17-4 lists five of the customers served during the first day of business.

Select the Customers routine from the Files window and enter the customer information from Fig. 17-4.

The Vendor File

In order to sell your products to your customers, you must first purchase them from vendors. Initial purchases were made from five vendors. Figure 17-5 lists these vendors with the information that *DacEasy* would need for the vendor file.

Select the Vendors option from the Files window and enter the vendor information given in Fig. 17-5.

The Product/Inventory File

The complete inventory for a hardware store can be quite large—on a per-item basis—and can be difficult to control. The owner of Parts and Parcels wants to keep a detailed inventory, using *DacEasy Accounting*, and has assigned unique inventory numbers to each product the store stocks.

Figure 17-6 gives information about ten of the items the store will carry.

You should enter these items through the Product option from the Files window.

The Services File

The store offers some services to its customers. These involve decorating, construction, and gardening. *DacEasy Accounting* permits Parts and Parcels to set up a separate services file. Although services do not contribute to assets (as do inventory items), they do contribute to revenue, and can contribute to expenses.

Figure 17-7 list six services offered by Parts and Parcels. These should be entered through the Services selection from the Files window.

Building the Company Payroll Files

Start-up for the Payroll Module

Before setting up the employee file, you must complete the setup procedures for *DacEasy Payroll*. These procedures are described in Chapter 9. Figure 9-2 indicates the number of employees to include for Parts and Parcels

The Payroll Control File

Figure 9-4 includes all the information to be entered into the Payroll Control File. This work screen is automatically displayed during the installation and setup procedures. It can be modified, later, by entering the Files window and selecting the Control option (see Fig. 9-5).

```
┌──────────────────────────────────────────────────────────────────────────────┐
│ Customer Code :   WEIR01           Type (O=Open B=Balance):  O                  │
│ Name          :   Weir Lighting Fixtures      Sales Person  :  WYNN             │
│ Contact       :   Sam Charger                 G/L Department:  01               │
│ Address       :   4312 S. Socket Street       Discount %    :     3.00          │
│ City          :   Ninety Six       State :  SC Discount Days :     10            │
│ Zip Code      :   29666-    Tel : (803)555-3467 Due days     :     30           │
│ Tax Id. Number:   15-1234567-2                Message Code  :  1                │
│ Credit Limit       :     5000.00                                                │
│ Credit Available :     5000.00                                                  │
│ Month Int. Rate  :   0.00        Sales Tax Code    :   4 Rate: 5.000            │
├──────────────────────────────────────────────────────────────────────────────┤
│ Customer Code :   WEIR02           Type (O=Open B=Balance):  O                  │
│ Name          :   Weir, P. Annie              Sales Person  :  PART             │
│ Contact       :                               G/L Department:  02               │
│ Address       :   1313 Garrote Neck           Discount %    :     0.00          │
│ City          :   Saluda           State :  SC Discount Days :      0            │
│ Zip Code      :   29138-    Tel : (803)555-2086 Due days     :     30           │
│ Tax Id. Number:   (none)                       Message Code  :  1               │
│ Credit Limit       :      500.00                                                │
│ Credit Available :      500.00                                                  │
│ Month Int. Rate  :   1.50        Sales Tax Code    :   4 Rate: 5.000            │
├──────────────────────────────────────────────────────────────────────────────┤
│ Customer Code :   PAMS01           Type (O=Open B=Balance):  O                  │
│ Name          :   Pam's Spades/Garden Shop    Sales Person  :  WYNN             │
│ Contact       :   Pam Mulch                   G/L Department:  01               │
│ Address       :   123 Pine Bark Circle        Discount %    :     3.00          │
│ City          :   Greenwood        State :  SC Discount Days :     10            │
│ Zip Code      :   29646-    Tel : (803)555-9875 Due days     :     30           │
│ Tax Id. Number:   15-7623459-2                 Message Code  :  1               │
│ Credit Limit       :     2000.00                                                │
│ Credit Available :     2000.00                                                  │
│ Month Int. Rate  :   0.00        Sales Tax Code    :   4 Rate: 5.000            │
├──────────────────────────────────────────────────────────────────────────────┤
│ Customer Code :   VOLT01           Type (O=Open B=Balance):  O                  │
│ Name          :   Volten, Rhea                Sales Person  :  PART             │
│ Contact       :                               G/L Department:  02               │
│ Address       :   P.O. Box 3423               Discount %    :     0.00          │
│ City          :   Hodges           State :  SC Discount Days :      0            │
│ Zip Code      :   29653-    Tel : (803)555-1578 Due days     :     30           │
│ Tax Id. Number:   (none)                       Message Code  :  1               │
│ Credit Limit       :      500.00                                                │
│ Credit Available :      500.00                                                  │
│ Month Int. Rate  :   1.50        Sales Tax Code    :   4 Rate: 5.000            │
├──────────────────────────────────────────────────────────────────────────────┤
│ Customer Code :   BILD01           Type (O=Open B=Balance):  O                  │
│ Name          :   Bildah Supply, Inc.         Sales Person  :  WYNN             │
│ Contact       :   J. Bildah, Foreman          G/L Department:  01               │
│ Address       :   5432 Brickyard Blvd.        Discount %    :     3.00          │
│ City          :   Greenwood        State :  SC Discount Days :     10            │
│ Zip Code      :   29646-    Tel : (803)555-2745 Due days     :     30           │
│ Tax Id. Number:   15-0980976-2                 Message Code  :  1               │
│ Credit Limit       :     8000.00                                                │
│ Credit Available :     8000.00                                                  │
│ Month Int. Rate  :   0.00        Sales Tax Code    :   4 Rate: 5.000            │
└──────────────────────────────────────────────────────────────────────────────┘
```

Fig. 17-4. Sample customer records to be used with Parts and Parcels tutorials. Enter through the Files option on the DacEasy Accounting Main Menu.

```
Vendor Code      :  SHAD01              Type (O=Open B=Balance):  O
Name             :  Shady Vore Lumber Company    Territory      :  WEST
Contact          :  Bubba Vore, President       Type           :  WD
Address          :  543 Barron Hills Canyon     Discount %     :  2.00
City             :  St. Arbor       State  :  AZ  Discount Days :  10
Zip Code         :  85899-    Tel : (602)555-1234  Due days     :  30
Tax Id. Number:  23-4561239-0                  Message Code   :  2
Credit Limit     :      15000.00
Credit Available :      15000.00
                               Sales Tax Code    :    0 Rate:  3.000

Vendor Code      :  SHOV01              Type (O=Open B=Balance):  O
Name             :  Shovell Shovels, Inc.       Territory      :  NMID
Contact          :  B.S. Shovells, Acct. Rep.   Type           :  HW
Address          :  Fourth Elyzer Plaza         Discount %     :  3.00
City             :  Patty           State  :  IL  Discount Days :  10
Zip Code         :  60799-    Tel : (618)555-4567  Due days     :  30
Tax Id. Number:  34-5412098-7                  Message Code   :  2
Credit Limit     :       8000.00
Credit Available :       8000.00
                               Sales Tax Code    :    7 Rate:  6.500

Vendor Code      :  NUTS01              Type (O=Open B=Balance):  O
Name             :  Nuts-to-You, Inc.           Territory      :  NMID
Contact          :  Douglas Clark, Sales Rep.   Type           :  FA
Address          :  546 Pecan Grove             Discount %     :  0.00
City             :  Brazil          State  :  IN  Discount Days :   0
Zip Code         :  47911-    Tel : (219)555-6543  Due days     :  45
Tax Id. Number:  32-7609098-9                  Message Code   :  2
Credit Limit     :       2500.00
Credit Available :       2500.00
                               Sales Tax Code    :    0 Rate:  3.000

Vendor Code      :  PAIN01              Type (O=Open B=Balance):  O
Name             :  Paint By the Numbers, Inc.  Territory      :  EAST
Contact          :  Vinnie Van Gogh             Type           :  PT
Address          :  Green Fields Mall           Discount %     :  1.50
City             :  Plaster         State  :  TN  Discount Days :  15
Zip Code         :  38654-    Tel : (615)555-1029  Due days     :  30
Tax Id. Number:  92-2323142-0                  Message Code   :  1
Credit Limit     :      12000.00
Credit Available :      12000.00
                               Sales Tax Code    :    3 Rate:  4.500

Vendor Code      :  SINK01              Type (O=Open B=Balance):  O
Name             :  The Sink Whole              Territory      :  NWST
Contact          :  L. Beau Trapp, Jr.          Type           :  PL
Address          :  4 Thunder Lane              Discount %     :  0.00
City             :  Shower Head     State  :  SD  Discount Days :   0
Zip Code         :  57813-    Tel : (605)555-5601  Due days     :  45
Tax Id. Number:  52-1212345-6                  Message Code   :  2
Credit Limit     :       7500.00
Credit Available :       7500.00
                               Sales Tax Code    :    7 Rate:  6.500
```

Fig. 17-5. Sample vendor records to be used with Parts and Parcels tutorials.
Enter through the Files option on the DacEasy Accounting Main Menu.

240

Product Code	: PAINT01	Description	: Paint, Wt Base Gal		
Measure	: CASE	Fraction	: 4	Dept.	: 01
Bin	: P01	Vendor	: PAIN01	Minimum	: 25
Sales Price	: 75.800	Taxable(Y/N): Y		Reorder	: 10

Product Code	: PAINT02	Description	: Paint, Wt Base Qt		
Measure	: CASE	Fraction	: 12	Dept.	: 01
Bin	: P02	Vendor	: PAIN01	Minimum	: 10
Sales Price	: 83.400	Taxable(Y/N): Y		Reorder	: 10

Product Code	: PIGMENT99	Description	: Pigment, Asst Pt		
Measure	: CASE	Fraction	: 24	Dept.	: 01
Bin	: P03	Vendor	: PAIN01	Minimum	: 4
Sales Price	: 102.000	Taxable(Y/N): Y		Reorder	: 4

Product Code	: GARDEN01	Description	: Hoe, Garden		
Measure	: UNIT	Fraction	: 1	Dept.	: 02
Bin	: G01	Vendor	: SHOV01	Minimum	: 6
Sales Price	: 19.950	Taxable(Y/N): Y		Reorder	: 6

Product Code	: GARDEN09	Description	: Hose, Garden 25Ft		
Measure	: UNIT	Fraction	: 1	Dept.	: 02
Bin	: G03	Vendor	: SHOV01	Minimum	: 6
Sales Price	: 11.880	Taxable(Y/N): Y		Reorder	: 6

Product Code	: BOARD01	Description	: 2x4, Pine Stud 8Ft		
Measure	: BDFT	Fraction	: 1	Dept.	: 01
Bin	: W01	Vendor	: SHAD01	Minimum	:9000
Sales Price	: 0.170	Taxable(Y/N): Y		Reorder	:3000

Product Code	: BOARD51	Description	: Plywood, 3/4 4x8		
Measure	: SHET	Fraction	: 1	Dept.	: 01
Bin	: W07	Vendor	: SHAD01	Minimum	: 75
Sales Price	: 32.950	Taxable(Y/N): Y		Reorder	: 25

Product Code	: CONDUIT01	Description	: Conduit, Alum 16Ft		
Measure	: UNIT	Fraction	: 1	Dept.	: 01
Bin	: E05	Vendor	: SINK01	Minimum	: 125
Sales Price	: 8.590	Taxable(Y/N): Y		Reorder	: 25

Product Code	: CONDUIT07	Description	: Conduit, Plas 50Ft		
Measure	: COIL	Fraction	: 1	Dept.	: 01
Bin	: E23	Vendor	: SINK01	Minimum	: 25
Sales Price	: 21.500	Taxable(Y/N): Y		Reorder	: 10

Product Code	: WARES17	Description	: Oven, Toaster M1203		
Measure	: UNIT	Fraction	: 1	Dept.	: 03
Bin	: H41	Vendor	: NUTS01	Minimum	: 6
Sales Price	: 29.950	Taxable(Y/N): Y		Reorder	: 3

Fig. 17-6. Sample product records to be used with Parts and Parcels tutorials.
Enter through the Files option on the DacEasy Accounting Main Menu.

Start-up in the Payroll Files Window

After you have completed the initial installation procedures for *DacEasy Payroll*, the payroll main menu is displayed. Several pieces of information must be provided in

```
┌──────────────────────────────────────────────────────────────────────┐
│ ┌──────────────────────────────────────────────────────────────────┐ │
│ │ Service Code  : SOILTEST01     Description : Soil, Prelim Test    │ │
│ │ Measure       : HOUR           Fraction    :   4        Dept.  : 02│ │
│ │ Sales Price   :     30.000     Taxable(Y/N): Y                    │ │
│ ├──────────────────────────────────────────────────────────────────┤ │
│ │ Service Code  : WATERTEST01    Description : Water, Chem Test     │ │
│ │ Measure       : HOUR           Fraction    :   4        Dept.  : 02│ │
│ │ Sales Price   :     30.000     Taxable(Y/N): Y                    │ │
│ ├──────────────────────────────────────────────────────────────────┤ │
│ │ Service Code  : PAINTSERV01    Description : Painting, Interior   │ │
│ │ Measure       : HOUR           Fraction    :   4        Dept.  : 01│ │
│ │ Sales Price   :     37.500     Taxable(Y/N): Y                    │ │
│ ├──────────────────────────────────────────────────────────────────┤ │
│ │ Service Code  : CONSTRUCT08    Description : Construction, Renov  │ │
│ │ Measure       : HOUR           Fraction    :   4        Dept.  : 01│ │
│ │ Sales Price   :     55.000     Taxable(Y/N): Y                    │ │
│ ├──────────────────────────────────────────────────────────────────┤ │
│ │ Service Code  : DECOR01        Description : Consulting, Decor    │ │
│ │ Measure       : HOUR           Fraction    :   4        Dept.  : 03│ │
│ │ Sales Price   :     42.500     Taxable(Y/N): Y                    │ │
│ ├──────────────────────────────────────────────────────────────────┤ │
│ │ Service Code  : DECOR09        Description : Decor, Interior      │ │
│ │ Measure       : HOUR           Fraction    :   4        Dept.  : 03│ │
│ │ Sales Price   :     42.500     Taxable(Y/N): Y                    │ │
│ └──────────────────────────────────────────────────────────────────┘ │
└──────────────────────────────────────────────────────────────────────┘
```

Fig. 17-7. Sample services records to be used with Parts and Parcels tutorials.
Enter through the Files option on the DacEasy Accounting Main Menu.

the Files options window on the main menu. Be sure Files is highlighted and press <ENTER>.

The Department Files

When the Files window is displayed, select the Departments option. You must then enter your department information and the codes for exceptions to the normal payroll information. We will choose to set up only one payroll department and that setup is described in Chapter 9. Figures 9-7, 9-8, and 9-9 provide the information to be entered in the departments file. All of the information should be entered before you continue with this chapter.

The Income Tax Tables

After completing the department information, select the Tax Table option from the Files window. This routine permits you to enter information that is specifically needed for determining federal and state income taxes, among other things. Figure 9-10 shows the window for selecting the state tax tables in the payroll process. We selected Table 58 for South Carolina, which is the location of our company.

Figure 9-11 shows the South Carolina tax tables and the other information we must provide. For our tutorial, enter the information as it is given in this figure. Chapter 9 contains complete discussions of the information required for the tax tables.

Start-up in the Payroll Options Window

Three items require information that is entered through the Options window of the main menu—screen colors, printer codes, and password protection. The discussion presented earlier in this chapter is appropriate for all three options and you should review that discussion before continuing.

Be sure to provide all the necessary information in the Options window.

Setting Up the Employee File

The Employee File must be completed before continuing. Employee information is entered by selecting the Employee option from the Payroll Files window.

Two full-time, and three part-time employees, are paid weekly by Parts and Parcels. Figure 17-8 provides all of the relevant information for the five employees.

Starting the Accounting Process

So far, we have presented all the information you need to set up *DacEasy* for a small hardware store. You should follow all of the procedures to complete that set up. The rest of the chapter describes the start-up of the Parts and Parcels hardware store. The descriptions include all of the accounting procedures involved in starting-up a small business.

We squeezed several things into Parts and Parcels operations although these things could not happen (probably) during such a short time. The idea, of course, is to provide you with models for the accounting process, regardless of time factors.

Printing the Working Lists

Before beginning the first day's accounting work, you will want to print lists of your files so you can refer to them as you enter your accounting information. Specifically, you need a list of accounts, a list of vendor codes, a list of customer codes, a list of inventory and services numbers, and a list of employees.

To print your chart of accounts, select the Print option in Financials options *DacEasy Accounting* Main Menu.

To print your customer and vendor lists, select the Reports option from the *DacEasy Accounting* Main Menu. The accounts receivable "directory" option prints the customer list and the accounts payable "directory" option prints the vendor list. Also from the Reports window, you can select the Inventory option to print your "product listing" and the "service report."

The employee list can be printed from the *DacEasy Payroll* module—which means you must exit *DacEasy Accounting* and start the payroll module. From the Payroll main menu, select the Reports option to print the "employee directory."

Using *DacEasy Graph + Mate*

If you are not using *DacEasy Graph + Mate*, you need to print copies of your lists as references for account numbers and codes. Keep these copies in your work area so you can quickly find the appropriate information when it is needed in your recordkeeping.

If you are using *DacEasy Graph + Mate*, your lists are really just a printed copy to be used for infrequent reference. To work with your files and codes, press <ALT + F10> for the *DacEasy Graph + Mate* Menu. Chapter 6 discusses *DacEasy Graph + Mate* and its capabilities.

```
┌──────────────────────── Employee Data ────────────────────────┐
│ No.COAR01                                                      │
│ Name ..:Coard, Wynn Doe                                        │
│ Address:10 Payne Lane                                          │
│ City ..:Greenwood        State  SC   Zip 29646-                │
│ Phone  (803)555-5454     Social Security 888-11-5555           │
│ Sex(M/F) M Marital(S/M) M Origin                               │
├──────────────────────────── Dates ────────────────────────────┤
│    Birth     Hire      Raise    Review   Promotion  Termination│
│   01/21/47  01/01/87  06/01/87                                 │
├──────────────────── Payment Information ───────────────────────┤
│ Dept  1    Parts and Parcels    │ Vacation: Date  06/01/87  Freq W│
│ Title Owner/Manager             │ Hrs    1.540                 │
│ Pay Suspended(Y/N) N            │ Acrd   0.000                 │
│ Freq(W/B/S/M) W                 │ Paid   0.000                 │
│ Type(H/S/C) S                   │ Sick Time: Date 01/01/87  Freq W│
│ Amount 18575.00                 │ Hrs    0.770                 │
│ Ovt1       0.00                 │ Acrd   0.000                 │
│ Ovt2       0.00                 │ Paid   0.000                 │
├──────────────────────── Tax Information ───────────────────────┤
│ Marital Code(1-4) 3     EIC(0-2)  0                            │
│ Exempt(Y/N)  FICA N     FUTA N    SUTA N                       │
│ Allowances:  Federal  2       State 2                          │
│ State Tax Table No.   58      SOUTH CAROLINA                   │
├──────── Earnings ────────┬──────── Deductions ─────────────────┤
│ Code Description  Frq  Amount/Rate │ Code Description  Frq  Amount/Rate│
│  9   Bonuses          100.0000     │  21  Union Dues    M      57.5000 │
└────────────────────────────────────────────────────────────────┘
```

```
┌──────────────────────── Employee Data ────────────────────────┐
│ No.ROUT01                                                      │
│ Name ..:Router, Bitsy                                          │
│ Address:234 Drillman Road                                      │
│ City ..:Hodges           State  SC   Zip 29653-                │
│ Phone  (803)555-8741     Social Security 987-65-4321           │
│ Sex(M/F) F Marital(S/M) S Origin                               │
├──────────────────────────── Dates ────────────────────────────┤
│    Birth     Hire      Raise    Review   Promotion  Termination│
│   11/22/69  01/01/87                                           │
├──────────────────── Payment Information ───────────────────────┤
│ Dept  1    Parts and Parcels    │ Vacation: Date            Freq│
│ Title Parttime Clerk            │ Hrs    0.000                 │
│ Pay Suspended(Y/N) N            │ Acrd   0.000                 │
│ Freq(W/B/S/M) W                 │ Paid   0.000                 │
│ Type(H/S/C) H                   │ Sick Time: Date           Freq│
│ Amount    4.19                  │ Hrs    0.000                 │
│ Ovt1       0.00                 │ Acrd   0.000                 │
│ Ovt2       0.00                 │ Paid   0.000                 │
├──────────────────────── Tax Information ───────────────────────┤
│ Marital Code(1-4) 1     EIC(0-2) 0                             │
│ Exempt(Y/N)  FICA N     FUTA N    SUTA N                       │
│ Allowances:  Federal  1       State 1                          │
│ State Tax Table No.   58      SOUTH CAROLINA                   │
├──────── Earnings ────────┬──────── Deductions ─────────────────┤
│ Code Description  Frq  Amount/Rate │ Code Description  Frq  Amount/Rate│
│                                    │                               │
└────────────────────────────────────────────────────────────────┘
```

Fig. 17-8. Sample employee records to be used with Parts and Parcels tutorials. Enter through the Files option on the DacEasy Payroll Main Menu.

```
─────────────────── Employee Data ───────────────────
┌──────────────────────────────────────────────────────────────────────────┐
│ No.PART01                                                                  │
│ Name ..:Partment, Notmai D.                                                │
│ Address:"C" Next Isle                                                      │
│ City ..:Abbeville          State  SC   Zip 29620-                          │
│ Phone  (803)555-3409       Social Security 222-33-4444                     │
│ Sex(M/F) F Marital(S/M) M  Origin                                          │
│ ─────────────────────────── Dates ───────────────────────────             │
│     Birth       Hire        Raise    Review   Promotion   Termination      │
│    01/21/63   01/01/87     06/01/87                                        │
│ ────────────────────── Payment Information ──────────────────────         │
│ Dept  01   Parts and Parcels    │ Vacation: Date  06/01/87   Freq W        │
│ Title Sales Clerk               │ Hrs    1.540                             │
│ Pay Suspended(Y/N) N            │ Acrd   0.000                             │
│ Freq(W/B/S/M) W                 │ Paid   0.000                             │
│ Type(H/S/C) H                   │ Sick Time: Date            Freq          │
│ Amount     5.75                 │ Hrs    0.000                             │
│ Ovt1       8.63                 │ Acrd   0.000                             │
│ Ovt2      11.50                 │ Paid   0.000                             │
│ ────────────────────── Tax Information ──────────────────────            │
│ Marital Code(1-4) 2     EIC(0-2)  0                                        │
│ Exempt(Y/N)  FICA N     FUTA N     SUTA N                                  │
│ Allowances:  Federal   1     State 1                                       │
│ State Tax Table No.   58    SOUTH CAROLINA                                 │
│ ──────── Earnings ────────        ──────── Deductions ────────           │
│ Code Description  Frq  Amount/Rate  Code Description  Frq  Amount/Rate      │
│   9   Bonuses           100.0000     21  Union Dues    M      57.5000       │
└──────────────────────────────────────────────────────────────────────────┘
─────────────────── Employee Data ───────────────────
┌──────────────────────────────────────────────────────────────────────────┐
│ No.REAL01                                                                  │
│ Name ..:Real, Rod N.                                                       │
│ Address:Fish Lakes Drive                                                   │
│ City ..:Chappells          State  SC   Zip 29037-                          │
│ Phone  (803)555-1209       Social Security 999-88-2222                     │
│ Sex(M/F) M Marital(S/M) S  Origin                                          │
│ ─────────────────────────── Dates ───────────────────────────             │
│     Birth       Hire        Raise    Review   Promotion   Termination      │
│    03/12/69   01/04/87                                                     │
│ ────────────────────── Payment Information ──────────────────────         │
│ Dept  01   Parts and Parcels    │ Vacation: Date            Freq           │
│ Title Parttime Clerk            │ Hrs    0.000                             │
│ Pay Suspended(Y/N) N            │ Acrd   0.000                             │
│ Freq(W/B/S/M) W                 │ Paid   0.000                             │
│ Type(H/S/C) H                   │ Sick Time: Date            Freq          │
│ Amount     4.00                 │ Hrs    0.000                             │
│ Ovt1       0.00                 │ Acrd   0.000                             │
│ Ovt2       0.00                 │ Paid   0.000                             │
│ ────────────────────── Tax Information ──────────────────────            │
│ Marital Code(1-4) 1     EIC(0-2) 0                                         │
│ Exempt(Y/N)  FICA N     FUTA N     SUTA N                                  │
│ Allowances:  Federal   1     State 1                                       │
│ State Tax Table No.   58    SOUTH CAROLINA                                 │
│ ──────── Earnings ────────        ──────── Deductions ────────           │
│ Code Description  Frq  Amount/Rate  Code Description  Frq  Amount/Rate      │
│                                                                            │
└──────────────────────────────────────────────────────────────────────────┘
```

Fig. 17-8. Continued

```
┌──────────────────────── Employee Data ─────────────────────────────┐
│ No.COAR02                                                           │
│ Name ..:Coard, Stension                                             │
│ Address:10 Payne Lane                                               │
│ City ..:Greenwood          State  SC   Zip 29646-                   │
│ Phone  (803)555-3409       Social Security 666-00-9090              │
│ Sex(M/F) M Marital(S/M) S  Origin                                   │
│ ─────────────────────────── Dates ─────────────────────────────    │
│    Birth       Hire      Raise     Review    Promotion   Termination│
│    08/15/70    01/05/87                                              │
│ ──────────────────── Payment Information ───────────────────────    │
│ Dept  1    Parts and Parcels     │ Vacation: Date          Freq     │
│ Title Parttime Clerk             │ Hrs     0.000                    │
│ Pay Suspended(Y/N) N             │ Acrd    0.000                    │
│ Freq(W/B/S/M) W                  │ Paid    0.000                    │
│ Type(H/S/C) H                    │ Sick Time: Date         Freq     │
│ Amount     4.19                  │ Hrs     0.000                    │
│ Ovt1       0.00                  │ Acrd    0.000                    │
│ Ovt2       0.00                  │ Paid    0.000                    │
│ ─────────────────────── Tax Information ─────────────────────────  │
│ Marital Code(1-4) 1      EIC(0-2) 0                                 │
│ Exempt(Y/N)  FICA N      FUTA N      SUTA N                         │
│ Allowances:  Federal  1      State 1                                │
│ State Tax Table No.   58     SOUTH CAROLINA                         │
│ ──────────── Earnings ───────────── ─────────── Deductions ──────── │
│ Code Description  Frq  Amount/Rate │ Code Description  Frq  Amount/Rate│
│                                    │                                 │
└─────────────────────────────────────────────────────────────────────┘
```

Fig. 17-8. Continued

Setting Up the Company

We went to our local banker and borrowed $50,000 to open and operate a hardware store. With the borrowed money and an amount representing our personal investment, we are ready to go into business.

We plan to sell a full line of building supplies and hardware, electrical supplies and equipment, and plumbing fixtures. (And, of course, there will be the obligatory toaster oven and toy sections.)

We have also decided to use *DacEasy Accounting* to keep the books and *DacEasy Payroll* to pay our force of two full-time, and three part-time, employees. We also will be using *DacEasy Graph + Mate* so we can view our files and backup our data as our needs dictate.

Accounting for the Working Capital

In addition to the $50,000 loan for Parts and Parcels, the owner has put up $25,000. The total amount represents our working capital. Before we can buy merchandise to sell, we must put our working capital in the bank—and we must account for it in our bookkeeping system.

It's easy to see that we need to add the $75,000 to one of the "Cash in Banks" accounts. And since we will be using the money to set up our operation, we want to put it in the checking account—account number 11021. From this account, we will write checks for purchases from vendors. Placing the two amounts in this account means that two "debits" have been placed in the system. Consequently, we must match these debits with "credits" totaling the same amount.

The $25,000 is an investment by the owner of the company. In effect, the company will owe this amount back to the owner, at some point in time. Our chart of accounts contains a capital account for "stockholders equity"—another term for "owners' investment." That account number is 3, and it is a general account that contains detail accounts where we make direct entries, accounting for the value of the owners' stock in the company. We will make a direct entry to account number 31011, which holds the face value—the "par value"—of that stockholders equity. This account is a "credit" account and will balance against $25,000 of the cash deposit.

The remaining $50,000 is a liability that can easily be assigned to account number 2202 for long-term notes payable. This account is also a "credit," balancing the rest of the cash deposit.

To translate all of this into accounting transactions and enter it into the general ledger in *DacEasy Accounting*:

(1) From the main menu, select the Transactions option.

(2) The Transactions window contains an option for the General Ledger, which permits you to enter transactions. Select this option to enter the first work screen.

(3) The cursor stops on the top line so you can enter a "journal" code. Journals are used for direct entry in the general ledger. Different journals let you enter information that does not come through one of the accounting modules.

Journal Codes

Five journal codes are used by *DacEasy Accounting* to identify transactions from different modules. Those are "AP" for transactions from accounts payable, "AR" for accounts receivable, "PO" for purchase orders, "BI" for billing and customer invoices, and "IN" for inventory and services. Entries in these journals might be made only from the individual modules. Likewise, correcting errors for these journals must be made in the modules and cannot be made directly into the general ledger. It is not possible to make a direct entry into one of these journals.

Our current entries deal exclusively with cash transactions; so we will create a "cash journal" into which we enter the transactions described above. We can use any two-character code (using alphabetic or numeric characters) for a journal name. We will code ours "CA" for cash.

Type the two letter journal code and press <ENTER>, the cursor moves to the "Transaction #" field. Each time a series of direct entries are made into a journal, we will be asked to enter a new transaction number and the system will record the transactions by these numbers. Using the journal code and transaction number, we can re-call and review any transaction that has already been entered.

A transaction can contain any number of entries. Figure 11-8 shows our first transaction in the cash journal. The total of the debits must equal the total of the credits or our books will be out of balance.

When you type the transaction number, the current system date is displayed. It can be changed, if necessary, however, be careful when changing dates within the system because *DacEasy* uses dates to record and report the order of transactions. You can accept the displayed date by pressing <ENTER>. The following steps detail the actual transaction entries:

(1) The cursor moves to the "account number" column. Because we are placing money into our checking account, enter account number 11021 for that account. Press <ENTER>. The program checks the chart of accounts to make sure that the account exists. If it does, the account name is automatically displayed.

(2) Type "Personal Investment" in the "Description" column to indicate the owners' investment.

(3) The cursor then moves to the "debit" column. Enter the proper amount of the personal investment ($25,000—without the dollar sign and without the comma). Press <ENTER>.

(4) The cursor moves to the next line so the balancing amount can be entered. We chose to place the "credit" for the personal investment in account number 31011. This account is an "owners' equity" account and retains the amount the company owes the owner.

(5) Following the model for the first entry in this transaction, enter the description, press <ENTER> to move from the debit to the credit column. In the credit column, enter part or all of the balancing amount. Part of the amount can be entered if another amount is to be added to balance the difference.

(6) Continue entries until every dollar is accounted for twice (see Fig. 11-8).

If you make a mistake entering a transaction, move the cursor to the beginning of the transaction line and press <ALT+D>. The line will be deleted and you can add in the line, or lines, that will correct the error. If you want to delete the entire transaction without processing it into the accounting system, press <F6> while the cursor is in the first column.

Once the entry is completed, let *DacEasy* know you have finished by pressing the <F10> key. The system will then total your entries, making sure that the total for the debits equals the total for the credits. If the transaction does not balance, you cannot go on.

The Transaction Module

There are several transaction work screens that can be used throughout the *DacEasy* modules. Each of these work screens are used as described above, and the procedures for totaling debits and credits are the same. In addition to the entry process, error correction procedures are similar throughout *DacEasy*.

When a Transaction Does Not Balance

When you process a transaction and the totals of the debits and credits entered on the transaction work screen are equal (and, thus, their subtracted difference is zero), *DacEasy* accepts the transaction and displays a new blank transaction screen.

If the totals are not "in balance" (that is, the debits and credits are not equal), *DacEasy* displays a message to let you know that one of four things must happen: (1) you must debit an additional amount; (2) you must credit an additional amount; (3) you must edit one of the entries already entered; or you must decide to let the system make a temporary credit to the "journal difference" account—account number "D."

In the first two cases, you can enter the amounts to the proper accounts and the proper columns, as described in the next section. In the last case, *DacEasy* automatically assigns the "journal difference"—the amount the transaction is out of balance—so you can go on to another transaction. Correcting errors in the recordkeeping system is discussed later in the chapter.

Editing a Transaction Entry

If you find that you have made a mistake in a transaction entry, return to the entry by using the <Up Arrow> to move to that entry line. You can then move the cursor left or right to correct the error.

DacEasy permits you to correct any entry made in a journal or a module until the entry is actually posted at the end of the period. Therefore, if you find an error 10 days after it is made, and if you have not completed the posting process for the period the entry was made, you can correct the entry.

In Chapter 21, we discuss the "posting" process, through which all entries from journals and modules are posted officially to the general ledger. This process finalizes the entries for the period of the posting, (most often a calendar month).

(Correcting errors after the posting *process is* completed must be made through "reversing journal entries."

When You Cannot Find the Mistake

There will be times when you have completed your entries and they do not balance. You have double-checked everything, and you simply cannot find the mistake. In these instances, you must go back to research your original information more closely—but you would like to finish the current work session before digging through all those paper records.

You must, however, balance the current transaction before you can go on or quit.

DacEasy provides a means to balance the current transaction although there is an obvious mistake. The difference—that is, the amount that is causing the imbalance—can be credited to the "journal difference" account (account number D). *DacEasy* can automatically enter the difference without you calculating it, if you tell it to.

If your transaction is out of balance—the debit entries do not equal the credit entries—the system displays a message when you enter the <F10> to process. You can choose to review the entries and make the necessary adjustments. If it is still out of balance, however, and you cannot find a problem with your entries, the error must be in the original documents.

In this case, you can instruct *DacEasy* to place the difference into account number D by pressing the <F2> key in the "account number" column on the current work screen. The difference is recorded and you can continue with the next transaction work screen. Figure 17-9 shows such an entry.

Clearing the Journal Difference Account

Whenever account number D is not zero, your books are out-of-balance. You should not perform end-of-period routines when this account is not empty.

Once the error in your information is found, return to the transaction where the difference was entered. From the Main Menu, pass through the general ledger menu to the transaction work screen. Enter the appropriate journal code and the transaction number for the entries to be adjusted. The entries in that transaction are displayed, including the journal difference amount.

Move the cursor to the journal difference line and press <ALT+D> to delete that line from the transaction and enter the appropriate lines and complete balancing the transaction.

Summing Up Error Corrections

DacEasy permits you to correct mistakes in your journals until entries are officially posted to the general ledger. When errors cannot be readily corrected, *DacEasy* allows you to balance the current transaction by placing the amount of the error in the "journal difference" account until you can find the error and make the appropriate debits and credits to zero the voucher difference account.

```
                       GENERAL LEDGER TRANSACTION ENTRY
  Journal.. :CA          Transaction #..:0001          Date..:10/29/88

  Acct.#    Account Name             Description        Debit      Credit

  11021   Checking Account    Personal Investment     25000.00
  31011   Par Value           Personal Investment                 25000.00
  11021   Checking Account    Loan Proceeds           50000.00
  2202    Notes Payable       Loan Proceeds                        5000.00
  D       Journal Difference  Reconcile Trans. Differ.            45000.00



  Total Debits :    75000.00    | Total Credits :  75000.00

F1-Help F2-Difference F6-Delete F9-Auto Entry F10-Process ALT D-Delete line
```

Fig. 17-9. Using the Journal Difference when a transaction does not balance.
Press <F2> to automatically enter the difference.

```
GENERAL LEDGER TRANSACTION ENTRY
Journal.. :CA        Transaction #..:0002        Date..:10/29/88

Acct.#   Account Name          Description           Debit        Credit

11021    Checking Account    Loan for Building Buy   65000.00
2201     Mortgages Payable   Loan for Building Buy                65000.00




Total Debits :      65000.00      | Total Credits :    65000.00

F1-Help F2-Difference F6-Delete F9-Auto Entry F10-Process ALT D-Delete line
```

Fig. 17-10. Accounting for a loan to buy a building. *The cash is put in the bank after the loan is approved for mortgage.*

Setting Up Shop

In addition to the bank note for $50,000 (to be used for operating the business), Parts and Parcels has also borrowed $65,000 to buy the building where the store will be set up.

Accounting for the Cash

We will again debit ''checking'' and credit long-term ''mortgages payable.'' Figure 17-10 summarizes the transaction, which puts the money into the checking account so it can be spent for the building. The balancing amount is a liability owed by the business to the bank.

```
GENERAL LEDGER TRANSACTION ENTRY
Journal.. :CA        Transaction #..:0003        Date..:10/29/88

Acct.#   Account Name          Description         Debit          Credit

12051    Original Value      Purchase Building    65000.00
11021    Checking Account    Purchase Building                   65000.00




Total Debits :      65000.00     | Total Credits :    65000.00

F1-Help F2-Difference F6-Delete F9-Auto Entry F10-Process ALT D-Delete line
```

Fig. 17-11. Transaction for buying a building. *One asset is debited and the other is credited.*

Paying for the Building

Once the check is written to purchase the building, the accounting transaction can be handled as a simple transfer of assets—that is, the amount of the check can be moved from "checking" to "original value of buildings" under fixed assets. Figure 17-11 shows the entries necessary to make that transfer.

Note that a "credit" was written to the checking account because we had to decrease the asset. The balancing "debit" was written to the original building value account so that that asset would be increased. The net assets of the business do not change as a result of the asset transfer.

Buying a Truck for Deliveries

Using part of the remaining cash, we will purchase a delivery truck. Because the truck—like the building—is a fixed asset, we can make journal entries to transfer assets from checking to vehicles. Figure 17-12 describes the transaction.

Accounting for Furniture and Fixtures

One last transfer of assets is necessary before we can get down to the business of purchasing inventory items to be sold to customers. This transaction accounts for the furniture and fixtures that were included in the purchase price of the building. Although all of the furnishings, lighting, and plumbing were included in the price, they should be treated as separate assets.

The value of the contents of the building has been estimated at $25,000. Therefore, this amount must be transferred from the original value of the building to the value of furniture and fixtures. The transfer is summarized in Fig. 17-13.

Completing the General Ledger Transactions

When the last cash transaction has been entered and processed, press <ESC>

```
                       GENERAL LEDGER TRANSACTION ENTRY
   Journal.. :CA          Transaction #..:0004           Date..:10/29/88

   Acct.#    Account Name        Description            Debit        Credit

   12011   Original Value     Truck Purchase          12995.00
   11021   Checking Account   Truck Purchase                        12995.00



   Total Debits :    12995.00      Total Credits :    12995.00

 F1-Help F2-Difference F6-Delete F9-Auto Entry F10-Process ALT D-Delete line
```

Fig. 17-12. Transaction for buying a delivery truck. One asset is debited and the other is credited.

```
┌────────────────────────────────────────────────────────────────────┐
│ ┌──────────────────────────────────────────────────────────────┐   │
│ │                GENERAL LEDGER TRANSACTION ENTRY               │   │
│ │ Journal.. :CA          Transaction #..:0005     Date..:10/29/88│  │
│ │ ─────────────────────────────────────────────────────────────│   │
│ │ Acct.#   Account Name         Description      Debit    Credit│   │
│ │ ─────────────────────────────────────────────────────────────│   │
│ │ 12021  Original Value   Adjust for Furn/Fixtures 25000.00     │   │
│ │ 12051  Original Value   Adjust for Furn/Fixtures      25000.00│   │
│ │                                                               │   │
│ │                                                               │   │
│ │ ─────────────────────────────────────────────────────────────│   │
│ │ Total Debits :   25000.00  │ Total Credits :  25000.00        │   │
│ └──────────────────────────────────────────────────────────────┘   │
│ F1-Help F2-Difference F6-Delete F9-Auto Entry F10-Process ALT D-Delete line │
└────────────────────────────────────────────────────────────────────┘
```

Fig. 17-13. Transaction for adjusting assets to include the contents of the building.

```
Date : 11/16/88              Parts and Parcels, Inc.          Page no. 1
Time : 01:16 AM                  #2 Byfore Avenue
                              Greenwood, S.C. 29646
                                 803/555-1685

                          General Ledger Journal Report

Journal                                                              Post
Trans.#  Date     Acct. Account Name   Description    Debits   Credits ed?
-------  -------- ----- -------------- ------------- --------- -------- ---
CA 0001 10/29/88 11021 Checking Account Personal Investment 25000.00        NO
                 11021 Checking Account Loan Proceeds       50000.00        NO
                 2202  Notes Payable    Loan Proceeds                50000.00 NO
                 31011 Par Value        Personal Investment         25000.00 NO
                                        TOTAL TRANSACTION : 75000.00 75000.00
CA 0002 10/29/88 11021 Checking Account Loan for Building Buy 65000.00       NO
                 2201  Mortgages Payabl Loan for Building Buy        65000.00 NO
                                        TOTAL TRANSACTION : 65000.00 65000.00
CA 0003 10/29/88 12051 Original Value   Purchase Building   65000.00        NO
                 11021 Checking Account Purchase Building            65000.00 NO
                                        TOTAL TRANSACTION : 65000.00 65000.00
CA 0004 10/29/88 12011 Original Value   Truck Purchase      12995.00        NO
                 11021 Checking Account Truck Purchase               12995.00 NO
                                        TOTAL TRANSACTION : 12995.00 12995.00
CA 0005 10/29/88 12021 Original Value   Adjust for Furn/Fixtu 25000.00      NO
                 12051 Original Value   Adjust for Furn/Fixtu       25000.00 NO
                                        TOTAL TRANSACTION : 25000.00 25000.00
                                        TOTAL TRANSACTION :242995.00 242995.00
              # OF ENTRIES PRINTED  : 12
```

Fig. 17-14. The General Ledger Journal Report after transactions were entered for Parts and Parcels startup. An actual report has more detail.

```
Date : 11/16/88                    Parts and Parcels, Inc.                Page no. 1
Time : 09:11 PM                       #2 Byfore Avenue
                                    Greenwood, S.C. 29646
                                       803/555-1685

                               G/L Account Activity Detail Report
                                   Complete Monthly Activity

Journal
Trans.# Date     Acct. #  Account Name     Description         Debits      Credits  Posted?
------- -------- ------   ---------------- -----------         ---------   -------- -------
                 11021 Checking Account  BEGINNING BALANCE        0.00
CA 0001 10/29/88                         Personal Investment   25000.00                NO
CA 0001 10/29/88                         Loan Proceeds         50000.00                NO
CA 0002 10/29/88                         Loan for Building Buy 65000.00                NO
CA 0004 10/29/88                         Truck Purchase                   12995.00     NO
CA 0003 10/29/88                         Purchase Building                65000.00     NO
                                         CURRENT BALANCE       62005.00

                 12011 Original Value    BEGINNING BALANCE        0.00
CA 0004 10/29/88                         Truck Purchase        12995.00                NO
                                         CURRENT BALANCE       12995.00

                 12021 Original Value    BEGINNING BALANCE        0.00
CA 0005 10/29/88                         Adjust for Furn/Fixtu 25000.00                NO
                                         CURRENT BALANCE       25000.00

                 12051 Original Value    BEGINNING BALANCE        0.00
CA 0003 10/29/88                         Purchase Building     65000.00                NO
CA 0005 10/29/88                         Adjust for Furn/Fixtu            25000.00     NO
                                         CURRENT BALANCE       40000.00

                 2201  Mortgages Payable BEGINNING BALANCE                    0.00
CA 0002 10/29/88                         Loan for Building Buy            65000.00     NO
                                         CURRENT BALANCE                  65000.00

                 2202  Notes Payable     BEGINNING BALANCE                    0.00
CA 0001 10/29/88                         Loan Proceeds                    50000.00     NO
                                         CURRENT BALANCE                  50000.00

                 31011 Par Value         BEGINNING BALANCE                    0.00
CA 0001 10/29/88                         Personal Investment              25000.00     NO
                                         CURRENT BALANCE                  25000.00

                                         TOTAL TRANSACTION  :   242995.00 242995.00

                 # OF ENTRIES PRINTED  : 12
```

Fig. 17-15. The General Ledger Account Activity Detail Report. *Summarizes all Parts and Parcels transactions. An actual report has more detail.*

to return to the Transactions window. To print a summary of the transactions, choose to print the general ledger journals from the Journals window. You will be asked for a range of journals and a range of dates. You can press <ENTER> to print from the first to the last journal, and from the first to the last date. The first page will be ''1.''

Note that, for the next printing of the journals, you can enter the next page number and the notebook containing your journal printouts will have pages that are consecutively numbered.

Journal printouts give you a summary of each transaction that was entered. The summary also includes transactions from other modules—after we have some activity in those modules. Figure 17-14 gives an abbreviated sample of the General Ledger Journal Report. A complete report is included in Appendix D (Report D.1).

Once the journals are printed, the Journals window is displayed. You can now print the "general ledger activity report." This report summarizes each account, showing any activity and the balances. Basically, it shows the same information as the journal report, except that it lists transactions by account numbers and the journal lists transactions by transaction number. Transactions can be ranked by date or number.

Figure 17-15 shows an abbreviated sample of the General Ledger Account Activity Detail Report. Report D.2, in Appendix D, includes the complete report.

Posting Transactions to the General Ledger

Once you have completed your transactions for the day, and after you have printed your journals and detail reports, post the day's transactions to the general ledger.

Before posting, however, you should make a backup copy of your data files. In *DacEasy Graph + Mate* the backup can be made by pressing <ALT + F10>. (Figure 6-10 shows the *DacEasy Graph + Mate* backup windows.) If you are not using *DacEasy Graph + Mate*, you must use the BACKUP command from DOS. Consult your DOS manual for instructions.

After backing up your files, return to the Posting option on the *DacEasy Accounting* Main Menu.

Answer "yes" to the continuation question and enter the month for which the current transactions are to be posted. Transactions dated in other months will not be posted. Our example uses October but you should use the month that is current on your system.

After posting is completed, *DacEasy* prints the total debits and credits posted.

Printing the Trial Balance Report

The trial balance report includes beginning balances for each account at the beginning of the period, the total activity in each of these accounts during the period, and the current balance at the end of the current period. The trial balance includes only transactions that have been posted to the general ledger. Transactions that have not been posted are not included.

The trial balance report can be printed by selecting option #5 from the General Ledger Menu. You can limit its detail to different levels of accounts but it is probably best to accept all five levels and print all accounts (by pressing <ENTER> in the "from" and "to" fields).

Reprinting the Journals and Account Activity Report

You can, after posting your transactions, reprint the general ledger journals and the account activity detail report. These reports will indicate that all transactions have been posted.

Summary

In this chapter, we discussed the procedures for setting up DacEasy Accounting *and* DacEasy Payroll *for Parts and Parcels.*

We also discussed the basic accounting procedures for starting a new company. Admittedly, the procedures are elementary, and the actual start-up procedures for a company can be much more complex. The process of accounting for monetary transactions, however, is stressed (rather than the start-up procedures for a small business).

Printing lists of accounts and codes was described, and the process for using them discussed.

The use of debits and credits to increase, and decrease various account values, was illustrated. The company's assets, liabilities, and owners' equity were described in relation to the value of the company.

Tutorial 2: Buying and Selling

If you are using the tutorials to learn about *DacEasy Accounting*, all activities described in the previous chapter must be completed before you begin this chapter. The setup and start-up information presented in Chapter 17 are necessary for accurate recordkeeping in this phase of our tutorials.

Buying from Your Vendors

To make the most of *DacEasy's* integrated approach to recordkeeping, you want to use the Purchasing module when buying items for your store to sell. The best reason for doing this is the automatic inventory control feature, the automatic links to your accounts payable, and the automatic check writing to your vendors—all is, in addition to providing you with a complete purchasing process. *DacEasy* automatically numbers each purchase order for you, beginning with the information you gave it earlier.

You can also purchase services through the purchase order module. These services would be listed in your services file and all the appropriate records would be kept, automatically, by *DacEasy Accounting*.

You can also purchase items and services through the purchase order module that are to be used for the operation of your business, rather than for re-sale. The value of these items are appropriately posted to expenses and assets based on the account numbers setup in the purchasing and billing codes table (see Figs. 7-11 and 7-12).

Finally, all the information you placed in your vendor file, product file, and services file is immediately available each time you enter the code for one of those.

Because *DacEasy Accounting* does so much for you through the purchasing (and billing) module, be sure that your purchasing, receiving, and returning procedures are fully integrated and that all information concerning them is entered regularly, frequently, and correctly.

You can create purchase orders and match them to merchandise received, and to invoices received, for the merchandise you order. If you must return items to the vendor, you can create a merchandise return form to accompany the returned merchandise.

All inventory and services records are automatically updated and revised to reflect ordered, received, and returned items. With this information, you can print reports of all the activity within the purchasing module.

Access to Vendor and Inventory Codes

If you are not using *DacEasy Graph + Mate*, you need to print your lists of vendors and products. You also need a printed copy of your purchasing and billing codes (see Figs. 7-11 and 7-12). With *DacEasy Graph + Mate*, you can "pop-up" the codes from both these files.

Creating a Purchase Order

In the *DacEasy Accounting* Main Menu (Fig. 5-1), select the Transactions module. From the Transactions window, select Purchasing.

To create your first purchase order, elect to "enter purchase orders" from the Purchasing transactions window (see Fig. 11-1).

An empty purchase order is displayed on your screen and the cursor is in the Purchase Order # field. If you are creating a new purchase order, simply press the <ENTER> key and the next available purchase order number is printed for you. Because we entered the number "01000" in the "Invoice/Purchase Order (PO) Numbers" default options routine (see Fig. 17-3) in the last chapter, the first PO number that is displayed for Parts and Parcels will be "01001."

Later, if you want to see, or edit a purchase order already created, enter the purchase order number and the completed purchase order will be displayed.

The Vendor Code

When the PO number is displayed, the cursor will move to the Vendor Code field. From your vendor list, enter the code for the vendor to whom the order will be sent.

If you are using *DacEasy Graph + Mate*, press <ALT + F10> to open the window. Select "FileView" to view data files. Another window will open, giving you a list of these files. Select the Vendors (A/P) file. Figure 18-1 shows the result.

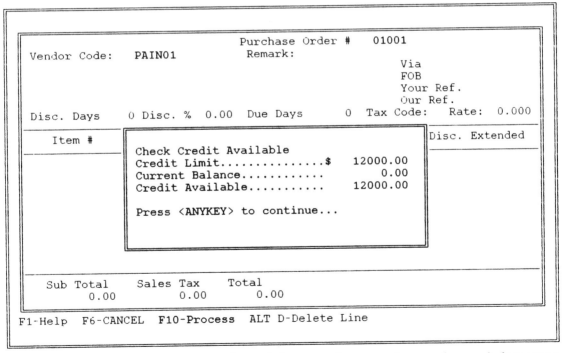

```
 ┌─0.0% of Total─────────────────────────────────────────────────────────────┐
 │ Vendor            Vendor         Area Telephone     Credit      Current    │
 │ Number            Name           Code Number        Limit       Balance    │
 │ ───────  ───────────────────────  ───  ────────  ────────────  ────────── │
 │ NUTS01  Nuts-to-You, Inc.          219 555-6543      2500.00         0.00  │
 │ PAIN01  Paint By the Numbers, Inc. 615 555-1029     12000.00         0.00  │
 │ SHAD01  Shady Vore Lumber Company  602 555-1234     15000.00         0.00  │
 │ SHOV01  Shovell Shovels, Inc.      618 555-4567      8000.00         0.00  │
 │ SINK01  The Sink Whole             605 555-5601      7500.00         0.00  │
 │                                                                            │
 │                                                                            │
 │                                                                            │
 └────────────────────────────────────────────────────────────────────────── │
 Home End, L R U D, Tab STab, PgUp PgDn, Esc, P)aste, F1=Help F10=Go, Ctrl-W
```

Fig. 18-1. DacEasy Graph+Mate's view of the Vendor File. *It can be accessed by pressing <ALT+F10> and selecting "FileView."*

In the *DacEasy Graph+Mate* window, the first vendor code is highlighted and can be moved up or down with the arrow keys. When the appropriate code is highlighted, press the <P> key to "paste" the code into the purchase order. The window will disappear and the highlighted code is placed on the Purchase Order.

Fig. 18-2. When a vendor code is entered on a purchase order, a window opens to show the current status of your account with that vendor.

Once the vendor code is entered, either manually or from *DacEasy Graph + Mate*, a window opens to show the status of your account with that vendor. Figure 18-2 shows a sample for our first purchase order. When any key is pressed, the vendor's name and address is printed, automatically, onto the Purchase Order. Other information about the vendor is also ready for use as you complete your order.

We are going to buy paint. For the vendor code, select vendor code PAIN01 from your vendor list. When the code is entered, the vendor's name and address is displayed automatically. Press the <ENTER> key to move the highlight to the "Remark" field on the Purchase Order.

The Remark Field

You will be able to enter up to three lines of information that you want your vendor to know in the Remark Field. These lines can be used to give the vendor special instructions about your order, or about delivery of your order. Each line can have as many as 20 characters. If you do not want to make remarks on your Purchase Order, press <ENTER> three times to move the cursor to the next field.

Enter two lines: (1) "SHIP OVERNIGHT," and (2) "LAND CARRIER ONLY." Press <ENTER> after each and <ENTER> again to skip the third remark line.

The Via and F.O.B. Fields

You can name the carrier in the "Via" field, if you prefer to use one type of carrier more than another. To leave the discretion of a carrier up to the vendor, just press <ENTER>.

Enter "LAND EXPRESS" as the name of the carrier of your choice.

The cursor's next stop is at the "free-on-board" field. (We had to look it up, too.) You can enter as many as 15 characters to name the location from which your shipping charges will start. To leave the field blank, press <ENTER>.

Leave this field blank for our example.

The Reference Number

You will be asked to give a reference number (labeled "Your Ref"), which will identify you to the vendor. If you have an account number, or an identification number that is used by the vendor to identify you and your orders, enter it in this field. The code can contain as many as six characters.

For this example, assume that the vendor has assigned our company an account number. Type A-123 and press <ENTER>.

The cursor will then permit you to enter additional reference information for this order. The information can contain as many as six characters. Since the vendor information is already complete, this field might be used to designate a specific customer or job for which the merchandise is to be used. The information placed here is for your use only and will not be of any value to the vendor in completing your order.

For our purchase order, enter the Purchase Order number.

To leave either of the reference fields blank, press <ENTER> while the cursor is in that field.

Discount and Tax Information

Discount and tax information for the vendor is read from the vendor file and displayed automatically. You can change the information by backspacing and re-typing, or you can accept each field by pressing <ENTER> as it is displayed.

For our example, use the values that *DacEasy* has obtained from the vendor file we created in Chapter 17.

Listing the Merchandise to be Ordered

DacEasy controls your inventory by using the information placed on your purchase orders and matching it to the inventory numbers in your product file.

You cannot place any item on a purchase order unless, or until, that item is listed in your inventory or it can be included in the purchase order codes for non-inventory items. In other words: You cannot order legal pads, using the *DacEasy* purchase order module, until legal pads are included in your inventory or classified as office supplies (see Fig. 7-11).

Our order is for two sizes of white base paint, to which we will add pigment to create our custom colors. The order also includes the pigment.

To enter the first item, use inventory code PAINT01, typing it at the cursor (which is located in the "Item #" column), and press <ENTER>. The description of that inventory item is displayed by *DacEasy*.

The cursor moves to the "Ordered" field so you can enter the number of items you want. For now, order 30 cases. Enter the number "30."

Next, enter the vendors "unit price"—the price for each case. Type "51.85" and press <ENTER>. (When entering prices, never type the dollar sign or use commas— and leave out our quotation marks.) If you have placed a previous order for this item with this vendor, the last purchase price is automatically displayed and you can accept it or change it, as needed.

The "Disc" column is included on the Purchase Order so you can enter any special price breaks the vendor might offer you. This percentage indicates you are to receive a discount, in addition to the discount for paying early. The percentage should be entered as the percent itself, and not as its decimal equivalent (for example, three and one-half percent would be entered as "3.5" and not as .035). A different discount rate can be entered for each item on the Purchase Order.

When the <ENTER> key is pressed at the "Disc" field, the "Extended" price is automatically calculated by multiplying the number of items ordered by the unit price, and subtracting the amount equal to the discount percentage. The total cost for the item is displayed.

Additional lines can be added as needed. Complete your sample purchase order to match PO #01001 in Fig. 18-3.

Making Comments on Your Purchase Order

If you need to add an explanation to any item on your purchase order, enter the letter "D" in the "Item #" field at the left side of the PO. Then type as many as 40 characters per line, to give the explanations the vendor will need. The "D" is not printed

```
                                     Purchase Order #     01001
Vendor Code:    PAIN01               Remark:
Paint By the Numbers, Inc.             SHIP OVERNIGHT          Via LAND EXPRESS
Vinnie Van Gogh                        LAND CARRIER ONLY       FOB
Green Fields Mall                                              Your Ref. A-123
Plaster         TN  38654-                                     Our Ref.  01001
Disc. Days      15 Disc. %  1.50  Due Days      30  Tax Code: 3 Rate:  4.500
─────────────────────────────────────────────────────────────────────────────
    Item #            Desc. Ordered                   Price   Disc.    Extended
─────────────────────────────────────────────────────────────────────────────
   PAINT01          Paint, Wt Base Gal
                        30.000                        51.850   0.00     1555.50
   PAINT02          Paint, Wt Base Qt
                        10.000                        51.000   0.00      510.00
   PIGMENT99        Pigment, Asst Pt
                         4.000                        51.600   0.00      206.40
─────────────────────────────────────────────────────────────────────────────
  Sub Total       Sales Tax      Total
  2271.90          102.24       2374.14
```

```
                                     Purchase Order #     01002
Vendor Code:    NUTS01               Remark:
Nuts-to-You, Inc.                                             Via OVERNIGHT LAND
Douglas Clark, Sales Rep.                                     FOB
546 Pecan Grove                                               Your Ref.
Brazil          IN  47911-                                    Our Ref.  01002
Disc. Days       0 Disc. %  0.00  Due Days      45  Tax Code: 0 Rate:  3.000
─────────────────────────────────────────────────────────────────────────────
    Item #            Desc. Ordered                   Price   Disc.    Extended
─────────────────────────────────────────────────────────────────────────────
   WARES17          Oven, Toaster M1203
                        12.000                        14.560   0.00      174.72




─────────────────────────────────────────────────────────────────────────────
  Sub Total       Sales Tax      Total
   174.72           5.24        179.96
```

Fig. 18-3. Sample purchase order information to be used with Parts and Parcels tutorials. Enter the data through the Purchasing window from the Transactions option on the DacEasy Accounting Main Menu.

on the purchase order. See PO #01005 in Fig. 18-3 for an example of the on-screen entry of messages. Appendix D contains an actual copy of the purchase orders we are creating here. To see the results of entering a comment, see PO #01005 in Report D-7.

The comment facility is especially important when you place an order by telephone. Because *DacEasy* will not know about the order until you enter it into the purchase order system. It is important to enter the order as though it were just being made. You can, however, use the comment option to include a message such as ''CONFIRMATION OF TELEPHONE ORDER. PLEASE DO NOT DUPLICATE.'' Then you can mail the

```
                          Purchase Order #   01003
Vendor Code:   SHAD01      Remark:
Shady Vore Lumber Company  PARTIAL ORDER         Via OVERNITE
Bubba Vore. President      ACCEPTED--RUSH        FOB
543 Barron Hills Canyon                          Your Ref. (NONE)
St. Arbor       AZ  85899-                        Our Ref.   01003
Disc. Days    10 Disc. %  2.00  Due Days    30  Tax Code: 0 Rate:  3.000
```

Item #	Desc. Ordered	Price	Disc.	Extended
BOARD01	2x4, Pine Stud 8Ft			
	9000.000	0.095	0.00	855.00
BOARD51	Plywood, 3/4 4x8			
	75.000	21.470	0.00	1610.25

```
Sub Total    Sales Tax    Total
  2465.25       73.96     2539.21
```

```
                          Purchase Order #   01004
Vendor Code:   SHOV01      Remark:
Shovell Shovels. Inc.      IMMEDIATE             Via OVERNIGHT
B.S. Shovells, Acct. Rep.  DELIVERY              FOB
Fourth Elyzer Plaza        DESIRED               Your Ref. PART24
Patty           IL  60799-                        Our Ref.   01004
Disc. Days    10 Disc. %  3.00  Due Days    30  Tax Code: 7 Rate:  6.500
```

Item #	Desc. Ordered	Price	Disc.	Extended
GARDEN01	Hoe, Garden			
	6.000	12.250	0.00	73.50
GARDEN09	Hose, Garden 25Ft			
	6.000	7.500	0.00	45.00

```
Sub Total    Sales Tax    Total
   118.50        7.70      126.20
```

Fig. 18-3. Continued

PO normally, or recognize it as a not-to-be-mailed order if the vendor does not need a written confirmation.

Shipping, Handling, and Other Non-Inventory Items

Non-inventory items, such as shipping, handling, insurance, and others, are sometimes needed on your purchase orders. These can be included if they have been included in the purchasing and billing codes tables (Figs. 7-11 and 7-12).

When these items are included on a Purchase Order, *DacEasy* is able to account for the costs by posting the amounts to the accounts listed in the table. Freight, insurance, and packaging are samples of normal Purchase Order entries that are not inventory items.

To include one of these items on your purchase order, type the letter ''C'' (for ''code'') in the ''Item #'' field and a blank space and the number for the code you want

```
                        Purchase Order #    01005
Vendor Code:    SINK01   Remark:
The Sink Whole           IMMEDIATE          Via OVERNITE TRUCK
L. Beau Trapp, Jr.       DELIVERY           FOB
4 Thunder Lane           REQUESTED          Your Ref. (NONE)
Shower Head     SD  57813-                  Our Ref.  01005
Disc. Days      0 Disc. %  0.00  Due Days   45  Tax Code: 7 Rate:  6.500

   Item #       Desc. Ordered                Price    Disc.    Extended

   CONDUIT01     Conduit, Alum 16Ft
                 125.000                     5.810    0.00      726.25
   D            All aluminimum conduit must be in 16 ft.

   D            lengths.  None may be shorter than that.

   CONDUIT07     Conduit, Plas 50Ft
                 25.000                      17.950   3.50      448.75
   C 1          Freight
                                                                25.00

   Sub Total    Sales Tax     Total
   1184.29       75.35      1259.64
```

```
                        Purchase Order #    01006
Vendor Code:    NUTS01   Remark:
Nuts-to-You, Inc.        NEEDED IMMEDIATELY.  Via OVERNIGHT EXPR.
Douglas Clark, Sales Rep. PLEASE SHIP         FOB
546 Pecan Grove          OVERNIGHT EXPRESS.   Your Ref. (NONE)
Brazil          IN  47911-                    Our Ref.  01006
Disc. Days      0 Disc. %  0.00  Due Days   45  Tax Code: 0 Rate:  3.000

   Item #       Desc. Ordered                Price    Disc.    Extended

   C 8          #C-8972X Desktop Calculator, Electronic
                                                                319.98
   C 1          Freight
                                                                12.00
   C 2          Insurance


   Sub Total    Sales Tax     Total
     335.98       9.60       345.58
```

Fig. 18-3. Continued

to use. From Fig. 7-11, choose the number "1" if you want to include "freight" on your PO.

Note that the letter "C" and the code number are not printed on the purchase order. See PO #01005 and PO #01006 in Fig. 18-3 as a sample of non-inventory code uses.

Including Items for Operation of the Business

DacEasy Accounting allows you to purchase, with a purchase order, non-inventory items that are to be used for business operations rather than for re-sale. In order to place such items on a purchase order, they must be categorized to fit one of the purchasing codes in the purchase order and billing code tables (Figs. 7-11 and 7-12).

The main reason for using purchase orders to buy these non-inventory items is so *DacEasy* can keep track of your assets, expenses, and other transactions—automatically—if they can be posted to the proper accounts in the general ledger. This is the purpose of the purchase order and billing code tables.

PO #01006 illustrates the process used for placing such an order. On that purchase order, we chose to buy a desktop calculator to be used in daily operations. We did not want to place the calculator in our product inventory so we chose to categorize it as office equipment (code 8 in the purchase order and billing codes tables). To place that item on a purchase order, we entered the letter "C" followed by a space and an "8" to indicate the code for "office equipment." The words "Office Equipment" were printed in the "Description" field, but the cursor is placed at the beginning of the field so we can type over those words. We typed the catalog number and description for the calculator we wanted to buy. We were then able to type in the price and other items that related to the purchase.

DacEasy does not update inventory for such items, but it does update our assets account (number 12031, from the codes table) when we receive the calculator from the vendor.

Totaling the Purchase Order

Figure 11-3 shows a work screen where a sample PO was created. The bottom line of the screen lists four options for operating on that purchase order. One of these options is "Process" the PO. This is done by pressing <F10> to tell *DacEasy Accounting* to total the purchase order, calculate discounts and taxes, and permit confirmation of the information on the bottom of the work screen.

The sub-total will equal the sum of the "Extended" fields, including all inventory items, services, and non-inventory items. The sales tax displays and can be modified if needed. It includes sales tax only on items sold by vendors marked as taxable in the vendor file and on non-inventory items marked as taxable in the purchasing codes table. Non-taxable items will not be taxed although they may be on the PO.

Then the total amount for the purchase order is calculated and displayed.

Finishing the Purchase Order

When everything on the purchase order is correct, press <F10>. The current PO will be filed to your disk and another blank PO displayed. Complete all purchase orders in Fig. 18-3.

To quit entering purchase orders, press <ESC> while the cursor is at the purchase order number field.

Printing Purchase Orders

Once you have completed all the purchase orders for this work session, you will want to print them so they can be mailed to vendors.

You can print purchase orders on plain paper or on pre-printed professional forms. Dac Software sells forms that are specifically designed for use with *DacEasy Accounting*. Because *DacEasy Accounting* and Payroll are so popular, other companies also sell forms and checks designed for these programs. (Appendix D contains copies of purchase orders you create in this tutorial. These are printed on plain paper.)

From the Purchasing transactions window, select the option to "print purchase orders." Figure 18-4 shows the purchase order printing options. You must answer each question, or provide the indicated information, before printing can begin. The following explains all of these options:

(1) Printing Packing Slips (Y/N)?: If you choose to print packing slips, copies of your purchase orders are printed, but the pricing information is omitted. This is an excellent control device for your receiving department.Strongly we recommend that you print packing slips as well as purchase orders so you can control receiving merchandise, as well as purchasing it.

If you choose to print packing slips, the printing routine is run once to print the slip and again to print the purchase orders. (You can print PO's first if you want.)

Some multi-copy pre-printed forms let you print the purchase orders and not carbon the pricing information on one of the copies for the receiving department.

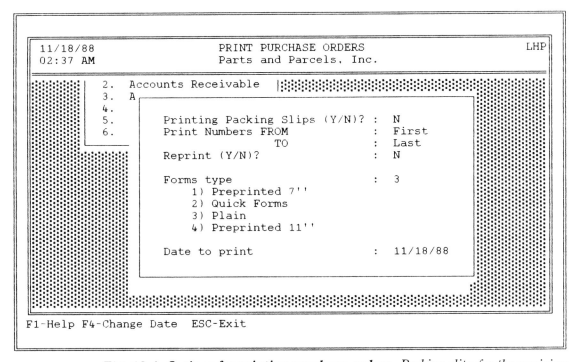

Fig. 18-4. Options for printing purchase orders. *Packing slips for the receiving department and other various forms are included.*

(2) Print Number From and To: You can give a range of Purchase Order's to be printed, entering the beginning and ending numbers for that range. If you want to print only one purchase order, enter the same number in both fields. If you want to print all PO's, press <ENTER> in both fields (the result of this action is shown in Fig. 18-4).

(3) Reprint (Y/N)?: If you answer "No" for reprints, the program prints only those PO's that have not been previously printed. If you answer "Yes," all previously printed purchase orders are re-printed. If you have changed a purchase order since it was last printed, a "No" includes it in the printout, a "Yes" leaves it out.

(4) Forms Type: If you are using pre-printed forms (from *DacEasy*, NEBS, Colwell, or some other supplier), use either the 7-inch form, the 11-inch form, or "Fast Forms", and the program will adjust its printed information to fit within the lines on these pre-printed purchase orders. If you want *DacEasy* to print the PO on plain white paper, select the appropriate option.

(5) Date to Print: The current system date is displayed and you can press <ENTER> if you want the date printed on your Purchase Order. If you want to use some other date, you can enter the correct date.

Once the date is confirmed, a window opens and reminds you to put your forms in the printer and align them. An alignment pattern is printed at the location of the print head. If that pattern is not printed at the very top of the form, adjust and reprint the pattern. When the pattern is printed immediately under the perforation on the form, take your printer "off-line" and press the "form feed" control. The form on which the pattern is printed is fed out and the next form is aligned for printing correctly. Then put your printer back "on-line."

You must perform the "form feed" as described above. If you do not, your forms will not be properly aligned when printing begins.

When you indicate that the forms are correctly aligned, *DacEasy* begins to print your purchase orders. You can stop the printing at any time by following the instructions you see on the screen.

Copies of all purchase orders are included in Appendix D (Reports D-3 through D-8).

Posting Purchase Orders

When your purchase orders are complete and ready to mail, you need to post them to the *DacEasy* system. Posting purchase orders is done in the Posting window in the Main Menu of *DacEasy Accounting*. The posting process updates your inventory records to include items "on-order," and it should be done daily.

Purchase orders must be posted before you start receiving items you have ordered. If you create an "after-the-fact" purchase order (although we all know we would never approve such a purchase), you must post the purchase order before marking the items received. If you do not, the purchases will not be correctly recorded in inventory.

A strong word of caution is appropriate at this time. Be sure that you have printed all your purchase orders, current merchandise received forms, and merchandise returned forms before you start the posting process. If you do not print the forms before posting, you will not be able to print them at all.

You should also make a backup copy of your files before beginning the posting process.

Because of the implications of posting your orders, returns, and items received, you should consider giving this responsibility to one, and only one, person. If one employee posts a set of purchase orders immediately after entering and printing them, the posting process might also post items received before the forms are printed. Consequently, you could lose your audit trail for these items.

After posting is completed, you can check the status of any inventory item by returning to the Main Menu and selecting the Files option. When the maintenance work screen appears, enter the inventory number for an item you've ordered. The "on-order" information will be included on the screen.

After checking to be sure everything is as it should be, print the Purchases Journal. The journal list all the purchases that have been posted and becomes your audit trail for those purchases.

Receiving Merchandise From Your Vendors

Because each of your purchase orders stated that you needed overnight delivery, your vendors shipped during the night and the materials were waiting at the store when you arrived for work the next morning. (We never said this was the actual real world.)

Using the "enter merchandise received" routine from the Purchasing transactions window will ensure that your recordkeeping is complete and accurate. All items received should be entered as received—whether or not it is what you ordered. If you receive items you did not order or do not want, these are accounted for when they are received and when they are returned. Your audit trails will be complete in your purchasing and receiving departments and in your inventory.

Receiving Merchandise

The receiving department (even if that's you) should have the packing list printed at the same time the Purchase Orders were printed. As the merchandise is received, mark the forms to indicate the actual counts. These are compared to the packing slips that accompany the merchandise from the vendor.

Both sets of packing slips (yours and the vendors') are sent to the business office for processing in *DacEasy Accounting*. The information marked on these forms will be entered into the accounting system.

From the *DacEasy Accounting* Main Menu, select the Transactions option. From this window, select Purchasing, to enter information about merchandise received.

An empty merchandise received form is displayed and the cursor positioned in the field for you to enter a purchase order number. Enter the number "01001" and press <ENTER>.

Editing the Merchandise Received Form

The vendor information for your first Purchase Order is displayed, press <ENTER>

several times to move the cursor through the fields at the top of the form. You can edit any of these fields before pressing <ENTER> if you need to.

One field in the top section of the form must be updated so accounts payable can print the checks for the invoice that accompanies your merchandise. The field named "Your Ref." must be updated to contain the first six characters of the vendor's invoice number, or some other number, that will be identified by accounts payable as an invoice number. The system cannot print a check for the merchandise if this number is missing.

For our example, use the vendor invoice number A23409.

When the number is entered, the cursor can be moved into the merchandise area. The cursor will highlight the "Item #" for first PO item. If that item was not received, use the <Down Arrow> to move to the next item on the PO. For our sample, press <ENTER> to move the cursor to the "Received" field. The cursor will then flash in the field where the number received will be placed.

For our example, type the number "25" and press <ENTER>. The difference between the number ordered and number received is displayed as a backorder, and the price from the Purchase Order is displayed. The price can be changed if the price on the invoice is different from the price on the purchase order. If the price is correct, press <ENTER> to accept it.

Enter any discount percentage that might apply to the item and press <ENTER>. The extended price is displayed. Press <ENTER> to confirm the extended price and

```
     Merchandise Received from Purchase Order #      01001
Vendor Code:    PAIN01              Remark:
Paint By the Numbers, Inc.         SHIP OVERNIGHT        Via LAND EXPRESS
Vinnie Van Gogh                    LAND CARRIER ONLY     FOB
Green Fields Mall                                        Your Ref. A-123
Plaster          TN  38654-                              Our Ref.   01001
Disc. Days       15 Disc. %  1.50  Due Days      30  Tax Code: 3 Rate:   4.500

   Item #          Desc. Ordered     Received Back Ord.     Price    Disc. Extended

PAINT01      Paint, Wt Base Gal
             30.000      25.000       5.000               51.850  0.00  1296.25
PAINT02      Paint, Wt Base Qt
             10.000      10.000       0.000               51.000  0.00   510.00
PIGMENT99    Pigment, Asst Pt
             4.000       4.000        0.000               51.600  0.00   206.40




  Sub Total     Sales Tax     Total                            Net to Pay
   2012.65        90.57      2103.22                             2103.22

F1-Help  F6-CANCEL  F10-Process  ALT D-Delete Line
```

Fig. 18-5. The work screen for entering merchandise received for purchase order #01001. "Net to Pay" *should equal the amount on the invoice.*

move the cursor to the next item. Repeat the process for receiving merchandise.

For this example, enter ''10'' as the number of PAINT02 received, accept the displayed price, and give no discount information. For PIGMENT99, enter ''4'' as received with no price change and no discount. Figure 18-5 shows the results of your efforts.

Complete the merchandise received form for PO #01002, marking everything as received with constant prices and no discounts. The vendor did, however, add a shipping charge of $9.18. This amount must be added, using one of the codes from the purchase order and billing codes tables (Figs. 7-11 and 7-12). We will use code ''1,'' as shown in Fig. 18-6. The vendor invoice number is 00908.

For PO #01003, note that only 6,000 boardfeet of item BOARD01 were received. All other items where received as ordered, and for the prices shown. No discounts were given on invoice, #4723-A.

Complete the merchandise received form for PO #01004 to indicate that everything was received. Item GARDEN01, however, was priced at $10.77 instead of $12.25. Make the adjustment by backspacing over the wrong price and typing in the correct price. Other items are priced as ordered. The invoice number is KB4301.

When you complete the form for PO #01005, indicate that all items were received but change the special freight charge to zero because the order was greater than $1,000 (a discount we were not aware of when we placed the order). The invoice was numbered 213450.

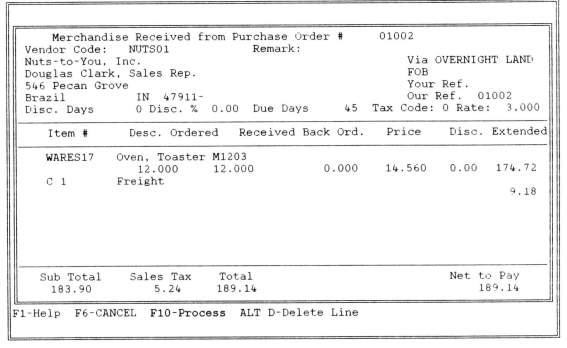

```
      Merchandise Received from Purchase Order #       01002
Vendor Code:    NUTS01              Remark:
Nuts-to-You, Inc.                               Via OVERNIGHT LAND
Douglas Clark, Sales Rep.                       FOB
546 Pecan Grove                                 Your Ref.
Brazil          IN  47911-                      Our Ref.   01002
Disc. Days       0 Disc. %  0.00  Due Days      45 Tax Code: 0 Rate:   3.000

     Item #        Desc. Ordered   Received Back Ord.   Price    Disc. Extended

    WARES17     Oven, Toaster M1203
                  12.000     12.000          0.000     14.560    0.00   174.72
    C  1        Freight
                                                                         9.18



   Sub Total     Sales Tax     Total                         Net to Pay
    183.90          5.24      189.14                          189.14

F1-Help   F6-CANCEL   F10-Process   ALT D-Delete Line
```

Fig. 18-6. Adding unanticipated charges when merchandise is received. The vendor added a freight charge.

For PO #01006, simply confirm receipt (without regard for numbers received). *DacEasy* is interested only in the dollar amounts that are to be posted to the general ledger and has no interest in the number of items bought or received since these numbers are not posted to the inventory. Confirm receipt of the items (we still must pay for them) and use the vendor's invoice number KB4398. None of the prices changed and no charges were added.

Following the processing procedure of the last merchandise received form, press < ESC > to return to the Purchasing window to print the merchandise received forms. Copies of these merchandise received forms can be seen in Appendix D (Reports D-9 through D-14).

Matching Received Merchandise to Vendor Invoices

The totals at the bottoms of your received merchandise forms should match the totals on the invoices you received from your vendors. These provide you with immediate information when you are ready to pay your vendors. In addition, the invoice number in the ''Your Ref.'' field at the top of the form, helps *DacEasy* find the appropriate information when you begin to pay your vendors.

Printing the Purchase Journal

Whenever you want a complete record of purchases, print the Purchase Journal from the Journals window options. The Purchase Journal can be printed after receiving items from vendors. Items are not considered ''purchased'' until they are received and marked as such in the merchandise received module.

The Purchase Journal has two pages. The first contains a summary of purchases, listed by ''vendor department,'' which is the same as the vendor type on the work screen in Files. The gross price given on the first page is actually the gross cost of the merchandise before taxes. Taxes are included in a separate column, as is the total amount for the PO.

The second page includes an inventory and codes summary, listed by department number and non-inventory codes from the purchase order and billing codes tables. The number of items received, their cost, an average cost per unit, and other data is included on the second page.

Reports D-15 and D-16 in Appendix D include both pages of the Purchase Journal.

Posting Merchandise Received

Once your forms for merchandise received are completed, you should post them to the *DacEasy* system. Posting updates your inventory records and moves items ''on-order'' to items ''on-hand.''

A strong word of caution is appropriate at this time. Be sure that you have printed all your purchase orders, merchandise received forms, and merchandise returned forms before you start the posting process. If you have received merchandise during the day, you should also print the Purchase Journals before posting. If you do not print these forms and journals before posting, you will not be able to print them at all.

You should also make a backup copy of your files before beginning the posting process.

Because of the implications of posting your orders, returns, and items received, you should consider giving this responsibility to one, and only one, person. If one employee posts a set of purchase orders immediately after entering and printing them, the posting process might also post items received before these forms are printed. Consequently, you can lose your audit trail for these items received.

After posting is completed, you can check the status of any inventory item by returning to the main menu and selecting the Files option. When the maintenance work screen appears, enter the inventory number for an item you've ordered. The "on-order" information for backordered items is included and the number of items "on-hand" updated and displayed.

What Posting Does for Purchases and Merchandise Received

The posting process performs several important functions such as, updates to the general ledger transaction file, the inventory file, the accounts payable open invoice file, the vendor file, and several other files within the system.

Figure 18-7 shows the status of each vendor's account—that is, the status of your accounts payable after receiving the merchandise and completing the posting routine. This view is through a *DacEasy Graph + Mate* window.

Figure 18-8 shows the status of an inventory item—PAINT01—after the posting process is completed. The view is from within the Files window for products in your inventory.

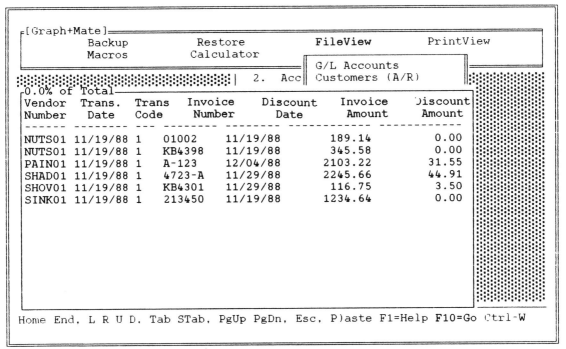

Fig. 18-7. DacEasy Graph + Mate "FileView" window for the Accounts Payable Open Invoice file. This tells you what you owe and when it is due.

```
 11/19/88                  PRODUCT FILE MAINTENANCE                  LHP
 11:10 AM                   Parts and Parcels, Inc.
  Product Code  : PAINT01      Description : Paint, Wt Base Gal
  Measure       : CASE         Fraction     :    4      Dept.   : 01
  Bin           : P01          Vendor       : PAIN01
  Sales Price   :      75.800  Taxable(Y/N): Y
  Last Sale Date:              Minimum      :    25     Reorder :   10
  Last Purch. Date :11/19/88 Lst.Purch.Price :    51.850
  Std. Cost     :      0.000   Avg. Cost    :    51.850
  On Hand   Units :       25.000  Dollars   :     1296.250
  Committed Units :        0.000
  On Order  Units :        5.000
 ══════════════════════ STATISTICAL INFORMATION ══════════════════
            Yr.Bef.Lst Last Year This Year  Forecast   Variance     %
  Units Purch. :      0         0       25         0       -25    -100.0
  $ Purchase   :      0         0     1296         0     -1296    -100.0
  Units Sold   :      0         0        0         0         0       0.0
  $ Sales      :      0         0        0         0         0       0.0
  $ Cost       :      0         0        0         0         0       0.0
  $ Profit     :      0         0        0         0         0       0.0
  Times Turn   :    0.0       0.0      0.0       0.0         0       0.0
  Gross Return :      0         0        0         0         0       0.0

F1-Help   F6-Delete   F7-Enter Stock   F10-Process   ESC-exit
```

Fig. 18-8. The inventory record after posting purchase and merchandise received. "On-order" units reflect a backorder.

Printing the P.O. Status Report

After posting your purchases and merchandise received to the accounting system, you can print the P.O. Status Report from the Journals window. This report lists all purchase orders that are unfilled, or which have backorders outstanding. This report is discussed in Chapter 15 and a copy of the report printed for this tutorial in Appendix D (Report D-17).

Selling to Your Customers

To make the most of *DacEasy*'s integrated system of recordkeeping, you want to use the Billing module when selling to your customers. This module lets you create an invoice for each sale, list all items purchased and all non-inventory charges. You probably will want to use that module for all cash-and-carry sales, as well as credit and purchase order sales. Sales not made through the Billing module must be posted to accounts receivable manually.

You can also sell services through the Billing module. Services would be listed in your services file and all the appropriate records automatically kept by *DacEasy Accounting*.

You can also sell items and services through the Billing module that were used for your business rather than for re-sale. The value of these items are appropriately posted to revenues and assets, based on the account numbers that were set up in the purchasing and billing codes tables (see Figs. 7-11 and 7-12).

Because *DacEasy Accounting* does so much for you through the billing (and purchase order) module, you should be sure that your sales and return procedures are fully integrated, and that all information is entered regularly, frequently, and correctly.

The Billing transactions window (Fig. 11-6) gives you complete control of selling and invoicing. You can create invoices, and match them to merchandise sold. If a customer returns an item, you can create a sales return form to accompany the returned merchandise.

All inventory and services records are automatically updated and revised to reflect sales and returned items. From this information you can print reports of all of the activity within the billing module.

All the information in your customer file and your inventory/product file is immediately available each time you enter an appropriate code. Services might also be invoiced, and all accompanying accounting activity recorded automatically within the accounting system.

If you are not using *DacEasy Graph + Mate*, you need to print lists of customers and products when you use the Billing module. With *DacEasy Graph + Mate*, you can "pop-up" the codes from each file.

When to Use an Invoice

The invoice can be filled out at the time of the sale, or the sales ticket can be used to enter the invoice at a later date.

You might want to establish a "dummy" customer to which all cash sales are credited so that you do not have to create a new customer record each time a new customer comes in for a small item. A "dummy" customer permits the system to credit sales and debit cash-on-deposit when the deposit is made daily. In addition, all inventory records would be current if you use the invoice as a sales ticket, listing items purchased for the cash sale. Chapter 14 includes a complete discussion of "point-of-sale" accounting.

You might also want to use a sales ticket that is not dependent on immediate keyboard entry of a sale. This approach to cash sales can create a sales ticket, with a carbon for your records, at the point-of-sale and then transfer the information from the sales ticket to the computer, some point after the sale.

Whether you use a "point-of-sale" or a "sales-ticket" approach, you must use inventory numbers to indicate items sold. *DacEasy* can control your inventory only if you tell it exactly what has been sold (and bought) each and every time a sale (or purchase) takes place.

Creating an Invoice

From the *DacEasy Accounting* Main Menu, select the Transactions option, then select the Billing module from the Transactions window. To create your first invoice, elect to "enter invoices" from the Billing window (Fig. 11-6).

When the invoice work screen is displayed, the cursor is at the "invoice number" field. Press <ENTER> to display the next available number, or type in the number of an invoice you have already created and want to review. For our example, press <ENTER> to create a new invoice. The cursor moves to the "customer code" field.

When you enter the customer code, a window opens in the middle of the screen, showing the current status of that customer's account. The credit limit and the balance available within that limit is displayed. When you press any key to continue, the name and address is displayed. You can edit any of these fields, or press <ENTER> to move through them, until the cursor stops in the field for "remarks". You can enter a shipping address, if it is different from the original customer address, or any other comment that might be appropriate. You have three lines of 20 characters.

The cursor will stop at the "Via" field and at the "FOB" field. Enter the appropriate information for those, referring to the definitions in the purchase orders section.

You can then enter two reference numbers. The first is a reference code, or number, that the customer recognizes and helps the customer keep track of his or her purchases. This code might be a purchase order number or a check number. The second reference is a code that you use for your recordkeeping. In our examples, we use the invoice number. To skip either or both, press <ENTER> the appropriate number of times.

Discount information and due days are displayed automatically. *DacEasy* retrieves this information from the existing customer file.

Entering Items Purchased by a Customer

The process for entering items to be purchased by the customer is similar to completing purchase order forms (described earlier in the chapter).

Items to be sold must have an inventory number that can be entered in the first column of the invoice, and that can be confirmed by *DacEasy* when it looks for the number and description of the product. In addition to using inventory numbers in the "Inv. #" column, enter a code from the billing codes table or the letter "D" if you want to type a descriptive comment.

Entering Non-Inventory Items

You can, however, include non-inventory items, such as freight or insurance for shipped items, by typing the letter "C," followed by a space and the code from the billing codes table (see Fig. 7-12).

In addition, you can sell non-inventory items, such as old trucks and other assets used in the business. The billing codes table contains items for these sales, and revenue are posted to the accounts provided for these transactions.

Note that the letter "C" and the number that follows it are not printed on the invoice.

Adding Comments

You can also add comments or explanations for entries on the invoice. To do this, type the letter "D" in the "Inv. #" column and press <ENTER>. The cursor moves to the right and permits you to type as many as 40 characters on the line. Use as many lines as you need. The "D" will not be printed on the invoice and spaces between the lines are omitted.

Totaling the Invoice

When all items have been entered for the current invoice, press <F10> to tell

```
                                 Invoice #   01001
Customer Code: WEIR01           Remark:
Weir Lighting Fixtures          Ship to address       Via Truck
Sam Charger                     at left.              FOB
4312 S. Socket Street                                 Your Ref. 884356
Ninety Six        SC   29666-                         Our Ref.   01001
Disc. Days        10 Disc. %  3.00  Due Days    30  Tax Code: 4 Rate:  5.000

   Inv. #       Desc. Ordered    Shipped  Back Ord.    Price   Disc.   Extended

   PAINT01   Paint. Wt Base Gal
               5.002        5.002        0.000     75.800  0.00     416.90
   CONDUIT01 Conduit. Alum 16Ft
               3.000        3.000        0.000      8.590  0.00      25.77

 Sub Total    Sales Tax     Total    Pmt.Ref.  Payment $   Net to Pay
  442.67       22.13       464.80                0.00        464.80
```

```
                                 Invoice #   01002
Customer Code: VOLT01           Remark:
Volten, Rhea                    Cash and carry.       Via
                                                      FOB
P.O. Box 3423                                         Your Ref. Ck3104
Hodges            SC   29653-                         Our Ref.   01002
Disc. Days        0 Disc. %  0.00  Due Days    30  Tax Code: 4 Rate:  5.000

   Inv. #       Desc. Ordered    Shipped  Back Ord.    Price   Disc.   Extended

   GARDEN09 Hose. Garden 25Ft
               1.000        1.000        0.000     11.880  0.00      11.88
   BOARD51  Plywood, 3/4 4x8
               2.000        2.000        0.000     32.950  0.00      65.90
   PAINT02  Paint, Wt Base Qt
               0.002        0.002        0.000     83.400  0.00      13.90

 Sub Total    Sales Tax     Total    Pmt.Ref.  Payment $   Net to Pay
   91.68        4.58        96.26     Cash       96.26         0.00
```

Fig. 18-9. Sample invoice information to be used with Parts and Parcels tutorials. Enter through the Billing Transaction Window.

DacEasy to "process" the billing. Subtotals and taxes are calculated (from information in the customer file) and a total displayed.

Advance Payments and Cash Sales

If there is an advance payment, such as a cash sale, you can reference it, and its amount, before *DacEasy* calculates and displays the "net to pay." Simply enter a code (up to six characters) in the reference field—a word like "CASH" might do—and the amount tendered in the advance payment field. The "net to pay" will, of course, be zero.

```
                                    Invoice #   01003
Customer Code: WEIR01           Remark:
Weir Lighting Fixtures          Ship to address      Via Truck
Sam Charger                     at left.             FOB
4312 S. Socket Street                                Your Ref. 883982
Ninety Six        SC  29666-                         Our Ref.   01003
Disc. Days        10 Disc. %  3.00  Due Days    30  Tax Code: 4 Rate:  5.000
─────────────────────────────────────────────────────────────────────────
   Inv. #        Desc. Ordered    Shipped  Back Ord.   Price   Disc. Extended
─────────────────────────────────────────────────────────────────────────
   CONDUIT07     Conduit, Plas 50Ft
                    30.000      25.000      5.000     21.500  3.50    518.69



   Sub Total     Sales Tax     Total    Pmt.Ref.  Payment $   Net to Pay
    518.69        25.93       544.62                 0.00       544.62
```

```
                                    Invoice #   01004
Customer Code: BILD01           Remark:
Bildah Supply, Inc.             Ship to: New School  Via Truck
J. Bildah, Foreman              Rt2, Booker Road     FOB
5432 Brickyard Blvd.            Greenwood, SC 29646  Your Ref. PO7129
Greenwood         SC  29646-                         Our Ref.   01004
Disc. Days        10 Disc. %  3.00  Due Days    30  Tax Code: 4 Rate:  5.000
─────────────────────────────────────────────────────────────────────────
   Inv. #        Desc. Ordered    Shipped  Back Ord.   Price   Disc. Extended
─────────────────────────────────────────────────────────────────────────
   BOARD01       2x4, Pine Stud 8Ft
                  2500.000    2500.000     0.000      0.170   2.00    416.50
   CONDUIT01     Conduit, Alum 16Ft
                    80.000      80.000     0.000      8.590   2.00    673.46
   PAINT01       Paint, Wt Base Gal
                    35.000      19.002    15.002     75.800   2.00   1448.54
   D             Backorders guaranteed in 3 work days.

   C 1           Delivery and unloading.
                                                                      50.00

   Sub Total     Sales Tax     Total    Pmt.Ref.  Payment $   Net to Pay
   2588.50        126.93      2715.43                0.00      2715.43
```

Fig. 18-9. Continued

Creating Invoices for Parts and Parcels

Sample Invoices

Figure 18-9 contains information for six invoices that you should enter in Parts and Parcels records. After they have been entered through the Billing module, we will trace them through inventory and to accounts receivable.

Special Situations in Samples

As we discuss the sample invoices in Fig. 18-9, we point out the special non-inventory items included, and the results of selling items that you don't have.

```
                                   Invoice #   01005
Customer Code: PAMS01          Remark:
Pam's Spades/Garden Shop        Picked up.          Via
Pam Mulch                                           FOB
123 Pine Bark Circle                                Your Ref. Ck0789
Greenwood       SC  29646-                          Our Ref.   01005
Disc. Days      10 Disc. %  3.00  Due Days    30  Tax Code: 4 Rate:   5.000

   Inv. #         Desc. Ordered   Shipped  Back Ord.    Price      Disc. Extended

 GARDEN01           Hoe, Garden
                       6.000        6.000      0.000     19.950   0.00      119.70


   Sub Total     Sales Tax     Total      Pmt.Ref.   Payment $   Net to Pay
    119.70         5.99       125.69      Cash        125.69       0.00
```

```
                                   Invoice #   01006
Customer Code: PAMS01          Remark:
Pam's Spades/Garden Shop        On-site service.    Via
Pam Mulch                                           FOB
123 Pine Bark Circle                                Your Ref. 880034
Greenwood       SC  29646-                          Our Ref.   01006
Disc. Days      10 Disc. %  3.00  Due Days    30  Tax Code: 4 Rate:   5.000

   Inv. #         Desc. Ordered   Shipped  Back Ord.    Price      Disc. Extended

 SOILTEST01        Soil, Prelim Test
                       3.002        3.002      0.000     30.000   0.00      105.00


   Sub Total     Sales Tax     Total      Pmt.Ref.   Payment $   Net to Pay
    105.00         5.25       110.25                   0.00       110.25
```

Fig. 18-9. Continued

Invoice #01001

The first sample invoice is for a small company that deals with lighting fixtures. The order is referenced for the company's purchase order number ("Your Ref.") and our invoice ("Our Ref."). Enter the inventory number and the quantity ordered for each item purchased.

Note that the quantity for product PAINT01 is entered as a decimal fraction. The fractional part of inventory items is discussed in Chapter 8. We entered the decimal number "5.2" to indicate that we had sold 5 complete cases and 2 fractional parts of a case. The fraction part indicated in the inventory record for PAINT01 is 4—meaning that there are four cans of paint in one case. Thus, the "5.2" that we entered is translated by *DacEasy* to "5 ¾" cases.

When we pressed <ENTER> after typing "5.2," *DacEasy* changed the fraction to "5.002." This is done because *DacEasy* can accept fractional parts in the inventory file up to "999."

You can check *DacEasy*'s arithmetic by calculating the extended cost. Each case costs $75.80. The extended cost is exactly 5 ½ times that cost.

Pressing <F10> moves the cursor to the "Pmt.Ref." field, where you can enter a reference to the method of payment if you want. For this invoice, no payment has been made and the total amount is currently due.

Invoice #01002

The second invoice is a cash-and-carry purchase made by an individual. The customer's reference is the number on the check with which the bill was paid.

One of the items on the invoice is a fractional part of the case. PAINT02, in the inventory list "12" as the fraction of the unit—indicating that there are 12 cans of paint in each case. The ".002" was entered as "0.2" to indicate we had sold two cans out of a case. The extended cost is exactly $2/12$—or $1/6$—of the price for one case.

The purchases are standard and the totals are calculated by *DacEasy*. Note that the "net to pay" is zero because the individual's check has been handled as an immediate payment. The invoice was created so *DacEasy* could adjust the inventory, post the appropriate revenue account, and eventually post the correct bank account.

Invoice #01003

The lighting fixture company came back that day and placed an order for 30 coils of plastic conduit piping. Note that a purchase order is referenced for the customer.

When the desired quantity (30) is keyed in and <ENTER> is pressed, the "shipped" column specifies 25 items and the "backorder" column specifies five. *DacEasy* knew, from the inventory, that there were only 25 coils in stock and it automatically backordered the balance. The extended price includes only the 25 items shipped—minus a three and one-half percent discount. When <F10> is pressed, *DacEasy* totals and displays the bottom line. The cursor is placed in the "sales tax" field so the tax amount can be confirmed. When <F10> is pressed again, the invoice is filed and another empty invoice is displayed.

Invoice #01004

The contractor who placed the order for which the fourth invoice was written requested that the materials be shipped to a construction site. The shipping address is given at the top of the invoice. The invoice, itself, is mailed to the customer's regular address.

The customer requested more paint than was in stock and *DacEasy* automatically backordered the balance, billing only for the quantity shipped. The seller entered a message on the invoice to indicate that the backordered items would be delivered within three working days. A "D" in the inventory number column allows entry of the message.

Because the items were to be delivered and unloaded outside the free delivery area, a delivery charge was added to the invoice. The charge is not for an inventory item and can only be entered if the billing codes table includes a code under the billing column.

Line 1 contains the "freight" reference code that was entered in the inventory number column. When *DacEasy* automatically enters "Freight" following the code, we just typed "Delivery and unloading" so it overwrote the word "Freight."

Totals, as always, are calculated by *DacEasy*, using the tax rates in the customer's record. You must press <F10> twice to file the invoice.

Invoice #01005

The customer to whom the fifth invoice was issued picked up the merchandise and paid for it with a check. That check is referenced on the invoice. The completion of the invoice was normal, with the advance payment fields used to designate the cash transaction and the advance payment. The balance due is zero.

Invoice #01006

The sixth invoice is for services rather than products. For the soil testing services, we charge by the hour and, according to the services file, for every quarter-hour (or part thereof, as they say). The testing took three and one-half hours and was entered on the invoice as "3.2," which is translated to mean "3 and ¾" hours. The extended cost is exactly 3½ × 30, which is the hourly rate.

Although we have not included a sample invoice for selling assets, you could create an invoice for any item listed in the billing codes table (see Fig. 7-12).

Completing the Invoices

When all invoices have been entered, return to the Billing Menu by pressing <ESC> when the cursor is in the "invoice number" field of the next blank work screen.

Printing Invoices

From the Billing transactions window (Fig. 11-6), elect to "print invoices." Your options are the same as print purchase orders (see Fig. 18-4). Assume you do not want packing slips (at this time), do not want to re-print invoices, and you want to print all invoices on plain white paper instead of on pre-printed forms. Accept the date as it is displayed—although you can change it if you need to give a date other than the current date.

The printed invoices include most of the information you saw on the work screens and one important other piece of data: The date payment is due. This date is calculated from information in the customers record.

Copies of the invoices printed from these examples are included in Appendix D (Reports D-18 through D-23).

The Sales Journal

After you print invoices for your customers, print the Sales Journal so you can have a complete and concise record of the sales for the current period. This option is selected from the Billing transactions window (Fig. 11-6).

The first page of the Sales Journal contains a list of all invoices, sorted by customer department. The gross sales are listed and totaled, the sales taxes are listed and totaled, and the total of each invoice is listed and totaled. The amounts paid are included and used in calculating the balance to be paid.

The second page contains an inventory summary, sorted by department. This list includes units and fractions sold, sales price, and an average price per unit sold. The total for sales on this page matches the total for sales listed on the first page.

Both pages of the report are included in Appendix D (Reports D-24 and D-25).

Posting Invoices and Sales

In order to update your inventory and accounts receivable, you must run the Posting routine for the Billing module.

Before you run that routine, however, print all invoices, returns, and journals listed in the Billing transactions window and in the Billing reports window.

As with any posting process in *DacEasy Accounting*, you should backup your files before starting the process.

Summary

You will understand all the implications of buying and selling through DacEasy Accounting *if you study the sample data presented in this chapter and the reports that have resulted from entry of those data. Copies of all reports are in Appendix D.*

This chapter described, in detail, the process for purchasing merchandise to sell in your store. We traced several examples through the process and seen the results of posting them to the accounting system. You have seen the reports that indicate the updates to inventory and accounts payable—updates that are done automatically when the posting process is completed.

This chapter also described, in detail, the process of selling and billing for merchandise. We presented several examples and have seen the results of posting to the accounting system. Samples of invoices, reports, and update screens were given. These updates are completed automatically by DacEasy Accounting.

19

Tutorial 3: Hiring and Firing

Chapter Goals
- *This chapter will describe the use of the* DacEasy Payroll *module during the regular operation of a business. We will discuss all the standard procedures for data entry and processing, the payroll registers, automatic calculation, check printing, and the end-of-period routines.*

After completing our work in the accounting module, we must pay the people who have been pushing our wares and pleasing our patrons. The basic payroll data was setup in Chapter 9, and the basic employee information for Parts and Parcels was provided in Chapter 17.

To start the payroll module from your fixed disk, without *DacEasy Graph + Mate*, enter the following commands from the DOS prompt:

```
CD \ DEP3 <ENTER>
DEP3 <ENTER>
```

To start the payroll module, with *DacEasy Graph + Mate*, enter the following commands at the DOS prompt:

```
CD \ GRAFMATE <ENTER>
GM <ENTER>
```

If installation and setup procedures have been completed, the *DacEasy Payroll* Main Menu (Fig. 9-5) is displayed.

An Overview of the Payroll Process

From the main menu, select the option for payroll processing. The Payroll Process window (Fig. 11-11) is displayed. It contains the logical process for working with the payroll module. If these steps are followed in sequence your payroll records will be updated and your payroll checks printed.

The first step in using the payroll program is to enter the exceptions for the current period's payroll. When exceptions are completed, instruct *DacEasy* to calculate all the deductions, based on the information in each employee's record. Calculations can be different for each employee because each employee has a separate record.

After deduction calculations are completed, print and examine the payroll register, which is a list of the complete payroll. Any errors detected in the register can be corrected in the system before checks are printed. Whenever corrections are made, a new register should be printed.

When you are satisfied with the payroll register, print the payroll checks. The checks will be compared to the payroll register and to the check register, which is printed immediately after the checks are printed. At this time, incorrect checks can be voided and new checks printed.

When all payroll checks are printed and correct, print a final checks register, a department and codes summary, and then post the payroll data to the accounting system.

The last step in the payroll process includes the end-of-period routines, which post the proper amounts to the general ledger and compile data for quarterly reports, federal W-2 forms, and other reports.

Once payroll is complete, print the payroll reports that summarize payroll activity and allow you to examine any areas in your payroll costs that might need review.

The File routines can be run each time a new employee is hired, or an existing employee quits, is fired, or promoted. Changes in base salaries, wages, and in tax rates, are also entered through maintenance routines.

Figure 17-8 provides information for the five employees of Parts and Parcels. Using the procedures described in Chapter 9 and Chapter 17, enter the employee information (if you have not done so already).

Printing an Employee Directory

Before starting the payroll process, print a payroll directory for reference as you enter data. If you are not using *DacEasy Graph + Mate*, the list should be near your work station as a primary source of employee information. If you are using *DacEasy Graph + Mate*, much of the employee information is available on-screen and your printed list is used only when the on-screen data is not sufficient.

To print a complete employee list, select Payroll Reports from the Main Menu. The Reports window is displayed and you can print the employee directory.

The directory prints a one-page record for each employee. Each record contains all the information entered through the Files option. The directory also contains all of the quarter-to-date and year-to-date information that can be useful if reprinted regularly.

Printing a Department General Ledger Interface Table

Part of the information you will need to enter employee data is contained in the department general ledger interface tables. You will need the earnings codes shown in Fig. 9-8 and the withholdings codes in Fig. 9-9. You can print each of these by using the "print screen" feature of your computing system.

From the main menu, select the Files option. The Files window is displayed (see Fig. 9-5). Choose the option for departments. When the first work screen is shown, enter your first department number (in our example, we have only one). When the data is displayed, hold down the <SHIFT> key and press the <PRTSC> key to print the screen to the printer. Use the <PgDn> key to display the next screen and repeat the process to print it. Finally, press <PgDN> for the third screen and print it. Repeat for each department.

Once you have printed all screens, return to the main menu. With this information in-hand you are ready to begin payroll processing.

Payroll Data Entry

From the main menu of the payroll module, select the Process option to begin the payroll data entry process at the end of each pay period. The Payroll Processing Menu (Fig. 11-11) is displayed. Select the option for "data entry." Fig. 19-1 shows a sample work screen. You must then provide the payroll period (weekly, monthly, etc.). Parts and Parcels employees are all paid weekly.

The payroll data entry process is used only when there is an exception to the information provided in an individual's employee record, or in the payroll control file (Fig. 9-4). If your payroll is stable from one period to the next, you will never use this routine. If, however, you have varying hours for some employees, or overtime hours for others, this routine permits you to enter these exceptions to the employee's files before printing checks.

Depending on the code you enter in this routine (see Fig. 19-1), *DacEasy Payroll*

```
┌─────────────────────────────────────────────────────────────────────────┐
│                                                                           │
│  Emp.  #   REAL01 Name   Real, Rod N.              Dept   1   Parts and Parcels │
│  ┌─────────────────────────────────────────────────────────────────────┐  │
│  │                          Tax Base            Current Period: Weekly   │  │
│  │  Dept Code Description   Fed State   Number  Rate or %      Amount    │  │
│  │                                                                       │  │
│  │   1    2    Hourly        T    T     27.000     4.0000      108.00    │  │
│  │                                                                       │  │
│  │                                                                       │  │
│  │    Total Earnings   :        108.00 │ Total Deductions  :       0.00  │  │
│  │    Total Hrs worked :         27.000│ Total Liabilities :       0.00  │  │
│  └─────────────────────────────────────────────────────────────────────┘  │
│  F1-Help   F6-Delete   F10-Process   Alt_D-Line                           │
│                                                                           │
└─────────────────────────────────────────────────────────────────────────┘
```

Fig. 19-1. Entering exceptions to the regular payroll. *The employee worked only 27 hours instead of the normal 40.*

adjusts the amount of the specified payroll checks. If no exceptions are listed for an employee, the payroll check is written as indicated in the employee file and the payroll control file.

The following information might assist you in completing this work screen. The main thing to remember, however, is that this routine is done only if there is a change in an employee's file.

Employee Number and Name. In the payroll data entry work screen enter the code "REAL01" where the cursor is flashing in the "employee number" field to begin entering data for that employee. The employee's name is automatically displayed, as is the department to which the employee was originally assigned.

Department Number. If the employee is to be paid for work done outside the original department (and if other departments have been defined in the setup process), enter the appropriate amount here. If the exception is in the original department, enter the amount shown at the top of the screen.

Code. The cursor will move to the "code" field, where you must enter the exception code. The exception code can be an earnings code, a deductions code, or an employer liability code. The earnings codes (01 through 15), and deductions codes (16 through 30), come from the department general ledger interface tables (Figs. 9-8 and 9-9). Employer liability codes are defined below and are not included in the interface table.

Code 31: Employer FICA Liability
Code 32: FUTA
Code 33: SUTA
Code 34: Defined by system user
Code 35: Defined by system user
Code 36: Defined by system user
Code 40: Tips reported to employer

Figure 19-1 illustrates a situation in which an employee worked fewer than the 40 hours entered in the Payroll Control File (see Fig. 9-4). Normally, *DacEasy* would use the 40 hours to automatically calculate the wages for employees paid an hourly rate. The employee, however, whose name appears at the top of Fig. 19-1 worked only 27 hours during the first week Parts and Parcels was open. Because 27 hours is an exception to the information included in the Payroll Control File, it must be entered here. *DacEasy* will then use the 27 hours to over-ride the normal 40-hour week for waged employees.

The 37 codes available for defining exceptions to normal pay patterns make *DacEasy* a powerful and flexible tool to handling your payroll needs. This flexibility can be seen in the following example (which we will not enter into our tutorial).

An employee is hired at an hourly rate, and is paid an additional amount, based on the number of items he is able to produce. In the department general ledger interface table for earnings (Fig. 9-8), the employer can use code 10 to indicate "piece work." The account can be included to place the actual amounts paid for piece work in the proper accounts in the general ledger. The appropriate "type" would be given (see Chapter 9) and the amount-per-piece entered as the rate. The appropriate tax codes would be entered.

On pay day, the employer finds that the employee has worked the full 40 hours (at $4.65 per hour), and has produced 109 "pieces." He has been promised 87.5 cents per piece. The employer would enter the piece work information on a screen like that shown in Fig. 19-1. Code 10 would be placed in the second column, and the description would be displayed automatically. The tax information would be displayed but could be edited. The cursor then stops in the "number" column, where the employer would type in "109" as the number of pieces completed. The "rate" would be automatically displayed, as would the "amount."

The code would tell *DacEasy* how to calculate the proper pay amount.

There would be no need to enter the hours because they were normal and are used to calculate the base pay for this employee. The Payroll Register showed that this employee received earnings from two sources—the hourly rate and his piece work. The paycheck is written for the total amount.

As with the earnings codes, the deductions codes and the liabilities codes provide instructions to *DacEasy* for calculating payroll when there are exceptions to the normal calculation.

Tax Base Types. The next two fields match the "tax base" fields for federal and state withholdings that are also shown beside the salary field on the department general ledger interface table. Each can be changed, if needed, or accepted by pressing <ENTER>.

Number. The "number" column is used to provide specific information used in calculating payroll. For salaried employees (Code 1), the number represents the number of days to pay in the current pay period. For employees paid by the hour (Code 2), the number represents the number of hours to pay. For overtime (Code 3 or Code 4), the number represents the number of overtime hours—not the total number of hours worked. For employees who report tips (Code 5), the amount is the actual amount of the tips to be paid. In all cases, the code determines how *DacEasy* calculates a payroll exception.

Amount to Pay. For most situations, the calculated amount to pay is automatically displayed. For some—such as tips—you have to enter the amount. This amount can either be, the amount to pay, or an amount that is added to the normal pay for a particular employee. It might also designate additional amounts to be deducted (if you use codes 16 through 30) or additional amounts of employer liability (if you use codes 31 through 36, or code 40).

More than one code can be entered for one employee.

When you have completed entering data for a particular employee, press <F10> to go on to the next employee.

Entering Data for the Parts and Parcels Employees

All Parts and Parcels employees worked during the first week that the store was open. Complete the information shown in Fig. 19-1 before continuing with the payroll tutorial. In addition, another part-time employee—Bitsy Router (ROUT01)—worked only 14.5 hours that week. Enter this information before going on.

Figure 19-2 shows the entry for employee PART01. She worked overtime during the first week. Her normal salary is calculated when we start the automatic payroll

```
┌──────────────────────────────────────────────────────────────────────────┐
│  Emp. #  PART01 Name  Partment, Notmai D.        Dept  1   Parts and Parcels │
│  ┌────────────────────────────────────────────────────────────────────┐   │
│  │                    Tax Base              Current Period: Weekly      │   │
│  │  Dept Code Description  Fed State  Number  Rate or %      Amount      │   │
│  │  ──────────────────────────────────────────────────────────────     │   │
│  │   1    3    Overtime #1  T   T      5.000      8.6300       43.15     │   │
│  │                                                                      │   │
│  │                                                                      │   │
│  │                                                                      │   │
│  │  ─────────────────────────────┬──────────────────────────────────   │   │
│  │   Total Earnings   :    43.15  │ Total Deductions  :         0.00     │   │
│  │   Total Hrs worked :    0.000  │ Total Liabilities :         0.00     │   │
│  └────────────────────────────────────────────────────────────────────┘   │
│  F1-Help   F6-Delete   F10-Process   Alt_D-Line                            │
└──────────────────────────────────────────────────────────────────────────┘
```

Fig. 19-2. Entering overtime pay. *An employee worked 5 hours overtime. Code "3" tells DacEasy Payroll to add the amount to regular pay.*

generation. The information in Fig. 19-2, however, is used by *DacEasy* to add the appropriate amount of overtime pay to her wages. Enter the information in Fig. 19-2 before proceeding.

The other two employees will be paid normally this week. Do not enter any special information for them because their salaries are calculated in the automatic generation of normal payroll.

Automatic Payroll Generation

From the Payroll Process option, you can calculate normal payroll after completing payroll data entry for exceptions. This automatically calculates payroll and deductions for each employee, using information from the employee records. It also calculates all employer liabilities for matching FICA amounts and other payroll amounts.

A window opens and you will be asked to identify the type of payroll to calculate (weekly, monthly, etc.).

Figure 19-3 includes the options for generating regular payroll. If exceptions exist, they will be accounted for and the calculated amounts automatically adjusted.

When your options are entered, press <ENTER> to pass through all listed items, the calculation is done automatically.

If you have employees paid for differing periods—that is, some paid weekly and others paid bi-weekly—you must run the calculation routine again.

Printing the Payroll Register

The Payroll Register can be printed by selecting the appropriate option from the Payroll Process window (Fig. 11-11). It should be printed before printing payroll checks.

The Payroll Register includes a summary of payroll activity for each employee for whom checks will be written. You should examine it to be sure that there are no discrepancies, and that you are not about to write a check for several million inappropriate dollars.

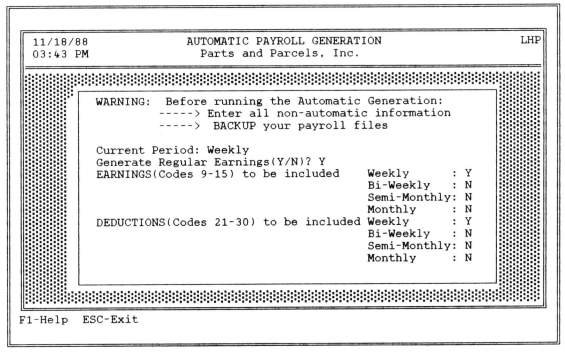

```
 11/18/88                  AUTOMATIC PAYROLL GENERATION                LHP
 03:43 PM                    Parts and Parcels, Inc.


       WARNING:  Before running the Automatic Generation:
                 -----> Enter all non-automatic information
                 -----> BACKUP your payroll files

       Current Period: Weekly
       Generate Regular Earnings(Y/N)? Y
       EARNINGS(Codes 9-15) to be included      Weekly     : Y
                                                Bi-Weekly  : N
                                                Semi-Monthly: N
                                                Monthly    : N
       DEDUCTIONS(Codes 21-30) to be included  Weekly     : Y
                                                Bi-Weekly  : N
                                                Semi-Monthly: N
                                                Monthly    : N




 F1-Help   ESC-Exit
```

Fig. 19-3. Automatic payroll calculations are made using information in the employee file unless exceptions are entered in processing.

The Payroll Register includes the code and description for each type of pay received by each employee. The number of hours is printed for each waged employee and the number of days paid is listed for each salaried person. Overtime and other exceptions-to-normal are listed and totaled. Total earnings are listed by pay type.

Each type of deduction, calculated by *DacEasy*, is coded, named, and totaled. The net pay is calculated and displayed for each employee. The employer's liabilities for social security (FICA), Federal unemployment tax (FUTA), and State unemployment tax (SUTA) are also included.

Totals for each employee, each department, and for the whole payroll are given.

Separate reports must be printed for waged employees and for salaried employees. In Appendix D, Report D-26 and Report D-27 show the results of printing the Payroll Register for Parts and Parcels, based on the information given above.

Printing Payroll Checks

If you were operating your business at this point, you would need payroll checks. These can be purchased from *DacEasy* (their advertisements surely accompanied their software), or from other suppliers that provide forms especially designed for *DacEasy*. For our tutorial, we recommend that you use blank white paper.

When you have confirmed that the amounts on the Payroll Register are correct, you are ready to begin the process of printing the payroll checks. Be sure your printer is ready and that your checks (or blank paper) are aligned to your satisfaction. The program will print an alignment pattern that will void the first check each time.

Once the payroll checks are printed, *DacEasy* reverses the names as they are copied from the employee files, printing the first name before the last name.

The checks should be visually scanned for accuracy and compared to the Payroll Register that was printed earlier.

Printing the Payroll Checks Register

The Payroll Checks Register is your official record of checks printed. It should not be confused with the Payroll Register, which is the list of checks that are to be printed. These reports are a "before-and-after" payroll accuracy test.

When you elect to print the report, you will be asked if you want to include paid, unpaid, or both paid and unpaid checks. "Paid" refers to any check that has cleared the bank. The register lists these checks as "not paid" because they have not been paid by the bank. The "paid" terminology does not refer to employees—it refers only to the check clearing the bank. Thus, you will (probably) want to print only the unpaid checks, or both, at this point.

Report D-28, in Appendix D, illustrates the Check Register Report that resulted from printing the payroll checks for the five employees of Parts and Parcels. The report is sorted by check number.

DacEasy provides a routine to reconcile the check register—"Check Reconciliation"— and it can be found in the Periodic window of the Main Menu. If you select this option, you can enter check numbers and mark them paid or void. You mark only those checks that have cleared your bank.

After clearing these checks, re-print your check register to include paid, unpaid, or both types of checks. You can also purge paid checks monthly so that your register contains only outstanding checks. The purge feature for payroll checks is also listed in in the Periodic routines.

If you have additional paychecks to write for employees who are paid by a period other than weekly, return to the *DacEasy Payroll* Main Menu and re-start the payroll processing procedures. These procedures must be repeated for every differing pay cycle.

Printing Department Reports

You can print a detailed report, by department, that includes all the activity in the payroll, deductions, and employer liability codes found in the department general ledger interface table (Figs. 9-8 and 9-9). Each code is listed with the persons and amounts that affect the accounts represented by those codes. Total activity is given for each account.

A detail report and a summary report are available from the Department Report option in the Process window of the main menu.

In Appendix D, Reports D-29 and D-30 are pages of the detail report for departments and codes. Report D-31 is the summary report for each of the accounts represented by the codes in each of the departments.

Post Payroll Data

The payroll posting routine posts the period's transactions to the employee records and creates the journal entries (in the payroll journal code "PY") that will be posted to the accounting system, if you are interfacing with *DacEasy Accounting*. The transaction number in the journal is a four-digit number which includes using the month and day of the end-of-period routines.

Before posting payroll data, you should backup your data files.

When the posting process is complete, the period payroll general ledger transaction summary report is printed. It lists the total activity in each of the accounts named in each department general ledger interface table. Report D-32, in Appendix D, contains the results of posting the payroll data from our examples for Parts and Parcels.

Cancel Automatic Generation

If you need to enter special payroll information that requires the suspension of normal payroll information, you can "cancel automatic generation" of the normal payroll. This feature is not used often, but it is provided for those few times.

End-of-Period Routines

There are six end-of-period procedures we can run: (1) print the monthly payroll report, (2) end-of-month process, (3) print payroll quarterly report, (4) end-of-quarter process, (5) print W-2 and 1099 forms, and (6) end-of-year process. Figure 19-4 shows the window for processing payroll periods.

Print Payroll Quarterly Report

The payroll quarterly report is one of the most important reports that a business can complete and submit to government agencies. It lists wages subject to FICA taxes, withholding taxes, and state unemployment taxes (SUTA).

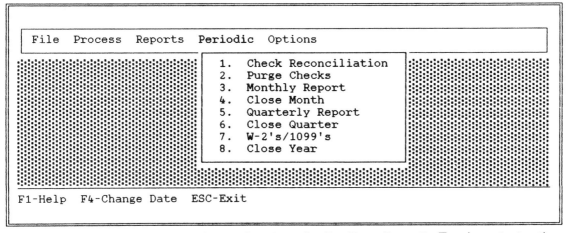

Fig. 19-4. End-of-Period options for DacEasy Payroll. *Two important options are the quarterly report and W-2 Forms.*

When you select this option, *DacEasy* will ask for a range of states for which to print the quarterly reports. For Parts and Parcels, South Carolina is the only state in which employees were paid. The range would be entered as "From SC" and "To SC."

Report D-33, in Appendix D, is a sample report printed from the data entered in the earlier parts of this chapter.

End-of-Quarter Process

The end-of-quarter process clears all quarter-to-date amounts, clearing those fields for new data in a new quarter. Be sure to print all your quarter reports before running this routine because this routine clears all data that will be used in quarterly reports.

Print W-2 Forms

The standard "one-up/six-deep" W-2 Forms must be printed. These can be obtained from Dac Software, Inc., or from any other agency that provides standard W-2 Forms.

The W-2 format is approved by the IRS, including the sub-totaling of every 41 forms, with sub-totals printed on every 42nd form.

End-of-Year Process

The last option is the end-of-year process, which clears all yearly data. You must print all quarterly reports and W-2 Forms before running this routine. All quarter-to-date and year-to-date totals in the employee records are cleared.

Summary

This chapter detailed using the DacEasy payroll module to pay your employees. Exceptions to normal payroll procedure is discussed in-depth and examples are given. The sequential steps to completing the payroll process are described. Sample data is included for Parts and Parcels.

20

Tutorial 4: Giving and Receiving

Chapter Goals
- *This chapter deals with the cash flow of the business. In the first section, we look at the accounting for revenue from cash sales and from payment of invoices. In the second section, we pay expenses for merchandise received and discuss paying for services and utilities. We also discuss direct entries to accounts receivable and accounts payable. Direct entries are used to record transactions that are not entered through billing or purchasing.*

  As we go through the entry and posting processes, we will print the related statements, journals, and reports.

After we set up the business, buy our inventory, sell items to customers, and pay our employees, we must refine the process of accounting for funds. The accounting system is designed to let us know whether or not we are making a profit. In order to tell us this, we must let the system know something about our income and our expenses.

Making Money: The Tide Flows In

There are many ways to make money in our business. There are, however, only two basic ways to take money: (1) take payment when the sale is made, or (2) take payment after selling the item on credit.

Accounting for funds is done through the accounts receivable module, where all cash receipts, advance payments, and payments on invoices are entered and posted. Once all cash receipts are accounted for in accounts receivable, we can determine part of the worth of the business.

From an accounting standpoint, the money is placed, eventually, in account number 11021, our "checking account." This deposit increases our amount of cash and will, therefore, be a "debit" to the account. The corresponding "credit"—to keep things in balance—must be made to accounts receivable for items purchased on credit, or to sales, for items purchased with cash.

Therefore, to make a deposit to our cash account, we must make the appropriate "journal entries" that move the money out of *DacEasy*'s accounts receivable and sales. In effect, we must instruct *DacEasy* which accounts are affected by the revenue generated by the business. Fortunately, *DacEasy* already knows (from the account numbers listed in the general ledger interface table—Fig. 7-14) the accounts to be posted. Thus consequently, when a cash sale is made, and the invoice is marked paid, or when a payment on an invoice is received, and entered into accounts receivable, *DacEasy* automatically posts the proper amounts to the appropriate accounts.

To make a direct entry to accounts receivable, the appropriate account numbers must be provided when the transaction is entered. Once the posting process is complete, these accounts are updated with the new amounts.

Once the proper accounts are named, and after posting procedures are completed for the appropriate journals, the amounts are removed from each customer's record so that printed statements reflect the payments, whether or not the payments are made in advance.

Advance Payments and Cash Sales

When Parts and Parcels opened for business, two customers made cash payments. These cash payments were entered on the invoices with a resulting balance of zero. These two sales represent the first income for the business.

DacEasy Accounting permits you to enter cash sales, and advance payments treated as cash sales, in the invoice and billing system so that inventory records and customer records can be maintained. This approach works well in updating records without having to do it manually. All the accounting procedures are handled by *DacEasy Accounting*.

See Chapter 14 for a discussion of "point-of-sale" accounting and Chapter 18 for a specific discussion of invoices #01002 and #01005, on which cash sales were recorded.

Figure 18-9 contains a list of all the invoices that we entered earlier. The two we received cash payments for total $222.58. This amount is never entered into accounts receivable because it is received at the time the sales were made. The total of the other four invoices, $3,840.35, is placed in accounts receivable when the posting routine is run from the Billing module.

Payments on Invoices

Some customers will pay on the invoice, whether they take the invoice with them, or you mail it to them. When you receive payment on an invoice, treat it as a cash sale for the day it is received, and enter it into the accounting system through the Accounts Receivable module.

To do this, select Accounts Receivable from the Transactions window on the *DacEasy Accounting* Main Menu. The Accounts Receivable window (Fig. 20-1) is displayed. From this menu, you can choose to enter data from two routines, either directly to accounts

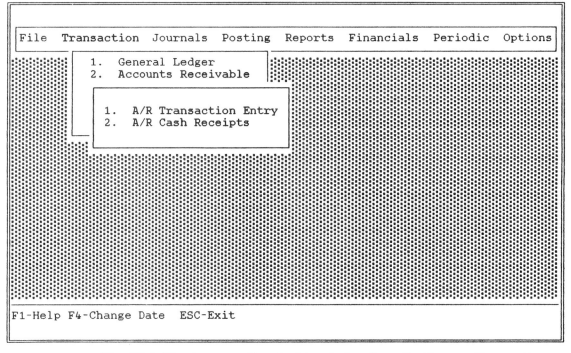

```
┌────────────────────────────────────────────────────────────────────────┐
│ ┌──────────────────────────────────────────────────────────────────────┐ │
│ │ File   Transaction  Journals  Posting  Reports  Financials  Periodic  Options │ │
│ │        ┌──────────────────────────┐                                       │ │
│ │        │ 1.   General Ledger       │                                       │ │
│ │        │ 2.   Accounts Receivable  │                                       │ │
│ │        │  ┌─────────────────────────┐                                      │ │
│ │        │  │ 1.   A/R Transaction Entry │                                   │ │
│ │        │  │ 2.   A/R Cash Receipts     │                                   │ │
│ │        │  └─────────────────────────┘                                      │ │
│ │                                                                            │ │
│ │                                                                            │ │
│ │                                                                            │ │
│ │                                                                            │ │
│ │                                                                            │ │
│ │                                                                            │ │
│ │ F1-Help  F4-Change Date    ESC-Exit                                        │ │
│ └──────────────────────────────────────────────────────────────────────┘ │
└────────────────────────────────────────────────────────────────────────┘
```

Fig. 20-1. The Accounts Receivable window from the Transactions option on the DacEasy Accounting Main Menu.

receivable or, through cash receipts so *DacEasy* can automatically put those amounts in the proper accounts.

For our example choose to enter cash receipts to account for the two checks we received in the mail today. Figure 20-2 and Fig. 20-3 demonstrate entering payments through the cash receipts routine.

To enter the payment shown in Fig. 20-2, follow the procedure outlined in the next several paragraphs.

Transaction Number. Press <ENTER> in the "Transaction #" field and *DacEasy* will assign the next available number to the transaction. If you enter a specific number, however, and the transaction assigned to that number exists, the transaction work screen is displayed and you can edit the transaction.

Customer Code and Name. Enter the customer code. The customer name is displayed automatically. If you enter an incorrect code, press <CTRL+X> to clear the work screen and start again. For our first example, enter the customer code shown in Fig. 20-2. Once the code is entered, a window displays the current status of the account, indicates the credit limit, the current balance, and the current credit available.

Transaction Type. When the cursor stops in the "Transaction Type" field, a window opens on the screen to indicate acceptable entries. You can enter a "P" for payment by check or cash, or you can enter an "A" to indicate that the transaction

```
                 CASH RECEIPTS AND ADJUSTMENTS
 Transaction # :0001                        Date     : 11/20/88
 Customer Code :WEIR01                       Check #  : 3475
         Name :Weir Lighting Fixtures        Amount   :      450.86
 Transac. Type :P                            Applied  :      450.86
 Account #      :11021   Checking Account    To Apply :        0.00
 ─────────────────────────────────────────────────────────────────
 Inv. #   Date      Due       Amount   Disc.Avail  Amt.Applied  Disc.taken
 ─────────────────────────────────────────────────────────────────
 01001   11/19/88 12/19/88    464.80      0.00       450.86       13.94
 01003   11/19/88 12/19/88    544.62     16.34         0.00        0.00


F1-Help F2-Advance F5-Balance F6-Delete F8-Sort F9-Auto apply F10-Process
```

Fig. 20-2. A customer paid one of two invoices. Amounts are posted to accounts receivable and checking.

is an adjustment to the original account. For this sample, we received a check in the mail. Type ''P.''

Account Number. For a payment such as the one we are now entering, *DacEasy* assigns the ''checking account'' number as the account that the revenue is sent to when the transaction is completed. This account number comes from the general ledger interface table as the standard account such transactions are sent to. You can, however, change this account number if you need to for a particular transaction. Press < ENTER> to accept the given account number.

```
                 CASH RECEIPTS AND ADJUSTMENTS
 Transaction # :0002                        Date     : 11/20/88
 Customer Code :BILD01                       Check #  : 12397
         Name :Bildah Supply, Inc.           Amount   :     2633.97
 Transac. Type :P                            Applied  :     2633.97
 Account #      :11021   Checking Account    To Apply :        0.00
 ─────────────────────────────────────────────────────────────────
 Inv. #   Date      Due       Amount   Disc.Avail  Amt.Applied  Disc.taken
 ─────────────────────────────────────────────────────────────────
 01004   11/19/88 12/19/88   2715.43      0.00      2633.97       81.46


F1-Help F2-Advance F5-Balance F6-Delete F8-Sort F9-Auto apply F10-Process
```

Fig. 20-3. A payment is accepted for invoice #01004. Accounts are automatically adjusted when accounts receivable are posted.

Date. The current system date is provided, but can be changed simply by typing over it. You can press <ENTER> to accept the date given, or change the date. The current system date is used by *DacEasy* to determine whether or not your customer qualifies for available discounts for prompt payment.

Check Number. Enter the number of the check your customer sent. If the customer paid with something other than a check, enter a reference that is a unique reminder about this customer's transaction. For our sample, use the customer's check number 3475.

Amount, Applied, and To Apply. The amount of the check or payment must be entered in the "Amount" field. This amount must be the exact amount of the check or payment—not the amount of the invoice. Type in the amount and press <ENTER>. The "Applied" and "To Apply" fields will be skipped and are updated as you enter amounts for each invoice in the bottom section of the work screen.

"Applied" is updated as you apply parts of the check to various invoices listed on the screen. For example, if there are four invoices listed for one customer, and a payment is received, you assign the necessary amounts to each of these invoices as you mark them paid. The "Applied" field will continuously show the total of these amounts as they are applied. The "To Apply" field shows the amount you have left to apply—it subtracts the amounts applied from the amount of the check and displays the difference. The "To Apply" amount should be zero before you end this transaction.

For our example, the customer sent a check for $450.86. Enter this number in the "Amount" field and press <ENTER>. The cursor will skip the next two fields.

Invoice Information. All invoices with non-zero balances are listed in the bottom section of the work screen. The cursor will stop in the "Amt.Applied" field, skipping over the invoice date, the due date, the invoice amount, and the discount available. In the "Amt.Applied" field, enter the amount from the check to be applied to the invoice on that line.

DacEasy automatically applies the appropriate amount for the current invoice line if you press the <F9> key while the cursor is in the "Amt.Applied" field. The options line at the bottom of the screen indicates all the options available on this work screen.

When you press <ENTER> for the amount to be applied to this invoice, the cursor moves to the "Disc. taken" field (the abbreviation means "discount taken"). Enter the portion of the available discount that you are giving the customer. For our example, the payment came in before the discount period expired; so the full discount applies. Enter 13.94 for invoice #01001.

When you entered the "Amt.Applied" on this line, you should have noticed that the "Applied" field at the top of the screen changed. It automatically adjusted to reflect the application of the given amount, and the "To Apply" field automatically adjusted to show what was left.

The check did not include enough money to apply an amount to invoice #01003, which is also outstanding for this customer.

To end the entry for this customer, press <F10> and the information will be processed.

When the next empty work screen is displayed, repeat this process and enter the information for a payment received from Bildah Supply, Inc. Figure 20-3 shows this transaction.

Entering Accounts Receivable Transactions

All cash receipts are entered on the invoice, or through the Accounts Receivable module. There are times when receipts are affected but no payment has been made. For these situations, enter transactions directly into the Accounts Receivable module.

For whatever reason, we have decided to void invoice #01006. To do this, select the "transaction entry" option from the Accounts Receivable window (Fig. 20-1). An empty work screen similar to that shown in Fig. 20-4 is displayed.

The cursor stops at the field for the transaction number. If you are making a new entry, simply press <ENTER> and the next available transaction number is displayed. If you want to review or change a previously entered transaction, enter that transaction number.

To make the entries for our example, press <ENTER>. The transaction number shown in Fig. 20-4 is #0003, which implies that two other transactions have taken place since the last posting. These two transactions were the two payments we received and entered above.

Once the customer number is entered, the customer name is automatically displayed. A window also displays the current status of the account for that customer. If the customer number was entered incorrectly, press <CTRL+X> to clear the work screen and start again.

The cursor moves to the field that you will enter the transaction code. Your options are listed in a small window that opens on the screen.

Invoice. Type an uppercase "I" if the cash receipt is accompanied by an invoice

```
               ACCOUNTS RECEIVABLE TRANSACTION ENTRY
 Trans. #   : 0003                Reference/Check #   : 880034
 Customer # : PAMS01              Transaction Date    : 11/19/88
 Cust. Name : Pam's Spades/Garden Shop  Due Date      : 12/19/88
 Trans. Code: C                   Discount Date       : 11/29/88
 Invoice #  : 01006               Discount Available  :        0.00

 Acct.#    Account Name       Description              Debit      Credit

 11051   Accts Rec'ble Module  Invoice #01006 Voided.            110.25
 4102    Sales Dept. 02        Invoice #01006 Voided.   110.25

 Total Debits :       110.25    | Total Credits :       110.25

 F1-Help F6-Delete F9-Auto Entry F10-Process ALT D-Delete line
```

Fig. 20-4. Voiding an invoice within accounts receivable. *Two accounts must be adjusted.*

that did not come through the Billing module. You can then make entries that would be charged to the appropriate account.

Debit. A debit is used for additional charges to the invoice for the customer. This might happen if a customer paid with a bad check, for which you charge a fee.

Credit. A credit would be used for additional adjustments that decrease the amount of the invoice. Samples of adjustments might include correcting an overcharge, or giving an additional discount.

For our sample, enter a "C" for credit because we are voiding the entire invoice, which will generate a credit to the customer. After entering the letter, type in the "Invoice #" as a reference for the customer and the store.

The "Reference/Check #" field permits you to further identify the credit. We have decided to use the customer's purchase order number so that he can cross-reference the transaction to the canceled purchase.

The dates and discounts available are supplied by *DacEasy* and the cursor moves to the column labeled "Acct. #." The first account number is given by *DacEasy* and it is the number for "accounts receivable." For our sample, the number is 11051, from our chart of accounts. The "Account Name" is automatically displayed and the cursor stops to permit entry of a description.

Type "Invoice #01006 Voided" and press <ENTER>. The invoice amount is $110.25 and must be credited to accounts receivable because it will no longer be charged to that account. Enter the amount in the "Credit" column. (Note that the cursor skipped the Debit column for entry to account #11051.)

Once the credit is entered, the cursor moves to the next line so you can make the balancing entry. For our purpose, we will debit sales for Department 02 so that that department does not show a sale it did not have. When the account number (4102) is entered, the account name is automatically displayed and the description given on the previous line is automatically repeated here. This description can be changed. Pressing <ENTER> to accept the description places the cursor in the "Debit" column, where you should enter $110.25 to balance the credit on the preceding line.

After completing this entry, press <F10> to process the transaction.

Adding Finance Charges for Late Payment

If you have given a finance charge percent in a customer's record, *DacEasy* automatically calculates and adds it when you elect to "generate finance charges" from the Accounts Receivable window in the Periodic routines (Fig. 20-5).

Part of each customer's record is a field for "due days." The number placed in this field is used to calculate the due date—by counting the number of days from the invoice date. If the current date is past the due date, *DacEasy* will calculate the appropriate finance charges.

If you assess finance charges, you should select this routine only once a month. The best time to do this is immediately before you print your customer statements for mailing.

We have no late payments in such a short period of time and will skip this option for now.

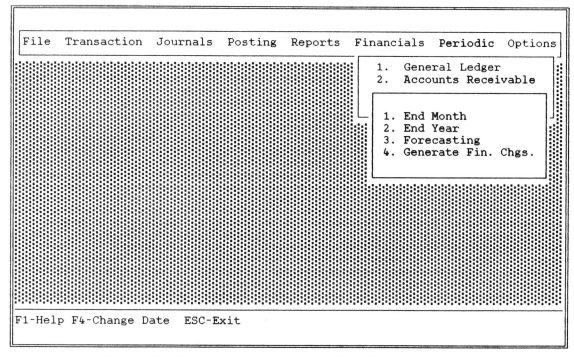

```
┌────────────────────────────────────────────────────────────────────┐
│ ┌──────────────────────────────────────────────────────────────────┐ │
│ │ File  Transaction  Journals  Posting  Reports  Financials  Periodic  Options │
│ │                                        ┌─────────────────────────┐ │
│ │:::::::::::::::::::::::::::::::::::::::::│ 1.   General Ledger      ::│ │
│ │:::::::::::::::::::::::::::::::::::::::::│ 2.   Accounts Receivable ::│ │
│ │:::::::::::::::::::::::::::::::::::::::│ ┌───────────────────────┐ :::│ │
│ │:::::::::::::::::::::::::::::::::::::::└─│ 1. End Month          │─┘::│ │
│ │:::::::::::::::::::::::::::::::::::::::::│ 2. End Year           │:::│ │
│ │:::::::::::::::::::::::::::::::::::::::::│ 3. Forecasting        │:::│ │
│ │:::::::::::::::::::::::::::::::::::::::::│ 4. Generate Fin. Chgs.│:::│ │
│ │:::::::::::::::::::::::::::::::::::::::::└───────────────────────┘:::│ │
│ │:::::::::::::::::::::::::::::::::::::::::::::::::::::::::::::::::::::::│ │
│ │ F1-Help  F4-Change Date   ESC-Exit                               │ │
│ └──────────────────────────────────────────────────────────────────┘ │
└────────────────────────────────────────────────────────────────────┘
```

Fig. 20-5. The Accounts Receivable Periodic window.

Printing the Cash Receipts Journal and the Accounts Receivable Journals

Before posting your cash receipts and accounts receivable transactions, print the Cash Receipts Journal and the Accounts Receivable Journals. These journals are listed in the Journals window (Fig. 15-1) from the main menu. The Cash Receipts Journal is shown in Report D-34 in Appendix D. The Accounts Receivable Journals are shown in Reports D-35 and D-36.

The Cash Receipts Journal lists the two transactions that were entered as cash payments. The Accounts Receivable Journal lists the transaction in which one invoice was voided. The General Ledger Transfer Summary, the second part of the Accounts Receivable Journal, lists the accounts in the chart of accounts that were affected by voiding the invoice.

Posting the Accounts Receivable

When you select the option to post the transactions you've entered into accounts receivable (see Fig. 20-6), you are reminded to back up your files. You should do this so your files won't be lost if there is a computer problem while the posting process is running.

When you are ready to post your transactions, answer ''yes'' to the question about continuing. The posting process is automatic.

Return to the *DacEasy Accounting* Main Menu when the posting process is complete.

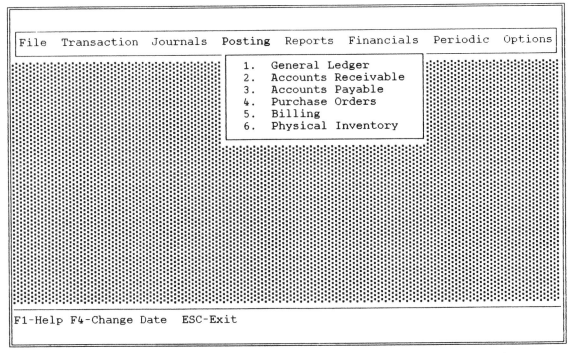

```
┌────────────────────────────────────────────────────────────────────────┐
│                                                                          │
│  File   Transaction  Journals  Posting  Reports  Financials  Periodic  Options │
│ ┌──────────────────────────────┐ ┌─────────────────────────────┐        │
│ ░░░░░░░░░░░░░░░░░░░░░░░░░░░░░░░│ 1.   General Ledger           │░░░░░░░░░░ │
│ ░░░░░░░░░░░░░░░░░░░░░░░░░░░░░░░│ 2.   Accounts Receivable      │░░░░░░░░░░ │
│ ░░░░░░░░░░░░░░░░░░░░░░░░░░░░░░░│ 3.   Accounts Payable         │░░░░░░░░░░ │
│ ░░░░░░░░░░░░░░░░░░░░░░░░░░░░░░░│ 4.   Purchase Orders          │░░░░░░░░░░ │
│ ░░░░░░░░░░░░░░░░░░░░░░░░░░░░░░░│ 5.   Billing                  │░░░░░░░░░░ │
│ ░░░░░░░░░░░░░░░░░░░░░░░░░░░░░░░│ 6.   Physical Inventory       │░░░░░░░░░░ │
│                                                                          │
│                                                                          │
│ F1-Help  F4-Change Date   ESC-Exit                                       │
└────────────────────────────────────────────────────────────────────────┘
```

Fig. 20-6. The Posting window for ending periods in the journals.

Checking the General Ledger Journals Report

To check the results of all the entries made for accounts receivable, go to the Journals window and print the General Ledger Journal Report. This report contains all the transactions that have been posted in purchasing, billing, accounts receivable, accounts payable (after we complete the next section of this chapter), and all other transactions that were posted from other modules, or directly to the general ledger, itself. In effect, all these transactions are stored in journals that are waiting to be posted to the general ledger.

From the *DacEasy Accounting* Main Menu, select the Journals option. Then, from that window, (Fig. 15-1), choose the "G/L Journal." A sample of the report based on the first day of operation for Parts and Parcels is shown in Report D-37 and Report D-38 in Appendix D.

From this report, you can trace every transaction that was entered up to this point. Note that most of the transactions listed in the report came from summary information from other modules. The appropriate account numbers come from the general ledger interface table (Fig. 7-14), which tells *DacEasy* the account numbers to use when posting transactions in these modules.

Printing Customer Statements

One last procedure is left in the process of making money. This involves the need to send statements to customers who have account balances that are due.

From the main menu, select the Reports option. The Accounts Receivable reports window (Fig. 15-9) contains options for printing customers statements. Depending on your needs, you can have the report sorted by one of four pieces of information. Select the one that you want and enter its number at the cursor.

You will then be asked for a range of statements to print. If you would like to print a statement for only one customer, enter the code or name (depending on your sort selection) in the "From" field and the "To" field. Only the statement for that one customer will be printed. If you want all the statements printed, press <ENTER> in the "From" field and again in the "To" field.

You will be asked for a closing date, with the current date being displayed. You can accept the current date (with <ENTER>), or you can change it. Be careful when changing the date because some invoices might be excluded if they fall outside that date.

Select the option to print on plain paper.

The statements will include all transactions in the given period, including the current invoices posted in the Billing module and the payments posted in the Accounts Receivable module.

Sample statements for customers of Parts and Parcels are included in Appendix D, listed from Report D-39 through Report D-42. One customer did not have a statement printed because no activity took place in the current period.

Spending Money: The Tide Flows Away Again

To date, we have made purchases from five different vendors. Assuming that one or more of these invoices have been received, we will work our way through the process of paying our vendors.

The Accounts Payable module, in the Transactions window (Fig. 20-7), is used to enter all vendor payments. The Accounts Payable module uses information from our purchase orders and from the merchandise received forms to create the Accounts Payable Open Invoice file, which stores all of the information on the bills we owe. Using *DacEasy Graph + Mate*, we can look into the open invoice file at any time by pressing <ALT + F10> and selecting the appropriate options.

We are also going to pay utilities and other non-inventory items that do not originate in the purchase order routine of the Purchasing module. Although you do not have inventory numbers for these items, you must have vendor records to which the amounts due, and paid, can be assigned a code in the purchase order codes table (Fig. 7-11).

The Paying Process

In order to pay your debts, enter the Accounts Payable module and select the option "enter payments." For each vendor, indicate whether you want *DacEasy* to write the check, whether you paid the invoice with a handwritten check, whether there is an adjustment to be made to the invoice, or whether to pay the whole invoice (or only a portion).

After you provide this information, give instructions to the program to print a report about the checks to be written. From this report, you can confirm payment and catch any errors. When everything is ready, instruct *DacEasy* to print the checks you've

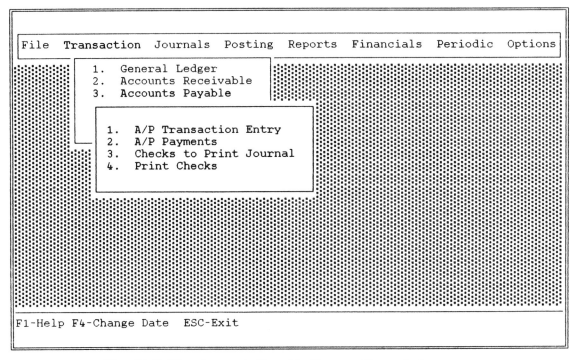

Fig. 20-7. The Accounts Payable Transaction window.

designated. When the checks are printed, print the reports that will constitute the audit trail for these vendor payments.

The last step in the process is to mail the checks to the vendors and other creditors.

Gathering the Information

To start paying our vendors, we need our Purchase Journal Reports (Reports D-15 and D-16 in Appendix D), copies of our Merchandise Received forms (Reports D-9 through D-14), and the invoices from our vendors. Ordinarily, invoices accompany the merchandise, or arrive shortly after the merchandise is received.

Other information that can be very helpful when paying of our vendors is the accounts payable statements. These statements give a summary of each vendor's account and details the amounts we owe each vendor. We recommend that you print these statements from the Reports module menu (Fig. 12-4) before you continue with your check writing. These statements can also be used to determine your "cash requirements" before you start marking invoices to pay. The vendor statements for our tutorial are included in Appendix D (Reports D-43 through D-47).

With these resources at your disposal, you can make decisions about paying vendors and other creditors before you actually begin the payment process. This gives you control of your check-writing procedures based on your cash requirements and your cash availability (which can be checked in the Files module, using account number #11021 in the chart of accounts routine).

Starting the Payment Process

We will continue with the daily operation of Parts and Parcels by entering several payments and transactions, describing the process, and tracing the results through the accounting system. When you are ready to begin, select Accounts Payable from the Transactions window. The Accounts Payable window (Fig. 20-7) contains all the options needed to pay our vendors.

Preparing to Pay Invoices

For now, we'd simply like to print checks for the amounts we owe vendors from whom we purchased the products we sell. Select the option to "enter payments."

Figure 20-8 details the first payment we will make. The following will help build an understanding of the entries for this work screen.

Transaction Number. The transaction number serves two purposes. It displays the next available number if you press <ENTER>, without typing a number or code, or it displays a previously entered transaction so it can be edited if you enter the number of the transaction. The second feature lets you cancel a check if it has not been printed. Press <ENTER> to get the next transaction number (which is #0001 for our sample).

Vendor Code and Vendor Name. Enter the code for the first vendor you want to pay. The name will be automatically displayed. For our example, enter NUTS01 and press <ENTER>. You will also see the current status of your account with that vendor in a window in the middle of the screen. The window also displays any messages you might have indicated in the vendor file. These messages come from the message file shown in Fig. 7-22.

Transaction Type. When the cursor is located in this field, your options are displayed in a window on the work screen. If you want *DacEasy* to write the check to pay this vendor, type a "K." If the invoice has already been paid, or will be paid with

```
                    PAYMENTS AND ADJUSTMENTS
  Transaction # :0001                          Date    : 11/20/88
  Vendor    Code :NUTS01                        Check # :
            Name :Nuts-to-You, Inc.             Amount  :      189.14
  Transac. Type :K                              Applied :      189.14
  Account #     :                               To Apply :       0.00

  Inv. #    Date       Due        Amount   Disc.Avail  Amt.Applied  Disc.taken

  01002    11/19/88 01/03/89     189.14       0.00       189.14        0.00
  KB4398   11/19/88 01/03/89     345.58       0.00         0.00        0.00


 F1-Help F2-Advance F5-Balance F6-Delete F8-Sort F9-Auto apply F10-Process
```

Fig. 20-8. Instructing DacEasy Accounting to write a check for a vendor. Only one of the invoices is to be paid at this time.

a handwritten check, type the letter "P" and press <ENTER>. If you are making an adjustment in this vendor's information, enter an "A" to let *DacEasy* know.

Because we want *DacEasy* to write the check to NUTS01, you enter the letter "K."

Account Number. The cursor skips the account number, or prints the number for the checking account (from the chart of accounts), depending on the type of transaction you entered above. If the checking account number is displayed, you can change it or you can press <ENTER> to accept it.

Date. The current system date is displayed. You can change it or accept it. At any point later in the transaction, you can press <F4> to change the date if you need to.

Check Number. If you entered a "K" to designate the "transaction type," the cursor will not stop in this field because the check number is automatically assigned when you start the check printing process. If you enter "P" or "A," the cursor stops in this field so you can enter a reference number, or the number of the check you wrote manually.

Amount, Applied, and To Apply. If you entered "K" to instruct *DacEasy* to write your checks, the cursor skips these three fields. These fields, however, are updated as you enter amounts in the lower part of the screen. If you entered one of the other two options ("P" or "A"), the cursor stops in the "Amount" field (where you enter the amount of the transaction) but skips the other two fields, leaving these to be updated as amounts are assigned to each line in the lower part of the work screen.

For our example, the cursor skips these fields and stops in the "Amt.Applied" ("amount applied) field in the bottom section.

Invoice Number, Invoice Date, Due Date, Invoice Amount, and Discount Amount. The first five columns of information for vendors is automatically displayed. All open invoices are listed, giving the invoice number, invoice date, due date, invoice amount, and the amount of any available discount.

The invoice number comes from the "Your Ref." field on the Received Merchandise forms. The discount amount is calculated only if the current date is within the discount period offered by the vendor (and included in the vendor's record). If the current date is past the discount date, the discount will be displayed as zero.

Amount Applied. The cursor stops in this field after you have completed the top part of the work screen. If there are several open invoices for a vendor, you can designate the portion of your payment that is to be applied to each invoice. You can also elect to enter only part of the due amount if there is a reason for doing so.

If there is only one invoice in the vendor record, press the <F9> key and *DacEasy* will automatically apply the correct amounts for the amount due and the discount taken.

When you press <ENTER> to accept the "Applied Amount," several things happen. Most noticeable is the cursor moves to the next field. Two fields, however, in the top part of the work screen are updated—"Applied" and "To Apply" change to indicate the status of the transaction. If you have given a "Transaction Type" of "K" (for the check to be written by *DacEasy*), these updates are not really important. They summarize your entries in the bottom part of the work screen.

If you indicated that the invoice was paid with a handwritten check, or that you are making an adjustment, the numbers in "Applied" and "To Apply" can be important because of their relationship to the "Amount" you entered in the field above them. The "To Apply" field indicates the balance available after you enter each "Amt.Applied" figure.

For our tutorial example, enter the amount $189.14 for Invoice #01002. We will not pay the other invoice at this time.

Discount Taken. If a discount is available for the displayed invoice, you can enter the amount in this field and the amount will be printed on the check stub as a reference for the vendor. The sum of the discount taken, and the amount applied, should equal to the invoice amount (unless you are making a partial payment).

For NUTS01, we get no discount (we might consider looking for another vendor, in this case).

We will not pay the second invoice due to NUTS01; thus it will be unchanged at this time. When the transaction is completed, press <F10> to tell *DacEasy* to process the given information. You completed work screen should be similar to the work screen shown in Fig. 20-8.

Figures 20-9 and 20-10 show additional payments that should be entered into the Accounts Payable module before you continue.

Note that Fig. 20-9 details a transaction that does not print a check from *DacEasy*. The "P" indicates that the invoice was paid with a handwritten check, and that the appropriate discount was taken. When we look at the reports that result from our payments, you will see the significance of recording vendor payment transactions in the *DacEasy* system.

When the last invoice is completed, press <F10> to process. The cursor is then displayed at the top of an empty transaction work screen. Press <ESC> while the cursor is in the "Transaction Number" field and *DacEasy* will file all the information you've entered. The Accounts Payable transactions window will be displayed.

```
                         PAYMENTS AND ADJUSTMENTS
   Transaction # :0002                          Date      : 11/20/88
   Vendor    Code :SHOV01                        Check #   : M0981
             Name :Shovell Shovels, Inc.         Amount    :      113.25
   Transac. Type :P                              Applied   :      113.25
   Account #     :11021  Checking Account        To Apply  :        0.00

   Inv. #   Date      Due       Amount    Disc.Avail  Amt.Applied  Disc.taken

   KB4301   11/19/88 12/19/88  116.75        0.00        113.25        3.50



F1-Help F2-Advance F5-Balance F6-Delete F8-Sort F9-Auto apply F10-Process
```

Fig. 20-9. Instructing DacEasy Accounting that the invoice for SHOV01 was paid with a handwritten check. See the "P" for Transaction Type, above.

```
                      PAYMENTS AND ADJUSTMENTS
  Transaction # :0003                       Date      : 11/20/88
  Vendor    Code :PAIN01                     Check #   :
            Name :Paint By the Numbers, Inc. Amount    :      2071.67
  Transac. Type :K                           Applied   :      2071.67
  Account #      :                           To Apply  :         0.00
  ─────────────────────────────────────────────────────────────────────
  Inv. #   Date      Due      Amount    Disc.Avail  Amt.Applied  Disc.taken
  ─────────────────────────────────────────────────────────────────────
  A-123   11/19/88 12/19/88 2103.22       0.00       2071.67       31.55


  F1-Help F2-Advance F5-Balance F6-Delete F8-Sort F9-Auto apply F10-Process
```

Fig. 20-10. Instructing DacEasy Accounting to write a check to pay the invoice for PAIN01. The "K" in Transaction Type designates A/P check.

Checking the Checks

Before you instruct *DacEasy* to print your checks, you must print three journals—the Checks to Print Journal (from the Accounts Payable transaction window in Fig. 20-7), the Accounts Payable Transactions Journal, and the Accounts Payable Payments Journal (both from the Journals window in Fig. 15-1). These journals provide you with information about checks to be printed, corrections and other direct entries to accounts payable, and handwritten checks or cash payments.

Checks to Print Journal. From the Accounts Payable window of the Transactions option, elect to print the Checks to Print Journal (see Fig. 20-7 for the window location). The Checks to Print Journal must be printed before you print your checks. It contains all the information about the checks you've told *DacEasy* to print. You should check the amounts and payees before continuing the check writing process. A sample report is shown in Report D-48 in Appendix D.

Transactions Journal. The Transactions Journal must be printed before you print your checks. It permits you to review the entries you've made through the transactions routine for accounts payable. This data summarizes the transactions which did not go through the purchasing routines. Errors can be detected and corrected before checks are printed.

If you select this option, after entering payments for the three vendors for our tutorial, you will receive a message indicating that there are no records for this journal. We made no entries in this routine from our tutorial and there is no sample report in Appendix D.

Payments Journal. If printed before checks are printed, the Payments Journal summarizes only the payments that have not gone through the *DacEasy* check writing process. The payment we documented in Fig. 20-9 is listed in the Payments Journal. If printed after accounts payable checks are printed, the Payments Journal summarizes all payments made to vendors. Report D-49 shows a sample of the Payments Journal (printed after checks were printed).

Printing the Checks

After confirming that *DacEasy* understands your instructions about printing checks, you should print those checks. Select the appropriate option from the Accounts Payable transaction window (Fig. 20-7).

DacEasy will then require four pieces of information (Fig. 20-11) to be used to print and post the amounts of your checks.

Reprint Checks (Y/N). If you have already printed your checks and have found an error, you must reprint check, or checks, so *DacEasy* knows not to make additional entries to accounts affected by the action. Since we are printing checks for the first time, answer ''N'' for reprints.

Date on Checks. The current system date is displayed. You can change the date, or you can press <ENTER> to accept it.

Checking Account Number. The account number from the chart of accounts (Fig. 7-2) for ''checking account'' is displayed. You can change it, or press <ENTER> to accept it. Be very careful if you change this number. Any new number must be an account from which you can write checks.

When we completed the work screens instructing *DacEasy* what to pay (Figs. 20-8 through 20-10), the ''Account Number'' field was skipped. The number on the Print Checks work screen (Fig. 20-11) is placed in this field now.

First Check Number. Enter the first check number to be printed. The first check, however, will be voided in the printer alignment process (unless you elect to skip the

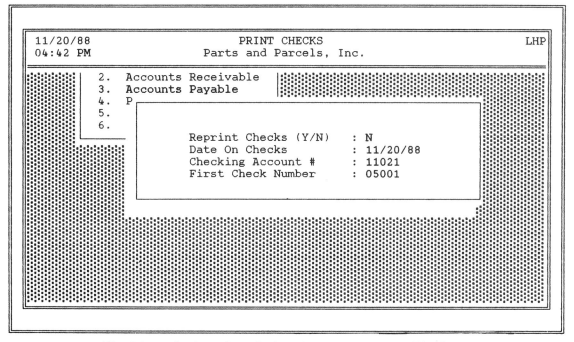

Fig. 20-11. Options for printing checks to vendors. *The first check number must be given. All amounts are automatically updated.*

alignment process). The number you give should be the number on the first check you will put in the printer. This number is printed on the check as a cross-reference and you should check to be sure that the printed number matches the number that was originally printed on the check when you ordered them.

Accounts payable checks can be ordered from Dac Software (see your package) or from one of several other vendors who sell Dac-specific forms.

When you press <ENTER> for your check number, you will be instructed to place your continuous form checks in the printer and to press <ENTER> when they are ready. An alignment pattern will be printed and should align on the perforation at the top of the first check stub. Once you have adjusted your forms and confirm that they are aligned properly, the first check will be voided and the other checks printed.

Printing the Payments Journal

When the printing is completed, remove your checks from the printer and replace your continuous forms paper with plain white paper. Then print the "Payments Journal" from the Account Payable Journals option on the Accounts Payable Menu (see Fig. 20-7). The "Payments Journal" list all payments entered through accounts payable, including those made with handwritten checks, or with adjustments made to the invoices. In Appendix D, Report D-49 contains the information we entered as part of this tutorial.

Voiding a Check

You can void a printed check, in the system, until the check is posted. To do this, return to the "enter payments" routine on the Accounts Payable Menu and enter the transaction number to which the check was originally assigned (this number can be found in the Checks Printed Journal—if it has been printed). Cancel the transaction by pressing <F6>. This process voids the check in *DacEasy*. Then reprint your journals for an official audit trail. (And don't forget to void the actual check.)

Posting Accounts Payable

When all your work is done for the day, post your transactions to the accounts payable journal, where the information is stored until it is posted to the general ledger.

From the Posting window, select the option to post the data. When the posting process is completed, a three-line summary will be printed (so be sure your printer is ready).

Printing the Payments Report

After posting all accounts payable transactions, print the Payments Report by making the appropriate selection from the Accounts Payable window in the Reports option (Fig. 12-4). (Do not confuse the Payments Report with the Payments Journal discussed earlier.)

The Payments Report can be sorted by date or by vendor. Reports D-50 and D-51 in Appendix D illustrate the two forms.

Summary

This chapter tracks the cash that comes and goes in a day-to-day operation. We accounted for sales and payment for the items purchased by our customers. We also accounted for purchases and payments for items sold to us by our vendors.

Transactions included direct entries into the accounts receivable and accounts payable journals and printing accounts payable checks to vendors.

21

Ending and Beginning Again

Chapter Goals
- *This chapter discusses the end-of-period routines that tie all accounting transactions together in the general ledger. We will assume that we have reached the end of the month and, then, the end of the year. The procedures for posting journals to the general ledger is explored and final reports and listings are printed.*

Posting data to various journals and ledgers is, typically, the signal of the end of an accounting period. In the last few chapters, we posted entries to the various journals in which we have been working. As the year wears on, summaries of this data must be posted to various ledgers—the most important of which is the general ledger. Ultimately, these ledgers become the records for our business and each of them contains information from various end-of-period routines.

The Meaning of End-of-Period

There are several periods that an accounting period might end. Typically, however, three periods are used for accounting purposes: (1) the calendar day, (2) the calendar month, and (3) the fiscal year. For payroll procedures, you might also be concerned about quarters and calendar years, since these are periods the Internal Revenue Service is concerned about.

Daily Routines

Daily routines have been discussed throughout the tutorial chapters. None of the other end-of-period routines can be completed until these daily tasks are completed. Daily tasks are discussed in Chapter 11 and Fig. 11-13 provides an outline of these procedures.

End-of-Month Routines

Each of the major accounting modules—the general ledger, accounts receivable, and accounts payable—requires end-of-month procedures. Each of these procedures accomplishes a different goal.

In accounts receivable, the end-of-month process deletes all open invoices that have zero balances. "Open invoice" customers that are not zero, are not deleted but carried forward with all detail included. The process calculates the balance to be carried forward as well as which customers are "balance forward" types. The balances carried forward are summaries, and all transaction details are deleted. Each non-zero invoice, whether open or balance forward, is aged, and the appropriate finance charges can then be added when the statements are printed. Balances are compiled and the net result is posted to the accounts receivable asset account.

In accounts payable, the end-of-month process parallels that for accounts receivable. It deletes all open invoices for which the balance due the vendor is zero and all details of purchases are deleted. For "open invoice" vendors, all non-zero invoices are retained, with full detail. The process also calculates the balances carried forward for those vendors who are "balance forward" types. The balances to be carried forward are summaries, and all details relating to these balances are deleted. Vendor invoices with balances are aged according to due date and the statements printed for internal use include appropriate finance charges. Balances are compiled and the net result is posted to the accounts payable liability account.

Before the end-of-month process is begun for the general ledger, all other monthly posting must be completed in all the accounting modules.

The end of the month is also the time to account for the depreciation of fixed assets. The amounts of depreciation are entered into the general journal, debited to the appropriate asset accounts and credited to the appropriate expense accounts. Depreciation should be entered and posted before the end-of-month routines are run.

The gross value of inventory on-hand is calculated—using the costing method you selected during the setup process—and that value is posted to the inventory asset account.

For the general ledger, the end-of-month process deletes all closed transactions that have been posted to the system. It does not delete open transactions or those that are carried forward for resolution in the next month. Current balances in all accounts are re-assigned as "previous balances" and taken into the next month as such.

Posting to the general ledger has the effect of closing the books for the month. Prior to posting, changes and corrections can be made in the different modules or routines. After posting, all changes must be entered as reversing or changing entries.

All daily posting to accounting modules must be completed before the end-of-month routines are run.

End-of-Year Routines

As with the monthly routines, each of the major accounting modules has its end-of-year process. For all four modules, historical data is deleted for the third year back, and moves last year's data into those slots. This year's data is then moved into the slots vacated by last year's, and a new current year is started with zero balances in the historical data.

Also, in inventory, you can ask *DacEasy* to print inventory count sheets for you so you can take physical counts of your stock. By using the physical inventory routine, you can enter your on-hand counts so *DacEasy* can compare these to its on-going counts and print reports of any discrepancies between the two. This process should be completed at least once a year, but regular monitoring of inventory will give you more control of your business.

The end-of-year routine for the general ledger clears all expense and revenue detail accounts to the "clear-to" account defined when you start the end-of-year process. These expense and revenue detail accounts and their general accounts at higher levels, are set to zero to start the new year. The "clear-to" account, then accumulates the "retained earnings" for the year, providing the amount for re-investment, pay back to the owners, or cumulative loss for the year (if negative).

Asset accounts, liability accounts, and owner equity accounts are not cleared, and their balances are carried forward as the financial foundation for the new year. Only the revenue and expense accounts are cleared and started fresh each year.

End-of-year routines are not run until all end-of-month routines are completed.

Preparing for The End

With the foundations laid in the section above, we will work our way through the end of the year for Parts and Parcels. Remember that we are doing this in a very short period of time and the results for a full year's business activity might look different from the small numbers we have posted to our accounts.

The end-of-period procedures post summaries of all journal transactions to the general ledger. These journal transactions are automatically entered into the individual journals when the posting processes are completed in each of the *DacEasy Accounting* modules. Before you begin an end-of-period routine, be sure you have posted all transactions to the appropriate journals in each module. All purchase order and billing transactions must be posted and all accounts payable, all accounts receivable, and general ledger transactions must be posted through these modules. Transactions that are not posted in these modules will not be posted to the general ledger during the end-of-period routines.

For Parts and Parcels, all daily posting—except in the general ledger— must be completed before continuing with the chapter. You can go through each module and do the posting if you are unsure of the status of those journals.

Depreciation as an End-of-Month Process

At this point, we have completed and posted all transactions, except for entering depreciation for the building, the truck, and the furnishings we have included in our fixed assets. Thus, we can begin our end-of-period routines as soon as we post depreciation.

For our company, we use the simple straight-line depreciation method for all our fixed assets. Each will be originally valued at its purchase price and depreciated by a fixed percentage over a period of years.

We account for depreciation through the cash journal, which is the same journal where we posted the amounts of the notes and the purchases of these fixed assets (Chapter 17).

Calculating the Depreciation

We have three depreciation values to calculate and account for:

The Building. The original cost of the building was $40,000 (after the value of its furnishing were taken from the overall purchase price) and its expected life is 25 years—or three hundred months. We can, then, determine that its value will decrease one-three-hundredth each month during that 25 year period. Therefore, the straight-line depreciation is $133.33 per month.

The Truck. The original cost of the truck was $12,995 and its expected life is four years—or 48 months. Therefore, the monthly depreciation is $270.73.

The Furniture and Fixtures in the Building. The original value of the furniture and fixtures in the building was set at $25,000. The life expectancy for these items is seven years—or 84 months. Therefore, the monthly depreciation would be $297.62.

Posting Depreciation to the Cash Journal

From the *DacEasy Accounting* Main Menu, select the Transactions option. From the Transaction window, choose the General Ledger. Figure 21-1 summarizes the entries in the cash journal.

The transaction number is ''0006'' because of our earlier entries for the general ledger.

The net effect of accounting for depreciation is to reduce assets—by posting a credit to a debit account—and to increase expenses—by posting a debit to a credit account. (Figure 3-3 summarizes these results.) In effect, the value of the building goes down with age, and this reduction in value—depreciation—is accumulated as an expense.

Printing the General Ledger Journal

After totaling the entries in the cash journal, and returning to the Transactions

```
                        GENERAL LEDGER TRANSACTION ENTRY
  Journal.. :CA              Transaction #..:0006          Date..:11/21/88

  Acct.#    Account Name              Description           Debit      Credit

  52035  Building               Oct 88 Depreciation       133.33
  12052  Accum. Depreciation    Oct 88 Depreciation                   133.33
  52032  Furniture & Fixtures   Oct 88 Depreciation       297.62
  12022  Accum. Depreciation    Oct 88 Depreciation                   297.62
  52031  Autos & Trucks         Oct 88 Depreciation       270.73
  12012  Accum. Depreciation    Oct 88 Depreciation                   270.73


  Total Debits :      701.68    |    Total Credits :      701.68

F1-Help F2-Difference F6-Delete F9-Auto Entry F10-Process ALT D-Delete line
```

Fig. 21-1. Depreciation decreases the value of assets and increases expenses.

window, you should print the journals entries that are about to be posted to the general ledger. These can be printed of the first option in the Journals window or the main menu.

The resulting printout will include all transactions posted from direct entry, and from the posting done in each of the other modules. Note that many of the transactions are summaries of system posting, or from specific modules. Reports D-52 and D-53 in Appendix D provide a summary of the General Ledger Journal.

Printing the General Ledger Account Activity Detail Journal

After printing the General Ledger Journal, print the General Ledger Account Activity Detail Journal. Do not choose to print page-by-page unless you want each account on a separate page.

The Activity Detail Journal gives you instant information about the action in each account in the general ledger. In addition, you can see the current balance for each account. Reports D-54 through D-58 are pages from the General Ledger Account Activity Detail Report, Complete Monthly Summary. Note that the amounts for depreciation are included but have not been posted.

Posting All Transactions to the General Ledger

When the account activity detail report is printed, and you have examined it and the journals to be sure that everything has been entered properly, you should begin the

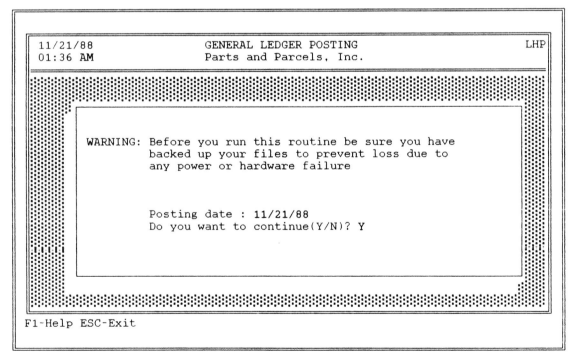

Fig. 21-2. General Ledger posting is completed when all transactions in a month have been finalized.

final posting to the general ledger.

Figure 21-2 shows the work screen where you can post to the general ledger. You are reminded to make your backup copies before you begin the actual posting process. It is important that you make backup copies of your files.

After giving the posting date, give the month you want posted and if the month is not the same as the current month, you are asked several times to confirm your decision to post. In our case, we would like to post the month of November 1988. As you work through this tutorial, however, you should post each month in which you worked with the data presented here.

Posting to the general ledger is an important process. Prior to posting, you can return to any transaction and change it, however, after posting, changes can only be made through reversing journal entries.

Printing Trial Balances

The last step in preparation for running the end-of-period routines is printing trial balances, which show the ending and beginning balances for each account in the chart of accounts. Trial balances can be printed from the Financials window of the main menu.

Choose to print all five levels of all the accounts, but print only those accounts that have had activity. Reports D-59 and D-60 in Appendix D show a sample of a trial balance report done before end-of-period processing.

Reprinting the Journals

Just to satisfy any curiosity you might have, you can reprint the journals to see what has happened since posting to the general ledger. You will find that all transactions are now marked ''yes'' for posted, if the dates of these transactions are within the month you specified for posting to the general ledger.

Printing Financial Statements

After any end-of-period processing, you should print the balance sheet/income statement, and the statement of changes in financial conditions. These forms are discussed in Chapters 12, 13, and 15. In Appendix D, Reports D-61 and D-62 are sample pages from the balance sheet, Report D-63 is a sample of the income statement, and Reports D-64 and D-65 are an abbreviated statement of changes in financial conditions.

End-of-Period Routines

We will complete the three end-of-month routines and discuss the results in relation to your daily and monthly recordkeeping.

After running the end-of-month routines, we will run all four end-of-year routines to close the books for the current year. Following all end-of-period routines, we will print all applicable reports.

End-of-Month Routines

From the main menu, select the Periodic routines. This window lists four modules in which end-of-month procedures can be run.

In succession, select the accounts receivable end-of-month routine, the accounts payable end-of-month routine, and the general ledger end-of-month routine. Each process prints *DacEasy*'s standard warning about backing up disks and posting to the appropriate journals.

The effect of these monthly routines is to delete transactions—including customer invoices, vendor invoices, and others that are no longer necessary to operate the recordkeeping system. Previous postings to the proper journals and ledgers has preserved summary data for all of these.

Reports D-67 and D-68, in Appendix D, show the results for the Trial Balance Report after running the end-of-month routines. Compare these two pages to Reports D-59 and D-60.

Quarterly Payroll Routines

In the Payroll module, you can print a monthly report that summarizes the payroll data for that period. You must print the Payroll Quarterly Report and complete the end-of-quarter process, which sets up the files for the new quarter. In both cases, these reports can be printed from the Periodic window of the Payroll Main Menu.

In Appendix D, Report D-66 is the first quarterly report for Parts and Parcels (based on our sample entries).

End-of-Year Payroll Routines

In the payroll module, you must print W-2 Forms before you complete the end-of-year process. These forms can be purchased from Dac Software, the IRS, or other vendors specializing in business forms.

DacEasy prints only on the "one-up/six-deep" W-2 format—that is, you must use the W-2 Forms that print one at a time, making five carbon copies. Your printer must be able to adjust to the thickness of so many forms.

When you start printing the W-2 Forms, a printer alignment pattern is printed on the first form. This pattern must be very close to the top perforation in order for the data to fit in the appropriate boxes. After printing the alignment pattern, do not use the form feed to bring the next form into line.

After printing W-2 Forms, run the payroll end-of-period routine, which will post the payroll activity to the proper accounts—in the payroll module.

End-of-Year Accounting Routines

From the Periodic window in *DacEasy Accounting*, select sequentially the end-of-year routines for accounts receivable, accounts payable, inventory, and the general ledger.

During the processing of the end-of-year routine for the general ledger, you are asked to give the "clear-to" account for your expenses and revenues. The totals from expenses and revenues are calculated and the amount obtained by subtracting the expenses from the revenues to determine profit (or—perish the thought—loss).

The "clear-to" account is a capital account in the category with owners' equity. Any profit must be added to the equity held by the owners. The profit is posted to account number #3288 for our example, to show the net gain for the year. The net gain is the "retained earnings" for the year. Following the end-of-year routines, all expense and revenue accounts are cleared to the "retained earnings" account and the chart of accounts is made ready for the new year.

Beginning The New Business Year

To start the new business year, your accounting system retians all assets, liabilities, and equity. All expenses and revenues from the year just ending are posted to retained earnings for that year. The expense and revenue accounts will be re-set to zero.

The first act of the new business year is to move those retained earnings—in our example, these are posted to account #3288—from the account for last year to the account number #33, Current Earnings. By moving the funds to this account, they are available for use in the current year's accounting system. They can be moved from this account to operating funds (eventually, to the checking account, paid to investors, or given back to the owner as payback for the personal investment (which is a liability to the company).

After placing retained earnings in the appropriate accounts for the new business year, you are ready to incur additional expenses and create new sources of revenue.

To see the effects of end-of-year posting, reprint some to the journals in the general ledger and the trial balances to see that new beginning balances have been posted and expense and revenue accounts set to zero. A sample of the trial balances for the beginning of the new business year is provided in Appendix D (Reports D-69 and D-70).

Summary

This chapter summarizes the purpose of the end-of-period routines, posts the depreciation of property and vehicles, and runs the end-of-month and end-of-year routines.

At this point, we have been through the major components of DacEasy Accounting *and* DacEasy Payroll. *The setup process was described in detail and the tutorial addresses the use of the software and the basics of accounting so that you can take advantage of both.*

APPENDIX   A

Using DacEasy Accounting
and Payroll on a Two
Diskette System

Our discussions in the main body of this book have focused on using *DacEasy Accounting* and *Payroll* with a fixed disk—sometimes called a hard disk. The purpose of this appendix is to provide information about using *DacEasy Accounting* and *Payroll* with a two-floppy disk drive system that has no fixed disk.

The Disadvantages of Diskettes

Before continuing with this appendix, please consider two distinct disadvantages to using a two-floppy disk drive system for your accounting operations.

(1) Floppy disks have limited space for storing your files. For PC- and XT-type computers, disk space is limited to 360Kb of storage space. This is enough space to keep accounting files for about 150 customers, 50 vendors, and 150 inventory items. For AT-type computers, disk space on the high-density diskettes is limited to approximately 1.2Mb of storage—or about four times that of the regular 5.25-inch double-density diskette.

If you are using a PS/2-type computer, your system might have 3.5-inch diskette drives instead of the "traditional" 5.25 inch drives. A double-density 3.5-inch diskette can hold 720Kb of data (twice the capacity of the 5.25-inch double-density diskette. A high-density 3.5-inch diskette can contain approximately 1.44Mb of data—just a little more than a high-density 5.25 inch floppy.

You need to consider your current accounting needs and projected growth—by analyzing the numbers of customers, vendors, products, and services—before deciding whether a two-floppy disk drive system is sufficient.

(2) You must handle no fewer than eight diskettes—two for *DacEasy Graph + Mate*, two for the *DacEasy Accounting* program, one for your accounting files, one for the *DacEasy Payroll* program, one for your payroll files, and your DOS disk. Manipulating this many disks can be a task in itself—even before you start taking care of your accounting and payroll needs.

Despite these disadvantages, using a two-floppy system is still better than keeping your records by hand.

Installation

As with the fixed disk system, there is an installation procedure to be followed to prepare *DacEasy* software for use with a floppy disk system. For each of the *DacEasy* modules, the installation process consists of running an "install program" and answering the questions that *DacEasy* asks during the installation process.

The CONFIG.SYS File

Before starting the installation of the accounting and payroll modules, you must be aware of a special file that is required for the smooth operation of your *DacEasy* software. It is not important that you understand the technical aspects of the operation of the file, but you must be sure that it exists before your software will work. The following discussion might provide some insight into the importance of this file.

In order to operate properly, *DacEasy Accounting* and *DacEasy Payroll* require that a set of "configuration" instructions be given to the computer when the computer is turned on. These instructions are contained in a file called CONFIG.SYS—an abbreviation for "system configuration." These instructions tell the computer to reserve enough space to allow *DacEasy* to have as many as 20 files open at one time. They also set aside enough memory for 16 file buffers so that *DacEasy* has space to temporarily store data as it reads from, and writes to, your data disks.

The CONFIG.SYS file must be on the disk you "boot" with. It cannot be placed on your *DacEasy* program disks, or on your data disks. Thus, you must be sure that your DOS disk—the one you boot with—contains the appropriate CONFIG.SYS file. The computer will look for the CONFIG.SYS files on the boot disk before it tries to load your software. Once found, the information is placed in memory so the computer can understand your system configuration.

If you are not sure that your "boot" disk contains the proper instructions in a CONFIG.SYS file, *DacEasy* can build the file for you. During the installation process for *DacEasy Accounting* and *DacEasy Payroll*, you will be asked about the file. You can select this option to let *DacEasy* take care of it for you. You will be asked for your DOS disk, which must be placed in drive A: when requested. *DacEasy* will check the existing CONFIG.SYS (if there is one) and add the appropriate instructions, as needed. If a CONFIG.SYS file does not exist, it is created and the appropriate instructions included.

After the CONFIG.SYS file exists, and is stored on your "boot" disk, the computer will use it each time it is turned on. You will not be required to re-create the file—unless you change "boot" disks.

Installing *DacEasy Accounting* for a Floppy System

Before you start the process of installing the accounting module, have on-hand three newly-formatted disks on which the program and files can be installed. Two of these disks are used for the *DacEasy Accounting* program. The third disk is used for your data files. You should create labels for each disk so they can be identified as "Program Disk #1," "Program Disk #2," and "Accounting Data Disk."

To install *DacEasy Accounting* for a floppy system, run the INSTALL program on the *DacEasy* Install/Program disk. Simply copying the files to another set of disks will not be sufficient.

The following steps detail the installation process for *DacEasy Accounting*:

(1) If your computer is not on, place your DOS disk in drive A: and boot. Provide the date and time information. When the DOS prompt—A>—is displayed, remove the DOS disk from drive A:.

(2) Place the *DacEasy Accounting* Install/Program Disk (Disk 1) in drive A:.

(3) Type INSTALL and press <ENTER>.

(4) You will be asked if *DacEasy* is to be installed on a floppy diskette or on a fixed disk. Select the option for "Floppy" system.

(5) The second screen displays information about the CONFIG.SYS file that is discussed earlier in this chapter. If you want *DacEasy* to make sure the file contains the necessary instructions, make the appropriate selection. The program will ask for your DOS disk, which you must insert into drive A:.The program will check your CONFIG.SYS file and modify or build it as needed. Once the CONFIG.SYS file is ready, you are instructed to re-insert your Install/Program Disk (Disk 1).

(6) Place your newly-labeled Program Disk #1 in drive B: and press the appropriate key (see the screen instructions). Files from the disk in drive A: are copied to the disk in drive B:.

(7) When instructed to do so, remove the Install/Program Disk from drive A: and insert the *DacEasy Accounting* Disk #2. Then replace the disk in drive B: with the newly-labeled Program Disk #2. When the appropriate key is pressed, files are copied from the original disk to the disk in drive B:.

(8) When the copying process has been completed successfully, a message is displayed confirming the installation. At this time, place your original disks in a safe place and use the copies you have just made.

(9) Your Accounting Data Disk is used when you start the accounting program.

After the installation process, your new Program Disk #1 will contain the *DacEasy Accounting* program, three files that contain setup information used by the *DacEasy* program, and the built-in report formats. The new Program Disk #2 contains the screen "overlay" files and help files that are used throughout the program.

When you are ready to use *DacEasy Accounting*, follow these steps:

(1) Place your DOS disk (with the CONFIG.SYS file) in drive A: and boot.

(2) When the DOS prompt is displayed, remove the DOS disk and insert Program Disk #1. You must also insert the Accounting Data Files disk in drive B: at this time.

(3) At the DOS prompt, type **DEA3** and press <ENTER>. The computer will read the program from the program disk, read the setup information from the appropriate files on the program disk, and ask you to insert Program Disk #2, and to press a key to continue.

(4) Program Disk #1 will not be used again (unless you decide to print a report) because the computer has all the information it needs in order to run the accounting program. Program Disk #2 remains in drive A: for the duration of your work session because it contains screen images and help screens that are used as you work. Data files are created on the Accounting Data Disk in drive B:, and this disk remains in the drive during the entire work session.

The installation process for *DacEasy Accounting* is completed after you provide the information for selecting a chart of accounts, and for the number of customers, vendors, and products. This process is discussed fully in Chapter 8 and in Chapter 17.

Figure 7-4 shows the number of records for each file used in the tutorial chapters. Note that we elected to use the built-in chart of accounts, in addition to using the number of record shown. At the bottom of the setup screen, you can see that there is not much disk space left on a standard double-sided, double-density disk when the setup information is used. (Figure 7-4 does not show this information, however, if you use the numbers given, there will be approximately 10,000 bytes of free disk space available for future growth.)

Installing *DacEasy Payroll* for a Floppy System

If you have installed *DacEasy Accounting* as described above, there is no need to worry about the CONFIG.SYS file again—because it was created during that installation. If you are using *DacEasy Payroll* and will not use the accounting module, you must be sure the CONFIG.SYS file is created. In this case, refer to the CONFIG.SYS File section of this chapter for a description and discussion of the CONFIG.SYS file.

In order to complete the *DacEasy Payroll* installation, you will need two newly-formatted disks. One should be labeled "Payroll Program Disk" and the other labeled "Payroll Data Disk."

To install *DacEasy Payroll*, use the following procedure:

(1) Boot your system with DOS in drive A:. Provide the date and time as needed.

(2) When the DOS prompt is displayed, remove the DOS disk and insert the *DacEasy*

Payroll Installation Disk (Disk 1) in drive A:. Place the Payroll Program Disk in drive B:.

(3) At the DOS prompt, type **INSTALL** and press <ENTER>. Specific files are copied from your original disk to the new disk in drive B:.

(4) When instructed, remove the Installation Disk from drive A: and replace it with the *DacEasy Payroll* Program Disk (Disk 2). Press the appropriate key to complete the installation process.

(5) A message will indicate that the installation has been successful, remove both disks and place your originals in a safe place. Use the newly-installed disks for all of your work.

When you are ready to use *DacEasy Payroll*, follow these steps:

(1) Place your DOS disk (with the CONFIG.SYS file) in drive A: and boot.

(2) When the DOS prompt is displayed, remove the DOS disk and insert the Program Disk. You must also insert the Payroll Data Files disk in drive B: at this time.

(3) At the DOS prompt, type **DEP** and press <ENTER>. The computer will read the program from the program disk, read the necessary setup information from the appropriate files on the program disk, and solicit the information it needs to work with your payroll data.

Refer to Chapters 9 and 17 for details on the continuing setup process. It is in this process that a major error can occur. You will be asked to insert your Installation disk so the program can copy the tax files from that disk to your Payroll Data Disk. If you use a disk other than your original Installation disk, the program will stop and exit to DOS, requiring you to start the process again. No real harm is done; it's just a major annoyance.

Once this process is completed, your Payroll Program Disk contains the payroll program, the help files, and the screen "overlays." Your Payroll Data Disk contains the current tax tables and all other data files that are created and used during the payroll process. The Payroll Program Disk remains in drive A: whenever the payroll module is used. The Payroll Data Disk remains in drive B:.

Installing *DacEasy Graph + Mate* for a Floppy System

DacEasy Graph + Mate can be installed on a floppy disk simply by copying all the files from the original diskettes to two, newly-formatted diskettes. This can be done using the following steps:

(1) Boot your system with DOS in drive A:. Enter the date and time, as needed.

(2) When the DOS prompt is displayed, remove the DOS disk and replace it with the original *DacEasy Graph + Mate* Disk 1. Place one, newly-formatted disk in drive B:.

(3) Type **COPY A:*.* B:** and press <ENTER>. The files on the disk in drive A: will be copied to the disk in drive B:.

(4) Repeat the process with *DacEasy Graph + Mate* Disk 2 and the second, newly-formatted diskette.

Once the copying process is completed, put the original *DacEasy Graph + Mate* disks in a safe place and always use the copies for your work.

The copies of *DacEasy Graph + Mate* should be labeled and added to your stack of disks.

Using *DacEasy Accounting* and *Payroll* with a Floppy System

After all the installation procedures are completed, you will have eight *DacEasy* disks. These include: two accounting program disks, one accounting data disk, one payroll program disk and one payroll data disk, two *DacEasy Graph + Mate* disks, and the DOS disk with the CONFIG.SYS file.

The following steps start *DacEasy Accounting*:

(1) Boot with the appropriate DOS disk in drive A:.

(2) Place the *DacEasy Graph + Mate* Disk 1 in drive A:.

(3) Type **GM** and press <ENTER>.

(4) *DacEasy Graph + Mate* is loaded and you can choose the application you want to work with.

(5) Select the accounting option and place the accounting Disk 1 in drive A: when instructed to do so. The accounting program and setup information is loaded. You are then instructed to insert the second program disk and press <ENTER>.

(6) The Main Menu is displayed and you can go to work.

(7) Program Disk #2 stays in drive A: while you are working.

The following steps start *DacEasy Payroll*:

(1) Boot with the appropriate DOS disk in drive A:.

(2) Place the *DacEasy Graph + Mate* disk in drive A:.

(3) Type **GM** and press <ENTER>.

(4) *DacEasy Graph + Mate* is loaded and you are able to select your application. Select the payroll option and, when instructed, insert your "application" disk—*DacEasy*'s way of saying, "Insert the payroll program disk."

(5) The payroll program and setup information is loaded.

(6) The Main Menu is displayed and you can go to work.

APPENDIX   B

Quick and Easy Batch
Files for Starting *DacEasy*

One of the most tedious aspects about starting *DacEasy Accounting* and *DacEasy Payroll* from a fixed disk is typing in commands. Each time you want to start one of the programs, you must type at least two commands following the DOS prompt. If we can reduce this number to one command and, if we can reduce the size of the command, we can start either program without the hassle of misspelled commands and without needing to learn DOS commands such as "change directory."

There are two ways to access your programs without typing several commands following the DOS prompt. One of these is to use a menu program that automatically loads and lists all of the available programs. You can then select an item from the menu and go to work.

In the absence of a menu, you might want to consider using "batch" files to start each program. Batch files are text files that contain a series of commands that are executed sequentially by DOS. By placing several commands in a batch file, you can simply type the name of the batch file and press <ENTER> to start the whole process. The batch file then sends all your commands to the computer.

For example, to start *DacEasy Accounting*, you must type the following series of commands.

```
CD \ DEA3 <ENTER>
DEA3 <ENTER>
```

These commands will change the disk directory to \DEA3, where *DacEasy Accounting* is located, and loads the accounting program.

To create a batch file that automatically sends these commands to the computer, type in the following set of commands at the DOS prompt.

```
COPY CON C:\ACCT.BAT <ENTER>
CD\DEA3 <ENTER>
DEA3 <ENTER>
<F6> <ENTER>
```

After the first line of the commands is typed in, the DOS prompt will not be displayed again until you press the <F6> key and <ENTER> to tell the computer you have completed the batch of commands. When these keys are pressed, the light on your fixed disk comes on as the computer saves the batch file, called ACCT.BAT to your disk.

From this point, you can simply type **ACCT** and press <ENTER>. The computer automatically changes directories and starts *DacEasy Accounting* for you.

The following steps create a batch file named PAY.BAT that automatically starts the payroll module for you.

```
COPY CON C:\PAY.BAT <ENTER>
CD\DEP3 <ENTER>
DEP3 <ENTER>
<F6> <ENTER>
```

The drive light comes on as the computer saves the file to your disk. From this point, you can type **PAY** and press <ENTER> to start *DacEasy Payroll*.

If you are using *DacEasy Graph+Mate*, you can build the following batch file to automatically start that program. From the Graph+Mate menu, you can select accounting or payroll without building the batch files described above.

```
COPY CON C:\GM.BAT <ENTER>
CD\GRAFMATE <ENTER>
GM <ENTER>
<F6> <ENTER>
```

When one file is saved to your fixed disk, you can simply type **GM** to start the Graph+Mate software.

1988 Tax Tables
for *DacEasy Payroll*

Appendix C contains information from the five state tax tables used by *DacEasy Payroll* in calculating deductions based on allowances and exemptions.

Table 1

Each state is included in Table 1. For each marital status code, you can select the appropriate tax table number to be placed in each employee record. For each employee, you must determine which of the tax tables listed in Table 1 must be applied to deductions. Once this is determined, the tax table number is placed in the employee record so *DacEasy* can find and use the appropriate information. If a state allows an exemption number or amount, this is also given in the appropriate column and should be placed in each employee's record.

The information included in Table 1 has been updated through January 1988. Dac Software, Inc. updates the tax information as needed, and will send, for a nominal fee, the newest updates at the beginning of each payroll year.

Table 2

Table 2 lists all the states that have no state income tax. Each of these states has a tax table number that must be placed in the employee record.

Table 3

Figure 9-11 shows a sample screen containing information used in the calculating of state tax withholdings (the screen shows the tax information for the state of South Carolina).

Table C-1. Tax Tables for all States and Other Entities.

STATE	MARITAL STATUS	TAX TABLE	STATE EXEMPTIONS NO.	AMOUNT	COMMENTS
Alabama	Single All Others	3 4	0 0	1500.00 0.00	$0.00 exemp if no A-4 $0.00 exemp if no A-4
Alaska	All	5	0	0.00	Table has DISF rate
Arizona	All	6	0	0.00	Check additional withholdings
Arkansas	Single Separately Jointly	7 7 7	2 1 2	0.00 0.00 0.00	0 exemp if no W-4 0 exemp if no W-4 0 exemp if no W-4
California	Single Married/1 Married/2 Head/House	8 9 9 10	0 0 0 0	1880.00 1880.00 3760.00 3760.00	0 or 1 allowance 2 or more allowances
Colorado	Single Married	11 12	0 0	0.00 0.00	
Connecticut	All	13	0	0.00	No State taxes
Delaware	All	14	0	0.00	
District of Columbia	Separately All Others	16 15	0 0	0.00 0.00	
Florida	All	17	0	0.00	No State taxes
Georgia	Single Separately Jointly Head/House	18 19 19 20	0 0 0 0	0.00 0.00 0.00 0.00	Because of rate structure, DAC-Easy programmed to determine exemptions.
Hawaii	Single Married	21 22	0 0	0.00 0.00	
Idaho	Single Marries	23 24	0 0	0.00 0.00	
Illinois	All	25	0	0.00	

Table C-1. Continued

STATE	MARITAL STATUS	TAX TABLE	STATE EXEMPTIONS NO.	STATE EXEMPTIONS AMOUNT	COMMENTS
Indiana	All	26	0	0.00	
Iowa	All	27 27	0 0	1200.00 3000.00	0 or 1 allowances 2 or more allowances
Kansas	Jointly All Others	29 28	0 0	0.00 0.00	
Kentucky	All	30	0	0.00	
Louisiana	All	31	* *	5000.00 15000.00	*If 0 or 1 exemption If 2 exemptions
Maine	Single Married	32 33	0 0	0.00 0.00	
Maryland	All	34	0	0.00	Put county piggyback %age in employee rcd
Massa-chusetts	All	35	0	0.00	
Michigan	All	36	0	0.00	
Minnesota	Single Married	37 70	0 0	0.00 0.00	
Mississippi	Single Married Head/House	38 38 38	0 0 0	2300.00 3400.00 1700.00	
Missouri	Sing/Marr Head/House Married w/1 Work	39 39 39 39	0 0 0 0	1200.00 1700.00 2400.00 2800.00	Self and spouse
Montana	All	40	0	0.00	
Nebraska	Single Married	41 75	0 0	0.00 0.00	

Table C-1. Continued

STATE	MARITAL STATUS	TAX TABLE	STATE EXEMPTIONS NO.	AMOUNT	COMMENTS
Nevada	All	42	0	0.00	No State taxes
New Hampshire	All	43	0	0.00	No State taxes
New Jersey	All	44	0	0.00	
New Mexico	Single Married	45 46	0 0	0.00 0.00	
New York State	Single Married	47 71	0 0	0.00 0.00	
New York City	Single Married	48 74	0 0	0.00 0.00	Due to tax structure DAC Easy calculates
North Carolina	Single Separately Jointly Head/House	49 49 49 49	0 0 0 0	1100.00 1100.00 2200.00 2200.00	
North Dakota	All	50	0	0.00	
Ohio	All	51	0	0.00	
Oklahoma	Single All Others	52 53	0 0	368.00 544.00	
Oregon	Single All	54 55	0 0	0.00 0.00	If 1 or 2 allowances If 3 or more allow's
Pennsylvania	All	56	0	0.00	
Rhode Island	Single Married	57 76	0 0	0.00 0.00	
South Carolina	All	58	0	0.00	
South Dakota	All	59	0	0.00	No State taxes

Table C-1. Continued

STATE	MARITAL STATUS	TAX TABLE	STATE EXEMPTIONS NO.	AMOUNT	COMMENTS
Tennessee	All	60	0	0.00	No State taxes
Texas	All	61	0	0.00	No State taxes
Utah	Single Married	62 73	0 0	0.00 0.00	
Vermont	All	63	0	0.00	
Virginia	All	64	0	0.00	
Washington	All	65	0	0.00	No State taxes
West Virginia	Single Married Head/House	66 67 72	0 0 0	0.00 0.00 0.00	
Wisconsin	All	68	0	0.00	Due to tax structure DAC Easy calculates
Wyoming	All	69	0	0.00	No State taxes

SOURCE: DacEasy Payroll manual and updates for July 1988.

Six fields on the screen—labeled "Field 1" through "Field 6"—contain specific information to be used in calculating withholdings. The bottom half of the screen is used to display the state's tax structure.

The information on this screen can be edited at any time and is considered to be part of *DacEasy*'s "open architecture"—a design that let's you modify the tax tables for your state if the laws change after you have your system in operation.

Table 3 lists all states that permit only one amount for an employee allowance, which is given in Field 1 of the state tax table. If the amount changes, you can change it so that your tax tables will be up-to-date.

Table 4

Table 4 lists the states that use only a tax percentage rate, which is placed in Field 5 for each of these states. The percentage can be changed if necessary.

Table 5

Table 5 lists all the states using several of the available fields. Each field is defined so you can make changes if the tax laws in your state change.

Table C-2. States With No State Income Tax (With Tax Table Numbers).

Alaska	5	Nevada	42	Tennessee	60		
Connecticut	13	New Hampshire	43	Texas	61	Wyoming	69
Florida	17	South Dakota	59	Washington	65		

Table C-3. States Using Only Field 1 for Amount of Allowance.

Colorado	11-12	Hawaii	21-22	New Jersey	44	W.Virginia	66-67
District of Columbia	15-16	Idaho	23-24	New Mexico	45-46		72
		Montana	40			Wisconsin	68
Georgia	18-20	Nebraska	41 75	Rhode Island	57 76		

Table C-4. States Using Only Field 5 for Tax Percentage Rate.

North Dakota	50	Pennsylvania	56	Utah	62
				Vermont	63

Table C-5. State Using Several Fields.

STATE	FIELD	EXPLANATIONS	TABLE
Alabama	1 2 3	State allowance amount Percentage of standard deduction Standard deduction limit	 3 4
Arizona	1 2 4	State allowance amount Basic withholding rate limit amount Next higher withholding rate	 6
Arkansas	2 3 4 5	Percentage of standard deduction Maximum amount of the standard deduction Personal tax credit for single with one exempt Amount for each dependent	 7
California	3	Amount of first allowance in Tax Credit Table	8 9 10
Delaware	1 3 4	Amount for one deduction Standard deduction for married employee Standard deduction for single employee	 14
Illinois	1 5	Amount for personal exemptions Tax percentage rate	 25
Indiana	1 5	Amount for personal exemptions Tax percentage rate	 26
Iowa	1 2 4	Annual credit amount for exemptions 1 and 2 Standard deduction percentage Credit amount for three or more exemptions	 27
Kansas	1 2 3 4 5	State exemption amount Standard deduction percentage Standard deduction minimum Standard deduction maximum Federal income tax deduction percentage	 28 29
Kentucky	1	Amount of tax credit for one exemption	30
Louisiana	1 3 4 5	Each exemption amount Personal exemptions Percentage for A part of tax formula Percentage for B part of tax formula	 31
Maine	1 2 3	Personal exemption amount Standard deduction percentage Standard deduction limit	 32 33

Table C-5. Continued

STATE	FIELD	EXPLANATIONS	TABLE
Alabama	1 2 3	State allowance amount Percentage of standard deduction Standard deduction limit	3 4
Arizona	1 2 4	State allowance amount Basic withholding rate limit amount Next higher withholding rate	6
Arkansas	2 3 4 5	Percentage of standard deduction Maximum amount of the standard deduction Personal tax credit for single with one exempt Amount for each dependent	7
California	3	Amount of first allowance in Tax Credit Table	8 9 10
Delaware	1 3 4	Amount for one deduction Standard deduction for married employee Standard deduction for single employee	14
Illinois	1 5	Amount for personal exemptions Tax percentage rate	25
Indiana	1 5	Amount for personal exemptions Tax percentage rate	26
Iowa	1 2 4	Annual credit amount for exemptions 1 and 2 Standard deduction percentage Credit amount for three or more exemptions	27
Kansas	1 2 3 4 5	State exemption amount Standard deduction percentage Standard deduction minimum Standard deduction maximum Federal income tax deduction percentage	28 29
Kentucky	1	Amount of tax credit for one exemption	30
Louisiana	1 3 4 5	Each exemption amount Personal exemptions Percentage for A part of tax formula Percentage for B part of tax formula	31
Maine	1 2 3	Personal exemption amount Standard deduction percentage Standard deduction limit	32 33

Table C-5. Continued

STATE	FIELD	EXPLANATIONS	TABLE
South Carolina	1 2 3 4	Personal exemption amount Standard deduction percentage Standard deduction maximum (1 exemption) Standard deduction maximum (2 or more exempts)	58
Virginia	1 3	Personal exemption amount Standard deduction amount	64

Reports from the Tutorials

This appendix contains the reports and printouts from the tutorial sections of the book, Chapters 17-21. Reports marked with an asterisk (*) are full-page printouts which have been compressed vertically for space considerations.

Report D.1

Parts and Parcels, Inc.
#2 Byfore Avenue
Greenwood, S.C. 29646
803/555-1685

General Ledger Journal Report

Journal Trans.#	Date	Acct. #	Account Name	Description	Debits	Credits	Posted?
CA 0001	10/29/88	11021	Checking Account	Personal Investment	25000.00		NO
		11021	Checking Account	Loan Proceeds	50000.00		NO
		2202	Notes Payable	Loan Proceeds		50000.00	NO
		31011	Par Value	Personal Investment		25000.00	NO
				TOTAL TRANSACTION :	75000.00	75000.00	
CA 0002	10/29/88	11021	Checking Account	Loan for Building Buy	65000.00		NO
		2201	Mortgages Payable	Loan for Building Buy		65000.00	NO
				TOTAL TRANSACTION :	65000.00	65000.00	
CA 0003	10/29/88	12051	Original Value	Purchase Building	65000.00		NO
		11021	Checking Account	Purchase Building		65000.00	NO
				TOTAL TRANSACTION :	65000.00	65000.00	
CA 0004	10/29/88	12011	Original Value	Truck Purchase	12995.00		NO
		11021	Checking Account	Truck Purchase		12995.00	NO
				TOTAL TRANSACTION :	12995.00	12995.00	
CA 0005	10/29/88	12021	Original Value	Adjust for Furn/Fixtures	25000.00		NO
		12051	Original Value	Adjust for Furn/Fixtures		25000.00	NO
				TOTAL TRANSACTION :	25000.00	25000.00	
				TOTAL TRANSACTION :	242995.00	242995.00	

OF ENTRIES PRINTED : 12

Report D.2

Parts and Parcels, Inc.
#2 Byfore Avenue
Greenwood, S.C. 29646
803/555-1685

G/L Account Activity Detail Report
Complete Monthly Activity

Journal Trans.#	Date	Acct. #	Account Name	Description	Debits	Credits	Posted?
		11021	Checking Account	BEGINNING BALANCE	0.00		
CA 0001	10/29/88			Personal Investment	25000.00		NO
CA 0001	10/29/88			Loan Proceeds	50000.00		NO
CA 0002	10/29/88			Loan for Building Buy	65000.00		NO
CA 0004	10/29/88			Truck Purchase		12995.00	NO
CA 0003	10/29/88			Purchase Building		65000.00	NO
				CURRENT BALANCE	62005.00		
		12011	Original Value	BEGINNING BALANCE	0.00		
CA 0004	10/29/88			Truck Purchase	12995.00		NO
				CURRENT BALANCE	12995.00		
		12021	Original Value	BEGINNING BALANCE	0.00		
CA 0005	10/29/88			Adjust for Furn/Fixtures	25000.00		NO
				CURRENT BALANCE	25000.00		
		12051	Original Value	BEGINNING BALANCE	0.00		
CA 0003	10/29/88			Purchase Building	65000.00		NO
CA 0005	10/29/88			Adjust for Furn/Fixtures		25000.00	NO
				CURRENT BALANCE	40000.00		
		2201	Mortgages Payable	BEGINNING BALANCE		0.00	
CA 0002	10/29/88			Loan for Building Buy		65000.00	NO
				CURRENT BALANCE		65000.00	
		2202	Notes Payable	BEGINNING BALANCE		0.00	
CA 0001	10/29/88			Loan Proceeds		50000.00	NO
				CURRENT BALANCE		50000.00	
		31011	Par Value	BEGINNING BALANCE		0.00	
CA 0001	10/29/88			Personal Investment		25000.00	NO
				CURRENT BALANCE		25000.00	
				TOTAL TRANSACTION :	242995.00	242995.00	

OF ENTRIES PRINTED : 12

Report D.3*

```
                        Parts and Parcels, Inc.
                          #2 Byfore Avenue
                         Greenwood, S.C. 29646
                            803/555-1685
                        P u r c h a s e   O r d e r
```

```
        PAIN01                                    Ship to/Remarks
     Paint By the Numbers, Inc.                   SHIP OVERNIGHT
     Vinnie Van Gogh                              LAND CARRIER ONLY
     Green Fields Mall
     Plaster TN 38654
```

```
              Date 11/18/88    No. 01001 Page  1  Due Date  12/18/88
     ---------------------------------------------------------------------------
     Via LAND EXPRESS    FOB        Disc.days 15 Disc.% 1.50 Net Days 30  Your #A-123  Our #01001
     ---------------------------------------------------------------------------
     Inventory #  Description              Ordered  Unit Price Disc.%  Extended Price
     ---------------------------------------------------------------------------
     PAINT01     Paint, Wt Base Gal         30.000   51.850             1555.50
     PAINT02     Paint, Wt Base Qt          10.000   51.000              510.00
     PIGMENT99   Pigment, Asst Pt            4.000   51.600              206.40

     ---------------------------------------------------------------------------
                                                     Sub-total          2271.90
                                                     Tax                 102.24
                                                     Total              2374.14

                                                     Net to Pay         2374.14
                                                     -----------
```

Report D.4*

Parts and Parcels, Inc.
#2 Byfore Avenue
Greenwood, S.C. 29646
803/555-1685
P u r c h a s e   O r d e r

NUTS01
Nuts-to-You, Inc.
Douglas Clark, Sales Rep.
546 Pecan Grove
Brazil IN 47911

Ship to/Remarks

Date 11/18/88   No. 01002 Page 1 Due Date 01/02/89

Via OVERNIGHT LAND   FOB   Disc.days   Disc.% 0.00 Net Days 45   Your #   Our #01002

Inventory #	Description	Ordered	Unit Price	Disc.%	Extended Price
WARES17	Oven, Toaster M1203	12.000	14.560		174.72

Sub-total	174.72
Tax	5.24
Total	179.96
Net to Pay	179.96

Report D.5*

SHAD01
Shady Vore Lumber Company
Bubba Vore, President
543 Barron Hills Canyon
St. Arbor AZ 85899

Ship to/Remarks
PARTIAL ORDER
ACCEPTED--RUSH

Date 11/18/88   No. 01003 Page 1 Due Date   12/18/88

Via OVERNITE   FOB   Disc.days 10 Disc.% 2.00 Net Days 30 Your #(NONE) Our #01003

Inventory #	Description	Ordered	Unit Price	Disc.%	Extended Price
BOARD01	2x4, Pine Stud 8Ft	9000.000	0.095		855.00
BOARD51	Plywood, 3/4 4x8	75.000	21.470		1610.25

Sub-total	2465.25
Tax	73.96
Total	2539.21
Net to Pay	2539.21

340

Report D.6*

```
                    Parts and Parcels, Inc.
                       #2 Byfore Avenue
                     Greenwood, S.C. 29646
                        803/555-1685
                    P u r c h a s e   O r d e r
```

```
   SHOV01                                    Ship to/Remarks
   Shoveil Shovels, Inc.                     IMMEDIATE
   B.S. Shovellis, Acct. Rep.                DELIVERY
   Fourth Elvzer Plaza                       DESIRED
   Fatty IL 60799
```

```
              Date 11/18/88    No. 01004 Page  1  Due Date  12/18/88
--------------------------------------------------------------------------------
Via OVERNIGHT      FOB         Disc.days  10 Disc.% 3.00 Net Days  30  Your #PART24  Our #01004
--------------------------------------------------------------------------------
Inventory #  Description                 Ordered  Unit Price Disc.%  Extended Price
--------------------------------------------------------------------------------
GARDEN01     Hoe, Garden                  6.000    12.250                    73.50
GARDEN09     Hose, Garden 25Ft            6.000     7.500                    45.00

--------------------------------------------------------------------------------
                                                    Sub-total          119.50
                                                    Tax                  7.70
                                                    Total              126.20

                                                    Net to Pay         126.20
                                                    -----------
```

Report D.7*

Parts and Parcels, Inc.
#2 Byfore Avenue
Greenwood, S.C. 29646
803/555-1685
P u r c h a s e   O r d e r

SINK01   Ship to/Remarks
The Sink Whole   IMMEDIATE
L. Beau Trapp, Jr.   DELIVERY
4 Thunder Lane   REQUESTED
Shower Head SD 57813

Date 11/18/88   No. 01005 Page 1 Due Date 01/02/89

Via OVERNITE TRUCK   FOB   Disc.days   Disc.% 0.00 Net Days 45 Your #(NONE) Our #01005

Inventory #   Description   Ordered Unit Price Disc.% Extended Price
----
CONDUIT01   Conduit, Alum 16Ft   125.000   5.810   726.25
            All aluminium conduit must be in 16 ft.
            lengths. None may be shorter than that.
CONDUIT07   Conduit, Plas 50Ft   25.000 17.950   3.50   433.04
            Freight   25.00

                                                        Sub-total   1184.29
                                                        Tax   75.35
                                                        Total   1259.64

                                                        Net to Pay   1259.64

342

Report D.8*

NUTS01
Nuts-to-You, Inc.
Douglas Clark, Sales Rep.
546 Pecan Grove
Brazil IN 47911

Ship to/Remarks
NEEDED IMMEDIATELY.
PLEASE SHIP
OVERNIGHT EXPRESS.

Date 11/18/88   No. 01006 Page 1 Due Date 01/02/89

Via OVERNIGHT EXPR.   FOB   Disc.days   Disc.% 0.00 Net Days 45 Your #(NONE) Our #01006

Inventory #	Description	Ordered	Unit Price	Disc.%	Extended Price
#C-8972X	Desktop Calculator, Electronic				319.98
	Freight				12.00
	Insurance				4.00

Sub-total	335.98
Tax	9.60
Total	345.58
Net to Pay	345.58

343

Report D.9*

Parts and Parcels, Inc.
#2 Byfore Avenue
Greenwood, S.C. 29646
803/555-1685
M e r c h a n d i s e   R e c e i v e d

PAIN01
Paint By the Numbers, Inc.
Vinnie Van Gogh
Green Fields Mall
Plaster TN 38654

Ship to/Remarks
SHIP OVERNIGHT
LAND CARRIER ONLY

Date 11/19/88   No. 01001 Page 1 Due Date 12/19/88

Via LAND EXPRESS   FOB   Disc.days 15 Disc.% 1.50 Net Days 30 Your #A-123 Our #01001

Inventory #	Description	Ordered	Received	Backorder	Unit Price	Disc.%	Extended Price
PAINT01	Paint, Wt Base Gal	30.000	25.000	5.000	51.850		1296.25
PAINT02	Paint, Wt Base Qt	10.000	10.000	0.000	51.000		510.00
PIGMENT99	Pigment, Asst Pt	4.000	4.000	0.000	51.600		206.40

Sub-total	2012.65
Tax	90.57
Total	2103.22
Net to Pay	2103.22

Report D.10*

M e r c h a n d i s e   R e c e i v e d

NUT501   Ship to/Remarks
Nuts-to-You, Inc.
Douglas Clark, Sales Rep.
546 Pecan Grove
Brazil IN 47911

Date 11/19/88   No. 01002 Page 1 Due Date 01/03/89

Via OVERNIGHT LAND   FOB   Disc.days   Disc.% 0.00 Net Days 45 Your #   Our #01002

Inventory #	Description	Ordered	Received	Backorder	Unit Price	Disc.%	Extended Price
WARES17	Oven, Toaster M1203	12.000	12.000	0.000	14.560		174.72
	Freight						9.18

Sub-total	183.90
Tax	5.24
Total	189.14
Net to Pay	189.14

Report D.11*

Parts and Parcels, Inc.
#2 Byfore Avenue
Greenwood, S.C. 29646
803/555-1685
M e r c h a n d i s e   R e c e i v e d

```
  SHAD01                                                Ship to/Remarks
  Shady Vore Lumber Company                             PARTIAL ORDER
  Bubba Vore, President                                 ACCEPTED--RUSH
  543 Barron Hills Canyon
  St. Arbor AZ 85899


            Date 11/19/88      No. 01003 Page  1  Due Date  12/19/88
  ------------------------------------------------------------------------------
  Via OVERNITE       FOB          Disc.days  10 Disc.% 2.00 Net Days  30  Your #4723-A  Our #01003
  ------------------------------------------------------------------------------

  Inventory #   Description      Ordered    Received  Backorder Unit Price  Disc.%   Extended Price
  ------------------------------------------------------------------------------
  BOARD01       2x4, Pine Stud 8Ft  9000.000  6000.000  3000.000    0.095              570.00
  BOARD51       Flywood, 3/4 4x8      75.000    75.000     0.000   21.470             1610.25


  ------------------------------------------------------------------------------
                                                          Sub-total    2180.25
                                                          Tax            65.41
                                                          Total        2245.66

                                                          Net to Pay   2245.66
                                                          -----------
```

Report D.12*

```
  SHOV01                                          Ship to/Remarks
  Shovell Shovels, Inc.                           IMMEDIATE
  B.S. Shovells, Acct. Rep.                       DELIVERY
  Fourth Elyzer Plaza                             DESIRED
  Patty IL 60799

             Date 11/19/88    No. 01004 Page  1  Due Date   12/19/88
-------------------------------------------------------------------------------
Via OVERNIGHT      FOB         Disc.days  10 Disc.% 3.00 Net Days  30  Your #KB4301  Our #01004
-------------------------------------------------------------------------------
Inventory #   Description      Ordered   Received Backorder Unit Price Disc.%   Extended Price
-------------------------------------------------------------------------------
GARDEN01      Hoe, Garden       6.000      6.000    0.000     10.770                 64.62
GARDEN09      Hose, Garden 25Ft 6.000      6.000    0.000      7.500                 45.00


-------------------------------------------------------------------------------
                                                           Sub-total    109.62
                                                           Tax            7.13
                                                           Total        116.75

                                                           Net to Pay   116.75
                                                           ------------
```

Report D.13*

SINK01   Ship to/Remarks
The Sink Whole   IMMEDIATE
L. Beau Trapp, Jr.   DELIVERY
4 Thunder Lane   REQUESTED
Shower Head SD 57813

Date 11/19/88   No. 01005 Page 1 Due Date 01/03/89

Via OVERNITE TRUCK   FOB   Disc.days   Disc.% 0.00 Net Days 45 Your #213450 Our #01005

Inventory #	Description	Ordered	Received	Backorder	Unit Price	Disc.%	Extended Price
CONDUIT01	Conduit, Alum 16Ft	125.000	125.000	0.000	5.810		726.25
	All aluminium conduit must be in 16 ft.						
	lengths. None may be shorter than that.						
CONDUIT07	Conduit, Plas 50Ft	25.000	25.000	0.000	17.950	3.50	433.04
	Freight						0.00

                                            Sub-total   1159.29
                                            Tax   75.35
                                            Total   1234.64

                                            Net to Pay   1234.64

Report D.14*

M e r c h a n d i s e   R e c e i v e d

NUTS01   Ship to/Remarks
Nuts-to-You, Inc.   NEEDED IMMEDIATELY.
Douglas Clark, Sales Rep.   PLEASE SHIP
546 Pecan Grove   OVERNIGHT EXPRESS.
Brazil IN 47911

             Date 11/19/88   No. 01006 Page   1 Due Date 01/03/89

Via OVERNIGHT EXPR.   FOB   Disc.days   Disc.% 0.00 Net Days 45 Your #KB4398 Our #01006

Inventory #	Description	Ordered	Received	Backorder	Unit Price	Disc.%	Extended Price
	#C-8972X Desktop Calculator, Electronic						319.98
	Freight						12.00
	Insurance						4.00

                                                    Sub-total   335.98
                                                    Tax   9.60
                                                    Total   345.58

                                                    Net to Pay   345.58

349

Report D.15

Date : 11/19/88
Time : 10:34 AM

Parts and Parcels, Inc.
#2 Byfore Avenue
Greenwood, S.C. 29646
803/555-1685

Page no. 1

PURCHASE JOURNAL REPORT

Type	Vend. Dept.	PO. Number	Vendor Code	Name	Date	Gross	Tax	Total
PURCHASE FA	01002	NUTS01	Nuts-to-You, Inc.	11/19/88	183.90	5.24	189.14
PURCHASE FA	01006	NUTS01	Nuts-to-You, Inc.	11/19/88	335.98	9.60	345.58
				Purchase Total :		519.88	14.84	534.72
				Department Total :		519.88	14.84	534.72
PURCHASE HW	01004	SHOV01	Shovell Shovels, Inc.	11/19/88	109.62	7.13	116.75
				Purchase Total :		109.62	7.13	116.75
				Department Total :		109.62	7.13	116.75
PURCHASE PL	01005	SINK01	The Sink Whole	11/19/88	1159.29	75.35	1234.64
				Purchase Total :		1159.29	75.35	1234.64
				Department Total :		1159.29	75.35	1234.64
PURCHASE PT	01001	PAIN01	Paint By the Numbers, Inc	11/19/88	2012.65	90.57	2103.22
				Purchase Total :		2012.65	90.57	2103.22
				Department Total :		2012.65	90.57	2103.22
PURCHASE WD	01003	SHAD01	Shady Vore Lumber Company	11/19/88	2180.25	65.41	2245.66
				Purchase Total :		2180.25	65.41	2245.66
				Department Total :		2180.25	65.41	2245.66
				Grand Totals :		5981.69	253.30	6234.99

350

Report D.16

Date : 11/19/88
Time : 10:34 AM

Parts and Parcels, Inc.
#2 Byfore Avenue
Greenwood, S.C. 29646
803/555-1685

Page no. 2

PURCHASE JOURNAL REPORT
SUMMARY BY INVENTORY AND CODE

Dept.	Type	Item/Acct #	Description	Units	Amount	Avg./Unit	Last P.Price	% Variance
	CODE	12031	Office Equipment		319.98			
	CODE	52082	Insurance		4.00			
	CODE	52081	Freight		21.18			
			Code total :		345.16			
			Department Total :		345.16			
01	PRODUCT	BOARD01	2x4, Pine Stud 8Ft	6000.000	570.00	0.10	0.00	0.00
01	PRODUCT	BOARD51	Plywood, 3/4 4x8	75.000	1610.25	21.47	0.00	0.00
01	PRODUCT	CONDUIT01	Conduit, Alum 16Ft	125.000	726.25	5.81	0.00	0.00
01	PRODUCT	CONDUIT07	Conduit, Plas 50Ft	25.000	433.04	17.32	0.00	0.00
01	PRODUCT	PAINT01	Paint, Wt Base Gal	25.000	1296.25	51.85	0.00	0.00
01	PRODUCT	PAINT02	Paint, Wt Base Qt	10.000	510.00	51.00	0.00	0.00
01	PRODUCT	PIGMENT99	Pigment, Asst Pt	4.000	206.40	51.60	0.00	0.00
			Product total :		5352.19			
			Department Total :		5352.19			
02	PRODUCT	GARDEN01	Hoe, Garden	6.000	64.62	10.77	0.00	0.00
02	PRODUCT	GARDEN09	Hose, Garden 25Ft	6.000	45.00	7.50	0.00	0.00
			Product total :		109.62			
			Department Total :		109.62			
03	PRODUCT	WARES17	Oven, Toaster M1203	12.000	174.72	14.56	0.00	0.00
			Product total :		174.72			
			Department Total :		174.72			
			Grand Totals :		5981.69			

Report D.17

Date : 11/19/88
Time : 11:20 AM

Parts and Parcels, Inc.
#2 Byfore Avenue
Greenwood, S.C. 29646
803/555-1685

Page no. 1

PO STATUS REPORT

Vend. Type	PO. Number	Vendor Code	Name	Date	Gross	Tax	Total	Status	Printed
PT	01001	PAIN01	Paint By the Numbers, Inc		259.25	0.00	259.25	Backorder	NO
			Department Total :		259.25	0.00	259.25		
WD	01003	SHAD01	Shady Vore Lumber Company		285.00	0.00	285.00	Backorder	NO
			Department Total :		285.00	0.00	285.00		
			Grand Totals :		544.25	0.00	544.25		

Report D.18*

WEIR01   Ship to/Remarks
Weir Lighting Fixtures   Ship to address
Sam Charger   at left.
4312 S. Socket Street
Ninety Six SC 29666

Date 11/19/88   No. 01001 Page 1 Due Date   12/19/88

Via Truck   FOB   Disc.days 10 Disc.% 3.00 Net Days 30 Your #884356 Our #01001

Inventory #	Description	Ordered	Shipped	Backorder	Unit Price	Disc.%	Extended Price
PAINT01	Paint, Wt Base Gal	5.002	5.002	0.000	75.800		416.90
CONDUIT01	Conduit, Alum 16Ft	3.000	3.000	0.000	8.590		25.77

                                              Sub-total   442.67
                                              Tax   22.13
                                              Total   464.80

                                              Net to Pay   464.80

Report D.19*

I n v o i c e

```
    VOLT01                                          Ship to/Remarks
    Volten, Rhea                                    Cash and carry.

    P.O. Box 3423
    Hodges SC 29653

               Date 11/19/88    No. 01002 Page  1  Due Date  12/19/88
-----------------------------------------------------------------------------------
Via            FOB           Disc.days    Disc.% 0.00 Net Days  30  Your #Ck3104  Our #01002
-----------------------------------------------------------------------------------
Inventory #   Description    Ordered   Shipped  Backorder Unit Price Disc.%  Extended Price
-----------------------------------------------------------------------------------
GARDEN09      Hose, Garden 25Ft    1.000    1.000    0.000    11.880              11.88
BOARD51       Plywood, 3/4 4x8      2.000    2.000    0.000    32.950              65.90
PAINT02       Paint, Wt Base Qt     0.002    0.002    0.000    83.400              13.90


-----------------------------------------------------------------------------------
                                                        Sub-total      91.68
                                                        Tax             4.58
                                                        Total          96.26
                                                        Payment    (   96.26)
                                                        Net to Pay      0.00
                                                        -----------
```

353

Report D.20*

```
                        Parts and Parcels, Inc.
                           #2 Byfore Avenue
                         Greenwood, S.C. 29646
                             803/555-1685
                          I n v o i c e
```

```
     WEIR01                                    Ship to/Remarks
     Weir Lighting Fixtures                    Ship to address
     Sam Charger                               at left.
     4312 S. Socket Street
     Ninety Six SC 29666
```

```
             Date 11/19/88    No. 01003 Page  1  Due Date   12/19/88
    ----------------------------------------------------------------------------
    Via Truck        FOB           Disc.days  10 Disc.% 3.00 Net Days  30  Your #883982  Our #01003
    ----------------------------------------------------------------------------
    Inventory #   Description       Ordered    Shipped   Backorder Unit Price  Disc.%   Extended Price
    ----------------------------------------------------------------------------
    CONDUIT07    Conduit, Plas 50Ft  30.000    25.000     5.000    21.500     3.50          518.69
    ----------------------------------------------------------------------------
                                                                  Sub-total                518.69
                                                                  Tax                       25.93
                                                                  Total                    544.62

                                                                  Net to Pay               544.62
                                                                  -----------
```

Report D.21*

BILD01   Ship to/Remarks
Bildah Supply, Inc.   Ship to: New School
J. Bildah, Foreman   Rt2, Booker Road
5432 Brickyard Blvd.   Greenwood, SC 29646
Greenwood SC 29646

Date 11/19/88   No. 01004 Page 1 Due Date 12/19/88

Via Truck   FOB   Disc.days 10 Disc.% 3.00 Net Days 30 Your #PO7129 Our #01004

Inventory # Description   Ordered   Shipped   Backorder Unit Price Disc.% Extended Price
----

Inventory #	Description	Ordered	Shipped	Backorder	Unit Price	Disc.%	Extended Price
BOARD01	2x4, Pine Stud 8Ft	2500.000	2500.000	0.000	0.170	2.00	416.50
CONDUIT01	Conduit, Alum 16Ft	80.000	80.000	0.000	8.590	2.00	673.46
PAINT01	Paint, Wt Base Gal	35.000	19.002	15.002	75.800	2.00	1448.54
	Backorders guaranteed in 3 work days.						
	Delivery and unloading.						50.00

                                                Sub-total   2588.50
                                                Tax   126.93
                                                Total   2715.43

                                                Net to Pay   2715.43

Report D.22*

PAMS01   Ship to/Remarks
Pam's Spades/Garden Shop   Picked up.
Pam Mulch
123 Pine Bark Circle
Greenwood SC 29646

Date 11/19/88   No. 01005 Page   1 Due Date   12/19/88

Via   FOB   Disc.days 10 Disc.% 3.00 Net Days 30 Your #Ck0789 Our #01005

Inventory #   Description   Ordered   Shipped   Backorder   Unit Price Disc.%   Extended Price
----
GARDEN01   Hoe, Garden   6.000   6.000   0.000   19.950   119.70

                                                                 Sub-total   119.70
                                                                 Tax   5.99
                                                                 Total   125.69
                                                                 Payment   (125.69)
                                                                 Net to Pay   0.00

Report D.23*

Parts and Parcels, Inc.
#2 Byfore Avenue
Greenwood, S.C. 29646
803/555-1685
I n v o i c e

PAMS01   Ship to/Remarks
Pam's Spades/Garden Shop   On-site service.
Pam Mulch
123 Pine Bark Circle
Greenwood SC 29646

             Date 11/19/88   No. 01006 Page 1 Due Date 12/19/88

Via   FOB   Disc.days 10 Disc.% 3.00 Net Days 30 Your #880034 Our #01006

Inventory #   Description   Ordered   Shipped Backorder Unit Price Disc.%   Extended Price
----
SOILTEST01   Soil, Prelim Test   3.002 @   30.000   105.00

                                                                  Sub-total   105.00
                                                                  Tax   5.25
                                                                  Total   110.25

                                                                  Net to Pay   110.25

Report D.24

Date : 11/19/88   Parts and Parcels, Inc.   Page no. 1
Time : 01:16 PM   #2 Byfore Avenue
                                   Greenwood, S.C. 29646
                                      803/555-1685

                                   SALES JOURNAL REPORT

Type	Cust. Dept.	Inv/Ret Number	Customer Code	Name	Date	Gross	Tax	Total	Amount Pd	Net To Pay
INVOICE	01	01001	WEIR01	Weir Lighting Fixtures	11/19/88	442.67	22.13	464.80	0.00	464.80
INVOICE	01	01003	WEIR01	Weir Lighting Fixtures	11/19/88	518.69	25.93	544.62	0.00	544.62
INVOICE	01	01004	BILD01	Bildah Supply, Inc.	11/19/88	2588.50	126.93	2715.43	0.00	2715.43
INVOICE	01	01005	PAMS01	Pam's Spades/Garden Shop	11/19/88	119.70	5.99	125.69	125.69	0.00
INVOICE	01	01006	PAMS01	Pam's Spades/Garden Shop	11/19/88	105.00	5.25	110.25	0.00	110.25
				Invoice Total :		3774.56	186.23	3960.79	125.69	3835.10
				Department Total :		3774.56	186.23	3960.79	125.69	3835.10
INVOICE	02	01002	VOLT01	Volten, Rhea	11/19/88	91.68	4.58	96.26	96.26	0.00
				Invoice Total :		91.68	4.58	96.26	96.26	0.00
				Department Total :		91.68	4.58	96.26	96.26	0.00
				Grand Totals :		3866.24	190.81	4057.05	221.95	3835.10

357

Report D.25

Date : 11/19/88
Time : 01:16 PM

Parts and Parcels, Inc.
#2 Byfore Avenue
Greenwood, S.C. 29646
803/555-1685

Page no. 2

SALES JOURNAL REPORT
SUMMARY BY INVENTORY AND CODE

Dept.	Type	Item/Acct #	Description	Units	Amount	Avg./Unit	Sale Price	% Variance
	CODE	4301	Freight		50.00			
			Code total :		50.00			
			Department Total :		50.00			
01	PRODUCT	BOARD01	2x4, Pine Stud BFt	2500.000	416.50	0.17	0.17	-2.00
01	PRODUCT	BOARD51	Plywood, 3/4 4x8	2.000	65.90	32.95	32.95	0.00
01	PRODUCT	CONDUIT01	Conduit, Alum 16Ft	83.000	699.23	8.42	8.59	-1.93
01	PRODUCT	CONDUIT07	Conduit, Plas 50Ft	25.000	518.69	20.75	21.50	-3.50
01	PRODUCT	PAINT01	Paint, Wt Base Gal	25.000	1865.44	74.62	75.80	-1.56
01	PRODUCT	PAINT02	Paint, Wt Base Qt	0.002	13.90	83.40	83.40	0.00
			Product total :		3579.66			
			Department Total :		3579.66			
02	PRODUCT	GARDEN01	Hoe, Garden	6.000	119.70	19.95	19.95	0.00
02	PRODUCT	GARDEN09	Hose, Garden 25Ft	1.000	11.88	11.88	11.88	0.00
			Product total :		131.58			
02	SERVICE	SOILTEST01	Soil, Prelim Test	3.002	105.00	30.00	30.00	0.00
			Service Total :		105.00			
			Department Total :		236.58			
			Grand Totals :		3866.24			

Report D.26

Date : 11/18/88
Time : 03:55 PM

Parts and Parcels, Inc.
Hardware the Easy Way
#2 Byfore Avenue
Greenwood, SC 29646

Page no. 1

WEEKLY PAYROLL REGISTER : HOURLY

Code Employee Name	Cd	Earnings Description	Number	Amount	Cd	Deductions Description	Amount	Net to Pay	Liabilities Description	Amount
COAR02 Coard, Stension	2	Hourly	40.000	167.60	16	FWH Tax	16.49		FICA	12.59
					17	FICA	12.59		FUTA	0.50
					18	SWH Tax	4.82		Disab. Ins.	38.75
		Total		167.60			33.90	133.70		51.84
PART01 Partment, Notmai D.	2	Hourly	40.000	230.00	16	FWH Tax	26.55		FICA	20.51
	3	Overtime #1	5.000	43.15	17	FICA	20.51		FUTA	0.82
					18	SWH Tax	11.60		Disab. Ins.	38.75
		Total		273.15			58.66	214.49		60.08
REAL01 Real, Rod N.	2	Hourly	27.000	108.00	16	FWH Tax	7.55		FICA	8.11
					17	FICA	8.11		FUTA	0.32
					18	SWH Tax	2.17		Disab. Ins.	38.75
		Total		108.00			17.83	90.17		47.18
ROUT01 Router, Bitsy	2	Hourly	14.500	60.76	16	FWH Tax	0.46		FICA	4.56
					17	FICA	4.56		FUTA	0.18
					18	SWH Tax	0.79		Disab. Ins.	38.75
		Total		60.76			5.81	54.95		43.49
Total 1 Parts and Parcels	2	Hourly	121.500	566.36	16	FWH Tax	51.05		FICA	45.77
	3	Overtime #1	5.000	43.15	17	FICA	45.77		FUTA	1.82
					18	SWH Tax	19.38		Disab. Ins.	155.00
		Total		609.51			116.20	493.31		202.59
Company Totals	2	Hourly	121.500	566.36	16	FWH Tax	51.05		FICA	45.77
	3	Overtime #1	5.000	43.15	17	FICA	45.77		FUTA	1.82
					18	SWH Tax	19.38		LIABILITY	155.00
		Total		609.51			116.20	493.31		202.59

Report D.27

Date : 11/18/88
Time : 03:56 PM

Parts and Parcels, Inc.
Hardware the Easy Way
#2 Byfore Avenue
Greenwood, SC 29646

Page no. 1

WEEKLY PAYROLL REGISTER : SALARY

Code	Employee Name	Cd	Description	Number	Amount	Cd	Description	Amount	Net to Pay	Description	Amount
			--------- Earnings ---------------				----- Deductions ---------			--- Liabilities ------	
COAR01	Coard, Wynn Doe	1	Salary	5.000	357.21	16	FWH Tax	33.53		FICA	26.83
						17	FICA	26.83		FUTA	1.07
						18	SWH Tax	15.74		Disab. Ins.	38.75
			Total		357.21			76.10	281.11		66.65
Total 1	Parts and Parcels	1	Salary	5.000	357.21	16	FWH Tax	33.53		FICA	26.83
						17	FICA	26.83		FUTA	1.07
						18	SWH Tax	15.74		Disab. Ins.	38.75
			Total		357.21			76.10	281.11		66.65
	Company Totals	1	Salary	5.000	357.21	16	FWH Tax	33.53		FICA	26.83
						17	FICA	26.83		FUTA	1.07
						18	SWH Tax	15.74		LIABILITY	38.75
			Total		357.21			76.10	281.11		66.65

Report D.28

Date : 11/19/88
Time : 05:21 PM

Parts and Parcels, Inc.
Hardware the Easy Way
#2 Byfore Avenue
Greenwood, SC 29646

Page no. 1

CHECK REGISTER REPORT

Check #	Date	Code	Employee Name	Earnings	Deductions	Net Paid	Paid?
009001	11/19/88		V O I D				
009002	11/19/88	COAR02	Coard, Stension	167.60	33.90	133.70	No
009003	11/19/88	PART01	Partment, Notmai D.	273.15	58.66	214.49	No
009004	11/19/88	REAL01	Real, Rod N.	108.00	17.83	90.17	No
009005	11/19/88	ROUT01	Router, Bitsy	60.76	5.81	54.95	No
009006	11/19/88		V O I D				
009007	11/19/88	COAR01	Coard, Wynn Doe	357.21	76.10	281.11	No
			Checks Total 5	966.72	192.30	774.42	
			Voided 2				

Report D.29

Parts and Parcels, Inc.
Hardware the Easy Way
#2 Byfore Avenue
Greenwood, SC 29646

PAYROLL DEPARTMENT REPORT

Department : 1 Parts and Parcels
Payroll Type: Weekly.

Emp #	Employee Name	Cd	Description	Acct #	Number	Debits	Credits
COAR01	Coard, Wynn Doe	1	Salary		5.000	357.21	
			Total Acct.	520111	5.000	357.21	
COAR02	Coard, Stension	2	Hourly		40.000	167.60	
PART01	Partment, Notmai D.				40.000	230.00	
REAL01	Real, Rod N.				27.000	108.00	
ROUT01	Router, Bitsy				14.500	60.76	
			Total Acct.	520112	121.500	566.36	
PART01	Partment, Notmai D.	3	Overtime #1		5.000	43.15	
			Total Acct.	520114	5.000	43.15	
COAR01	Coard, Wynn Doe	16	FWH Tax				33.53
COAR02	Coard, Stension						16.49
PART01	Partment, Notmai D.						26.55
REAL01	Real, Rod N.						7.55
ROUT01	Router, Bitsy						0.46
			Total Acct.	210411			84.58
COAR01	Coard, Wynn Doe	17	FICA				26.83
COAR02	Coard, Stension						12.59
PART01	Partment, Notmai D.						20.51
REAL01	Real, Rod N.						8.11
ROUT01	Router, Bitsy						4.56
			Total Acct.	210412			72.60
COAR01	Coard, Wynn Doe	18	SWH Tax				15.74
COAR02	Coard, Stension						4.82
PART01	Partment, Notmai D.						11.60
REAL01	Real, Rod N.						2.17
ROUT01	Router, Bitsy						0.79
			Total Acct.	210416			35.12
COAR01	Coard, Wynn Doe	31	FICA			26.83	26.83
COAR02	Coard, Stension					12.59	12.59
PART01	Partment, Notmai D.					20.51	20.51
REAL01	Real, Rod N.					8.11	8.11
ROUT01	Router, Bitsy					4.56	4.56

Report D.30

Parts and Parcels, Inc.
Hardware the Easy Way
#2 Byfore Avenue
Greenwood, SC 29646

PAYROLL DEPARTMENT REPORT

Department : 1   Parts and Parcels
Payroll Type: Weekly.

Emp #	Employee Name	Cd	Description	Acct #	Number	Debits	Credits
			Total Acct.	520131		72.60	
				210413			72.60
COAR01	Coard, Wynn Doe	32	FUTA			1.07	1.07
COAR02	Coard, Stension					0.50	0.50
PART01	Partment, Notmai D.					0.82	0.82
REAL01	Real, Rod N.					0.32	0.32
ROUT01	Router, Bitsy					0.18	0.18
			Total Acct.	520132		2.89	
				210414			2.89
COAR01	Coard, Wynn Doe	34	Disab. Ins.			38.75	38.75
COAR02	Coard, Stension					38.75	38.75
PART01	Partment, Notmai D.					38.75	38.75
REAL01	Real, Rod N.					38.75	38.75
ROUT01	Router, Bitsy					38.75	38.75
			Total Acct.	520134		193.75	
				210418			193.75
			Checking	11022			774.42
						1235.96	1235.96

Report D.31

Parts and Parcels, Inc.
Hardware the Easy Way
#2 Byfore Avenue
Greenwood, SC 29646

Page no. 1

PAYROLL DEPARTMENT REPORT

Department : 1   Parts and Parcels
Payroll Type: Weekly.

Cd	Description	Acct #	Number	Debits	Credits
1	Salary	520111	5.000	357.21	
2	Hourly	520112	121.500	566.36	
3	Overtime #1	520114	5.000	43.15	
16	FWH Tax	210411			84.58
17	FICA	210412			72.60
18	SWH Tax	210416			35.12
31	FICA	520131		72.60	
		210413			72.60
32	FUTA	520132		2.89	
		210414			2.89
34	Disab. Ins.	520134		193.75	
		210418			193.75
	Checking	11022			774.42
				1235.96	1235.96

Report D.32

Parts and Parcels, Inc.
Hardware the Easy Way
#2 Byfore Avenue
Greenwood, SC 29646

Page no. 1

WEEKLY PAYROLL G/L TRANSACTION CODE PY1118

Account #	Debits	Credits
11022		774.42
210411		84.58
210412		72.60
210413		72.60
210414		2.89
210416		35.12
210418		193.75
520111	357.21	
520112	566.36	
520114	43.15	
520131	72.60	
520132	2.89	
520134	193.75	
Totals:	1235.96	1235.96

Report D.33

FAYROLL QUARTERLY REPORT

Social Security	Employee Name	Taxable FICA Wages	Taxable Wages	State Unemployment Wages	State
666-00-9090	Coard, Stension	167.60	167.60	0.00	SC
888-11-5555	Coard, Wynn Doe	357.21	357.21	0.00	SC
222-33-4444	Partment, Notmai D.	273.15	273.15	0.00	SC
999-88-2222	Real, Rod N.	108.00	108.00	0.00	SC
987-65-4321	Router, Bitsy	60.76	60.76	0.00	SC
5	Totals for Page :	966.72	966.72	0.00	
5	Totals for State : SC	966.72	966.72	0.00	

Report D.34

ACCOUNTS RECEIVABLE CASH RECEIPTS JOURNAL

Tran. No.	Acct #	Cust.	Customer Name	Invoice#	Date	Chk #	Type	Inv. Amount	Disc. Taken	Chk. Amount
0001	11021	WEIR01	Weir Lighting Fixtures	01001	11/20/88	3475	PMT.	464.80	13.94	450.86
0002	11021	BILD01	Bildah Supply, Inc.	01004	11/20/88	12397	PMT.	2715.43	81.46	2633.97
			Acct. Total:					3180.23	95.40	3084.83
			Grand Total: # of Transactions 2					3180.23	95.40	3084.83

Report D.35

Date : 11/19/88
Time : 11:53 AM

Parts and Parcels, Inc.
#2 Byfore Avenue
Greenwood, S.C. 29646
803/555-1685

Accounts Receivable Journal

Tran No.	Custom. Code	Customer name	Invoice#	Date	Ref. # Chk. #	Due Date	Discount Date	Discount Available	Trans. Type	Debit	Credit
0003	PAMS01	Pam's Spades/Garden Sh	01006	11/19/88	880034	12/19/88	11/29/88		CREDIT		
	11051	Accts Rec'ble Module			Invoice #01006 Voided.						110.25
	4102	Sales Dept. 02			Invoice #01006 Voided.					110.25	
								Totals:	TRANSACTION 2	110.25	110.25
								Grand Total :	TRANSACTIONS 2	110.25	110.25

Report D.36

Date : 11/19/88
Time : 11:53 AM

Parts and Parcels, Inc.
#2 Byfore Avenue
Greenwood, S.C. 29646
803/555-1685

GENERAL LEDGER TRANSFER SUMMARY

Acct #	Acct. name	Description	Debit	Credit
11051	Accts Rec'ble Module	Summary From AR Post		110.25
4102	Sales Dept. 02	Summary From AR Post	110.25	
		Summary Total :	110.25	110.25

Report D.37

Parts and Parcels, Inc.
#2 Byfore Avenue
Greenwood, S.C. 29646
803/555-1685

General Ledger Journal Report

Journal Trans.#	Date	Acct. #	Account Name	Description	Debits	Credits	Posted?
AR 1120	11/20/88	11021	Checking Account	Payments Summ.-AR Post	2633.97		NO
		11021	Checking Account	Payments Summ.-AR Post	450.86		NO
		4102	Sales Dept. 02	Summary From AR Post	110.25		NO
		5304	Sales Discounts	Payments Summ.-AR Post	95.40		NO
		11051	Accts Rec'ble Module	Summary From AR Post		110.25	NO
		11051	Accts Rec'ble Module	Payments Summ.-AR Post		3180.23	NO
				TOTAL TRANSACTION :	3290.48	3290.48	
BI 1119	11/19/88	11021	Checking Account	Billing Summary	221.95		NO
		11051	Accts Rec'ble Module	Billing Summary	3835.10		NO
		5101	COGS Dept. 01	Billing Summary	2500.48		NO
		5102	COGS Dept. 02	Billing Summary	72.12		NO
		11071	Inventory - Module	Billing Summary		2572.60	NO
		21042	Sales Tax Payable	Billing Summary		190.81	NO
		4101	Sales Dept. 01	Billing Summary		3579.66	NO
		4102	Sales Dept. 02	Billing Summary		236.58	NO
		4301	Freight	Billing Summary		50.00	NO
				TOTAL TRANSACTION :	6629.65	6629.65	
CA 0001	10/29/88	11021	Checking Account	Personal Investment	25000.00		YES
		11021	Checking Account	Loan Proceeds	50000.00		YES
		2202	Notes Payable	Loan Proceeds		50000.00	YES
		31011	Par Value	Personal Investment		25000.00	YES
				TOTAL TRANSACTION :	75000.00	75000.00	
CA 0002	10/29/88	11021	Checking Account	Loan for Building Buy	65000.00		YES
		2201	Mortgages Payable	Loan for Building Buy		65000.00	YES
				TOTAL TRANSACTION :	65000.00	65000.00	
CA 0003	10/29/88	12051	Original Value	Purchase Building	65000.00		YES
		11021	Checking Account	Purchase Building		65000.00	YES
				TOTAL TRANSACTION :	65000.00	65000.00	
CA 0004	10/29/88	12011	Original Value	Truck Purchase	12995.00		YES
		11021	Checking Account	Truck Purchase		12995.00	YES
				TOTAL TRANSACTION :	12995.00	12995.00	

Report D.38

Parts and Parcels, Inc.
#2 Byfore Avenue
Greenwood, S.C. 29646
803/555-1685

General Ledger Journal Report

Journal Trans.#	Date	Acct. #	Account Name	Description	Debits	Credits	Posted?
PO 1119	11/19/88	52082	Insurance	Purchase Order Summary	4.00		NO
		52091	Sales Tax/Purchases	Purchase Order Summary	253.30		NO
		2101	Accts Payable-Module	Purchase Order Summary		6234.99	NO
				TOTAL TRANSACTION :	6234.99	6234.99	
CA 0005	10/29/88	12021	Original Value	Adjust for Furn/Fixtures	25000.00		YES
		12051	Original Value	Adjust for Furn/Fixtures		25000.00	YES
				TOTAL TRANSACTION :	25000.00	25000.00	
PO 1119	11/19/88	11071	Inventory - Module	Purchase Order Summary	5636.53		NO
		12031	Original Value	Purchase Order Summary	319.98		NO
		52081	Freight	Purchase Order Summary	21.18		NO
PY 1118	11/18/88	520111	Salaries	PAYROLL POST SUMMARY	357.21		NO
		520112	Hourly	PAYROLL POST SUMMARY	566.36		NO
		520114	Overtime	PAYROLL POST SUMMARY	43.15		NO
		520131	FICA Employer	PAYROLL POST SUMMARY	72.60		NO
		520132	FUTA	PAYROLL POST SUMMARY	2.89		NO
		520134	Disability Insurance	PAYROLL POST SUMMARY	193.75		NO
		11022	Payroll Account	PAYROLL POST SUMMARY		774.42	NO
		210411	Federal Income W/H	PAYROLL POST SUMMARY		84.58	NO
		210412	FICA W/H Employee	PAYROLL POST SUMMARY		72.60	NO
		210413	FICA W/H Employer	PAYROLL POST SUMMARY		72.60	NO
		210414	FUTA	PAYROLL POST SUMMARY		2.89	NO
		210416	State Income W/H	PAYROLL POST SUMMARY		35.12	NO
		210418	Disability Insurance	PAYROLL POST SUMMARY		193.75	NO
				TOTAL TRANSACTION :	1235.96	1235.96	
				TOTAL TRANSACTION :	260386.08	260386.08	

OF ENTRIES PRINTED : 46

367

Report D.39*

BILD01
Bildah Supply, Inc.
J. Bildah, Foreman
5432 Brickyard Blvd.   Page 1
Greenwood, SC   29646   Closing Date : 11/20/88

Date	Invoice#	Due Date	CD	Description	Ref. #	Debits	Credits	Amount Due	Past Due	Days
11/19/88	01004	12/19/88	1	Invoice	P07129	2715.43				
11/20/88		11/20/88	4	Payment	12397		2633.97			
11/20/86		11/20/88	6	Discount Taken	12397		81.46	0.00		

		Total Balance	Past Due Balance	Days
		0.00	0.00	0

Thank you for your patronage. We hope
we will be able to serve you again soon.

Report D.40*

PAMS01
Pam's Spades/Garden Shop
Pam Mulch
123 Pine Bark Circle   Page 1
Greenwood, SC   29646   Closing Date : 11/20/88

Date	Invoice#	Due Date	CD	Description	Ref. #	Debits	Credits	Amount Due	Past Due	Days
11/19/88	01005	12/19/88	1	Invoice	Ck0789	0.00		0.00		
11/19/88	01006	12/19/88	1	Invoice	880034	110.25				
11/19/88		12/19/88	5	Credit	880034		110.25	0.00		

	Total Balance	Past Due Balance	Days
	0.00	0.00	0

Thank you for your patronage. We hope
we will be able to serve you again soon.

Report D.41*

Parts and Parcels, Inc.
#2 Byfore Avenue
Greenwood, S.C. 29646
803/555-1685
S t a t e m e n t

VOLT01
Volten, Rhea
P.O. Box 3423
Hodges, SC   29653

Page 1
Closing Date : 11/20/88

Date	Invoice#	Due Date	CD	Description	Ref. #	Debits	Credits	Amount Due	Past Due	Days
11/19/88	01002	12/19/88	1	Invoice	Ck3104	0.00		0.00		

		Total Balance	Past Due Balance	Days
		0.00	0.00	0

Thank you for your patronage. We hope
we will be able to serve you again soon.

Report D.42*

Parts and Parcels, Inc.
#2 Byfore Avenue
Greenwood, S.C. 29646
803/555-1685
S t a t e m e n t

WEIR01
Weir Lighting Fixtures
Sam Charger
4312 S. Socket Street
Ninety Six, SC   29666

Page 1
Closing Date : 11/20/88

Date	Invoice#	Due Date	CD	Description	Ref. #	Debits	Credits	Amount Due	Past Due	Days
11/19/88	01001	12/19/88	1	Invoice	884356	464.80				
11/20/88		11/20/88	4	Payment	3475		450.86			
11/20/88		11/20/88	6	Discount Taken	3475		13.94	0.00		
11/19/88	01003	12/19/88	1	Invoice	883982	544.62		544.62		

	Total Balance	Past Due Balance	Days
	544.62	0.00	0

Thank you for your promptness in paying
your bills. We appreciate it.

371

Report D.43*

```
                        Parts and Parcels, Inc.
                           #2 Byfore Avenue
                         Greenwood, S.C. 29646
                            803/555-1685
                          S t a t e m e n t

     NUT501
     Nuts-to-You, Inc.
     Douglas Clark, Sales Rep.
     546 Pecan Grove                          Page 1
     Brazil, IN   47911                       Closing Date : 11/20/88
-----------------------------------------------------------------------------

  Date  Invoice# Due Date CD Description    Ref. #   Debits  Credits Amount Due Past Due  Days
-----------------------------------------------------------------------------

11/19/88 01002   01/03/89 1  Purchase       01002   189.14           189.14
11/19/88 KB439B  01/03/89 1  Purchase       01006   345.58           345.58
-----------------------------------------------------------------------------

                                                             Total    Past Due
                                                             Balance   Balance Days
-----------------------------------------------------------------------------

                                                             534.72     0.00     0
-----------------------------------------------------------------------------
```

Report D.44*

```
                        Parts and Parcels, Inc.
                           #2 Byfore Avenue
                         Greenwood, S.C. 29646
                            803/555-1685
                          S t a t e m e n t

     PAIN01
     Paint By the Numbers, Inc.
     Vinnie Van Gogh
     Green Fields Mall                        Page 1
     Plaster, TN   38654                      Closing Date : 11/20/88
-----------------------------------------------------------------------------

  Date  Invoice# Due Date CD Description    Ref. #   Debits  Credits Amount Due Past Due  Days
-----------------------------------------------------------------------------

11/19/88 A-123   12/19/88 1  Purchase       01001   2103.22          2103.22
-----------------------------------------------------------------------------

                                                             Total    Past Due
                                                             Balance   Balance Days
-----------------------------------------------------------------------------

                                                             2103.22    0.00     0
-----------------------------------------------------------------------------
```

Report D.45*

```
                        Parts and Parcels, Inc.
                           #2 Byfore Avenue
                        Greenwood, S.C. 29646
                           803/555-1685
                        S t a t e m e n t


    SHAD01
    Shady Vore Lumber Company
    Bubba Vore, President
    543 Barron Hills Canyon                  Page 1
    St. Arbor, AZ   85899                    Closing Date : 11/20/88
--------------------------------------------------------------------------------

Date   Invoice# Due Date CD Description     Ref. #   Debits    Credits  Amount Due Past Due   Days
--------------------------------------------------------------------------------

11/19/88 4723-A  12/19/88  1  Purchase       01003   2245.66            2245.66


--------------------------------------------------------------------------------
                                                      Total     P a s t  D u e
                                                      Balance   Balance  Days
--------------------------------------------------------------------------------
                                                      2245.66    0.00      0
--------------------------------------------------------------------------------
```

Report D.46*

```
                        Parts and Parcels, Inc.
                           #2 Byfore Avenue
                        Greenwood, S.C. 29646
                           803/555-1685
                        S t a t e m e n t


    SHOV01
    Shovell Shovels, Inc.
    B.S. Shovells, Acct. Rep.
    Fourth Elyzer Plaza                      Page 1
    Patty, IL   60799                        Closing Date : 11/20/88
--------------------------------------------------------------------------------

Date   Invoice# Due Date CD Description     Ref. #   Debits    Credits  Amount Due Past Due   Days
--------------------------------------------------------------------------------

11/19/88 KB4301  12/19/88  1  Purchase       01004   116.75             116.75


--------------------------------------------------------------------------------
                                                      Total     P a s t  D u e
                                                      Balance   Balance  Days
--------------------------------------------------------------------------------
                                                      116.75     0.00      0
--------------------------------------------------------------------------------
```

Report D.47*

Parts and Parcels, Inc.
#2 Byfore Avenue
Greenwood, S.C. 29646
803/555-1685
S t a t e m e n t

SINK01
The Sink Whole
L. Beau Trapp, Jr.
4 Thunder Lane   Page 1
Shower Head, SD   57813   Closing Date : 11/20/88

Date	Invoice#	Due Date	CD	Description	Ref. #	Debits	Credits	Amount Due	Past Due	Days
11/19/88	213450	01/03/89	1	Purchase	01005	1234.64		1234.64		

	Total Balance	Past Due Balance	Days
	1234.64	0.00	0

Report D.48

Date : 11/20/88   Parts and Parcels, Inc.   Page no. 1
Time : 03:03 PM   #2 Byfore Avenue
                                      Greenwood, S.C. 29646
                                         803/555-1685

ACCOUNTS PAYABLE CHECKS TO PRINT JOURNAL

Tran. No.	Vendor	Vendor Name	Invoice#	Inv. Amount	Disc. Taken	Amt. to Pay
0001	NUTS01	Nuts-to-You, Inc.	01002	107.14	0.00	107.14
	Check Total:	# of Transactions	1	189.14	0.00	189.14
0003	PAIN01	Paint By the Numbers, Inc.	A-123	2103.22	31.55	2071.67
	Check Total:	# of Transactions	1	2103.22	31.55	2071.67
	Grand Total:	# of Transactions	2	2292.36	31.55	2260.81

Report D.49

Parts and Parcels, Inc.
#2 Byfore Avenue
Greenwood, S.C. 29646
803/555-1685

Page no. 1

ACCOUNTS PAYABLE PAYMENTS JOURNAL

Tran. No.	Acct #	Vendor	Vendor Name	Invoice#	Date	Chk #	Type	Inv. Amount	Disc. Taken	Chk. Amount
0004	11021	SHOV01	****** V O I D ******	VOID	11/20/88	005001	VOID	0.00	0.00	0.00
			Check Total: # of Transactions 1					0.00	0.00	0.00
0001	11021	NUTS01	Nuts-to-You, Inc.	01002	11/20/88	005002	CHECK	189.14	0.00	189.14
			Check Total: # of Transactions 1					189.14	0.00	189.14
0003	11021	PAIN01	Paint By the Numbers, Inc.	A-123	11/20/88	005003	CHECK	2103.22	31.55	2071.67
			Check Total: # of Transactions 1					2103.22	31.55	2071.67
0002	11021	SHOV01	Shovell Shovels, Inc.	KB4301	11/20/88	M0981	PMT.	116.75	3.50	113.25
			Check Total: # of Transactions 1					116.75	3.50	113.25
			Acct. Total:					2409.11	35.05	2374.06
			Grand Total: # of Transactions 4					2409.11	35.05	2374.06

Report D.50

Parts and Parcels, Inc.
#2 Byfore Avenue
Greenwood, S.C. 29646
803/555-1685

Page no. 1

PAYMENTS REPORT
Subtotals by Date

Vendor Code	Name	Invoice No.	Discount Available	Discount Date	Payment by Disc. Date	Due Date	Payment by Due Date	Remarks
NUTS01	Nuts-to-You, Inc.	01002	0.00	11/19/88	189.14	01/03/89	189.14	_____
		KB4398	0.00	11/19/88	345.58	01/03/89	345.58	_____
SINK01	The Sink Whole	213450	0.00	11/19/88	1234.64	01/03/89	1234.64	_____
		Sub-totals:	0.00		1769.36		1769.36	_____
NUTS01	Nuts-to-You, Inc.	01002	0.00		-189.14		-189.14	_____
PAIN01	Paint By the Numbers, Inc.	A-123	-31.55		-2071.67		-2103.22	_____
SHOV01	Shovell Shovels, Inc.	KB4301	-3.50		-113.25		-116.75	_____
		Sub-totals:	-35.05		-2374.06		-2409.11	_____
SHAD01	Shady Vore Lumber Company	4723-A	44.91	11/29/88	2200.75	12/19/88	2245.66	_____
SHOV01	Shovell Shovels, Inc.	KB4301	3.50	11/29/88	113.25	12/19/88	116.75	_____
		Sub-totals:	48.41		2314.00		2362.41	_____
PAIN01	Paint By the Numbers, Inc.	A-123	31.55	12/04/88	2071.67	12/19/88	2103.22	_____
		Sub-totals:	31.55		2071.67		2103.22	_____
	Totals :		44.91		3780.97		3825.88	_____

Report D.51

Parts and Parcels, Inc.
#2 Byfore Avenue
Greenwood, S.C. 29646
803/555-1685

PAYMENTS REPORT
Subtotals by Vendor

Vendor Code	Name	Invoice No.	Discount Available	Discount Date	Payment by Disc. Date	Due Date	Payment by Due Date	Remarks
NUTS01	Nuts-to-You, Inc.	01002	0.00	11/19/88	189.14	01/03/89	189.14	
		KB4398	0.00	11/19/88	345.58	01/03/89	345.58	
		01002	0.00		-189.14		-189.14	
		Sub-totals:	0.00		345.58		345.58	
PAIN01	Paint By the Numbers, Inc.	A-123	0.00	12/04/88	0.00	12/19/88	0.00	
		Sub-totals:	0.00		0.00		0.00	
SHAD01	Shady Vore Lumber Company	4723-A	44.91	11/29/88	2200.75	12/19/88	2245.66	
		Sub-totals:	44.91		2200.75		2245.66	
SHOV01	Shovell Shovels, Inc.	KB4301	0.00	11/29/88	0.00	12/19/88	0.00	
		Sub-totals:	0.00		0.00		0.00	
SINK01	The Sink Whole	213450	0.00	11/19/88	1234.64	01/03/89	1234.64	
		Sub-totals:	0.00		1234.64		1234.64	
	Totals :		44.91		3780.97		3825.88	

Report D.52

Parts and Parcels, Inc.
#2 Byfore Avenue
Greenwood, S.C. 29646
803/555-1685

General Ledger Journal Report

Journal Trans.#	Date	Acct. #	Account Name	Description	Debits	Credits	Posted?
AP 1120	11/20/88	2101	Accts Payable-Module	Payments Summ.-AP Post	2409.11		NO
		11021	Checking Account	Nuts-to-You, Inc-005002		189.14	NO
		11021	Checking Account	Paint By the Num-005003		2071.67	NO
		11021	Checking Account	Shovell Shovels,-M0981		113.25	NO
		4404	Purchase Discounts	Payments Summ.-AP Post		35.05	NO
				TOTAL TRANSACTION :	2409.11	2409.11	
AR 1120	11/20/88	11021	Checking Account	Payments Summ.-AR Post	2633.97		NO
		11021	Checking Account	Payments Summ.-AR Post	450.86		NO
		4102	Sales Dept. 02	Summary From AR Post	110.25		NO
		5304	Sales Discounts	Payments Summ.-AR Post	95.40		NO
		11051	Accts Rec'ble Module	Summary From AR Post		110.25	NO
		11051	Accts Rec'ble Module	Payments Summ.-AR Post		3180.23	NO
				TOTAL TRANSACTION :	3290.48	3290.48	
BI 1119	11/19/88	11021	Checking Account	Billing Summary	221.95		NO
		11051	Accts Rec'ble Module	Billing Summary	3835.10		NO
		5101	COGS Dept. 01	Billing Summary	2500.48		NO
		5102	COGS Dept. 02	Billing Summary	72.12		NO
		11071	Inventory - Module	Billing Summary		2572.60	NO
		21042	Sales Tax Payable	Billing Summary		190.81	NO
		4101	Sales Dept. 01	Billing Summary		3579.66	NO
		4102	Sales Dept. 02	Billing Summary		236.58	NO
		4301	Freight	Billing Summary		50.00	NO
				TOTAL TRANSACTION :	6629.65	6629.65	
CA 0001	10/29/88	11021	Checking Account	Personal Investment	25000.00		YES
		11021	Checking Account	Loan Proceeds	50000.00		YES
		2202	Notes Payable	Loan Proceeds		50000.00	YES
		31011	Par Value	Personal Investment		25000.00	YES
				TOTAL TRANSACTION :	75000.00	75000.00	
CA 0002	10/29/88	11021	Checking Account	Loan for Building Buy	65000.00		YES
		2201	Mortgages Payable	Loan for Building Buy		65000.00	YES
				TOTAL TRANSACTION :	65000.00	65000.00	
CA 0003	10/29/88	12051	Original Value	Purchase Building	65000.00		YES
		11021	Checking Account	Purchase Building		65000.00	YES
				TOTAL TRANSACTION :	65000.00	65000.00	

Report D.53

Farts and Parcels, Inc.
#2 Byfore Avenue
Greenwood, S.C. 29646
803/555-1685

General Ledger Journal Report

Journal Trans.#	Date	Acct. #	Account Name	Description	Debits	Credits	Posted?
CA 0004	10/29/88	12011	Original Value	Truck Purchase	12995.00		YES
		11021	Checking Account	Truck Purchase		12995.00	YES
				TOTAL TRANSACTION :	12995.00	12995.00	
CA 0005	10/29/88	12021	Original Value	Adjust for Furn/Fixtures	25000.00		YES
CA 0005	10/29/88	12051	Original Value	Adjust for Furn/Fixtures		25000.00	YES
				TOTAL TRANSACTION :	25000.00	25000.00	
CA 0006	11/21/88	52031	Autos & Trucks	Oct 88 Depreciation	270.73		NO
		52032	Furniture & Fixtures	Oct 88 Depreciation	297.62		NO
		52035	Building	Oct 88 Depreciation	133.33		NO
		12012	Accum. Depreciation	Oct 88 Depreciation		270.73	NO
		12022	Accum. Depreciation	Oct 88 Depreciation		297.62	NO
		12052	Accum. Depreciation	Oct 88 Depreciation		133.33	NO
				TOTAL TRANSACTION :	701.68	701.68	
PO 1119	11/19/88	11071	Inventory - Module	Purchase Order Summary	5636.53		NO
		12031	Original Value	Purchase Order Summary	319.98		NO
		52081	Freight	Purchase Order Summary	21.18		NO
		52082	Insurance	Purchase Order Summary	4.00		NO
		52091	Sales Tax/Purchases	Purchase Order Summary	253.30		NO
		2101	Accts Payable-Module	Purchase Order Summary		6234.99	NO
				TOTAL TRANSACTION :	6234.99	6234.99	
PY 1118	11/18/88	520111	Salaries	PAYROLL POST SUMMARY	357.21		NO
		520112	Hourly	PAYROLL POST SUMMARY	566.36		NO
		520114	Overtime	PAYROLL POST SUMMARY	43.15		NO
		520131	FICA Employer	PAYROLL POST SUMMARY	72.60		NO
		520132	FUTA	PAYROLL POST SUMMARY	2.89		NO
		520134	Disability Insurance	PAYROLL POST SUMMARY	193.75		NO
		11022	Payroll Account	PAYROLL POST SUMMARY		774.42	NO
		210411	Federal Income W/H	PAYROLL POST SUMMARY		84.58	NO
		210412	FICA W/H Employee	PAYROLL POST SUMMARY		72.60	NO
		210413	FICA W/H Employer	PAYROLL POST SUMMARY		72.60	NO
		210414	FUTA	PAYROLL POST SUMMARY		2.89	NO
		210416	State Income W/H	PAYROLL POST SUMMARY		35.12	NO
		210418	Disability Insurance	PAYROLL POST SUMMARY		193.75	NO
				TOTAL TRANSACTION :	1235.96	1235.96	
				TOTAL TRANSACTION :	263496.87	263496.87	

OF ENTRIES PRINTED : 57

378

Report D.54

Parts and Parcels, Inc.
#2 Byfore Avenue
Greenwood, S.C. 29646
803/555-1685

G/L Account Activity Detail Report
Complete Monthly Activity

Journal Trans.#	Date	Acct. #	Account Name	Description	Debits	Credits	Posted?
		11021	Checking Account	BEGINNING BALANCE	0.00		
CA 0001	10/29/88			Personal Investment	25000.00		YES
CA 0001	10/29/88			Loan Proceeds	50000.00		YES
CA 0002	10/29/88			Loan for Building Buy	65000.00		YES
CA 0004	10/29/88			Truck Purchase		12995.00	YES
CA 0003	10/29/88			Purchase Building		65000.00	YES
BI 1119	11/19/88			Billing Summary	221.95		NO
AR 1120	11/20/88			Payments Summ.-AR Post	2633.97		NO
AR 1120	11/20/88			Payments Summ.-AR Post	450.86		NO
AP 1120	11/20/88			Nuts-to-You, Inc-005002		189.14	NO
AP 1120	11/20/88			Paint By the Num-005003		2071.67	NO
AP 1120	11/20/88			Shovell Shovels,-M0981		113.25	NO
				CURRENT BALANCE	62937.72		
		11022	Payroll Account	BEGINNING BALANCE	0.00		
PY 1118	11/18/88			PAYROLL POST SUMMARY		774.42	NO
				CURRENT BALANCE	-774.42		
		11051	Accts Rec'ble Module	BEGINNING BALANCE	0.00		
BI 1119	11/19/88			Billing Summary	3835.10		NO
AR 1120	11/20/88			Summary From AR Post		110.25	NO
AR 1120	11/20/88			Payments Summ.-AR Post		3180.23	NO
				CURRENT BALANCE	544.62		
		11071	Inventory - Module	BEGINNING BALANCE	0.00		
PO 1119	11/19/88			Purchase Order Summary	5636.53		NO
BI 1119	11/19/88			Billing Summary		2572.60	NO
				CURRENT BALANCE	3063.93		
		12011	Original Value	BEGINNING BALANCE	0.00		
CA 0004	10/29/88			Truck Purchase	12995.00		YES
				CURRENT BALANCE	12995.00		
		12012	Accum. Depreciation	BEGINNING BALANCE	0.00		
CA 0006	11/21/88			Oct 88 Depreciation		270.73	NO
				CURRENT BALANCE	-270.73		
		12021	Original Value	BEGINNING BALANCE	0.00		
CA 0005	10/29/88			Adjust for Furn/Fixtures	25000.00		YES

Report D.55

Parts and Parcels, Inc.
#2 Byfore Avenue
Greenwood, S.C. 29646
803/555-1685

G/L Account Activity Detail Report
Complete Monthly Activity

Journal Trans.#	Date	Acct. #	Account Name	Description	Debits	Credits	Posted?
				CURRENT BALANCE	25000.00		
		12022	Accum. Depreciation	BEGINNING BALANCE	0.00		
CA 0006	11/21/88			Oct 88 Depreciation		297.62	NO
				CURRENT BALANCE	-297.62		
		12031	Original Value	BEGINNING BALANCE	0.00		
PO 1119	11/19/88			Purchase Order Summary	319.98		NO
				CURRENT BALANCE	319.98		
		12051	Original Value	BEGINNING BALANCE	0.00		
CA 0003	10/29/88			Purchase Building	65000.00		YES
CA 0005	10/29/88			Adjust for Furn/Fixtures		25000.00	YES
				CURRENT BALANCE	40000.00		
		12052	Accum. Depreciation	BEGINNING BALANCE	0.00		
CA 0006	11/21/88			Oct 88 Depreciation		133.33	NO
				CURRENT BALANCE	-133.33		
		2101	Accts Payable-Module	BEGINNING BALANCE		0.00	
PO 1119	11/19/88			Purchase Order Summary		6234.99	NO
AP 1120	11/20/88			Payments Summ.-AP Post	2409.11		NO
				CURRENT BALANCE		3825.88	
		210411	Federal Income W/H	BEGINNING BALANCE		0.00	
PY 1118	11/18/88			PAYROLL POST SUMMARY		84.58	NO
				CURRENT BALANCE		84.58	
		210412	FICA W/H Employee	BEGINNING BALANCE		0.00	
PY 1118	11/18/88			PAYROLL POST SUMMARY		72.60	NO
				CURRENT BALANCE		72.60	
		210413	FICA W/H Employer	BEGINNING BALANCE		0.00	
PY 1118	11/18/88			PAYROLL POST SUMMARY		72.60	NO

Report D.56

Parts and Parcels, Inc.
#2 Byfore Avenue
Greenwood, S.C. 29646
803/555-1685

G/L Account Activity Detail Report
Complete Monthly Activity

Journal Trans.#	Date	Acct. #	Account Name	Description	Debits	Credits	Posted?
				CURRENT BALANCE		72.60	
		210414	FUTA	BEGINNING BALANCE		0.00	
PY 1118	11/18/88			PAYROLL POST SUMMARY		2.89	NO
				CURRENT BALANCE		2.89	
		210416	State Income W/H	BEGINNING BALANCE		0.00	
PY 1118	11/18/88			PAYROLL POST SUMMARY		35.12	NO
				CURRENT BALANCE		35.12	
		210418	Disability Insurance	BEGINNING BALANCE		0.00	
PY 1118	11/18/88			PAYROLL POST SUMMARY		193.75	NO
				CURRENT BALANCE		193.75	
		21042	Sales Tax Payable	BEGINNING BALANCE		0.00	
BI 1119	11/19/88			Billing Summary		190.81	NO
				CURRENT BALANCE		190.81	
		2201	Mortgages Payable	BEGINNING BALANCE		0.00	
CA 0002	10/29/88			Loan for Building Buy		65000.00	YES
				CURRENT BALANCE		65000.00	
		2202	Notes Payable	BEGINNING BALANCE		0.00	
CA 0001	10/29/88			Loan Proceeds		50000.00	YES
				CURRENT BALANCE		50000.00	
		31011	Par Value	BEGINNING BALANCE		0.00	
CA 0001	10/29/88			Personal Investment		25000.00	YES
				CURRENT BALANCE		25000.00	
		4101	Sales Dept. 01	BEGINNING BALANCE		0.00	
BI 1119	11/19/88			Billing Summary		3579.66	NO
				CURRENT BALANCE		3579.66	
		4102	Sales Dept. 02	BEGINNING BALANCE		0.00	
BI 1119	11/19/88			Billing Summary		236.58	NO

Report D.57

Date : 11/21/88
Time : 00:57 AM

Parts and Parcels, Inc.
#2 Byfore Avenue
Greenwood, S.C. 29646
803/555-1685

Page no. 4

G/L Account Activity Detail Report
Complete Monthly Activity

Journal Trans.#	Date	Acct. #	Account Name	Description	Debits	Credits	Posted?
AR 1120	11/20/88			Summary From AR Post	110.25		NO
				CURRENT BALANCE		126.33	
		4301	Freight	BEGINNING BALANCE		0.00	
BI 1119	11/19/88			Billing Summary		50.00	NO
				CURRENT BALANCE		50.00	
		4404	Purchase Discounts	BEGINNING BALANCE		0.00	
AP 1120	11/20/88			Payments Summ.-AP Post		35.05	NO
				CURRENT BALANCE		35.05	
		5101	COGS Dept. 01	BEGINNING BALANCE	0.00		
BI 1119	11/19/88			Billing Summary	2500.48		NO
				CURRENT BALANCE	2500.48		
		5102	COGS Dept. 02	BEGINNING BALANCE	0.00		
BI 1119	11/19/88			Billing Summary	72.12		NO
				CURRENT BALANCE	72.12		
		520111	Salaries	BEGINNING BALANCE	0.00		
PY 1118	11/18/88			PAYROLL POST SUMMARY	357.21		NO
				CURRENT BALANCE	357.21		
		520112	Hourly	BEGINNING BALANCE	0.00		
PY 1118	11/18/88			PAYROLL POST SUMMARY	566.36		NO
				CURRENT BALANCE	566.36		
		520114	Overtime	BEGINNING BALANCE	0.00		
PY 1118	11/18/88			PAYROLL POST SUMMARY	43.15		NO
				CURRENT BALANCE	43.15		
		520131	FICA Employer	BEGINNING BALANCE	0.00		
PY 1118	11/18/88			PAYROLL POST SUMMARY	72.60		NO
				CURRENT BALANCE	72.60		
		520132	FUTA	BEGINNING BALANCE	0.00		
PY 1118	11/18/88			PAYROLL POST SUMMARY	2.89		NO

Report D.58

Parts and Parcels, Inc.
#2 Byfore Avenue
Greenwood, S.C. 29646
803/555-1685

G/L Account Activity Detail Report
Complete Monthly Activity

Journal Trans.#	Date	Acct. #	Account Name	Description	Debits	Credits	Posted?
				CURRENT BALANCE	2.89		
		520134	Disability Insurance	BEGINNING BALANCE	0.00		
PY 1118	11/18/88			PAYROLL POST SUMMARY	193.75		NO
				CURRENT BALANCE	193.75		
		52031	Autos & Trucks	BEGINNING BALANCE	0.00		
CA 0006	11/21/88			Oct 88 Depreciation	270.73		NO
				CURRENT BALANCE	270.73		
		52032	Furniture & Fixtures	BEGINNING BALANCE	0.00		
CA 0006	11/21/88			Oct 88 Depreciation	297.62		NO
				CURRENT BALANCE	297.62		
		52035	Building	BEGINNING BALANCE	0.00		
CA 0006	11/21/88			Oct 88 Depreciation	133.33		NO
				CURRENT BALANCE	133.33		
		52081	Freight	BEGINNING BALANCE	0.00		
PO 1119	11/19/88			Purchase Order Summary	21.18		NO
				CURRENT BALANCE	21.18		
		52082	Insurance	BEGINNING BALANCE	0.00		
PO 1119	11/19/88			Purchase Order Summary	4.00		NO
				CURRENT BALANCE	4.00		
		52091	Sales Tax/Purchases	BEGINNING BALANCE	0.00		
PO 1119	11/19/88			Purchase Order Summary	253.30		NO
				CURRENT BALANCE	253.30		
		5304	Sales Discounts	BEGINNING BALANCE	0.00		
AR 1120	11/20/88			Payments Summ.-AR Post	95.40		NO
				CURRENT BALANCE	95.40		
				TOTAL TRANSACTION :	263496.87	263496.87	

OF ENTRIES PRINTED : 57

Report D.59

Parts and Parcels, Inc.
#2 Byfore Avenue
Greenwood, S.C. 29646
803/555-1685

TRIAL BALANCE

Acct #	Account Name	BEGINNING BALANCE Debits	Credits	THIS MONTH Debits	Credits	CURRENT BALANCE Debits	Credits
1	ASSETS	0.00		143385.15		143385.15	
11	CURRENT ASSETS	0.00		65771.85		65771.85	
1102	CASH IN BANKS	0.00		62163.30		62163.30	
11021	Checking Account	0.00		62937.72		62937.72	
11022	Payroll Account	0.00		-774.42		-774.42	
1105	ACCOUNTS RECEIVABLE	0.00		544.62		544.62	
11051	Accts Rec'ble Module	0.00		544.62		544.62	
1107	INVENTORY	0.00		3063.93		3063.93	
11071	Inventory - Module	0.00		3063.93		3063.93	
12	FIXED ASSETS	0.00		77613.30		77613.30	
1201	AUTOS & TRUCKS NET	0.00		12724.27		12724.27	
12011	Original Value	0.00		12995.00		12995.00	
12012	Accum. Depreciation	0.00		-270.73		-270.73	
1202	FURNITURE & FIXT.NET	0.00		24702.38		24702.38	
12021	Original Value	0.00		25000.00		25000.00	
12022	Accum. Depreciation	0.00		-297.62		-297.62	
1203	OFFICE EQUIPMENT NET	0.00		319.98		319.98	
12031	Original Value	0.00		319.98		319.98	
1205	BUILDING NET	0.00		39866.67		39866.67	
12051	Original Value	0.00		40000.00		40000.00	
12052	Accum. Depreciation	0.00		-133.33		-133.33	
2	LIABILITIES		0.00		119478.23		119478.23
21	SHORT TERM LIABILITY		0.00		4478.23		4478.23
2101	Accts Payable-Module		0.00		3825.88		3825.88
2104	TAXES PAYABLE		0.00		652.35		652.35
21041	PAYROLL TAXES		0.00		461.54		461.54
210411	Federal Income W/H		0.00		84.58		84.58
210412	FICA W/H Employee		0.00		72.60		72.60
210413	FICA W/H Employer		0.00		72.60		72.60
210414	FUTA		0.00		2.89		2.89
210416	State Income W/H		0.00		35.12		35.12
210418	Disability Insurance		0.00		193.75		193.75
21042	Sales Tax Payable		0.00		190.81		190.81
22	LONG TERM LIABILITY		0.00		115000.00		115000.00
2201	Mortgages Payable		0.00		65000.00		65000.00
2202	Notes Payable		0.00		50000.00		50000.00
3	STOCKHOLDERS EQUITY		0.00		25000.00		25000.00
31	CAPTIAL STOCK		0.00		25000.00		25000.00
3101	COMMON STOCK		0.00		25000.00		25000.00
31011	Par Value		0.00		25000.00		25000.00
4	REVENUES		0.00		3791.04		3791.04
41	SALES		0.00		3705.99		3705.99
4101	Sales Dept. 01		0.00		3579.66		3579.66
4102	Sales Dept. 02		0.00		126.33		126.33

Report D.60

Date : 11/21/88
Time : 02:12 AM

Parts and Parcels, Inc.
#2 Byfore Avenue
Greenwood, S.C. 29646
803/555-1685

Page no. 2

TRIAL BALANCE

Acct #	Account Name	BEGINNING BALANCE Debits	BEGINNING BALANCE Credits	THIS MONTH Debits	THIS MONTH Credits	CURRENT BALANCE Debits	CURRENT BALANCE Credits
43	SHIPPING		0.00		50.00		50.00
4301	Freight		0.00		50.00		50.00
44	FINANCIAL INCOME		0.00		35.05		35.05
4404	Purchase Discounts		0.00		35.05		35.05
5	TOTAL EXPENSES	0.00		4884.12		4884.12	
51	COST OF GOODS SOLD	0.00		2572.60		2572.60	
5101	COGS Dept. 01	0.00		2500.48		2500.48	
5102	COGS Dept. 02	0.00		72.12		72.12	
52	GEN & ADMIN EXPENSES	0.00		2216.12		2216.12	
5201	PAYROLL	0.00		1235.96		1235.96	
52011	WAGES	0.00		966.72		966.72	
520111	Salaries	0.00		357.21		357.21	
520112	Hourly	0.00		566.36		566.36	
520114	Overtime	0.00		43.15		43.15	
52013	TAXES	0.00		269.24		269.24	
520131	FICA Employer	0.00		72.60		72.60	
520132	FUTA	0.00		2.89		2.89	
520134	Disability Insurance	0.00		193.75		193.75	
5203	DEPRECIATION	0.00		701.68		701.68	
52031	Autos & Trucks	0.00		270.73		270.73	
52032	Furniture & Fixtures	0.00		297.62		297.62	
52035	Building	0.00		133.33		133.33	
5208	SHIPPING	0.00		25.18		25.18	
52081	Freight	0.00		21.18		21.18	
52082	Insurance	0.00		4.00		4.00	
5209	TAXES (OTHER)	0.00		253.30		253.30	
52091	Sales Tax/Purchases	0.00		253.30		253.30	
53	FINANCIAL EXPENSES	0.00		95.40		95.40	
5304	Sales Discounts	0.00		95.40		95.40	
		============	============	============	============	============	============
		0.00	0.00	148269.27	148269.27	148269.27	148269.27

Number of Accounts printed 73

Report D.61

Date : 11/21/88
Time : 02:39 AM

Parts and Parcels, Inc.
#2 Byfore Avenue
Greenwood, S.C. 29646
803/555-1685

Page no. 1

BALANCE SHEET

Acct #	Account Name	Level 5	Level 4	Level 3	Level 2	Level 1
1	ASSETS					143385.15
11	CURRENT ASSETS				65771.85	
1102	CASH IN BANKS			62163.30		
11021	Checking Account		62937.72			
11022	Payroll Account		-774.42			
1105	ACCOUNTS RECEIVABLE			544.62		
11051	Accts Rec'ble Module		544.62			
1107	INVENTORY			3063.93		
11071	Inventory - Module		3063.93			
12	FIXED ASSETS				77613.30	
1201	AUTOS & TRUCKS NET			12724.27		
12011	Original Value		12995.00			
12012	Accum. Depreciation		-270.73			
1202	FURNITURE & FIXT.NET			24702.38		
12021	Original Value		25000.00			
12022	Accum. Depreciation		-297.62			
1203	OFFICE EQUIPMENT NET			319.98		
12031	Original Value		319.98			
1205	BUILDING NET			39866.67		
12051	Original Value		40000.00			
12052	Accum. Depreciation		-133.33			

```
                                                                ============
        TOTAL ASSETS                                              143385.15
```

Report D.62

Parts and Parcels, Inc.
#2 Byfore Avenue
Greenwood, S.C. 29646
803/555-1685

BALANCE SHEET

Acct #	Account Name	Level 5	Level 4	Level 3	Level 2	Level 1
2	LIABILITIES					119478.23
21	SHORT TERM LIABILITY				4478.23	
2101	Accts Payable-Module			3825.88		
2104	TAXES PAYABLE			652.35		
21041	PAYROLL TAXES		461.54			
210411	Federal Income W/H	84.58				
210412	FICA W/H Employee	72.60				
210413	FICA W/H Employer	72.60				
210414	FUTA	2.89				
210416	State Income W/H	35.12				
210418	Disability Insurance	193.75				
21042	Sales Tax Payable		190.81			
22	LONG TERM LIABILITY				115000.00	
2201	Mortgages Payable			65000.00		
2202	Notes Payable			50000.00		
						============
	TOTAL LIABILITIES					119478.23
3	STOCKHOLDERS EQUITY					25000.00
31	CAPTIAL STOCK				25000.00	
3101	COMMON STOCK			25000.00		
31011	Par Value		25000.00			
	CURRENT EARNINGS					-1093.08

	TOTAL EQUITY					23906.92
						============
	TOTAL LIABILITIES PLUS EQUITY					143385.15

387

Report D.63

Parts and Parcels, Inc.
#2 Byfore Avenue
Greenwood, S.C. 29646
803/555-1685

INCOME STATEMENT

Acct #	Account Name	Level 5	Level 4	Level 3	Level 2	Level 1
4	REVENUES					3791.04
41	SALES				3705.99	
4101	Sales Dept. 01			3579.66		
4102	Sales Dept. 02			126.33		
43	SHIPPING				50.00	
4301	Freight			50.00		
44	FINANCIAL INCOME				35.05	
4404	Purchase Discounts			35.05		
						============
	TOTAL REVENUE					3791.04
5	TOTAL EXPENSES					4884.12
51	COST OF GOODS SOLD				2572.60	
5101	COGS Dept. 01			2500.48		
5102	COGS Dept. 02			72.12		
52	GEN & ADMIN EXPENSES				2216.12	
5201	PAYROLL			1235.96		
52011	WAGES		966.72			
520111	Salaries	357.21				
520112	Hourly	566.36				
520114	Overtime	43.15				
52013	TAXES		269.24			
520131	FICA Employer	72.60				
520132	FUTA	2.89				
520134	Disability Insurance	193.75				
5203	DEPRECIATION			701.68		
52031	Autos & Trucks		270.73			
52032	Furniture & Fixtures		297.62			
52035	Building		133.33			
5208	SHIPPING			25.18		
52081	Freight		21.18			
52082	Insurance		4.00			
5209	TAXES (OTHER)			253.30		
52091	Sales Tax/Purchases		253.30			
53	FINANCIAL EXPENSES				95.40	
5304	Sales Discounts			95.40		
						============
	NET INCOME					-1093.08

388

Report D.64

Parts and Parcels, Inc.
#2 Byfore Avenue
Greenwood, S.C. 29646
803/555-1685

STATEMENT OF CHANGES IN FINANCIAL CONDITIONS

Acct #	Account Name	Last Yr - Yr. Bef. Last Sources	Uses	This Yr. - Last Yr. Sources	Uses	Current Period Sources	Uses
1	ASSETS		0.00		143385.15		143385.15
11	CURRENT ASSETS		0.00		65771.85		65771.85
1102	CASH IN BANKS		0.00		62163.30		62163.30
11021	Checking Account		0.00		62937.72		62937.72
11022	Payroll Account		0.00	774.42		774.42	
1105	ACCOUNTS RECEIVABLE		0.00		544.62		544.62
11051	Accts Rec'ble Module		0.00		544.62		544.62
1107	INVENTORY		0.00		3063.93		3063.93
11071	Inventory - Module		0.00		3063.93		3063.93
12	FIXED ASSETS		0.00		77613.30		77613.30
1201	AUTOS & TRUCKS NET		0.00		12724.27		12724.27
12011	Original Value		0.00		12995.00		12995.00
12012	Accum. Depreciation		0.00	270.73		270.73	
1202	FURNITURE & FIXT.NET		0.00		24702.38		24702.38
12021	Original Value		0.00		25000.00		25000.00
12022	Accum. Depreciation		0.00	297.62		297.62	
1203	OFFICE EQUIPMENT NET		0.00		319.98		319.98
12031	Original Value		0.00		319.98		319.98
1205	BUILDING NET		0.00		39866.67		39866.67
12051	Original Value		0.00		40000.00		40000.00
12052	Accum. Depreciation		0.00	133.33		133.33	
2	LIABILITIES		0.00	119478.23		119478.23	
21	SHORT TERM LIABILITY		0.00	4478.23		4478.23	
2101	Accts Payable-Module		0.00	3825.88		3825.88	
2104	TAXES PAYABLE		0.00	652.35		652.35	
21041	PAYROLL TAXES		0.00	461.54		461.54	
210411	Federal Income W/H		0.00	84.58		84.58	
210412	FICA W/H Employee		0.00	72.60		72.60	
210413	FICA W/H Employer		0.00	72.60		72.60	
210414	FUTA		0.00	2.89		2.89	
210416	State Income W/H		0.00	35.12		35.12	
210418	Disability Insurance		0.00	193.75		193.75	
21042	Sales Tax Payable		0.00	190.81		190.81	
22	LONG TERM LIABILITY		0.00	115000.00		115000.00	
2201	Mortgages Payable		0.00	65000.00		65000.00	
2202	Notes Payable		0.00	50000.00		50000.00	
3	STOCKHOLDERS EQUITY		0.00	25000.00		25000.00	
31	CAPTIAL STOCK		0.00	25000.00		25000.00	
3101	COMMON STOCK		0.00	25000.00		25000.00	
31011	Par Value		0.00	25000.00		25000.00	

Report D.65

Parts and Parcels, Inc.
#2 Byfore Avenue
Greenwood, S.C. 29646
803/555-1685

STATEMENT OF CHANGES IN FINANCIAL CONDITIONS

Acct #	Account Name	Last Yr - Yr. Bef. Last		This Yr. - Last Yr.		Current Period	
		Sources	Uses	Sources	Uses	Sources	Uses
4	REVENUES		0.00	3791.04		3791.04	
41	SALES		0.00	3705.99		3705.99	
4101	Sales Dept. 01		0.00	3579.66		3579.66	
4102	Sales Dept. 02		0.00	126.33		126.33	
43	SHIPPING		0.00	50.00		50.00	
4301	Freight		0.00	50.00		50.00	
44	FINANCIAL INCOME		0.00	35.05		35.05	
4404	Purchase Discounts		0.00	35.05		35.05	
5	TOTAL EXPENSES		0.00		4884.12		4884.12
51	COST OF GOODS SOLD		0.00		2572.60		2572.60
5101	COGS Dept. 01		0.00		2500.48		2500.48
5102	COGS Dept. 02		0.00		72.12		72.12
52	GEN & ADMIN EXPENSES		0.00		2216.12		2216.12
5201	PAYROLL		0.00		1235.96		1235.96
52011	WAGES		0.00		966.72		966.72
520111	Salaries		0.00		357.21		357.21
520112	Hourly		0.00		566.36		566.36
520114	Overtime		0.00		43.15		43.15
52013	TAXES		0.00		269.24		269.24
520131	FICA Employer		0.00		72.60		72.60
520132	FUTA		0.00		2.89		2.89
520134	Disability Insurance		0.00		193.75		193.75
5203	DEPRECIATION		0.00		701.68		701.68
52031	Autos & Trucks		0.00		270.73		270.73
52032	Furniture & Fixtures		0.00		297.62		297.62
52035	Building		0.00		133.33		133.33
5208	SHIPPING		0.00		25.18		25.18
52081	Freight		0.00		21.18		21.18
52082	Insurance		0.00		4.00		4.00
5209	TAXES (OTHER)		0.00		253.30		253.30
52091	Sales Tax/Purchases		0.00		253.30		253.30
53	FINANCIAL EXPENSES		0.00		95.40		95.40
5304	Sales Discounts		0.00		95.40		95.40
	Totals :	0.00	0.00	148269.27	148269.27	148269.27	148269.27

Report D.66

Parts and Parcels, Inc.
Hardware the Easy Way
#2 Byfore Avenue
Greenwood, SC 29646

PAYROLL QUARTERLY REPORT

Social Security	Employee Name	Taxable FICA Wages	Taxable Wages	State Unempl Wages	State
666-00-9090	Coard, Stension	167.60	167.60	0.00	SC
388-11-5555	Coard, Wynn Doe	357.21	357.21	0.00	SC
222-33-4444	Partment, Notmai D.	273.15	273.15	0.00	SC
999-88-2222	Real, Rod N.	108.00	108.00	0.00	SC
987-65-4321	Router, Bitsy	60.76	60.76	0.00	SC
5	Totals for Page :	966.72	966.72	0.00	
5	Totals for State : SC	966.72	966.72	0.00	

Report D.67

Date : 11/22/88
Time : 03:37 AM

Parts and Parcels, Inc.
#2 Byfore Avenue
Greenwood, S.C. 29646
803/555-1685

Page no. 1

TRIAL BALANCE

Acct #	Account Name	BEGINNING BALANCE Debits	BEGINNING BALANCE Credits	THIS MONTH Debits	THIS MONTH Credits	CURRENT BALANCE Debits	CURRENT BALANCE Credits
1	ASSETS	0.00		143385.15		143385.15	
11	CURRENT ASSETS	0.00		65771.85		65771.85	
1102	CASH IN BANKS	0.00		62163.30		62163.30	
11021	Checking Account	0.00		62937.72		62937.72	
11022	Payroll Account	0.00		-774.42		-774.42	
1105	ACCOUNTS RECEIVABLE	0.00		544.62		544.62	
11051	Accts Rec'ble Module	0.00		544.62		544.62	
1107	INVENTORY	0.00		3063.93		3063.93	
11071	Inventory - Module	0.00		3063.93		3063.93	
12	FIXED ASSETS	0.00		77613.30		77613.30	
1201	AUTOS & TRUCKS NET	0.00		12724.27		12724.27	
12011	Original Value	0.00		12995.00		12995.00	
12012	Accum. Depreciation	0.00		-270.73		-270.73	
1202	FURNITURE & FIXT.NET	0.00		24702.38		24702.38	
12021	Original Value	0.00		25000.00		25000.00	
12022	Accum. Depreciation	0.00		-297.62		-297.62	
1203	OFFICE EQUIPMENT NET	0.00		319.98		319.98	
12031	Original Value	0.00		319.98		319.98	
1205	BUILDING NET	0.00		39866.67		39866.67	
12051	Original Value	0.00		40000.00		40000.00	
12052	Accum. Depreciation	0.00		-133.33		-133.33	
2	LIABILITIES		0.00		119478.23		119478.23
21	SHORT TERM LIABILITY		0.00		4478.23		4478.23
2101	Accts Payable-Module		0.00		3825.88		3825.88
2104	TAXES PAYABLE		0.00		652.35		652.35
21041	PAYROLL TAXES		0.00		461.54		461.54
210411	Federal Income W/H		0.00		84.58		84.58
210412	FICA W/H Employee		0.00		72.60		72.60
210413	FICA W/H Employer		0.00		72.60		72.60
210414	FUTA		0.00		2.89		2.89
210416	State Income W/H		0.00		35.12		35.12
210418	Disability Insurance		0.00		193.75		193.75
21042	Sales Tax Payable		0.00		190.81		190.81
22	LONG TERM LIABILITY		0.00		115000.00		115000.00
2201	Mortgages Payable		0.00		65000.00		65000.00
2202	Notes Payable		0.00		50000.00		50000.00
3	STOCKHOLDERS EQUITY		0.00		25000.00		25000.00
31	CAPTIAL STOCK		0.00		25000.00		25000.00
3101	COMMON STOCK		0.00		25000.00		25000.00
31011	Par Value		0.00		25000.00		25000.00

392

Report D.68

Parts and Parcels, Inc.
#2 Byfore Avenue
Greenwood, S.C. 29646
803/555-1685

TRIAL BALANCE

Acct #	Account Name	BEGINNING BALANCE Debits	Credits	THIS MONTH Debits	Credits	CURRENT BALANCE Debits	Credits
4	REVENUES		0.00		3791.04		3791.04
41	SALES		0.00		3705.99		3705.99
4101	Sales Dept. 01		0.00		3579.66		3579.66
4102	Sales Dept. 02		0.00		126.33		126.33
43	SHIPPING		0.00		50.00		50.00
4301	Freight		0.00		50.00		50.00
44	FINANCIAL INCOME		0.00		35.05		35.05
4404	Purchase Discounts		0.00		35.05		35.05
5	TOTAL EXPENSES	0.00		4884.12		4884.12	
51	COST OF GOODS SOLD	0.00		2572.60		2572.60	
5101	COGS Dept. 01	0.00		2500.48		2500.48	
5102	COGS Dept. 02	0.00		72.12		72.12	
52	GEN & ADMIN EXPENSES	0.00		2216.12		2216.12	
5201	PAYROLL	0.00		1235.96		1235.96	
52011	WAGES	0.00		966.72		966.72	
520111	Salaries	0.00		357.21		357.21	
520112	Hourly	0.00		566.36		566.36	
520114	Overtime	0.00		43.15		43.15	
52013	TAXES	0.00		269.24		269.24	
520131	FICA Employer	0.00		72.60		72.60	
520132	FUTA	0.00		2.89		2.89	
520134	Disability Insurance	0.00		193.75		193.75	
5203	DEPRECIATION	0.00		701.68		701.68	
52031	Autos & Trucks	0.00		270.73		270.73	
52032	Furniture & Fixtures	0.00		297.62		297.62	
52035	Building	0.00		133.33		133.33	
5208	SHIPPING	0.00		25.18		25.18	
52081	Freight	0.00		21.18		21.18	
52082	Insurance	0.00		4.00		4.00	
5209	TAXES (OTHER)	0.00		253.30		253.30	
52091	Sales Tax/Purchases	0.00		253.30		253.30	
53	FINANCIAL EXPENSES	0.00		95.40		95.40	
5304	Sales Discounts	0.00		95.40		95.40	
		0.00	0.00	148269.27	148269.27	148269.27	148269.27

Report D.69

Date : 11/22/88
Time : 03:50 AM

Parts and Parcels, Inc.
#2 Byfore Avenue
Greenwood, S.C. 29646
803/555-1685

Page no. 1

TRIAL BALANCE

Acct #	Account Name	BEGINNING BALANCE Debits	BEGINNING BALANCE Credits	THIS MONTH Debits	THIS MONTH Credits	CURRENT BALANCE Debits	CURRENT BALANCE Credits
1	ASSETS	0.00		143385.15		143385.15	
11	CURRENT ASSETS	0.00		65771.85		65771.85	
1102	CASH IN BANKS	0.00		62163.30		62163.30	
11021	Checking Account	0.00		62937.72		62937.72	
11022	Payroll Account	0.00		-774.42		-774.42	
1105	ACCOUNTS RECEIVABLE	0.00		544.62		544.62	
11051	Accts Rec'ble Module	0.00		544.62		544.62	
1107	INVENTORY	0.00		3063.93		3063.93	
11071	Inventory - Module	0.00		3063.93		3063.93	
12	FIXED ASSETS	0.00		77613.30		77613.30	
1201	AUTOS & TRUCKS NET	0.00		12724.27		12724.27	
12011	Original Value	0.00		12995.00		12995.00	
12012	Accum. Depreciation	0.00		-270.73		-270.73	
1202	FURNITURE & FIXT.NET	0.00		24702.38		24702.38	
12021	Original Value	0.00		25000.00		25000.00	
12022	Accum. Depreciation	0.00		-297.62		-297.62	
1203	OFFICE EQUIPMENT NET	0.00		319.98		319.98	
12031	Original Value	0.00		319.98		319.98	
1205	BUILDING NET	0.00		39866.67		39866.67	
12051	Original Value	0.00		40000.00		40000.00	
12052	Accum. Depreciation	0.00		-133.33		-133.33	
2	LIABILITIES		0.00		119478.23		119478.23
21	SHORT TERM LIABILITY		0.00		4478.23		4478.23
2101	Accts Payable-Module		0.00		3825.88		3825.88
2104	TAXES PAYABLE		0.00		652.35		652.35
21041	PAYROLL TAXES		0.00		461.54		461.54
210411	Federal Income W/H		0.00		84.58		84.58
210412	FICA W/H Employee		0.00		72.60		72.60
210413	FICA W/H Employer		0.00		72.60		72.60
210414	FUTA		0.00		2.89		2.89
210416	State Income W/H		0.00		35.12		35.12
210418	Disability Insurance		0.00		193.75		193.75
21042	Sales Tax Payable		0.00		190.81		190.81
22	LONG TERM LIABILITY		0.00		115000.00		115000.00
2201	Mortgages Payable		0.00		65000.00		65000.00
2202	Notes Payable		0.00		50000.00		50000.00
3	STOCKHOLDERS EQUITY		-1093.08		25000.00		23906.92
31	CAPTIAL STOCK		0.00		25000.00		25000.00
3101	COMMON STOCK		0.00		25000.00		25000.00
31011	Par Value		0.00		25000.00		25000.00
32	RETAINED EARNINGS		-1093.08		0.00		-1093.08
3288	1988 Profit/(Loss)		-1093.08		0.00		-1093.08

Report D.70

Parts and Parcels, Inc.
#2 Byfore Avenue
Greenwood, S.C. 29646
803/555-1685

TRIAL BALANCE

Acct #	Account Name	BEGINNING BALANCE		THIS MONTH		CURRENT BALANCE	
		Debits	Credits	Debits	Credits	Debits	Credits
4	REVENUES		0.00		3791.04		3791.04
41	SALES		0.00		3705.99		3705.99
4101	Sales Dept. 01		0.00		3579.66		3579.66
4102	Sales Dept. 02		0.00		126.33		126.33
43	SHIPPING		0.00		50.00		50.00
4301	Freight		0.00		50.00		50.00
44	FINANCIAL INCOME		0.00		35.05		35.05
4404	Purchase Discounts		0.00		35.05		35.05
5	TOTAL EXPENSES	0.00		4884.12		4884.12	
51	COST OF GOODS SOLD	0.00		2572.60		2572.60	
5101	COGS Dept. 01	0.00		2500.48		2500.48	
5102	COGS Dept. 02	0.00		72.12		72.12	
52	GEN & ADMIN EXPENSES	0.00		2216.12		2216.12	
5201	PAYROLL	0.00		1235.96		1235.96	
52011	WAGES	0.00		966.72		966.72	
520111	Salaries	0.00		357.21		357.21	
520112	Hourly	0.00		566.36		566.36	
520114	Overtime	0.00		43.15		43.15	
52013	TAXES	0.00		269.24		269.24	
520131	FICA Employer	0.00		72.60		72.60	
520132	FUTA	0.00		2.89		2.89	
520134	Disability Insurance	0.00		193.75		193.75	
5203	DEPRECIATION	0.00		701.68		701.68	
52031	Autos & Trucks	0.00		270.73		270.73	
52032	Furniture & Fixtures	0.00		297.62		297.62	
52035	Building	0.00		133.33		133.33	
5208	SHIPPING	0.00		25.18		25.18	
52081	Freight	0.00		21.18		21.18	
52082	Insurance	0.00		4.00		4.00	
5209	TAXES (OTHER)	0.00		253.30		253.30	
52091	Sales Tax/Purchases	0.00		253.30		253.30	
53	FINANCIAL EXPENSES	0.00		95.40		95.40	
5304	Sales Discounts	0.00		95.40		95.40	
		============	============	============	===========	===========	===========
		0.00	-1093.08	148269.27	148269.27	148269.27	147176.19

Number of Accounts printed 75

Index

Index